FORM, GENRE, AND THE
STUDY OF POLITICAL DISCOURSE

FORM, GENRE, AND THE STUDY OF POLITICAL DISCOURSE

PN
239
.P64
F67
1986

Edited by
Herbert W. Simons
and
Aram A. Aghazarian

WITHDRAWN
Indiana
Purdue
Library
Fort Wayne

University of South Carolina Press

Excerpts from Samuel Beckett, *More Pricks Than Kicks*
(London: Chatto & Windus, 1934), *Proust* (New York:
Grove Press, Inc., 1970), and *The Unnamable* (Grove Press,
Inc., 1958), reprinted by permission of Grove Press, Inc.

Excerpts from Thomas Mann, *Joseph in Egypt*, translated by
H. T. Lowe-Porter (New York: Alfred A. Knopf, Inc., 1938),
reprinted by permission of Alfred A. Knopf, Inc.

Excerpts from Charles Tilly, "Repertoires of Contention in
America and Britain, 1750–1830," in Mayer N. Zald and
John D. McCarthy, eds., *The Dynamics of Social
Movements: Mobilization, Social Control, and Tactics.*
Copyright © 1979 by Little, Brown and Company, Inc.,
reprinted by permission of Little, Brown and Company, Inc.

Copyright © UNIVERSITY OF SOUTH CAROLINA 1986

Published in Columbia, South Carolina, by the
University of South Carolina Press

FIRST EDITION

Manufactured in the United States of America

Library of Congress Cataloging-in-Publication Data

Form, genre, and the study of political discourse.

   (Studies in rhetoric/communication)
   Bibliography: p.
   1. Rhetoric—Political aspects.   2. Political
oratory.   3. Literary form.   4. Presidents—
United States—Inaugural addresses.   5. Reagan,
Ronald—Oratory.   I. Simons, Herbert W., 1935–
II. Aghazarian, Aram A., 1932–   .   III. Series.
PN239.P64F67   1968   808.5'1'08832   86-16013
ISBN 0-87249-468-3

BB
1-27-88

To our families

Gayle and Michael　　　　　　　　*Lucy, Aram, and Lori*

CONTENTS

Contents

PREFACE

What value is there in identifying the forms that a given speech or other rhetorical act displays, or in fitting the act within one or another generic category? This is a book about rhetorical forms and genres of political discourse. Its primary interests are in assessing the possibilities and problems of form-and-genre scholarship, and in comparing alternative methods and perspectives. Featured in Part II of the book are several essays that focus on the presidential inaugural address as case-study material. While the dominant focus of this book is on political speechmaking, several of the contributors draw upon other examples of political influence, including television coverage of political events, political novels and films, treatments in textbooks of political issues, and so forth.

Most of the contributors to this anthology are in the field of speech communication. That field has contributed a good deal to form-and-genre scholarship since the mid-1960s, and we have sought here to review its accomplishments as well as its problems. So that we may introduce methods and perspectives from fields outside our own, we include essays by Richard A. Joslyn and Michael J. Shapiro, political scientists, and Robert J. Connors, a scholar of literary and rhetorical forms.

Several of the contributors take critical aim at form-and-genre scholarship. Joslyn was specifically urged to do so; Conley and McGee needed no such encouragement. We ourselves offer criticisms of the uses to which form-and-genre scholarship has been put, and particularly its use by critics in rendering evaluative judgments of a work. The primary function of such scholarship, we maintain, ought to be to identify and account for rhetorical regularities whether for purposes of theory-building and theory-testing, or as a vehicle for cultural and historical insights.

The first conference on rhetorical forms and genres was held in

Lawrence, Kansas, in 1976, cosponsored by the University of Kansas and the Speech Communication Association (SCA). It led to an anthology entitled *Form and Genre: Shaping Rhetorical Action*, which has exerted considerable influence. This book was born of a follow-up conference on form and genre—Temple University's Fourth Annual Conference on Discourse Analysis, March 17–19, 1983, hosted by the Department of Speech. Most of our authors contributed papers to that conference; Bruce E. Gronbeck and Herbert W. Simons contributed to both, as did the organizers of the first conference, Karlyn Kohrs Campbell and Kathleen Hall Jamieson. Although many of the symposiasts revised their papers or wrote new papers for this book, it nevertheless bears the imprint of the conference. We are indebted to all of the conference symposiasts as well as to the many who contributed to the discussions. In addition to our authors, they include Ronald H. Carpenter, Thomas W. Cooper, Robert T. Craig, Elliott Curson, Donald P. Cushman, Donald H. Ecroyd, Robert T. Friedenberg, Richard B. Gregg, Dan Hahn, Sarah Russell Hankins, Carl L. Kell, Ronald E. Lee, Mark Crispin Miller, Michael Pearson, Halford Ross Ryan, Ralph Towne, Richard W. Wilkie, Theodore Otto Windt, Jr., and Gary C. Woodward. We are grateful to Temple University for making the conference possible.

Two of the essays have appeared elsewhere. An earlier version of the Campbell and Jamieson essay appeared in *Presidential Studies Quarterly*; we thank the Center for the Study of the Presidency for permission to publish the revised version. The Shapiro essay, which appeared in *Political Theory*, seemed the perfect supplement to the conference essays; on reading it we knew it had to be included, and we thank the author for permission to reprint it.

Several of our contributors secured prepublication reviews and we arranged for others. We are grateful to Jane Blankenship, Karlyn Kohrs Campbell, Walter R. Fisher, Thomas Frentz, Roderick P. Hart, Kathleen Hall Jamieson, David Klemm, John R. Lyne, Howard Martin, Allan Megill, Michael Calvin McGee, Donovan Ochs, Calvin O. Schrag, Robert L. Scott, and Hermann Stelzner.

For their expert and patient support in bringing the manuscript into final form, we thank Dorothy Mewha and her staff, Sharon A. Smith and Cheryl D. Jones, and our departmental mainstays—Ronye Atkins and Diane Johnson.

Our most special thanks are reserved for Carroll C. Arnold. He encouraged us, wielded a sharp blue pencil, and made recommendations that helped to shape this book in fundamental ways.

CONTRIBUTORS

Aram A. Aghazarian, *Associate Professor, Department of Speech,* Temple University

Jane Blankenship, *Professor, Department of Communication Studies,* University of Massachusetts

Karlyn Kohrs Campbell, *Professor, Department of Speech-Communication,* University of Minnesota

Thomas Conley, *Associate Professor, Department of Speech Communication,* University of Illinois at Urbana-Champaign

Robert J. Connors, *Assistant Professor, Department of English,* University of New Hampshire

Bruce E. Gronbeck, *Professor, Department of Communication Studies,* University of Iowa

Roderick P. Hart, *Professor, Department of Speech Communication,* University of Texas at Austin

Kathleen Hall Jamieson, *Professor, Department of Speech Communication,* University of Texas at Austin

Richard A. Joslyn, *Associate Professor, Department of Political Science,* Temple University

Michael Calvin McGee, *Professor, Department of Communication Studies,* University of Iowa

Michael Osborn, *Professor, Department of Theatre and Communication Arts,* Memphis State University

Michael J. Shapiro, *Professor, Department of Political Science,* University of Hawaii

Herbert W. Simons, *Professor, Department of Speech,* Temple University

FORM, GENRE, AND THE
STUDY OF POLITICAL DISCOURSE

INTRODUCTION

There is an oft-told story out of the University of Iowa—it no longer matters whether it is correct in all of its details—about how Samuel Becker, for many years chairman of the Department of Speech and Dramatic Arts, was flown to São Paulo at the Brazilian government's expense to address its first annual Festival of the Arts on a theater-related subject of his own choosing. What made the lecture invitation more than a little surprising was that Sam's expertise lay in broadcast journalism, not theater. It turned out that the conference organizers had somehow mistaken Samuel Becker for the great Irish playwright Samuel Beckett. But the mixup was not discovered until after Becker had arrived in São Paulo. This was bad enough, but we are tempted to ask what Sam Becker should have done if, taking the situation to its most absurd, most Beckett-like extreme, he had become aware of the mixup only seconds before he was to address the audience. Should he have attempted to pass himself off as Beckett? But Beckett is a recluse; Beckett doesn't speak. Should he have attempted to sound like one of Beckett's more autobiographical characters—perhaps announcing that there would be a brief intermission while those assembled waited for Godot, or perhaps for Beckett himself? Failing to escape by a side exit during this mock intermission, should he have immediately improvised a one-character, one-act play about a character named Sam Becker who is mistaken for Sam Beckett and flown to Brazil? Or should he have simply announced that he was Sam Becker of the University of Iowa, begun a lecture on theater administration, and then waited for the audience to create Sam Beckett out of their own imaginations? Surely they would not have believed the truth.

In one of the essays in this book, a character from a Beckett play is quoted as saying, "I say what I'm told to say, that's all there is to it." To which those of us who spend much of our time in roles that are not of our choosing would probably offer at least limited assent, but then dismiss

3

the observation with a shrug of resignation. From childhood on, we are socialized to take roles, learn rules, employ the appropriate forms of speech in responding to what we take to be the "logic" of varying situations.

There is a marvelous essay by Erving Goffman about the roles, rules, and forms of the lecture—the typical lecture, as opposed to the Becker/Beckett absurdity.[1] In effect, Goffman explicates the lecture as a rhetorical genre. In what respects, he asks, is the lecture a distinctive speech type? How is it different, say, from the call to action, or the comedic performance, or the printed essay? Are there sufficient similarities between extemporaneous lectures and regularly scheduled ones, or between broadcast lectures and face-to-face ones, that we can speak coherently about the lecture as genre, rather than always having to refer to its subtypes? If so, what are the recurrent *forms* of the lecture—its characteristic features? What is there about the nature of the lecture situation that influences their recurrence?

Overall, says Goffman, the lecture situation carries audience expectations that the speaker will impart something of substantive value to the audience, and it imposes a concomitant obligation on the speaker to warrant the audience's conferral of intellectual authority. The lecturer is a performer but of a very special sort, and this gives rise to what is perhaps the cardinal rule: while the audience should ideally be carried away by the talk, it is the subject matter that should appear to do the carrying, not the lecturer's manner of presentation.

Thus, says Goffman, "the style is typically serious and slightly impersonal, the controlling intent being to generate calmly considered understanding, not mere entertainment, emotional impact, or immediate action."[2] But whatever the *form* of delivery of the lecture—whether read or memorized or presented as "fresh talk"—it should also give the impression of having been adapted to the immediate situation. This may be accomplished by such devices as amplification of a printed text or, in the case of extemporaneous speech, by making it appear a good deal "fresher" than it really is (e.g., through parenthetical utterances). What a lecturer brings to hearers in addition to the text, says Goffman,

is added access to himself and a commitment to the particular situation at hand. He exposes himself to the audience. He addresses the occasion. In both ways he gives himself up to the situation. And this ritual work is done under cover of conveying his text. No one need feel that ritual has become an end in itself. As the manifest content of a dream allows a latent meaning to be tolerated, so the transmission of a text allows for the ritual of performance.[3]

4

Goffman's observations about the lecture should not be surprising to readers of this book. Most will already be expert on the subject, having put in considerable time as lecturees, if not as lecturers. Indeed, the general processes of identifying and classifying kinds of discourse, of fitting them into one genre or another, of specifying their formal elements, and of accounting for them and formulating rules of a sort to guide future action are activities ordinary mortals use in sizing up situations, comparing and contrasting them to situations experienced in the past, and determining thereby how best to deal with them. What Goffman manages, in characteristic fashion, is to capture nuances of lecture functions (e.g., the need to perform and to appear not to perform) and details of lecture form (e.g., of overlaid keyings, text bracketings, and parenthetical utterances) that escape the average observer's attention. This sensitivity is one respect in which *good* generic scholarship differs from ordinary observation.

We have summarized only a small portion of Goffman's insightful comments about the lecture as rhetorical genre, but we have reviewed enough to suggest that not all of the situations we face are as anomalous as the situation Sam Becker confronted. It is as a result of the recurrence of situations—their typicality—that rhetorical practices recur, are emulated, and sometimes become conventionalized. This happens, not just in academic environs, but also, and perhaps most characteristically, in political settings.

RHETORICAL GENRES AND POLITICAL DISCOURSE

This book is about the study of forms and genres of rhetoric, especially rhetoric that is, broadly speaking, political. In modern scholarship the concepts of form and genre have been particularly prominent in literary studies, but the essays in this book explore the possibilities and the problems of generic scholarship that surveys discourse having to do with the practical conduct of public affairs.

The systematic study of rhetoric derives from the need, in ancient Greece and Rome, to train citizens in the art of legal and political oratory. Among the many meanings of "rhetoric" that have survived over the centuries is the sense of rhetoric as persuasion, and that is the sense in which the term is used in this book. We mean by rhetoric both the practice of persuasion and the systematic thought given to its practice; that is, the theory, art, or strategy informing the use of practical discourse—the study, as Aristotle put it, of "the available means of persuasion."

So conceived, rhetoric's close relationship to politics is apparent.[4] Our object, however, is not to treat comprehensively all aspects of rhetoric occurring in the conduct of public affairs; rather, it is to explore underlying conceptual and methodological issues that arise when one undertakes to study the nature and functions of forms and genres of political discourse. The central question of the book is: What are the advantages and disadvantages of focusing on forms and genres of talk when trying to understand political discourse? As the essays to follow show clearly, the answers to that question are not uniformly agreed on, nor have the possible foci of generic analysis been fully canvassed to date. The essays in Part I of this book are therefore exploratory and frequently argumentative. The studies comprising Part II are illustrative of generic approaches that could be taken in analyzing political discourse about public affairs. To highlight methodological possibilities, those studies focus on a single instance of a relatively unproblematic genre of political rhetoric: the American presidential inaugural. We introduce this volume by way of a preview and commentary on basic issues.

FORM, GENRE, AND SITUATION

One set of issues concerns the relationship between form and genre, and of both to situation. At times form and genre are treated as synonymous, as when Kenneth Burke speaks of Aristotle's classification of forensic, deliberative, and epideictic genres as "forms-in-the-large."[5] Others treat genres as "complexes" or "clusters" of forms, forms being elements of genres.[6] "Stripped of its aura of mystery," says Simons, "the term 'genre' vaguely denotes some type of categorization but is nonspecific about the nature of categorization or level of abstraction."[7] As regards "rhetorical genre," he notes, discourses have been variously classified by occasion, race, ideology, strategy, historical period, geographical location, intended effect, and various combinations thereof (e.g., respectively, inaugurals, black rhetoric, "women's liberation rhetoric," subversive rhetoric, nineteenth-century rhetoric, British rhetoric, rhetoric to stimulate).

Among the most popular images of form are those deriving from classifications of style and structure. Form is also treated as a shaper *of* content, or as a shape given *by* content. And form has been looked upon merely as a container into which content is poured.[8] Each of these images of form accords with what Michael Reddy refers to as the "*conduit* metaphor," a commonplace way of thinking about language that assumes that ideas (or meanings) are objects, linguistic expressions are containers, communication is sending.[9]

6

There are also various senses of *form as content*. It is often maintained, for example, that paraphrases never evoke quite the same meanings as the originals; that the style of a message always provides relational information (e.g., how the speaker regards the listener; how the speaker wishes to be perceived by the listener) if not substantive information; that seemingly minor alterations in form can significantly alter the content.

Yet another view holds that listeners impose form upon a work, or at least that they share in the process of "form-ation" with senders of messages. A variant of this *dialogic* view is Burke's notion of form as "the creation of an appetite in the mind of the auditor, and the adequate satisfying of that appetite."[10] Jane Blankenship in this volume incorporates Burke's well-known classification of forms (progressive, repetitive, conventional, and minor or incidental) into her model of form as energy.

No single conception of form dominates in contemporary rhetorical scholarship, but scholars have generally endorsed Edwin Black's view of rhetorical genres as related in some sense to situation, and as constituted by recurrent features or elements that can be described as forms.[11] Consistent with that view, Campbell and Jamieson offered a series of propositions about the relationships among form, genre, and situation. Their definitional statements are presupposed by some but not all contributors to this book:[12]

1. A genre is a constellation of recognizable forms bound together by an internal dynamic. It is from "a fusion of forms, not by its individual elements, that a genre is given its character."

2. The forms from which rhetorical genres are constituted "are of the kind that rhetoricians call 'strategies'—substantive and stylistic forms chosen to respond to situational requirements." Examples of substantive forms are modes of proof, canons of logic, *topoi*, motivational appeals, and the like. Stylistic forms include structural elements, patterns of personal display, as well as figures of speech such as metaphor and antithesis.

3. While the forms that comprise a genre "appear in isolation in other discourses," what is distinctive about their functioning within a genre "is the recurrence of the forms in constellation."

4. As constellations, rhetorical genres are not mere groupings of acts displaying significant similarities. Their substantive and stylistic elements are necessitated by situation, and they are joined to each other as well by an internal dynamic that remains virtually unchanged even as the elements themselves are altered somewhat over time.

5. Situations occasion generic patterns of rhetoric and can even be said to require them. When a community is "ruptured by death," for example, "persons must alter their relationship with the deceased and also confront their own mortality." Eulogies are thus "required to reknit the sundered community through rhetorical devices that appeal to the audience to carry on the works, to embody the virtues, or to live as the deceased would live."

In our view Campbell and Jamieson's conception of rhetorical genres as constellations of formal elements is useful, as is their notion that rhetorical genres are situationally grounded. There is, however, a need for a more fully developed view of situation and its influence on rhetorical choice. We are not convinced, for example, that the strategies persuaders select are always required by situation. We suspect, rather, that there is usually more than one way of coping with situational demands and more than one way of construing those demands and of interpreting them to others. Carolyn R. Miller comments in this connection that Campbell and Jamieson's "demand response" vocabulary is too objectivist in orientation.[13] While we believe that responses to situation tend to exhibit greater variability than is suggested by the Campbell-Jamieson formulation, theirs remains for us a convincing definitional statement.

Agreement on the term "genre" is less problematic than agreement as to the level of abstraction at which the term should be employed. Jackson Harrell and Wil A. Linkugel observed that generic classifications of rhetoric range from the immanent to the transcendent, that is, from obvious, occasion-related types such as the presidential inaugural to archetypal classifications embracing a wide array of these defacto types.[14] We propose that, unlike the companion term "genus" in biology, which stands taxonomically between class and species, the term "genre" can be reasonably used at any level of abstraction. Speechmaking, for example, is a genre, compared, say, with essay writing. In Aristotle's *Rhetoric* speechmaking is divided into forensic, deliberative, and ceremonial forms. As history has shown, these genres could be divided into subtypes. Aristotle distinguished also between lines of argument appropriate to the accused in the law tribunal and those appropriate to the accuser. One might go on to place the political apologia in the category of defensive forensic rhetoric. Similarly, alongside the accusatory rhetoric of the courtroom prosecutor, one might place political campaign advertisements that attack opponents. And one need not stop even at this level of specificity. For example, Rosenfield writes of mass-media apologias, as opposed to apologias delivered in face-to-face settings.[15] And the genre of the apologia might be divided further by type of mass medium, or by the nature of the accusation, or by defenses under conditions of actual guilt or innocence, and so forth. Thus "speechmaking" on one rung of the abstraction ladder and an apologia presented on television under conditions of admitted guilt on a more distant rung could each be said to represent a "genre" despite their obvious differences in levels and the fact that the apologia may be said to participate in the class "speechmaking." In our view it is not specificity that invites the generic name, but the presence of a characteristic set of formal elements given systematic play in response to a recurring situation.

ON THE MERITS OF GENERIC SCHOLARSHIP: Some Guiding Premises

A second set of issues to be addressed in this book concerns the merits of the generic approach to rhetorical discourse. What can we hope to gain from such scholarship in the way of theoretical and critical insights? Should we assume that every rhetorical work belongs to a genre, and only to that genre? Does every rhetorical creation stand in close enough relation to other works that understanding of work *A* is enhanced by study of the formal characteristics of works *E, I, O,* and *U?* What is the relationship between generic description and generic prescription? Is the "discovery" of a rhetorical genre's recurrent features anything more than an anthropological note about a culture or a subculture? Are genres fixed forms or do they change with every change in the experience patterns of audiences? In what sense, if at all, are political rhetors constrained by generic "rules"?

What, moreover, are the philosophical assumptions underlying references to "stable patterns," or to rhetorical works as "belonging" to a genre, or to generic "rules"? Is the search for stable or recurrent patterns reflective of an arcane, foundationalist epistemology? Does the very notion of generic "rules" presuppose a commitment to established ways of doing things and thus serve to perpetuate error and injustice? And where in the study of rhetorical genres are the ideas of creativity, originality, and improvisational freedom?

These are among the general questions considered in Part I of this book. In the opening chapter Connors sketches the history of generic criticism in literary theory and criticism, and provides a cautionary note for rhetorical critics regarding potential abuses of genre criticism. In chapter 2 Simons and Aghazarian offer a "rules-oriented" perspective on rhetorical genres. In the chapter that follows, Conley points to inherent taxonomical and philosophical problems in classifying works as complex as rhetorical discourses. Osborn next explores the nature and functions of a special form that recurs in persuasive rhetoric of many types: imagistic representation. McGee follows with an exploration of relations between communication praxis and the problem of form and structure, contrasting the theory of genres with his own functional approach to understanding rhetoric. In the final chapter of Part I, Shapiro draws attention to relevant work of European textualists, suggesting alternative "readings" that are possible when form in discourse is perceived as political expression. In sum, Part I of this volume provides a historical and theoretical overview of major problems and possibilities that deserve to be weighed by anyone considering whether and how to explore political rhetoric using the concepts "form" and "genre."

The essays in Part II continue our probe of problems and possibilities in the most practical way possible: through analysis of a sample of what is perhaps the most widely agreed-upon "genre" of American political discourse, the presidential inaugural. In the essays following Campbell and Jamieson's thoroughgoing explication of the genre, three critics committed to the proposition that Ronald Reagan's inaugural address of 1981 belongs, in fact, to a distinctive *class* or *kind* of political speaking offer critical comment on the event. They follow their own critical interests but work within the framework of theory of genres. In doing so they allow us to discern something of a range of insights that are possible using genre theory as a basis for critical inquiry. In Part III, political scientist Richard Joslyn casts a critical eye on the essays in Part II, asking what value such critiques have for enlarging understanding of contemporary political processes.

Our book is thus an inquiry into the uses and values of the concepts "form" and "genre" in the study of political rhetoric. Several issues raised by the chapters to follow deserve general, introductory identification. A first question about the merits of generic scholarship is what we can learn from the experience of using genre theory in literary studies. Well before "genre" became an important term in studies of political rhetoric, literary scholars were attempting to impose order upon their subject matter, to account for recurrent patterns, and to identify rules or principles that might guide both literary practice and the critical analysis of works that fall within a given genre. As is evidenced by Connors's review, the results have not always been regarded as felicitous. As literary theorists moved beyond such broad classifications as narrative, drama, and lyric to such "particulars" as the romance novel or the *Bildungsroman*, they found themselves increasingly frustrated by the complexities of

10

the task of taxonomizing their objects of study. Such genres as seemed recognizable were ordered according to a bewildering array of principles. And just when it seemed that a coherent deductive system of classification might be developed, the theorist would be confronted with exceptions sufficient in number, apparently, to *disprove* the rule.

Even more frustrating have been efforts to utilize generic classifications prescriptively as guides to literary practice or critical evaluation. For some genres, such as the epic, there were conventions galore; for others, such as the modern novel, there were apparently few, if any. More importantly, the very idea of *creative* writing—of originality—called into question the desirability of conformity to generic conventions. And, indeed, it was often the case that while one writer succeeded by close conformity to the rules, another succeeded by blatantly violating them. Little wonder that periods of intense interest in generic classification have been followed by cries of "Death to the systematizers!"

Still, one cannot *not* classify literary or rhetorical artifacts, any more than one can avoid categorizing natural objects in one's environment. To give a work any kind of reading or critique at all, one must first assume that it can be treated as some particular kind of thing; else, one would not know how to stand in relation to it. Although any single classification is bound to deflect attention from some of a given work's distinctive characteristics, there is no reason why the work cannot be classified in multiple ways. Thus, for example, one might profitably view Martin Luther King's letter from Birmingham Jail as black rhetoric, as southern rhetoric, as protest rhetoric, as ministerial, religious rhetoric, as a species of public letter-writing, and as an apologia of sorts—thus deriving a sense of the singularity of the work from an examination of its unique combination of commonalities with other works.

The fact is, moreover, that certain of our literary and rhetorical genres "exist" as cultural artifacts, and not just in the minds of classification-happy academics. The conventions associated with such forms as the epic and the presidential inaugural are known to message-makers and message recipients alike, and they can thus hardly be ignored by critics. Paul Hernadi reminds us that even the boldest departures from tradition take on meaning in relation to the conventions that they violate.[16] Heather Dubrow identifies a number of ways in which a writer might stand in relation to the conventions of a genre, each such act of conformity or deviation serving as a "code" of sorts that signals an attitude toward the genre, or to leading representatives of the genre, or to the culture as a whole.[17] Thus, for example, one poet will mock neoclassical generic pretensions by out-Homering Homer in the construction of an epic;

11

another will seek to "purify" the genre; another to modernize it. Similarly, Jamieson reflects upon the allusive character of oratorical prose in a discussion of how memorable synoptic phrases such as "making the world safe for democracy" get imitated, or mocked, or co-opted, and sometimes perverted in subsequent orations.[18] Just as it is possible to identify generic conventions, so may we classify the major forms and functions of departures from those conventions.

Between those who would add to our lists of generic categories, and those, such as Conley, in this volume, who believe that our categories have already proliferated to a point where there are nearly as many categories as there are cases, it needs to be remembered that categories serve diverse purposes. Genericists themselves frequently complain about each other's latest additions; but, while Carolyn Miller, for example, would focus upon de-facto genres (those for which there are names in ordinary language), and is critical of Walter R. Fisher's formalistic typologies, the fact is that Miller is mainly interested in cultural history, Fisher in generic comparison and theory building.[19] Except for such commonsense types as the presidential inaugural or the commencement address, the names given to rhetorical genres are typically designed as ways of looking at them, and perhaps of accounting for them. Thus, for example, when Kurt Ritter characterized presidential nomination speeches given at party conventions as "political jeremiads," he was suggesting their rootedness in Puritan culture and, before that, in the biblical injunctions of the prophet Jeremiah and his many followers.[20] Even structural likenesses to Puritan jeremiads constituted for Ritter evidence of a nonobvious tie to a foundational religious tradition. But Ritter also saw the acceptance speeches of modern-day politicians as impelled and constrained by other more immediate factors, such as whether the speakers were functioning as challengers or defenders of the administration in power at the time. This factor alone constituted sound reason in his view for division of the acceptance-speech genre into an "in-party" subgenre and an "out-party" subgenre. Again, we would not object. In analyzing any act or artifact, it is often helpful to move from the macroscopic to the microscopic, from the broadly generic to partic- ular subtypes, and to examine the work from a variety of generic perspectives as well. Admittedly some perspectives will not prove very helpful. It may also turn out that entire taxonomies were built on less-than-useful principles of classification, or, at the very least, that they were insufficiently inclusive. But there is always the possibility of choosing new classifications and new taxonomies, built on new princi- ples. Dubrow has suggested, for example, that literary genres are more akin to personality types than to biological types, and she would thus reclassify them accordingly.[21] Osborn, in this volume, challenges the study of depictions in rhetoric as though they were primarily linear and logical arguments. His proposed reconceptualization of rhetorical forms and functions would involve not so much a change in focus as a more inclusive study of "the roots of public rationality itself."

Even assuming that generic scholarship had not proved useful in literary studies—an assumption we would strongly contest—there remains the very real possibility that generic concepts and methods may prove more useful in the study of political rhetoric than they have in the study of literature. In arguing thus, we realize that we are begging the question of whether one may legitimately distinguish between literature and rhetoric, or, indeed, between literature and politics. By some recent accounts, everything is discourse, all life is a text, there is *only* literature; or there is *only* politics. And it is also argued that virtually all discourse, not least political discourse, is strategically selected, adapted to its ends—hence rhetorical.[22]

We think there is merit in a blurring of distinctions among the literary, the rhetorical, and the political—in a recognition, for example, that even the most seemingly innocuous pastoral poem may constitute a political statement of sorts and be rhetorically motivated.[23] We recognize, too, that some works of fiction have had great political impact (including a few that Osborn comments upon in this volume), and that most fiction writers strive to adapt to audience and situation at least in the sense of seeking to be at least minimally understood.

Still, we would argue that such prototypical rhetors as salesmen, editorialists, and politicians are far more constrained by situational factors than are poets, novelists, dramatists, and the like. For the politician responding to charges of wrongdoing in office, there is little opportunity to experiment with aesthetic conventions, or to consider the probable impact of the message on generations hence. What counts is responding, as political apologists have always done, to the demands of the immediate situation and to do so by offering convincing excuses or justifications. This makes political apologias relatively predictable—far more predictable and far more amenable to generic comparison than are poems, novels, or plays. It follows that the conventions associated with such rhetorical genres as the political apologia should have greater practical force—that is, greater prescriptive power—than those associated with literary genres.

The foregoing are among the assumptions that have guided this book's development. We are sensitive to the problems of "genre-alizing" about political rhetoric, and of bringing generic rules to bear in critical analyses of cases, but we are convinced that categorizing is inevitable, that generic proliferation isn't necessarily bad, and that placing a given work into a variety of generic categories may actually help us to fix upon its singularity. We assume, further, that rhetorical works are more amenable to generic analysis than are literary works, owing to the very nature of rhetoric as a practical, situational art. In maintaining that rhetors are more constrained by situation, we are in no way suggesting that they are slaves to generic rules; indeed, we think it possible to chart types of deviations from generic patterns, just as it has been possible to chart the patterns themselves.

We would add, finally, what perhaps needs no saying at this point, that political discourse falls more directly within the orbit of rhetorical theory than it does within the overlapping orbit of literary theory. Again, we are reluctant to overgeneralize. There is a rich storehouse of literary concepts, such as voice, distance, tone, and mood, which can be applied as well to political discourse as to works of fiction. Shapiro, in this volume, illustrates as well the potential benefits to be derived from treating political discourse metaphorically as literature, and even as narrative fiction. But these efforts at "de-familiarizing" political texts ought not to be construed as literal claims for the primacy of literary theory and criticism in the study of politics. If anything, Shapiro's "textual" analysis of a criminology text illustrates the book's pseudo-scientific, rhetorical character.

Whatever one's area of rhetorical or political interest, and whatever one's predilections for or against what are these days called "genre studies," it seems clear that the issues with which we are here contending virtually compel consideration. Except for Connors, Shapiro, and Joslyn, the contributors to this book all come from a tradition of rhetorical study focused on political speechmaking,[24] and it is in relation to these objects of scrutiny that the problems here discussed were first confronted by us. Rhetoricians operating from this "speech-communication" perspective have since come to study a considerable variety of nonoratorical genres, some of them identified as "genres," others labeled as rhetorical "types" or simply as "rhetorics."[25] In so doing, they have found themselves, together with scholars from other disciplines, confronting similar problems that arise when objects of study are approached as rhetoric.[26] Partly in consequence of social turbulence, so-called "rhetoric of" studies multiplied during the 1960s and 1970s: the "rhetoric of" historical and scientific discourse; popular culture and the fine arts; interpersonal, group, and organizational communications; and, especially, social move-

14

ments and social protest were explored both within and outside the speech-communication tradition.[27] Paralleling the emergence of structuralism in Europe, interest in roles and typologies in social science, the structure of arguments in philosophy, the functions of forms and genres in literature, and the nature and influences of rhetorical forms and genres began to develop in the United States following World War II. Especially influential among those associated with the speech-communication tradition in rhetorical studies were the writings of two literary critics, Kenneth Burke[28] and Northrop Frye.[29] The seminal work in rhetorical criticism per se was Edwin Black's *Rhetorical Criticism*, first published in 1965.[30] To a number of rhetorical critics, a generic approach to study of rhetoric seemed a welcome alternative to earlier, none-too-successful efforts to estimate and account for effects of rhetoric through evaluating the works' fulfillment of essentially classical prescriptions for composing speeches. As is indicated in several essays in this volume, some rhetorical critics have come to believe that systematic study of past practices and of situational factors that give rise to those practices can yield guiding principles and critical criteria for estimating the qualities and potentialities of rhetoric—principles and criteria more soundly based than the essentially pedagogical prescriptions of the classical tradition. One could, it is argued, legitimately criticize a eulogist if his or her rhetoric failed to fulfill the demands of eulogistic situations. One could applaud the effort if the rhetoric displayed the unity of form and function, of style and substance that eulogistic situations regularly call for in a given culture or subculture. Or, at the very least, one could presume the necessity of abiding by generic prescriptions, unless, in exceptional cases, there was clear and compelling reason to do otherwise. Our hope is that the collection of essays that follows will help readers to form their own judgments on the merits of such hypotheses.

Besides being promoted as a welcome alternative to neo-Aristotelian rhetorical criticism, the generic approach has been heralded as a humanistic alternative to a behavioral science of persuasion—what Nathan Maccoby once referred to as "the new scientific rhetoric."[31] We agree—or we would at least propose it as a useful complement to other modes of investigation.

Since the publication of *Communication and Persuasion* by a team of social psychologists at Yale University in 1953,[32] the behavioral approach to study of communication has spawned dozens of theories and hundreds of experiments. At the zenith of its popularity it was heralded as promising discovery of covering laws of persuasion, not much different from covering laws used in the physical sciences. While the sheer output of behavioral research is clearly impressive, the results are less so. We think this is in part because behavioral research has tended to ride roughshod over the contexts of persuasion, the very circumstances that give meaning and purpose to the interactants.[33] Like the behavioral approach, the generic approach seeks generalizations about persuasion and explanations for those generalizations, but the two approaches are quite different.

Broadly speaking, the behavioralist tends to do experiments; the genericist studies messages naturalistically. The behavioralist isolates variables in messages for purposes of research; the genericist seeks to understand how variables fit together to comprise patterns. The genericist looks for similarities in rhetorical patterns used by persuaders with similar roles in similar situations. The behavioralist looks for differences that make a difference in effects on audiences. In a sense, the behavioralist picks up where the genericist leaves off. Whereas the genericist is primarily interested in the actions of persuaders, the behavioralist is primarily interested in the reactions of persuadees. Finally, the generic approach to rhetorical research tends to be "rules-oriented" while the behavioral research tends to be "laws-oriented." In this last respect the generic approach has much in common with action theory, game theory, speech-act theory, symbolic interactionism, ethnomethodology, sociolinguistics, and rules-oriented communication theories. Simons and Aghazarian propose a rules-oriented generic approach in chapter 2.

SCOPE AND FUNCTIONS OF GENERIC SCHOLARSHIP

Before concluding this overview and commentary on basic issues, we should like to offer three additional points, each in the way of a call for a vast opening up of what it means to do "genre" scholarship. First, as regards the scope of our inquiry, it was noted earlier that some rhetoricians, identified with the speech-communication tradition, continue to restrict the purview of what they label as generic scholarship to studies of political oratory. This anomalous sense of "rhetorical genre" is a vestige, we suspect, of struggles for academic legitimacy begun earlier in the twentieth century. As scholars such as James Winans sought to develop programs in speech pedagogy and criticism in American universities, they looked for ways to define themselves on a par with their colleagues in English while at the same time justifying their separate identities. They did so by reminding their colleagues of the rootedness of classical rhetorical theory in the study of oratory, and then, having assumed the mantle of preserving the Greco-Roman tradition, they

16

sought to defend its oratorical emphasis by conceiving of rhetorical genres and of rhetorical criticism as oratorical counterparts of literary genres and literary criticism.

In this essay we have cited studies of oratorical and nonoratorical genres by scholars operating within and outside the speech-communication tradition. We think there is value in a cross-fertilization of perspectives, and we believe that, ultimately, the questions we have raised should be addressed, not just in the context of a study of political discourse, but as a multidisciplinary theory of discursive types.

As to just what acts and artifacts ought to count as genres of political rhetoric, we are unable to render an authoritative judgment, the problem being one of deciding what to exclude. This introduction has touched upon a variety of acts and artifacts, but it can hardly be said to have "covered" the territory. The study of political rhetoric must obviously include political campaigning, but surely it could not exclude such governmental activities as legislative hearings and negotiations, international diplomacy and propaganda, administrative rhetoric and the politics of social control. A list of political rhetorics might also include ostensibly nonpolitical messages that are known to influence political beliefs and attitudes, such as fairy tales that help to shape political attitudes and revisionist histories rewritten in response to changing political climates. The list would no doubt include political cartoons and newspaper editorials, but it might also include ordinary news reports as well as discussions of politics by rhetoricians and political scientists.

No doubt our readers will insist at this point that the catalogue be restricted. We ourselves would be willing to distinguish between paradigm and peripheral cases (e.g., between the politics of government and the politics of the boardroom or the bedroom), but we are sympathetic to Paul Valesio's view that rhetoric is a dimension—indeed "the political dimension"—in all discourse.[34]

The second point concerns the purposes of generic scholarship. All too often, in our view, generic scholarship has been bent to the purposes of rendering evaluative judgments on individual works. There have been few studies of patterns of rhetorical choice and variation over time, and there have been not enough comparative studies of variations in response to like rhetorical situations during any one period. The idea that "genre" is somehow exclusively "a critic's term" is one that gained popularity some time ago among literary scholars, and has since taken hold among rhetoricians. The idea was sustained by the methods that literary scholars customarily used to establish the distinguishing characteristics of a given genre—usually involving concentrated critical attention on a few generic specimens. We think there is real value in generic criticism of individual works, but there are surely other useful functions of generic scholarship, not the least of which are enhanced cultural and historical understanding.

Moreover, comparative generic studies can advance our theoretical understanding of persuasion, as Hart argues in this volume. When political scientist Stephen L. Wasby was asked to comment as an "outsider" on what he saw as the differences between the old and the new rhetorical studies, he said that the new represented fundamentally a shift in focus from the "particularistic or idiosyncratic in discourse" to a study of rhetorical regularities. The older scholarship, he said, had been "difficult for anyone to integrate in order to develop general explanations or theories."[35] Hart's computer-assisted generic comparisons provide an excellent example of theory-centered generic scholarship.

Lest these last comments fuel a conviction that we are "antihumanistic," or that we are more "scientoid" than "humanoid," we hasten to add, as our third and final point, that generic scholarship virtually requires a variety of methods to go with its variety of objectives. Elsewhere, one of our number called for more extensive use of scientific methods of research as a corrective to potential errors of observation and inference in the formulation of generalizations about distinguishing characteristics of a genre.[36] But there are times when much more anecdotal evidence is called for, as when nonobvious connections are being made between seemingly disparate rhetorical artifacts. The acknowledged master here is Kenneth Burke, and the example that springs to mind is his illustration of the varieties of situations that rhetors might "encompass" by way of the proverb "When the pitcher strikes the stone, or the stone the pitcher, it's bad for the pitcher."

Think of some primitive society in which an incipient philosopher, in disfavor with the priests, attempted to criticize their lore. They are powerful, he is by comparison weak. And they control all the channels of power. Hence, whether they attack him or he attacks them, he is the loser. And he could quite adequately size up this situation by saying, "Whether the pitcher strikes the stone, or the stone the pitcher, it's bad for the pitcher." Or Aristophanes could well have used it, in describing his motivation when, under the threats of political dictatorship, he gave up the lampooning of political figures and used the harmless Socrates as his goat instead. Socrates was propounding new values—and Aristophanes, by aligning himself with conservative values, against the materially powerless dialectician, could himself take on the role of the stone in the stone-pitcher ratio. Or the proverb could be employed to name the predicament of a man in Hitler's Germany who might come

18

forward with an argument, however well reasoned, against Hitler. Or a local clerk would find the proverb apt, if he would make public sport of his boss. These situations are all distinct in their particularities; each occurs in a totally different texture of history; yet all are classifiable together under the generalizing head of the same proverb.[37]

Freed from the constraints imposed upon it by any one discipline or school of thought, the concept of "genre" can provide yet another bridge between the humanities and the social sciences in the rapprochement that, according to Clifford Geertz, is already well under way.[38] Far from being just a critic's tool, it can be a vehicle for cultural and historical insights, and for theory-building and theory-testing as well. Whether as applied to political discourse or any other, generic scholarship ought to include figurative and not just literal comparisons and contrasts, studies of univocal responses to apparently dissimilar situations (as in the "pitcher-stone" example), as well as multivocal responses to seemingly similar situations.

Notes

1. Erving Goffman, *Forms of Talk* (Philadelphia: University of Pennsylvania Press, 1981), pp. 160–96.

2. Ibid., p. 165.

3. Ibid., p. 191.

4. Indeed, it may be argued that politics involves little more than persuading others and being persuaded by them. No doubt the power of tangible rewards and punishments influences political decisionmaking as well, but seldom are political decisions based solely on material inducements or on coercion or force. Almost always the influence agent attempts to change minds and not just behavior. And almost always the agent cares not just about immediate, substantive effects but also about reputation. Moreover, it needs to be remembered that the *perceived* value of political benefits depends often on how they are *labeled*, and this is yet another function of rhetoric. Using language to color perceptions, to build and maintain favorable images, and to influence behavior by changing minds is what persuasion is substantially about. For a discussion of these principles, see Herbert W. Simons, *Persuasion: Understanding, Practice, and Analysis* (2nd ed.; New York: Random House, 1986).

5. Kenneth Burke, *A Rhetoric of Motives* (Berkeley: University of California Press, 1969), pp. 69–78.

6. See Karlyn Kohrs Campbell and Kathleen Hall Jamieson, eds., *Form and Genre: Shaping Rhetorical Action* (Annandale, Va.: Speech Communication Association, 1978). Their lead essay reviews these and similar usages; see pp. 15–18.

7. Herbert W. Simons, " 'Genre-alizing' about Rhetoric: A Scientific Approach," in *Form and Genre: Shaping Rhetorical Action*, p. 33.

8. See Jane Blankenship and Barbara Sweeney's excellent summary in "The 'Energy' of Form," *Central States Speech Journal* 31(Fall 1980):172–83.

9. Michael Reddy, "The Conduit Metaphor," in A. Ortony, ed., *Metaphor and Thought* (Cambridge, Eng.: Cambridge University Press, 1979), pp. 284–324.

10. Kenneth Burke, *Counter-Statement* (Berkeley: University of California Press, 1931; 2nd ed., 1953), p. 31.

11. Edwin Black, *Rhetorical Criticism: A Study in Method* (New York: Macmillan, 1965).

12. See their lead chapter in Campbell and Jamieson, eds., *Form and Genre: Shaping Rhetorical Action*, esp. pp. 18–28. All quotations in the numbered paragraphs below are from this chapter.

13. Carolyn R. Miller, "Genre as Social Action," *Quarterly Journal of Speech* 70 (1984):152. Miller argues for a Schutzian view of genres as typified rhetorical actions based on popular understandings of how to act in particular situations. She views situational exigencies not as objective facticities, but as social constructions of danger, separateness, ignorance, and the like that provide rhetors with a way of explaining and legitimizing their intentions.

14. Jackson Harrell and Wil A. Linkugel, "On Rhetorical Genre: An Organizing Perspective," *Philosophy and Rhetoric* 11 (1978):262–81.

15. Lawrence W. Rosenfield, "A Case Study in Speech Criticism: The Nixon–Truman Analog," *Speech Monographs* 35 (1968):435–50.

16. Paul Hernadi, *Beyond Genre* (Ithaca, N.Y.: Cornell University Press, 1972).

17. Heather Dubrow, *Genre* (London: Methuen, 1982).

18. Kathleen Jamieson, "On Eloquence." Unpublished ms., n.d.

19. See Miller, "Genre as Social Action," p. 153. Also see Walter R. Fisher, "Genre: Concepts and Applications in Rhetorical Criticism," *Western Journal of Speech Communication* 44 (1980):288–99.

20. Kurt W. Ritter, "American Political Rhetoric and the Jeremiad Tradition: Presidential Nomination Acceptance Addresses, 1960–1976," *Central States Speech Journal* 31 (1980):153–71.

21. See Dubrow, *Genre*, pp. 115–18.

22. See, e.g., Paul Valesio, *Novantiqua: Rhetorics as Contemporary Theory* (Bloomington: Indiana University Press, 1980).

23. See, e.g., Burke on Gray's "Elegy," in *A Rhetoric of Motives*, pp. 123–27.

24. The most powerful, though not the original articulation of this scholarly interest, was an essay, "The Literary Criticism of Oratory," first published in 1925 by Herbert A. Wichelns of Cornell University and repeatedly anthologized since that date. (Reprinted in *Studies in Rhetoric and Public Speaking in Honor of James Albert Winans* [New York: Russell & Russell, 1962], pp. 181–216. The editor of this volume of essays is not identified.) "Rhetorical criticism lies at the boundary of politics (in the broadest sense)," wrote Wichelns; "its atmosphere is that of the public life, its tools are those of literature, its concern is with the ideas of the people as influenced by their leaders" (p. 215). This claim, it can be said, became the credo of a generation of scholars professionally associated with the study of speaking. Most who have in one way or another followed Wichelns's lead in historical and critical studies now belong to third and fourth generations of the tradition and tend to identify themselves as students of speech communication.

25. There is indeed a gap, to be discussed, between what they typically count

20

as "rhetorical genres" and their broad sense of rhetoric itself. Studies of nonoratorical genres are not uncommonly labeled as "movement" studies or as "media" studies. Or they are characterized as having used generic entitlements like "the rhetoric of the New Left" or "Black Power" rather casually, or, as Campbell and Jamieson put it, "without necessarily entailing a fully developed claim to generic particularity." Fisher's state-of-the-art review offers a "Catalogue," admittedly "nonexhaustive," of forty-two political genre studies. All, it turns out, are of speeches by prominent political figures. Fisher separately lists four "exemplary examples" of "the rhetoric of . . ." studies, but these he excludes from his all-important "Catalogue" because they largely perform a "theoretical," genre-characterizing function and are not examples of criticism.

26. There is at present a considerable movement toward viewing the discourse of the human sciences rhetorically. (See Herbert W. Simons, "Chronicle and Commentary on a Conference," *Quarterly Journal of Speech* 71 [1985]:52–64.)

27. Only a sampling of these studies is provided in the bibliography at the end of this volume. But other bibliographic sources are referred to. For "movement" studies, see in particular Herbert W. Simons, Elizabeth W. Mechling, and Howard N. Schreier, "The Functions of Human Communication in Mobilizing for Action from the Bottom Up: The Rhetoric of Social Movements," in C. C. Arnold and J. W. Bowers, eds., *Handbook of Rhetorical and Communication Theory* (Boston: Allyn & Bacon, 1984), pp. 794–95.

28. For an excellent introduction to Burkean ways of generalizing about rhetoric, see Burke's essay on "Traditional Principles of Rhetoric," in *A Rhetoric of Motives*, pp. 49–182. On the uses of rhetoric to "encompass situations," see Burke's *The Philosophy of Literary Form* (Berkeley: University of California Press, 1973), pp. 1–24.

29. Northrop Frye, *Anatomy of Criticism* (Princeton, N.J.: Princeton University Press, 1957).

30. Edwin Black offered generic scholarship as an alternative to traditional critical methods and proposed as prototypes two "clusters" of recurrent forms, the exhortative and the argumentative.

31. Nathan Maccoby, "The New 'Scientific' Rhetoric," in W. Schramm, ed., *The Science of Communication* (New York: Basic Books, 1963), pp. 41–53.

32. See C. I. Hovland, I. L. Janis, and H. H. Kelley, *Communication and Persuasion* (New Haven, Conn.: Yale University Press, 1953).

33. See Herbert W. Simons, "The Rhetoric of Science and the Science of Rhetoric," *Western Speech* 42 (1978):37–43.

34. Valesio, *Novantiqua*, p. 9.

35. Stephen L. Wasby, "Rhetoricians and Political Scientists: Some Lines of Converging Interest," *Southern Speech Journal* 36 (Spring 1971):237.

36. Herbert W. Simons, " 'Genre-alizing' about Rhetoric: A Scientific Approach," in Campbell and Jamieson, eds., *Form and Genre*, pp. 33–50.

37. Burke, *The Philosophy of Literary Form*, pp. 2–3.

38. Clifford Geertz, "Blurred Genres: The Refiguration of Social Thought," *American Scholar* 49 (1980):165–79.

PART I
THEORY AND METHOD

1

Robert J. Connors

GENRE THEORY IN LITERATURE

The attempt to understand phenomena by referring them to other phenomena both similar and dissimilar is one of the basic human conceptual activities. The oldest written records we have are concerned with lists of cattle and goats, differentiating one from the other and thus allowing ancient Mesopotamians to regulate and control their property. Only by careful application of taxonomically derived criteria were the ancient Israelites able to create a system of dietary laws guaranteeing them safe and palatable food sources. From the very earliest times the creation of classes into which to fit things, and reasons for the fitting, has been central to all our thought. This systematization has been peculiarly powerful in fields devoted to the intellectual understanding of difficult abstract concepts, and it has traditionally been an important part of discourse theories as they have evolved in both literary and rhetorical study. The other essays in this collection will treat the use and applicability of systematics in modern rhetorical theory; in this essay, however, I wish to shift up a level in generality and provide a context for the rest of the book by discussing taxonomic and generic theory as it has existed in Western culture for the last 2,500 years. In the ways that our culture has at different times relied on and dismissed taxonomically based understandings we can see a mirror of contemporary rhetorical genre studies as they have existed over the 1960s and 1970s.

Genre theory is almost as old as written language, and it has figured predominantly in the history of criticism. Since Edwin Black's deep critique in 1965 of what might be called neo-Aristotelian rhetorical criticism—the rather mechanical application of terms and classes from the *Rhetoric* to more recent speeches—there has been an understandable desire on the part of rhetoricians to seek more fruitful critical methods.[1] Genre studies have been important among these, and it is a bit ironic that we must turn to Aristotle for our understanding of the beginnings of taxonomic genre theory as it applies to works of the imagination.

Literary genres begin with Aristotle's *Poetics*, and all subsequent theories of literary genre have built on this work.

Aristotle's analysis of the literature of his time opens with the famous announcement, "Let us here deal with Poetry, its essence and its several species, with the characteristic function of each species . . . ."[2] Proceeding from his assumption that all art is one form or another of mimesis, Aristotle proposes three criteria by which poetic (i.e., literary) genres could be distinguished: first, works can be categorized by the different forms of rhythm, meter, and language they use, what Aristotle calls the "means of representation." Second, works can be classed by what they set out to treat, by what they choose as "objects of representation." Tragedy, for example, represents people as better than they are, comedy as worse. Finally, poems (and by "poems" we must remember that Aristotle meant "makings," that is, literary creations of any sort) can be distinguished by "manner of representations," that is, the narrative style and perspective(s) chosen by the author. Utilizing these criteria, Aristotle goes on in the *Poetics* to describe the three main sorts of poetry—tragedy, comedy, and epic—the three genres that were to provide the basis for generic literary theory through the eighteenth century. From Aristotle through the Renaissance period, these genres continued to rule, along with the lyric, which was generally admitted to exist in spite of the fact that Aristotle had not dealt with it in any depth.

What is interesting about Aristotle's genres is how quickly they took over as ways of discussing poetry and how quickly genre theory assumed what we now tend to think of as its neoclassical form—that is, as series of apodictic rules rather than as descriptions of existing phenomena.

Many post-Aristotelian commentators were, of course, mere pedants, "dull dogs who reproduced [Aristotle's] views without any of his merits," as Hamilton Fyfe puts it.[3] No later Greek commentator could speak of poetry without bowing to Aristotle and referring to the necessity of respecting generic proprieties. This is, of course, the famous principle of "literary decorum," the notion that certain subjects require appropriate formal treatment. In the *Poetics* we find Aristotle arguing that tragedy had developed over the years until it "stopped when it had found its own natural form." This assumes that there *are* natural, organically classifiable genres, and although Aristotle did not insist throughout on this sort of organic absolutism, it lies behind the insistence on decorum and propriety that fills the pages of later critics.

Even Horace, who is outside of Longinus the most perspicacious of the ancient critics, assumes in his *Ars poetica* of the first century B.C. the unquestionable necessity of decorum. For Horace, as for most of

Aristotle's followers, the genres have given and unchangeable attributes based on their relationship with human nature, and these attributes exist in an absolute world removed from mere audience desires and expectations. In a famous section of the *Ars*, Horace discusses the generic necessities of versification, appealing to the examples of Homer and Archilocus, concluding, "If I fail to keep and do not understand these well-marked shifts and shades of poetic forms, why am I hailed as a poet? Why through false shame do I prefer to be ignorant rather than to learn? A theme for Comedy refuses to be set forth in verses of Tragedy."[4] That Horace considered these generic constraints separate from mere audience expectations is shown by his later section that opens, "Now hear what I, and with me the public, expect."[5] It would be unfair to characterize Horace as mechanical or unyielding in the *Ars*; he does allow for some novelty and rule-bending, especially in comedy, but in comparison to his iconoclastic attitude toward derivative lyric poets of his own age in the other *Epistles* ("If novelty had been as offensive to the Greeks as it is to us, what in these days would be ancient? What would the public have to read . . . ?"),[6] the generic demands in the *Ars* are very rigid.

Horace's work centers primarily on satyric drama, a kind of tragedy, but he does mention other lesser genres, such as hymns, odes, lyric poetry, love poetry, and elegies. Quintilian, in Book 10 of the *Institutio*, also makes clear the fact that by the first century A.D. the Roman *literati* had accepted the generic discreteness of a number of different sorts of literature; he mentions no fewer than ten different genres: epic, elegy, lyric, iambic, satire, comedy, tragedy, history, oratory, and philosophy.[7] Most of the minor poetic genres were compacted in later commentators under the broad umbrella term "lyric poetry," which gradually came to stand beside tragedy, comedy, and epic as one of the four central genres. As the classical culture of Rome was gradually eroded between the time of Horace and A.D. 500, however, generic considerations were eroded along with most other purely literary theory. Epic is hardly mentioned, outside of Aristotle's strictures on it, after Longinus, and even comedy and tragedy as organic forms all but vanished. Classical stage drama seems to have been completely lost as a performing art following the sack of Rome in A.D. 415, and although a sort of debased handbook knowledge of literary genres continued to exist, the theory had little vitality.[8]

Definitions of tragedy and comedy did exist and remained almost unchanged from the fourth century to the Renaissance, as A. P. MacMahon has shown.[9] During this time, however, generic thought was kept vital not by literary theory, but by rhetorical theory as it was interpreted by medieval thinkers. Especially important throughout the Middle Ages was the *Rhetorica ad herennium*, which, although it contains nothing about literary genres, kept vital the generic motivation, inculcating generations of critics and scholars with the classical division of oratory into deliberative, judicial, and epideictic. These divisions, and indeed the entire taxonomic tendency of classical rhetoric, helped to keep alive the idea that a phenomenon is understood only when it can be classed and be itself divided into classes. Much of the logical genius of the medieval period is thus devoted to precise taxonomy, a crucial element in Scholastic thought.

As for the old literary genres, however, they fell on rather hard times. Medieval commentary on genre was nearly always circumscribed to comedy and tragedy, and medieval commentators added little or nothing to genre theory, keeping their remarks brief and conventional. Part of the problem, of course, was linguistic: the languages of theory and the languages of the people (and thus of most imaginative literature) were drawing apart after A.D. 900. Classical genre theory, developed to analyze the Greek and Latin literary corpus, seemed in many ways an unhelpful instrument when applied to the forms and prosody of the vulgate languages whose increasing popularity after A.D. 1200 made them ever more vital literary vehicles.

The first great work of vulgate literary criticism is, of course, Dante's fourteenth-century *De vulgare eloquentia*, which makes a case for vulgate poetry as being, if not the same as classical poetry, at least equal to it. Poetry in one's natural language, argued Dante, is more noble than carefully wrought artificialities in a grammatically learned language. Dante treats only poetry in this work, and it is intriguing to note that for him the important forms are all poetical and the old dramatic genres now exist only as stylistic indices. Dante introduces nonclassical genres thus: ". . . those who have written poetry in the vernacular have published their poems in many different metrical forms, some of them in *canzoni*, some in ballades, some in sonnets, and others in irregular and illegitimate metrical forms, as I will demonstrate later."[10] Dante opts for the *canzoni* as the noblest of the forms (probably because he used it so often himself), and in his next chapter discusses the three styles in which the *canzoni* may be sung, the tragic, the comic, and the elegiac: "Tragedy is an example of something in the higher style, comedy of something in the lower style, and elegy is to be understood as having the style of the miserable." For Dante, tragedy and comedy were no longer genres per se but styles, tones, to be adapted to the contemporary forms he considered vital.[11]

28

What is obvious about *De vulgari* is that Dante had considerably more important fish to fry than genre, and indeed, after Aristotle, generic considerations in literary theory do appear as a somewhat late, somewhat technical, and often somewhat precious and artificial factor. As Dante was exploring the possibilities of the vernacular in Italian, creating something genuinely new, in medieval France new poetic genres had hardly sprung up but they began quickly to atrophy, as the heavily artificial forms of rondeau, ballade, triolet, and villanelle completely stymied more natural forms of poetry. For poets of the Languedoc, this "fossilized formalism" as George Saintsbury refers to it, was stifling in its rule-bound absolutism.[12]

But the tendencies toward settled literary habits that marked the late medieval period were about to be shattered by the reawakening of scholarship, revolt, skepticism, and artistic awareness that we call the Renaissance. All of the uncritical reliance on the perceived wisdom of a limited number of often partial classical texts (not to mention the extreme power of churchly intellectual tradition) was called into question by a veritable explosion of classical rediscovery and consequent revaluation. In place of sterile reliance on the commonplaces from Horace and the *Ad herennium*, scholars now had full texts of the original Plato, Aristotle, Longinus, and Quintilian. Soon the passive, kind-bound recumbancy of the late medieval period was pierced by a number of competing schools of critical thought, and the questions of modes, forms, and genres were once again being eagerly asked and answered.

The most important generic question for Renaissance critics concerned the legitimacy of contemporary poetic forms that did not fit with classical genre theory. Especially after the reemergence of the *Poetics*, how could a critic deal with a work like Ariosto's *Orlando furioso*, which is undoubtedly a serious piece of work, yet which absolutely violated some of Aristotle's rules for epic? Antonio Sebastiano Minturno in his *Arte poetica*, published in 1563, asks the central question, "Is romance poetry?" and in a lengthy discussion concludes that it *is*, although not the same sort of poetry as the classical authors described. Although Minturno holds that romance is an *inferior* form of poetry, he still gives it formal credence because of the genius of the authors who have practiced it. Geraldi Cinthio had earlier argued that romance was the equal of heroic epic, and Minturno, while not in complete agreement, does give the new form general credence before proceeding to discuss the more traditional genres.

Other Renaissance critics, most importantly Julius Caesar Scaliger and Nicolas Boileau, used their grasp of classical learning to construct neoclassical systems, large portions of which were generic in orientation. The first book of Scaliger's famous *Poetices libri septem* of 1561 was devoted to a discussion of the different major and minor sorts of poetry, and Scaliger's opinionated vision of what was generically acceptable— what constituted true decorum—would be a neoclassical touchstone for over a century after the publication of the *Poetices*. Scaliger and the group of French poets called the Pleiade established neoclassicism as the essential sort of Renaissance criticism, but it was not until 1674, when Nicolas Boileau published his *Arte poetique*, a long, critical verse-poem, that neoclassicism assumed the commanding and rigid form that we now usually associate with it.

Boileau, who was often referred to as "the lawgiver of Parnassus," laid down in his *Arte* a whole series of unbreakable rules, based on the ancients and especially on Aristotle and Horace, for the construction of proper literature. Genre was an intrinsic and necessary element in Boileau's plan, of course, since the decorums of the genres were different. Boileau divided the genres into the modern, which he describes in Canto 2 as pastoral, elegy, ode, sonnet, epigram, ballade, madrigal, satire, and vaudeville, and the ancient, which are of course tragedy, comedy, and epic, and are treated at great length in Canto 3. Boileau's critical position, an almost servile surrender to the claims of ancient Greek and Latin practice, had a very powerful impact upon French literature, especially French drama. The genres he proposed as immutable would for years be assumed the only true ones, and most French writing would be bent to Boileau's rules. Much of Boileau's work is based, as he himself said, on the idea of good sense, and I would be unfair to him if I denied that much of his critical insight was keen. Finally, however, Boileau's demands for absolute generic propriety are confining and stifling to the genuine artistic spirit, which may be challenged and piqued by genre rules but which resents constraint. As Walter Scott put it in his *Life of Dryden*, such generic prescription "resembles the principle of an architect who should build all his houses with the same number of windows and of stories," and Henry Fielding, extending the criticism, claims that Boileau's rules "serve for no other purpose than to curb and restrain genius, in the same manner as it would have restrained the dancing master, had the many excellent treatises on that art laid it down as an essential rule that every man must dance in chains."[13]

These criticisms can lead us from the French school of criticism into the English. It is interesting to note that almost from the beginning of English vernacular criticism we can see an awareness of genre, an awareness of what generic knowledge and forms can *do* for a writer, and

30

yet a quick drawing away from the generic prescriptivism that marks Italian and then French neoclassicism. Sir Philip Sidney's *Defence of Poesy* of 1595, one of the first and certainly the first important vernacular critical treatise, is predictably prescriptive. It is written in the form of a classical oration, and the *divisio* puts forward Sidney's conception of the classes of discourse. Highest, in his mind, lie works of the religious realm—hymns, psalms, biblical books, and the like. The second sort of discourse is what we now call prose—philosophy, science, history, and so forth. The third sort is poetry proper, which is higher than prose because it is not "wrapped within the fold of the proposed subject." True poets "borrow nothing of what is, hath been, or shall be, but range, only reined with learned discretion, into the divine consideration of what may be, and should be." Within this third discourse class Sidney places heroic, lyric, tragic, comic, satiric, iambic, elegiac, pastoral, and other poetic forms. In the midst of his defense of poetry (which is to some degree an attack on prose), Sidney does have occasion to show his essentially neoclassical generic opinions, criticizing Chaucer's pastorals for nonclassical diction, chiding Elizabethan playwrights for failing to observe the dramatic unities and for stirring kinds of laughter "forbidden plainly by Aristotle."[14] Sidney is clearly still in thrall here to the older generic considerations of the ancients. But the great English vernacular literature of the Elizabethan period, written to no set generic prescription yet inarguably great, was about to knock the English importation of French neoclassicism into a cocked hat.

The most important English critical thought of the Restoration and the eighteenth century is a curious mixture of dependence on classical and Renaissance genre concepts and an inductive and flexible theory of art based on the growing body of English literature. It cannot be denied that genre and its decorums were important considerations for English critics or that most seventeenth-century critics were fairly doctrinaire about genre. Thomas Rymer became notorious for his splenetic dismissals of non-Aristotelian works, and even John Dryden, the greatest of Restoration critics (and poets) held what seem at times to be extreme opinions on any flouting of classical genres, as when he replied to Sir Robert Howard's anti-genre position in his *Defence of an Essay of Dramatic Poesy*: "If he means that there is no essential difference betwixt Comedy, Tragedy, and Farce, but what is only made by the people's taste, which distinguishes one of them from the other, that is so manifest an error, that I need not lose time to contradict it. Were there neither judge, taste, nor opinion in the world, yet they would differ in their natures . . . ."[15] The very names of many of Dryden's critical pieces show

31

his generic preoccupation: *Essay of Dramatic Poesy; Essay of Heroic Plays; Discourse on Satire.*[16]

And yet, much of Dryden's actual criticism and his personal observations of specific authors flies directly in the face of any traditional genericism; and in this inability to fit his specific commentary into a preordained terministic field, Dryden is the first modern critic. He pays abstract homage to Corneille's dogged worship of the Unities, but his real love (despite a claim for the more "correct" Ben Jonson) is Shakespeare, "the man who of all modern, and perhaps ancient poets, had the most comprehensive soul." Shakespeare's plays violate all generic decorums, admits Dryden, but he forgives all: "He needed not the spectacles of books to read Nature; he looked inwards, and found her there." Here is the voice of a romantic critic breaking through the neoclassical façade of Dryden's more abstract criticism, the same voice that admits that though the French "observe the laws of comedy, and decorum of the stage" more than English playwrights, the beauties of such stiff decorum "are indeed the beauties of a statue, but not of a man."

In his strange admixture of abstract defense of the generic proprieties and his practical acceptance of the genius of authors who defied them, Dryden sets an example that many eighteenth-century critics followed. The period itself was, of course, a paradoxical time of almost religious respect for classical truths as well as deep interest in the empirical truths of new discovery, a time when many intellectuals built up rigid systems of traditional belief to stave off what could easily be perceived as the chaos of novelty that increasingly surrounded them. For generic concepts, this meant an almost absolute acceptance (though not neoclassical worship) of generic distinctions in most of the published criticism, but also an increasingly flexible willingness to admit that true "genius" can proceed with only passing reference to the "rules" of generic acceptability. Genre is certainly a deep and abiding preoccupation of the eighteenth-century neoclassicists—how could it not be, important as it was to the criticism of the ancients?—but as the century moves along we see a shift from the hesitant Drydenian critique of "the rules" to a full-blown Wordsworthian romanticism, determined to credit individual genius rather than preordained constraints.

Alexander Pope,[17] for instance, tries in his famous *Essay on Criticism* to defend the classical proprieties:

> Those RULES of old discoverd, not divis'd,
> Are Nature still, but Nature methodiz'd ....
> Hear how learn'd Greece her useful rules indites,
> When to repress, and when indulge our Flights   [88–93].

Here Pope sounds very like Boileau (and in fact some of the conceits of the *Essay* do come directly from the *Arte*) in his reliance upon the critical precepts of Aristotle, but a few lines later the greatness of Chaucer and Shakespeare cannot be denied:

> Some beauties yet no Precepts can declare,
> For there's a happiness as well as care.
> Music resembles Poetry, in each
> Are nameless graces which no methods teach,
> And which a master-hand alone can reach.
> If, where the rules not far enough extend,
> (Since rules were made but to promote their end)
> Some lucky Licence answers to the full
> Th' intent propos'd, that Licence is a rule   [141–49].

Pope seems here to give full rein to any writer who can "snatch a Grace beyond the Reach of Art," whether he obeys the rules or not, and indeed he hastily draws back, crying, "Moderns, beware! or if you must offend/Against the precept, ne'er transgress its End,/Let it be seldom, and compell'd by need . . . ." If modern authors will not, Pope warns, have this care, "The Critic else proceeds without remorse,/Seizes your fame, and puts his laws in force" (163–68). This vision of the Genre Police, summoned by an aroused citizenry, was finally all that Pope dared to conclude on in the *Essay*. In the *Preface to Shakespeare*, however, Pope was somewhat bolder, defending the "rules of writing" but willing to admit that Shakespeare is great in spite of them. "To judge therefore of Shakespeare by Aristotle's rules, is like trying a man by the laws of one country, who acted under those of another."

Despite this willingness to pardon Shakespeare for his genius, Pope could not make the great leap that beckoned; the conclusion that great writers can succeed despite disobeying the rules never seemed to suggest that greatness could be achieved *by* disobeying the rules. In 1759 Edward Young began to make this case in *Conjectures on Original Composition*. He complained bitterly of the slavish practice of rule-whipped imitation of classical models that controlled much of the literature about him. "And why are originals so few?" he asks. ". . . because illustrious examples engross, prejudice, and intimidate." Young castigates the authors of his day for slavish adherence to neoclassical generic decorums, concluding that "Rules, like Crutches, are a needful aid to the Lame, tho' an Impediment to the Strong."[18]

The quietus was finally put to the neoclassical rules when Samuel Johnson, so classically conservative in much else, determined to attack them both in his *Rambler* papers and in his famous *Preface to Shakespeare*. In *Rambler* 156, from 1751, Johnson says, "the accidental prescriptions of authority, when time has procured their veneration, are often confounded with the laws of nature, and those rules are supposed coeval with reason, of which the first rise cannot be discovered."[19] Johnson then discusses the generic stage decorums of the critics, and he concludes resoundingly: "It ought to be the just endeavour of a writer to distinguish nature from custom, or that which is established because it is right, from that which is right only because it is established; that he may neither violate essential principles by a desire of novelty, nor debar himself from the attainment of beauties within his view, by a needless fear of breaking rules which no literary dictator had authority to enact."

This was practically the death knell for neoclassical worship of the stage rules, and after 1780 or so they were no longer taken seriously as prescriptions. But more was occurring during the eighteenth century than the rise and demise of neoclassical genre theory. This was, as well, the time when new genres were being launched in England and elsewhere. Hugh Blair in his *Lectures* of 1783 felt compelled to devote twelve entire lectures to genre, including a series of relatively predictable lectures on the traditional poetic genres—pastoral, lyric, didactic, descriptive, epic, tragic, and comic—but also including three lectures on prose compositions. This was a new departure, and Blair certainly popularized the idea of dividing prose into history, philosophy, dialogue, epistolary writing, and fictitious history. Defoe, Richardson, and Fielding were between 1710 and 1760 creating the novel form, which was hardly launched before it was dividing itself into subgenres: the romantic novel, the familiar novel, the gothic novel, the epistolary novel, the epic novel. True, Fielding tried to identify his *Tom Jones* with earlier generic forms, calling it "a comic epic in prose," but he must have been aware that such distinctions merely erased all traditional definitions. An epic could *not* be comic, could *not* be in prose, and still remain an epic. Meanwhile such poets as Gray, Cowper, and Blake were experimenting with poetic meter and content, consigning the elegant couplet form of the earlier Augustan age to the dustbin of poetic history. The revolution against generic decorums, which we see only haltingly in the criticism, was by 1795 going full steam ahead in the literature.

With the end of the eighteenth century we leave the last great intellectual era of respect for generic traditions. Never again would genre concepts be considered so absolute and important; never again would rebellion against them be condemned as a rebellion against the order of nature. It seems an era of certainty and innocence in certain ways, and we are led to ask why the eighteenth century was so concerned by genre questions. On one level, certainly, was the preoccupation with recapturing classical rationality, which meant an adoption of the powerful, if outdated, classical genre concepts. But just as important, I think, is the neoclassical obsession with order and structure as the only bulwark against chaos and irrationality, which always threaten. After the political confusion and turmoil of the Civil War, the Commonwealth, the Restoration, and the Glorious Revolution, the English were all too aware of how easily unreason could break through and rule. It may be that the conservatism of a Dryden, a Pope, or a Johnson owes as much to anxiety as to classical theory. With such anxiety reduced by the stable (though erratic) reigns of the Georges, the rage for order as the only defense against chaos lessened, and generic concepts were once again subject to revision.

It would be satisfying to report that the romantic writers and theorists moved in on genre theory like a demolition team and blew it up with bombs, but such is just not the case. Romantics were aware of traditional genre distinctions, but their interest was essentially in the individual phenomenon rather than in the context that may have shaped it. To use M. H. Abrams's figure, if neoclassical criticism wished art to mirror nature and created rather strict rules for the mirror's frame, romantic critics saw the artist as providing his own light rather than merely reflecting the light of nature. Since so much of romantic art refers to either the spirit of the age or the temperament and vision of the individual author, genre concepts tended to be (a) taken for granted as helpful but unimportant guides, (b) ignored, or (c) criticized as stifling.

It is clear, for instance, from William Wordsworth's *Prefaces* that he made no strenuous objection to the concept of genre, and that it was, in fact, the very water in which he swam. Wordsworth casually makes reference to various sorts of generic writers—philosopher, historian, scientist—in his famous *Preface* of 1800, and he gives no indication that genre is a repellent concept to him. In the lesser-known *Preface* of 1815, he shows, in fact, how deeply important to him the urge to classification is. In this short (and rather confused) piece, Wordsworth is determined to investigate that judgment by which "is determined what are the laws and appropriate graces of every species of composition."[20] After examining the "moulds of poetry"—which are essentially Sidney's poetic genres— Wordsworth announces that though these traditional genres are defensible, he will use a system of classifying the poems in his book that is different, though based on similar principles. Wordsworth's poems were arranged in a novel, complex, nonchronological set generally organized by the device of analogy with human life, beginning with childhood and proceeding to old age and immortality. It is clear that, although Wordsworth did not privilege the traditional genres, the *concept* of genre was important to him; as his oeuvre became large he became more and more concerned with the arrangement of it.

We see in romantic criticism none of the rule-worship of neoclassicism, but neither do we see any reduction of interest in genre as concept. What the romantics argued against was any *privileged* or *elitist* genre, any attempt to exclude works from consideration because they did not meet rigid expectations of class. If a poem was bad it was bad on its own merits; as Wordsworth put it, "The proper method of treating trivial and simple verses . . . is not to say, this is a bad kind of poetry, or, this is not poetry; but, this wants sense."[21] Coleridge in a fragment calls it absurd "to pass judgment on the works of a poet on the mere ground that they have been called by the same class-name as the works of other poets of other times and circumstances, or any ground indeed save that of their own appropriateness to their own end and being."[22] Yet order and classification were never far from Coleridge's obsessive mind, and some critics claim that his attempts to systematize a too unruly work led to the breakdown of his poetic power. Shelley, in his *Defense of Poetry*, mentions traditional metrical expectations but reports that "it is by no means essential that a poet should accommodate his language to this traditional form, so that the harmony, which is its spirit, be observed . . . . every great poet must inevitably innovate upon the example of his predecessors . . . ."[23]

These relatively benign rebellions against generic narrowness were the rule in England, but in France the revolt against genre was more violent. Victor Hugo *was* trying to blow convention up with bombs. Hugo, in his Prefaces to the *Odes et Ballades* of 1824 and 1826, is still fighting hard with the ghost of Boileau:

We hear all the time, concerning literary works, talk of the *dignity* of this genre, the *proprieties* of this other, the *strictures* of this one, the *allowances* of that one; *tragedy* forbids what *novels* permit, the *chanson* tolerates what the *ode* rejects, etc. The author of this book has the misfortune not to understand any of this. . . . Choose, then: the masterpiece of gardening or the works of nature, what is beautiful by convention or what is beautiful without 'the rules,' an artificial 'literature' or original poetry![24]

What was a won war for Wordsworth and Shelley in 1821 was still a battle for Hugo and the French romantics.

If the age of romanticism was in some senses a reaction against the rigid strictures of neoclassical genre theory, the Victorian age was in its turn a reaction against the individualist and anarchic tendencies in romanticism. Victorian criticism reflects a new awareness that genres cannot be denied, and Victorian literature tends to fall rigidly into established genres. There was very little innovation between 1840 and 1890 in genre theory; what we do see are apologies and explanations for the forms that do exist, and reasoned pleas why traditional forms should be respected.

The increasing philosophical acceptance of the idea of determinism and the gradual intellectual adoption of Darwin's concept of evolutionary change meant that the tone and milieu of Victorian thought were very different from those of romanticism. There seemed a sense, new in Western culture, of vast, faceless forces—historical, biological, economic—controlling the flow of daily life. Viewed from the standpoint of this ineluctable change and viscid organic development, the forms of literature were as helpless as everything else, and they obviously grew and developed according to immutable laws. Evolutionary theorists like Ferdinand Brunetière proposed that "the differentiation of genres works in history like that of the species in nature, progressively, by transition from the single to the multiple, from the simple to the complex, from the homogeneous to the heterogeneous."[25] Thus genres had evolved like organisms, from epic through the proliferation of genres of the nineteenth century. This view tended to see genre as an immutable and absolute expression of stages of cultural development rather than as voluntary efflorescence.

This element of determinism, of certainty that genres were the result of inarguable qualities in human nature, was shared by Matthew Arnold, probably the greatest critic of the later nineteenth century. (Arnold would, however, have argued that genre proceeds from unchanging human nature rather than from changing cultural development.) In direct contrast to the romantics, Arnold wished to cast back to the calm certainty of the ancients for the key to successful understanding of art. The ancients, he said, "at any rate, knew what they wanted in art, and we do not. It is this uncertainty that is disheartening, and not hostile criticism." The present-day writer, says Arnold, needs "a hand to guide him through the confusion" of modern critical and artistic cacophony. "Such a guide the English writer of the present day will nowhere find. Failing this, all that can be looked for, all indeed that can be desired, is, that his attention should be fixed on excellent models; that he may reproduce, at any rate, something of their excellence . . . ."[26] Arnold speaks little of genre per se—the very word was not in use in English criticism before the 1920s—but it is clear that he respects its concept as he does all of the "wholesome regulative laws" of poetry, which he begs his fellow artists to observe. Arnold's respect for genre was by no means the blind rule-worship of the neoclassicists—he admits that the Aristotelian rules cannot serve for all tragedy; rather, it was a considered view that classical art was shaped by simple good sense and attention to the realities of human nature.

Arnold was, however, hardly a prophet, and the remainder of nineteenth-century critical thought is distinguished by its relative lack of attention to genre concepts. In some senses romanticism never yielded, and we find the great critics of the later Victorian era engaged with literature and with authors on political, or personal, or aesthetic levels, but rarely in terms of genre. There was a tendency to regard authors as individual types whose works reflected genius insofar as they touched an audience emotionally or intellectually, but seldom did the essentially generic concepts behind aesthetic criticism come out openly. Walter Pater, for instance, sets out in his criticism to discover of Botticelli "what is the peculiar sensation, what is the peculiar quality of pleasure, which his work has the property of inciting in us, and which we cannot get elsewhere?"[27] Pater was interested not in generic constraints but in the "formula" used by each great individual artist to achieve his power, and this essentially romantic vision is much more typical of the nineteenth century than was Arnold's gloomy classicism. As George Saintsbury put it in 1904: "Feel; discover the source of feeling (or no-feeling, or disgust, as it will often be in the trivial cases); express the discovery so as to communicate the feeling: this can be done in every case."[28]

At this time genre criticism was essential but implicit; every book reviewer applied comparative, essentially generic tests to the work under review, but as a form of criticism it seldom was mentioned. It was not until 1902, when Benedetto Croce published his *Estetica*, that the essential romantic criticism of genre concepts was openly discussed. Croce proposed that there were two sorts of thinking about literature, the *logical* and the *aesthetic*, and claimed that the logical thinking that ends in concepts of genre excludes the aesthetic thought that takes in and appreciates works of literature. All aesthetic thought derives from contemplation of the individual work, said Croce, and "Error begins when we try to deduce the expression from the concept, and to find in what has taken its place the law of the thing whose place is taken. . . . This error is known as the *theory of artistic and literary kinds*." From this error, said Croce, "derive those erroneous modes of judgment and of

38

criticism, thanks to which, instead of asking before a work of art if it be expressive and what it expresses . . . they ask if it obeys the *laws* of epic or of tragedy, of historical painting or of landscape."[29] True artists, Croce said, always disobey generic strictures, and that is why they are true artists.

Irving Babbitt, in 1910, disagreed violently in his *The New Laokoon*, which took to task the romantic "mistiness" of Croce: "With his expansive view of beauty," says Babbitt, Croce "looks upon the whole attempt to set up literary and artistic *genres* as an unwarranted wedding of the intellect with aesthetic spontaneity. All the talk that has gone on in the past about the proper boundaries of the arts, and the confusion of the arts, is, as he would have us believe, a mere logomachy. 'A tempting doctrine, plausible and new!/What fools our fathers were if this be true.' "[30] Babbitt's insistence on the reality of genres was not as immediately influential as Croce's attack on them, but the generic position did gain strength in criticism after 1910.

In the 1920s begins what we usually call the New Critical period, the first specifically "modern" literary criticism. The hallmarks of New Criticism are, of course, close explications of the text of a work as it relates to itself, and various attempts to draw out inductively the different abstract qualities shared by great literary works. Genre was not, in other words, part of the *program* of New Criticism, but New Critics were constantly finding that generic questions vexed them in the midst of their other investigations. What effect, for instance, did the reading of other metaphysical love poems, the knowledge of their conventions, have on the reading of "To His Coy Mistress"? It was obviously an important question, and not one that could be dealt with by looking only at the poem's irony, or images, or ambiguities. The problem with actual investigation of genre theory for the New Critics was, however, that genres themselves seemed so arbitrary and unstable. There was little doubt that the generic expectations of readers were real, but there was also certainty that each reader brought a slightly different idea of what the operative genres were. As Wellek and Warren put it in *Theory of Literature*, "Genre in the nineteenth century and in our own time suffers from the same difficulty as 'period': we are conscious of the quick changes in literary fashion—a new literary generation every ten years, rather than every fifty."[31]

The New Critics were not, however, prepared to give up the idea of genre by any means, although New Criticism always emphasized that modern genres could never be regulative or prescriptive, as the neoclassical genres had been. "Modern genre theory is, clearly, descriptive. It

39

doesn't limit the number of possible kinds and doesn't prescribe rules to authors."[32] Genres become for the New Critics what we now tend to see them as—informing devices that tie together literary traditions with human expectations. "The totally familiar and repetitive pattern is boring; the totally novel form will be unintelligible—is indeed unthinkable. The genre represents, so to speak, a sum of aesthetic devices at hand, available to the writer and already intelligible to the reader. The good writer partially conforms to the genre as it exists, partly stretches it."[33]

The increasing professionalization of literary criticism after 1930 led to genre becoming something of a specialized cottage industry. A number of articles on leading genres appeared in literary magazines and genre theory was even enshrined in an entire book in 1945: *The Types Approach to Literature* by Irwin Ehrenpreis. As the discipline of literary studies matured, it was inevitable that it would take as grist for its mill as many perspectives as it could find. Generic theory was one way of looking at the old materials anew. It was a very powerful part of the approach used by a group of critics at the University of Chicago who have come to be called the "Chicago Formalists" or "Chicago Neo-Aristotelians" because they based a great deal of their method on Aristotle's method in the *Poetics*. These critics, most notably Elder Olson, R. S. Crane, and Richard McKeon, do not present prescriptive demands culled from Aristotle, of course, but their works do investigate the structure of audience expectations in the same way the *Poetics* does.

The great single modern theory of genres appeared, of course, in 1957: Northrop Frye's *Anatomy of Criticism*. Frye's book was profoundly influential in its time, and it remains an important statement, though a little-practiced critical perspective, today. Although only one of Frye's four essays in the *Anatomy* is called "Theory of Genres," the entire book is really about the necessity of using classification and generalization to make sense of the body of literature.

This is exactly what Frye thought that the New Critics, with their insistence on the individual, isolated work of art, did not do. One of the primary tasks of real criticism, said Frye,

is to outline the primary categories of literature, such as drama, epic, prose fiction, and the like. This at any rate is what Aristotle assumed to be the obvious first step in criticism. We discover that the critical theory of genres is stuck precisely where Aristotle left it. The way the word "genre" sticks out in an English sentence as the unpronounceable and alien thing it is. Most critical efforts to handle such generic terms as

40

"epic" and "novel" are chiefly interesting as examples of the psychology of rumor.[34]

Most of the *Anatomy*, not merely "Theory of Genres" (which is concerned with classifying literary works by their "radicals of presentation," whether they are designed to be acted, or spoken, or sung, or read silently), is concerned with the effort, as Frye put it, "not so much to classify as to clarify . . . traditions and affinities, thereby bringing out a large number of literary relationships that would not be noticed as long as there was no context for them."

This was exactly what Frye did in the *Anatomy*, which stands as the most serious attempt since Aristotle to shape an inclusive theory of literary relationships. Frye's essentially Jungian system of phases, archetypes, forms, and genres is too complex to be described here, but for several years it was assumed in critical circles that Frye had created the long-awaited synthesis and that most of criticism after him would be "normal science"—the mopping-up work of placing literary works into the Fryean framework.

Alas, it did not work out this way, largely because of the essential egotism of most critics, who became restive at the idea of laboring in another's vineyard all their professional lives. After around 1965, Fryean criticism, and generic criticism in general, were relegated to back benches as newer critical approaches—one hesitates to say "fads"—took center stage. If Frye broke the crumbling theoretical edifice of the New Criticism, then the history of criticism since Frye is one of succeeding waves of interest surrounding a theory or author and keeping the critical floor until undermined or replaced by another voice. There is today no clear ascendant—although deconstruction and feminist criticism seem in some ways the most widely credited. Structuralism, formalism, and phenomenology all have their devoted adherents as well, but none of these contemporary critical movements sees genre as an important concept. As Roland Barthes put it, "the Text does not come to a stop with (good) literature; it cannot be apprehended as part of a hierarchy or even a simple division of genres. What constitutes the Text is, on the contrary (or precisely), its subversive force with regard to old classifications."[35] For our purposes, it is necessary only to note that generic criticism in English is still carried on by literary scholars, but it is not an important theoretical component of any currently ascendant theory. There has been since 1968 a literary journal called *Genre* that specializes in generic criticism, but although respected it is not a mainstream journal in terms of current theory.

41

Perhaps the most interesting critical work currently being carried out in the general area of genre-oriented thought is that of the group of theorists called the "reader-response critics," most notably Stanley Fish and Wolfgang Iser. Fish's work has focused on the "interpretive strategies" used to decipher texts by members of "interpretive communities."[36] Such strategies within communities must be, of course, related to formal expectations of various sorts based on previous experience of similar works, and that is but another way of talking about genre. Generic questions are finally unavoidable for reader-response critics, because one central element of response must always be preconditioning.

In conclusion, however, it cannot be said that genre is a central theoretical consideration of modern literary criticism.[37] As we look back over the history of literary thought, it becomes obvious that generic criticism as a phenomenon has flourished during very early stages of an intellectual enterprise, when a literature is struggling to define itself; during periods of cultural anxiety, when established definitions are created as absolutes to shore up against perceived chaos; and during times when other critical methods have fallen into decay or have reached the end of their tether in some way. Genre continues to be an absolutely essential element in the transaction between authors and readers, but genre criticism always faces two dangers when it is applied consciously: first, the danger of solipsism, in which the critic uses intuitive ideas about the definition of genres that may not be shared by other readers; second, the danger of prescription, in which the critic uses her or his definition of genre to praise or damn works as they meet or fail to meet its specifications. Genre criticism has traditionally lost vitality through oversystematization, as in the Renaissance, and through attempts at literary regulation, as in the neoclassical period. As a result generic criticism has become a somewhat provincial branch of literary thought. Unless rhetorical criticism can avoid the solipsism and prescriptivism that always threaten to come with the territory of genre, it too may find that one of its potentially most useful perspectives has lost validity as a critical tool because it is too prone to abuse.

Notes

1. Edwin Black, *Rhetorical Criticism* (New York: Macmillan, 1965), chaps. 4–5.

2. Aristotle, *Poetics*, trans. W. Hamilton Fyfe (Cambridge, Mass.: Harvard University Press, 1973), p. 5.

3. Hamilton Fyfe, Introduction to Aristotle, *Poetics*, and Longinus, *On the Sublime*, p. xix.

4. Horace, *Satires, Epistles and Ars Poetica*, trans. H. Rushton Fairclough (Cambridge, Mass.: Harvard University Press, 1966), 2.86–89.

5. Horace *Ars* 1.153.

6. Horace *Epistles* 2.1.90–92.

7. Quintilian *Institutio Oratoria* 10.1.46–131.

8. For more information on this late classical and medieval genre theory, see the section on Evanthius, *De fabula*, and Donatus, *De comedia*, in Alex Preminger, O. B. Hardison, Jr., and Kevin Kerrane, *Classical and Medieval Literary Criticism* (New York: Frederick Ungar, 1974), pp. 299–309.

9. A. P. MacMahon, "Seven Questions on Aristotelian Definitions of Tragedy and Comedy," *Harvard Studies in Classical Philology* 40 (1929):97–198.

10. *Literary Criticism of Dante Alighieri*, trans. and ed. Robert S. Haller (Lincoln: University of Nebraska Press, 1973), 3.2.

11. Dante was certainly aware of the classical meanings of genre; he several times refers to the *Ars poetica* of "Horace, our master," at one point in the *Letters to Can Grande* even listing Horace's compilation of genres. He seems not to consider classical ideas of poetic genre very important. *The Divine Comedy*, as he explains, is called that mainly because it ends happily, in paradise.

12. George Saintsbury, *A History of Criticism and Literary Taste in Europe*, 3 vols. (Edinburgh: Wm. Blackwell & Sons, 1949), 2:6.

13. Quoted in *The Art of Poetry*, Albert S. Cook, ed. (Boston: Ginn & Co., 1892), pp. xlii–xliii. See this book for a translation of Boileau.

14. Sir Philip Sidney, "A Defence of Poesy," in Robert Kimbrough, ed., *Sir Philip Sidney: Selected Prose and Poetry* (Madison: University of Wisconsin Press, 1982), pp. 110–11, 151.

15. John Dryden, *An Essay of Dramatic Poesy* (Indianapolis, Ind.: Bobbs-Merrill, 1965), p. 81.

16. A preoccupation that Dryden shared with his age, which also produced Rymer's *Short View of Tragedy*, Farquhar's *Discourse upon Comedy*, Pope's *Essay on Criticism*, etc.

17. All quotations from Pope's Essay on Criticism are from Alexander Pope, *The Poetical Works of Alexander Pope*, Adolphus Williams Ward, ed. (New York: Thomas Y. Crowell, 1896). The final quotation in the paragraph, from Pope's *Preface to Shakespear*, is from *The Works of Alexander Pope*, 10 vols. (London: John Murray, 1886), 10:537.

18. Edward Young, *Conjectures on Original Composition, 1759* (Leeds, England: Scholar Press, 1966), pp. 17–28.

19. Quotations in this paragraph are from *Works of Samuel Johnson*, 12 vols. (London J. Longman etc., 1796), 6:96–100.

20. *Wordsworth's Prefaces & Essays on Poetry*, A. J. George, ed. (Boston: D. C. Heath, 1892), p. 41.

21. Ibid., *Preface* of 1800, p. 29.

22. "Classical and Romantic Drama," in Thomas M. Raysor, ed., *Coleridge's Shakespearean Criticism* 2 vols. (Cambridge, Mass.: Harvard University Press, 1930), 1:196.

23. "A Defense of Poetry," in David Lee Clark, ed., *Shelley's Prose* (Albuquerque: University of New Mexico Press, 1954), p. 280.

24. *Oeuvres Poetiques de Victor Hugo*, Pierre Albuny, ed. (Tours: Gallimard, 1969), pp. 280–81. My translation.

25. Ferdinand Brunetière, *L'Evolution des Genres dan l'Histoire de la Litterature*, quoted in Heather Dubrow, *Genre* (London: Methuen, 1982), p. 79.

26. Preface to *Poems*, 1853, in *The Poetical Works of Matthew Arnold*, C. B. Tinker and H. F. Loway, eds. (London: Oxford University Press, 1950), p. xxiv.

27. Walter Pater, *The Renaissance: Studies in Art and Poetry* (London: Macmillan, 1910), pp. 50–51.

28. Saintsbury, *History of Criticism*, 3:551.

29. Benedetto Croce, *Aesthetic*, trans. Douglas Ainslie (2nd ed.; London: Macmillan, 1929), pp. 36–37.

30. Irving Babbitt, *The New Laokoon* (Boston: Houghton Mifflin, 1910), p. 225. It was this book more than any other that introduced the French term *genre* into English criticism.

31. René Wellek and Austin Warren, *Theory of Literature* (New York: Harcourt, Brace, 1949), p. 242.

32. Ibid., p. 245.

33. Ibid., p. 225.

34. Northrop Frye, *Anatomy of Criticism: Four Essays* (Princeton, N.J.: Princeton University Press, 1957), p. 13.

35. Roland Barthes, "From Work to Text," in Josue V. Harari, ed., *Textual Strategies* (Ithaca, N.Y.: Cornell University Press, 1979), p. 75.

36. See Stanley Fish, "Interpreting the *Variorum*," *Critical Inquiry* 2 (1976):468–76.

37. See, however, Paul Hernadi's *Beyond Genre: New Directions in Literary Classification* (Ithaca, N.Y.: Cornell University Press, 1972) for a thoughtful and historically informed though oversystematized vision of what a modern genre theory would need to contain. Hernadi's challenge to the profession seems to have gone unanswered.

2

Herbert W. Simons and Aram A. Aghazarian

GENRES, RULES, AND POLITICAL RHETORIC:
Toward a Sociology of
Rhetorical Choice

Whereas rhetoricians have traditionally looked to the humanities for their formative ideas about genre, we draw extensively here upon social-scientific theory and research, exploring in particular the possibilities for casting research on genres of political rhetoric within a "rules" framework. Recall that we broached a distinction between rules and laws of persuasion in the introduction to this volume, the latter identified with efforts by behavioral social psychologists and other attitude-change researchers to formulate transhistorical, cross-cultural "covering laws" about message effects. Needed, we believe, is a rules-oriented "sociology of rhetorical choice" as a complement—if not an alternative—to a psychology of message effects. While "rules" perspectives in the social sciences are quite diverse, they are alike in their rejection of the epistemological assumptions on which covering laws of persuasion (and other phenomena) have been presumed to be discoverable through behavioral research.[1] Action theorists Rom Harré and Paul Secord, for example, distinguish sharply between actions (e.g., winks) and behaviors (e.g., blinks) and resist all efforts to reduce the one to the other, insisting that the study of social interaction respect its goal-oriented, context-dependent character.[2] In these respects, their own guiding assumptions might fairly be described as "humanistic."

The goal of a sociology of rhetorical choice, as we conceive it, is to make sense of the actions of persuaders, as opposed to the reactions of their audiences. Being better able to understand rhetorical choices should then place us in a better position to assess past performances and guide subsequent rhetorical efforts. We assume that amid the flux and uncertainty of rhetorical action, there exist levels of stability and predictability—made so by the very nature of rhetoric as a practical, pragmatic enterprise. Negotiators may do everything they can to keep their opponents guessing, but the very act of making their actions unpredictable is, at another level, highly predictable. That negotiators should keep

45

their opponents guessing is a rule of persuasion, albeit one that is stated so generally as to have little value. A rule is a generalization of the "as a rule" variety that is intended to cover types of practices, namely, genres, rather than specific acts. Rules may be formulated at various levels of abstraction, for example, for particular occasions or episodes, for delimited roles, for ongoing relationships of a certain type. Unlike laws such as the law of gravity, rules can never be cross-cultural and transhistorical. Laws of persuasion, if there be such, presumably reflect behavioral regularities that are biologically determined, like a dog's conditioned salivation to the sound of a bell that had been paired with food. Rules, by contrast, are expressions about human choice, and can thus be violated.

More specifically, we distinguish between descriptive rules and prescriptive rules. From evidence linking recurrent patterns of rhetoric to roles and situations, the researcher attempts to make explicit the generally tacit rules by which rhetors operate. Descriptions of this kind specify contingencies of choice without necessarily implying approval of that choice. It appears to be the rule in our culture, for example, that positions on technical and social issues tend to be promoted as "liberal" or "conservative" whether or not they have any intrinsic connection to those ideologies. Such, at least, is the impression one gets from the finding by Leahy and Mazur that positions expressed by leading proponents and opponents of nuclear power, fluoridation, and abortion tended, as a rule, to be linked by them to positions on the liberal-conservative continuum.[3] The investigators did not prescribe these seemingly arbitrary linkages; indeed, about the only reason they could provide for them was "historical accident." Nor did the investigators endorse the tendencies they observed for experts arrayed on either side of the three controversies to talk past each other, exploit ambiguities in their opponents' testimony, exaggerate the strength and significance of their own findings, and bend interpretations of neutral data to their own side's interest. These, as Leahy and Mazur described them, were merely recurrent patterns. Evidence of recurrence may in fact be used as the basis for criticizing institutionalized practices. Witness, for example, Mankiewicz and Swerdlow's castigation of television news programmers for featuring the dramatic, the sensational, and the visually interesting at the expense of substantial in-depth reporting.[4]

Prescriptive rules are judgments by an observer of what actions are called for in a given situation—called for in the sense of being appropriate or efficacious, but not necessarily wise or just. As Susan Shimanoff puts it, they are expressions of what behavior is obligated, preferred, or prohibited in certain contexts.[5] For some rules theorists, what is of paramount interest is explicating the rule—understanding what it is about the situation that makes the prescribed action particularly appropriate. Erving Goffman's essay on the lecture as genre (reviewed in our introduction) provides an example. For others of a more practical bent, explicating the rule is of less consequence than using it as the basis for assessing past practices or guiding future performances.[6] Much of the literature on counseling, community organizing, advertising, and other such "persuasion professions" exhibits a prescriptive rule-orientation, focusing as it does on techniques for role-accomplishment in particular types of situations. There is also, of course, an extensive popular literature on "making it" in our culture, dealing with such subjects as *Dress for Success*.[7] While much of that literature is insufficiently evidenced, one also finds books such as *In Search of Excellence* and *The Gamesman* based on careful research.[8] Campaign politics is an enterprise in which rule-making has become increasingly self-conscious and sophisticated. For example, a school for Republican congressional candidates, the subject of a *Moyers Journal* segment, offers advice on such genres as the formal announcement of candidacy, fundraisers, walking tours, political advertisements, political debates, press releases, and press conferences. At televised press conferences, for example, candidates are advised to adhere to such rules as the following:

Rule 1   Resist the temptation to talk a lot when you're feeling defensive; that's the time to say as little as possible.

Rule 2   Learn to speak directly into the camera when you're making a big point.

Rule 3   Use powerful, expressive language. None of those "wells" and "sos" and "maybes" that reveal you to be the confused thinker that you really are.

Rule 4   At the same time that you appear powerful, be warm, smile on occasion, indicate interest and affection. Put a twinkle in your eyes.

Rule 5   Help edit the late evening news for the television station by reserving one 30–60-second segment of your press conference for a newsworthy, well-edited, fluently delivered announcement or response to a question that everyone present will know is the segment that just has to be aired.

Particularly promising as a source of insights about the staging of rhetorical performances are the perspectives provided by action theorists, game theorists, symbolic interactionists, ethnomethodologists, and other rules theorists, even though the largest part of their work has been on patterns of informal interaction.[9] From Goffman, in particular, we derive a view of rhetoric as performative. Politics, we assume, is an arena of mixed-motive conflict, requiring of political actors that they stage-manage seemingly cooperative, socially sanctioned public performances while at the same time working to wrest advantages for themselves and for the groups with which they are aligned. This is not to say that political candidates, officeholders, lobbyists, protest leaders, and others whom we label as political actors never speak their own minds. Sometimes their interests coincide with their audiences' interests. Typically they have freedom of expression within the limits of institutionally imposed constraints. But calculations of partisan interests can never be entirely absent from the considerations of political actors and seldom are they free agents. To the extent that they have similar interests and confront similar pressures in similar situations, to that degree should their rhetoric be predictable and understandable. It is in this sense that study of roles and recurrent rhetorical situations provides evidence not only of what rhetors are *likely* to say and do, but also of what they probably *ought* to say and do, in ways that are not suggested either by extending the logics of literary theory and criticism or by relying exclusively for rhetorical prescriptions on behavioral studies of message effects.

The close connections between genre theory and rules perspectives have been noted by others. Carolyn R. Miller locates rhetorical genres within the semiotic realm of pragmatics, as opposed to syntactics (concerned exclusively with form) and semantics (concerned exclusively with meaning). What binds genre theory and rules perspectives together in investigations of rhetoric, she argues, is their "ethnomethodological" interest in "the knowledge that practice creates."[10]

Sharon D. Downey has offered a conception of genre that builds on the distinction between constitutive and regulative rules.[11] The former define the nature of the rhetorical undertaking, its essential characteristics; the latter are institutional norms of propriety or appropriateness that guide the performances of the actors. The lecture, for example, is said by Goffman to be "an institutionalized extended holding of the floor in which one speaker imparts his views on a subject, these thoughts comprising what can be called his 'text.'" The lecture is constituted further by its being different from other stand-up performances—from calls for action or comic routines, for example. To give a lecture is in effect to meet these minimal performance requirements. But the *appropriate* performance of a lecture is also guided by regulative rules: by the need to make the content appear a good deal "fresher" than it really is; by the permission usually granted the lecturer to hold the floor until the lecture has been completed; by the obligation, usually incumbent on lecturers, to save some time for discussion following the formal presentation; and so forth.

Rather than always inferring generic rules solely from evidences of recurring practices, it is possible to combine naturalistic study of rhetorical practices with behavioral research on message effects. Max Atkinson made ingenious use of the slow-motion video recorder in his study of techniques for eliciting prolonged and intense applause at political rallies.[12] Reliable applause-getters included calls for appreciation displays, "us/them" comparisons, elegantly worded antitheses, and three-part lists (e.g., "life, liberty, and the pursuit of happiness"). These, he noted, were accompanied by appropriate gestures and inflections. For example, when identifying the first and second parts of a three-part list, the rally speakers would end each phrase or sentence with a rising inflection so as to suggest that there was more to come, then lower their pitch and increase their volume as they uttered their third and final point.

Atkinson defends his preoccupation with applause-getters at political rallies on several grounds. First, rallies tend to be noisy affairs, with many stimuli competing for the listener's eyes and ears. Frequent and sustained applause provides evidence that the audience is giving close and favorable attention to the speech. Second, such applause is socially contagious, and, as it prompts even the normally reticent audience member to clap hands, it leads others who are present, including representatives of the media, to conclude that the speech was well received and hence to form favorable judgments themselves. Third, the media tend to highlight speech items that received the greatest applause.

Compare, now, the political-rally speech with the television speech, particularly one that is delivered without benefit of a live audience. Even when a television audience "eavesdrops" on a live presentation, argues Atkinson, the speaker had best adopt a more conversational style, as Ronald Reagan did in delivering what Alistair Cooke described as "the first conversational inaugural" in American history. Said Atkinson:

For those skilled in the traditional techniques of spellbinding oratory, the advent of mass television coverage is a very mixed blessing . . . . Practices which are visible, audible, and impressive to those sitting in the back row of an auditorium or debating chamber are likely to seem grossly exaggerated, unnatural, and even oppressive when viewed on a small screen from a distance of a few feet. A booming voice, poetic phrases, finely coordinated intonational cadences, and expressive non-verbal actions are unlikely to impress when witnessed at close quarters.[13]

Interestingly, Atkinson's microanalytic study of platform and television address represents a departure from his usual interest in interpersonal communication. Although rules theorists who focus on interpersonal communication have not made explicit reference to rhetorical genres, their perspectives have been applied to strategic symbolic actions. Frentz and Farrell, for example, applied their language-action paradigm to analysis of conversations among Richard Nixon and his co-conspirators in the attempted Watergate cover-up. It would not be difficult to extrapolate from this analysis generic rules for practices of a similar type (i.e., other collective cover-ups). In fact, rules theorists rely on such generalizations as they bring models of contextual influences to bear on particular cases. Frentz and Farrell, and Pearce and Cronen formulate models of "levels" of contextual influences, an idea that could be applied to rhetorical studies generally.[14] For Frentz and Farrell, "symbolic acts" are seen as fitting within particular sequences of goal-directed actions, known as "episodes." These sequences are shaped by normative characteristics of the type of encounter in which the interactants find themselves and, more broadly, by the encounter's "forms of life" in the Wittgensteinian sense. Similarly, Pearce and Cronen have offered a multileveled "rules" model of the coordinated management of meaning. According to their formulation, "streams of behavior" are said to take on meaning from the characteristics of particular "propositions" and "speech acts," which are themselves component parts of episodes. Understanding of the latter is informed, in turn, by knowledge of "cultural archetypes."

In the introduction to this volume we took exception to Campbell and Jamieson's conception of generic practices as univocal responses to the exigences of a situation. A rules-oriented generic perspective helps us to distinguish between situational requirements and strategic options. We shall illustrate.

In his content analysis of 145 confrontational questions asked at White House press conferences, Jack Orr discovered that while reporters had to strike a balance between avoiding tough questions, on the one hand, and appearing abrasive and disrespectful, on the other, they could walk this tightrope in a variety of ways.[15] One option was to present the President with an explicit criticism of his past conduct but attribute it to someone other than the reporter, then to follow the criticism with an open-ended question rather than a restricted-response question:

Mr. President, I apologize for this question before I ask it. The only reason I do is because I think you should have an opportunity to answer it. But I was in Richmond shortly after your reelection, at a public meeting, and a state senator, who was a Negro, got up and asked me, when is Mr. Nixon going to stop kicking the blacks around? And I thought you might like to respond to that.[16]

Another option used was to present oneself as the source of the criticism and ask a much more directive question, but soften the overall tone by making the criticism implicit rather than explicit:

Mr. President, sir, you indicated in January that an inflation policy would be forthcoming to the American people, but nothing has happened in eight months. Is it fair to say that you have failed to deliver on the promise?

Orr concluded, "When the literal content of reporters' words explicitly confront the President with criticism, reporters present themselves and question the President in a style consistent with deference to a Chief of State; but when their words are literally informative and only implicitly critical, reporters assume a style of self-presentation and questioning consistent with an interpellative assembly."[17] The important point to be drawn from Orr's study, for our purposes, is that situational requirements may be satisfied by a variety of rhetorical strategies.

It should be apparent at this juncture that while genericists have tended to focus on efforts at persuasion in one-to-many situations, and rules theorists have typically examined how dyads and small groups coordinate their behavior, we may quite profitably assume that rhetorical motives operate in both interactive relationships and one-to-many relationships. The concept of rule may be invoked to explain the choices of individual rhetors, just as has been done with less formal exchanges. One may derive generic rules for the performance of a given role from an analysis of the pressures and cross-pressures that persons in those roles confront, and draw upon those rules in assessing other comparable role-related performances.

Simons has shown how a sociologically oriented, rule-guided approach can be used in analyzing "collective rhetorics," the term he uses for messages by or in the name of groups or organizations.[18] Analyses of this kind begin from structural-functional assessments of role definitions. Being the leader of a protest movement, for example, means having to recruit supporters, mobilize them for action, raise funds, sell or impose a program of action to outsiders, and respond to counterpressures from opponents and governmental authorities.[19] Roles such as these largely

51

define the rhetorical purposes and functions of the individuals occupying them. We can often specify roles further for purposes of pinpointing rhetorical requirements for spokespersons. For example, we may wish to differentiate between the burdens of leading a protest movement seeking to promote radical change from the requirements of leading a moderate protest group seeking only reform. We can do so by specifying the common *and* the distinctive roles the leaders must perform.

For various situations there are predictable rhetorical problems, some of them unique to situations of that type, others much more common. For example, while protest-movement leaders share with mainstream politicians the problem of having to adapt their messages to widely different audiences, movement leaders tend to have fewer resources at their disposal, have less legitimacy, and to be encumbered by greater constraints on pragmatic decisionmaking. These and other problems have prompted movement theorists to formulate such rules as the following for reform-minded protest leaders:

Rule 1   Pressure upon adversaries should be applied persistently.

Rule 2   Tactics should be varied, should capitalize on gaffes and hypocritical acts by the opposition, and should in general be adapted to events of the period.

Rule 3   Among the tactics employed there should be some that go outside the experience of the opposition and that are in other ways satisfying for movement participants.

Rule 4   Leaders should work for media publicity while avoiding overexposure and resisting tendencies of the media to caricature movement groups.

Rule 5   The more sweeping the changes sought by a protest group, the more militant it must be in exerting pressure for change.

Rule 6   The more militant the movement's pressure tactics, the more effort must be expended to minimize the potential for backlash.

Let us pause at this juncture to review what a rules-oriented "sociology of rhetorical choice" might entail. We conceive of such an approach as a complement to the more psychologically oriented behavioral approach to persuasion, with its emphasis on message effects. We view it, as well, as a potential bridge between humanistically oriented rhetorical theorists and the many scientifically minded communication scholars who already invoke one or another conception of "rule" in theorizing about interactive relationships. Our sense of "rule" is as a "how to" generalization of the "as a rule" variety, intended to cover classes of rhetorical practice, rather than individual acts. Generic rules are usually tacit or implied rather than formal and explicit. They may stipulate particular techniques that experience has shown to be most efficacious in the handling of particular types of situations, or they may identify strategic options. They may be based on evidence of how rhetors characteristically respond to situational pressures, on the theoretically based speculations about how they should have responded, on evidence of actual effects, or some combination. Although some generic rules are prescriptive, they are not necessarily binding upon rhetors.

Having thus far sung the praises of a rules-oriented generic approach, it is time that we examined its most trenchant criticisms and considered what, if anything, can be done in light of them. To Conley's critique of classifications-in-general is added, in this volume, McGee's warning that generic scholarship, and particularly the social-scientific study of "rules for rhetors," can easily become formulaic. We would acknowledge that while generic scholarship can help to guide rhetorical practice, it is hardly a substitute for the prudential judgments of experienced persuaders. In persuading an audience, as in playing the stock market, being a contrarian, violating the rules, is sometimes the best rule of rules. At best, generic prescriptions are time-bound and culture-bound, and they are no wiser than the persuaders on whose collective experience and practice they are modeled. McGee's critique of transcendentalism—that is of the notion that there can be some outside, Archimedean point from which to vouchsafe knowledge claims—as well as his call for a self-reflective, self-reflexive, context-sensitive approach to discursive practice, is very much consistent with efforts both here and abroad to cast off objectivist pretensions and to turn our scholarship toward a search for wisdom and understanding.

Another very basic criticism of a rules-oriented generic approach is that it begs the question of whether the "rules" unearthed from an analysis of role requirements and situational constraints *ought* to be adhered to. The issue is brought to a head in Shapiro's critical commentary on James Q. Wilson's rhetoric. Here is a criminologist who brings to the readers of his textbook a clear and cogent view of crime and criminals, one that prompts Shapiro to reorder the book for his class. That Wilson is doing his job and the "crime-fighters" theirs is called into question only when one steps outside the mythic frames within which each operates; then the functions that the rhetors perform so well appear as dysfunctions, and their rhetoric loses its luster.

Much as we might prefer to occupy the high ground of impartiality, it must be admitted that generic criticism often serves uncritically as an

53

implicit endorsement of existing ways of doing things. What begins as a rule-of-thumb description of what it takes to succeed rhetorically in a given role easily becomes an ironclad prescription that implicitly sanctions and further legitimizes prevailing societal norms. Little wonder that "genre-alists," formalists, structuralists, and the like are sometimes accused of choosing sides in struggles between the forces of continuity and change, conservatism and rebellion, conventionality and innovation. Although we ourselves would prefer to remain neutrals, we recognize that, by training if not by inclination, the genericist tends to tilt in a conservatizing direction, if not a politically conservative one. Indeed, the very assumption that past practices ought to guide future actions is a conservative one. McGee and Shapiro are very persuasive on this point.

Still, these criticisms do not add up to a wholesale indictment of a rules-oriented generic approach. We would point out, first, that identification of generic rules does not necessarily imply moral approval; recall, for example, Mankiewicz and Swerdlow's derogatory treatment of newscasting rules. It was observed earlier, too, that as rhetors break with "the rules"—even to the point of rendering their discourse deliberately opaque or nonsensical (back to Beckett, once again)—their actions take on greater meaning in relation to the rules that they violate. For most radical or revolutionary movements, in any case, the issue is not one of abandoning rhetorical rules but of altering them. Even as libertarian movements for stream-of-consciousness literature or for Dadaist art declared themselves harbingers of a new freedom, their manifestos took on a hollow ring as one after another of them fell into a rigidified pattern of its own.[20] Not uncommonly, the "new" reveals itself to be strikingly similar to the old; witness, for example, the parallels to early Christianity that Kenneth Burke has identified in the rhetorics of modern political movements.[21]

Rather than abandoning a rules-oriented generic approach, we would urge genericists to utilize their talents for discovering order and coherence amid diversity and flux in an examination of how rhetors play off of existing genres, deviating ever so slightly from generic rules in some cases, breaking violently with them in others, but always, in effect, engaging in conversation with the past, and with their own cultures, while setting new precedents and helping to create new conventions in the process. Such a move, based on a dialectical merger of the oppositions with which we have been contending, would involve a radical historicizing of the entire subject of rhetorical genre, leading to greater understanding of processes of generic evolution and change. It would

54

also involve study of the interplay of modes of address at any one point in time: of the ways, for example, in which some rhetors combine or "hybridize" dominant forms; of the ways others parody or satirize them; and of the ways still others honor the conventions of an established genre like the inaugural while at the same time inscribing what Hart refers to as their unique "signatures" upon the work.

There are interesting parallels between what we are proposing be done in the study of political rhetoric and what has already been done in other fields. Goffman has identified a number of ways that social actors may "key off" from what he refers to as the two basic "frames" of experience, the natural and the social. A "key," says Goffman, is a systematic transformation of a primary form of experience, exemplified in the ways monkeys play at fighting (rather than engaging in the primary form of fighting itself) by nipping rather than biting, exaggerating threats and other such aggressive movements, and alternating between the roles of aggressor and victim. While the human's proclivity for keying off frames greatly exceeds the capacities for transformation identified by ethologists, and while methods of keying vary from culture to culture, there are recognizable patterns of transformation—"constellations of forms," to use Campbell and Jamieson's terminology—within our own culture.[22] There is, for example, a wide range of deceptive acts, ingeniously classified in a recent study by Hopper and Bell. These include teasings, white lies, ironic allusions, exaggerations, disguises, self-deceptions, and some forty additional "deception constructs," grouped into "families" of fictions, playings, lies, crimes, masks, and unlies on the basis of a statistical procedure known as hierarchical cluster analysis.[23] To Hopper and Bell's list of fabrications, Goffman identifies a host of other familiar "keys," including experiments, rehearsals, contests, dreams, rituals, and demonstrations. These "genres" of transformation are themselves amenable to keying, as when a television advertisement purports to display scientifically the benefits of one brand over another. Ultimately, says Goffman, our experiences of the real and the unreal are relational and contextual:

When we decide that something is unreal, the reality it isn't need not itself be very real, indeed, can be just as well a dramatization of events as the events themselves—or a rehearsal of the dramatization, or a painting of the rehearsal, or a reproduction of the painting. Any of these latter can serve as the original of which something is a mere mock-up, leading one to think that what is sovereign is relationship, not substance. (A valuable watercolor stored—for safekeeping—in a portfolio of reproduced masters is, in that context, a fake reproduction.)[24]

Earlier we pointed to the transformation in contemporary patterns of political speechmaking as a result of what some politicians apparently still regard as the "intrusion" of television onto the campaign scene. A particularly interesting model of generic transformation has been provided by historian Charles Tilly in a study of changes in forms of contention used by movement activists in England and the United States from 1750 to 1830.[25] At any given time and place, says Tilly, activists select from a well-defined repertoire of a collective actions a cluster that is relatively small compared to the range of options theoretically available to them. Tilly rejects both the notion that there are universal forms of contention and the image of calculating tacticians who seize every opportunity to press their advantage, yet he finds a place in his schemes of explanation for changes in modes of contention on both situational factors and also rhetorical invention and innovation. The idea of a repertoire, he says,

implies that the standard forms are learned, limited in number and scope, slowly changing and peculiarly adapted to their settings. Pressed by a grievance, interest or aspiration and confronted with an opportunity to act, groups of people who have the capacity to act collectively choose among the forms of action in their limited repertoire. The choice is not always cool or premeditated; vigilantes sometimes grab their guns and march off on the spur of the moment, while angry women make food riots. Nor are the performances necessarily frozen, regimented and stereotypical; demonstrators against the Stamp Act and the arrival of dutied tea often invented new ways of broadcasting their message and regularly responded to unanticipated contingencies by improvising. The repertoire is the repertoire of jazz or commedia dell'arte rather than of grand opera or Shakespearian drama. Nevertheless, a limited repertoire sets serious constraints on when, where and how effectively a group of actors can act.[26]

As to the importance of invention and innovation, Tilly notes:

Major mobilizations and conflicts such as those preceding the American Revolution on both sides of the Atlantic themselves reshaped the patterns of collective contention in Britain and America; Samuel Adams and John Wilkes helped invent forms of action which subsequently altered the choices available to aggrieved or ambitious groups of citizens . . . . The fragmentary evidence on Britain and America gives some encouragement to the idea of a flexible repertoire, with room for innovation and the occasional deliberate adoption of unfamiliar means of action. We see Englishmen innovating within the limits set by the petition march,

Americans adapting the devices of moral reprobation such as tarring and feathering or the mocking serenade to political ends.[27]

Tilly's observations about forms of contention can be generalized, we expect, to most other rhetorical situations. For any given task of responding to rhetorical situations of a certain type, there is likely to be a repertoire of standard responses, limited in number and scope, slowly changing, and peculiarly adapted to the situations giving rise to it. The repertoire is likely to be a flexible one, permitting, in Goffman's terms, numerous ways of keying off from established frames, and, on occasion, utilizing unfamiliar forms of response. With such notions as "frame" and "key," and with Tilly's idea of a flexible repertoire, we are in a better position to develop a sociology of rhetorical choice that admits of order and diversity, permanence and change.

Notes

1. Robert P. Sanders and Donald P. Cushman, "Rules, Constraints, and Strategies in Human Communication," in C. C. Arnold and J. W. Bowers, eds., *Handbook of Rhetorical and Communication Theory* (Boston: Allyn & Bacon, 1984), pp. 230–70. For rules approaches to persuasion quite different from our own, see Kathleen Kelley Reardon, *Persuasion: Theory and Context* (Beverly Hills, Calif.: Sage Publications, 1981), and Mary John Smith, *Persuasion and Human Action* (Belmont, Calif.: Wadsworth, 1982).

2. Rom Harré and Paul Secord, *The Explanation of Social Behavior* (Oxford: Basil Blackwell, 1972).

3. Peter Leahy and Allan Mazur, "A Comparison of Movements Opposed to Nuclear Power, Fluoridation, and Abortion," in L. Kriesberg, ed., *Research in Social Movements, Conflict, and Change* (Greenwich, Conn.: JAI Press, 1978), 1:143–54.

4. Frank Mankiewicz and Joel Swerdlow, *Remote Control: Television and the Manipulation of American Life* (New York: Time Books, 1978).

5. See Susan Shimanoff, *Communication Rules* (Beverly Hills, Calif.: Sage Publications, 1980), p. 57.

6. See, e.g., Saul Alinsky, *Rules for Radicals* (New York: Random House, 1971); Salvador Minuchin and H. Charles Fishman, *Family Therapy Techniques* (Cambridge, Mass.: Harvard University Press, 1981).

7. John T. Molloy, *Dress for Success* (New York: Warner Books, 1975).

8. Thomas J. Peters and Robert H. Waterman, Jr., *In Search of Success: Lessons from America's Best-Run Companies* (New York: Warner Books, 1982); Michael Maccoby, *The Gamesman: Winning and Losing the Career Game* (New York: Simon & Schuster, 1976).

9. For a review of research on communication rules, see Sanders and Cushman, "Rules, Constraints, and Strategies in Human Communication," and Shimanoff, *Communication Rules*.

10. Carolyn R. Miller, "Genre as Social Action," *Quarterly Journal of Speech* 70 (May 1984):155.

11. Sharon D. Downey, "The Evolution of Rhetorical Genres," paper presented at the Speech Communication Association annual convention, Louisville, Ky., in 1982.

12. Max Atkinson, *Our Master's Voices: The Language and Body Language of Politics* (London: Methuen, 1984).

13. Ibid., pp. 174–75.

14. Thomas S. Frentz and Thomas B. Farrell, "Language-action: A Paradigm for Communication," *Quarterly Journal of Speech* 62 (December 1976):333–49. W. Barnett Pearce and Vernon Cronen, *Communication, Action, and Meaning: The Creation of Social Realities* (New York: Praeger, 1980).

15. C. Jack Orr, "Reporters Confront the President: Sustaining a Counterpoised Situation," *Quarterly Journal of Speech* 66 (February 1980):17–32.

16. Ibid., p. 29.

17. Ibid., p. 31.

18. Herbert W. Simons, "Genres, Rules and Collective Rhetors: Applying the Requirements-Problems-Strategies Approach," *Communication Quarterly* 30 (Summer 1982):181–88.

19. Herbert W. Simons, Elizabeth W. Mechling, and Howard N. Schreier, "The Functions of Human Communication in Mobilizing for Action from the Bottom Up: The Rhetoric of Social Movements," in *Handbook of Rhetorical and Communication Theory*, p. 829.

20. See Tom Wolfe, *The Painted Word* (New York: Farrar, Straus and Giroux, 1975).

21. Kenneth Burke, *Attitudes toward History* (Boston: Beacon Press, 1961).

22. Erving Goffman, *Frame Analysis: An Essay on the Organization of Experience* (New York: Harper & Row, 1974).

23. Robert Hopper and Robert A. Bell, "Broadening the Deception Construct," *Quarterly Journal of Speech* 67 (1981):287–302.

24. Goffman, *Frame Analysis*, pp. 560–61.

25. Charles Tilly, "Repertoires of Contention in America and Britain, 1750–1830," in M. N. Zald and J. D. McCarthy, eds., *The Dynamics of Social Movements: Resource Mobilization, Control, and Tactics* (Cambridge, Mass.: Winthrop, 1979).

26. Ibid., p. 131.

27. Ibid., p. 154.

3

Thomas Conley

THE LINNAEAN BLUES:
Thoughts on the Genre Approach

I have written elsewhere about issues in generic criticism in both ancient and contemporary discussions.[1] In what follows here, I wish to consider some general limitations inherent, I believe, in efforts to organize phenomena, including discourses, according to kinds. Since this is a book about rhetorical criticism, I shall illustrate many of those limitations by reference to recent arguments in rhetorical criticism which propose that critics isolate and examine genres of rhetorical practice.

Though one would hardly know it from a reading of the recent literature, the same sorts of issues as those that currently concern rhetoricians were debated repeatedly in the past. Benedetto Croce, for instance, in rebelling against formalism and classicism, argued that the only two things about a literary work that matter are its "purity" and the uniqueness of "the intuition by which it is itself."[2] He was clearly wrong. A work may warrant our esteem not just because it is unique but also because it fulfills the demands of its genre.

But Ferdinand Brunetière, one of Croce's bêtes noires, was wrong, too, when he attempted to apply, in a rigorous and systematic way, the theory of evolution to literary history and criticism.[3] The essential problem with Brunetière's approach—as with any such systematic approach to criticism—is that it decontextualizes as it classifies, deflecting attention away from the particular actuality of a work over to the class or category of which it is said to be a member.[4]

Recent genre criticism in the field of rhetoric, I believe, shares some of the tendencies exhibited in Brunetièrére's attempts to construct a "natural history" of literature on a scientific model; and shares, as well, some of the problems. I am not yet convinced, as genericists seem to be, that genre criticism is likely to overcome those tendencies, much less that it is likely to demonstrate that patterns of appropriate response to rhetorical situations are predictable.

Accordingly, I shall be arguing in this paper that anyone who adheres

59

rigorously to the principles of genre criticism as they have recently been formulated is bound to suffer from the Linnaean Blues. To understand what that means, we shall first have to look briefly at what Linnaeus did, and then at what proponents of genre criticism have done. After this review, I shall offer some suggestions as to how some of the difficulties experienced by proponents of genre criticism might be overcome and briefly explore some implications for thinking about rhetorical criticism broadly conceived.

LINNAEUS

The contributions of Carl Linnaeus (1707–78) to systematic biology have been long and widely discussed. His definitions and classifications *per genus et differentiam*[5] of some 6,000 species of plants and more than 4,000 species of animals in his *Systema Naturae* (1758) constitute a monumental achievement that no biologist since has been able to surpass.[6]

Linnaeus's system can be illustrated from almost any page of *Systema Naturae*, but his treatment of the genus *Fulica*—the family of European coots—is particularly instructive, since it reveals both the genius of the system and its problems. The description of the genus reads: "*Fulica*: Rostrum convexum; Mandibula superiore margine supra inferiorem fornicata; Mandibula inferior, pone apice gibba. *Frons* calva. *Pedes* tetradactyli, sublobati."[7]

Within the genus *Fulica*, Linnaeus distinguished four species, each provided with a specific epithet (*atra, chloropus, porphyrio, spinosa*) as well as a species number. Next to this designation comes the name of the genus (abbreviated to *F.*), followed by the differentia (which define the *nomen specificum legitimum*); and then, below this, synonyms, references to literature, a statement of distribution, and sometimes other information.

atra	1. *F.* fronte calva, corpore nigro, digitis lobatis
chloropus	2. *F.* fronte calva, corpore nigro, digitis simplicibus
porphyrio	3. *F.* fronte calva, corpore violaces, digitis simplicibus
spinosa	4. *F.* fronte carunculata, corpore variegato, humeris spinosis digitis simplicibus, ungue postico longissimo.[8]

Linnaeus's list summarizes each characteristic, enabling one to distinguish one species from another, for example, the flanged or lobed toes (*digiti lobati*) of the coot proper (*F. atra*), the violet plumage (*corpus violaceum*) of the purple coot (*F. porphyrio*), or the very long hind claw

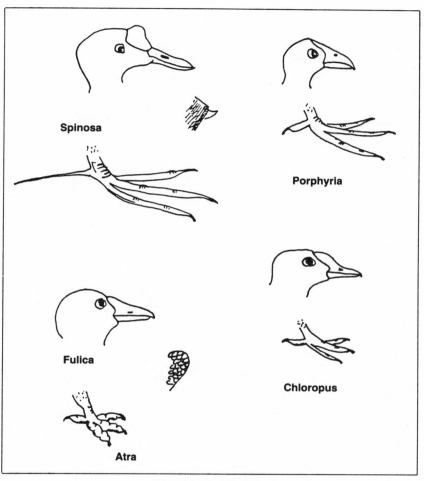

Spinosa

Porphyria

Fulica

Chloropus

Atra

The Genus Fulica

(*unguis posticus longissimus*) and the spur on the wing (*humerus spinosa*) of *F. spinosa*.

When we compare Linnaeus's definition of the genus *Fulica* with the definitions of the species, however, we can see some interesting peculiarities. According to the generic definition, all of the species should have *frons calva*, yet *F. spinosa* is distinguished from the other three species in having a *frons carunculata*. If one were to look for a good example of the genus *Fulica*, therefore, *F. spinosa* would have to be rejected. The generic description also calls for *pedes sublobati*, but *F. chloropus* and *F. porphyrio* are described as having smooth toes (*digitis simplicibus*) and in that respect are distinguished from *F. atra*, which does have *digiti lobati*. Linnaeus's first species, *atra*, is in fact the only one that agrees with the generic definition.

Linnaeus should, of course, have framed his generic description so that it applied to all the species. But evidently Linnaeus took a species well known to him,[9] and based his description of the genus on that species. When Linnaeus later came to know other species that he considered congeneric with the original species by their general appearance or the sum of their characteristics, but which diverged from the characteristics of the genus as originally stated in *Systema Naturae*, he put them in the same genus while, even in the later editions, leaving the original generic description as it was.

This account of Linnaeus's problems with coots suggests a number of questions, which, to my mind, are as relevant to genre criticism as they are to systematic biology, as both of them attempt to force experience to capitulate to rationality. First, how compatible are things to such classification? The differences among the various species of coots are small in number. What happens when you try to erect taxonomies for vastly more complex sets of differences?[10] Second, is the operation by which one classifies things a deductive or an inductive one? Linnaeus never resolved that problem in his own mind. There is a question as to whether genre critics will ever be able to resolve it in theirs. And third, what critical advantage can such classifications have? There is no doubt that Linnaeus's system was extremely useful to scientists who tried in his generation to make sense, in terms of what they already knew, of all the new specimens of living things they were introduced to as a result of the explosion of exploration and trade. But does that instance of demonstrated utility justify any attempt at all to classify unruly and largely unpredictable objects of scientific or scholarly scrutiny?[11] The relevance of these questions to the genre approach will become increasingly evident as we examine some of the more influential papers done along that line.

THE GENUS *APOLOGIA*

In an article that has been quite influential,[12] Ware and Linkugel propose a "conceptualization of the apologetic genre" and a division of it into four "subgenres." "Apologetic discourses," they claim, "constitute a distinct *form* of public address, a family of speeches with sufficient elements in common so as to warrant a legitimately [*sic*] generic status."[13] Drawing on the analytic resources of Robert P. Abelson's four modes of the resolution of belief dilemmas,[14] Ware and Linkugel divide the genre apologia into four species according to what they see as the basic strategies available to the apologist:

1. Denial—involves *negation* of allegations as to facts, sentiments, objects, or relationships; *consistent with* "audience's meaning or affect for whatever is in question" (pp. 275f.).
2. Bolstering—*reinforces* the existence of a fact, sentiment, object, or relationship; *consistent with* the audience's meaning or affect and involving a measure of identification with the audience (p. 277).
3. Differentiation—*separates* facts, sentiments, objects, or relationships from "some larger context within which the audience presently *views* that attribute" (p. 278); accompanied by a *change* in the audience's meanings.
4. Transcendence—*joins* some fact, sentiment, object, or relationship with some large context within which the audience does *not* view that attribute; accompanied by a *change* in the audience's meanings (p. 280).

This rigorous schema of the possible strategic decisions available to an apologist "forces" a critic to discern which choice (of the four) a given strategy represents within the framework of the factor terminology. "Speakers," Ware and Linkugel assure us, "usually assume one of the four major rhetorical postures when speaking in defense of their characters," each founded on one of the four species outlined above.[15]

As rigorous as the schema is, however, problems crop up as soon as the speeches they use as examples are looked at closely. The most important examples, one notices first, all involve "denial," in terms consistent not only with the audience's "meaning or affect" for what is in question, but also with the prosecution's interpretation of the admitted "facts" and the opposition's representation of the "sentiments" germane to the respective cases. Clarence Darrow's "They Tried to Get Me" is placed in the "subgenre" defined by the strategy of transcendence on the basis of a few quotes from very early in the speech; yet Darrow, in fact, uses all four strategies, or species, of apologia.[16] Likewise, in the case of the speech of Marcus Garvey, which they use as an example, it is hard to maintain that Garvey's "basic rhetorical posture" was one of transcendence. Garvey not only "denies"; he also "differentiates."[17] Both Darrow and Garvey spend a fair amount of time "bolstering," as well.[18] In fact, all of the "species" of apologia seem to be at work in all of the examples Ware and Linkugel cite.[19]

It cannot even be argued, moreover, that the "main thrust" of each speech can be used as a means of discriminating among the various species of apologia. In both the Darrow speech and the Garvey speech, the main thrust seems to be *none* of the strategies of apology described by Ware and Linkugel; for, in both, the main thrust is to the effect that the prosecution never proved its case beyond a reasonable doubt due to the poor quality of the testimony the prosecution introduced.[20] This strategy, very common in both civil and criminal defenses, seems to have no place within the schema of species laid out by Ware and Linkugel.

What we see in the speeches, in short, are not exemplars of genera or of species, but very complicated arguments using all of the strategies available to the accused and persecuted—and then some. This is possible, and reasonable, because the "strategies" in question are not genres or species, but *loci*, places, lines of argument, which can be combined (or not) with other *loci* depending on the nature of the case and the constitution of the audience/jury.[21] Speeches are, after all, more complicated than coots.[22]

DISPOSITIO PRACTICA/DISPOSITIO THEORETICA

The kinds of problems Ware and Linkugel have in defining genres and subgenres are in some ways similar to problems that Linnaeus encountered, and recognized, in his work. The central problem for him, as we have suggested, is, Which is prior, induction or deduction? Linnaeus's method involved a conflict between the a priori approach of division *per genus et differentia*—the *dispositio theoretica*, as he called it—and the empirical approach, the *dispositio practica*.[23] This conflict was, of course, overshadowed by the precision of terminology and orderly arrangement that Linnaeus bequeathed to his successors, from his student, Solander, through von Humboldt, to Darwin. The important difference between Linnaeus and Linkugel et al., however, is that, whereas Linnaeus's schemata were meant only to organize and define, Linkugel et al. have in view something more precisely critical. They seek eventually to establish normative standards against which to measure the quality of speakers and their speeches.[24]

In that respect, the labors of the genre critics in the field of rhetoric are closer to those of eighteenth-century neoclassical literary critics and, particularly, of early nineteenth-century social and literary philosophers such as Johann Herder than to those of Linnaeus.[25] Neoclassical critics

had a way of arriving before a literary work or project with a prefabri-
cated set of genres in hand, and tried to fit everything into that set,
sometimes successfully, sometimes not. Herder, on the other hand, went
about it somewhat differently. He took a vast range of literary material
available to him from European and Eastern literatures and tried to
organize it, using types—genres, if you will—of societies and social
relationships as his framework.[26] Interestingly, Herder came up with a
set of literary genres similar to the genres of neoclassical criticism, which
critics of that school assumed to be universal and perennial: lyric, epic,
and dramatic.[27]

Although Herder did not use his "empirically" established genres in
quite the same way as did the critics of the seventeenth and eighteenth
centuries, subsequent critics found in his work more justification for
continuing to do what they had been doing. They continued to work
deductively, normatively, prescriptively, until the romantic criteria of
"genius" and "sincerity" finally took hold.[28] But the lesson remains
clear: if the end is adjudicative criticism, the organization of discursive
wholes into genera and species, no matter how "empirical" its basis may
be, tends naturally to assimilate itself to the deductive a priori.

Ideally, of course, the genre approach should be neither deductive nor
inductive but "dialectical" in nature, playing off the general against the
particular, the inexorably historical against the seemingly novel—which,
to be sure, often turns out to be not so novel, after all.[29] The way up and
the way down are the same, as Heraclitus taught. Thus, in principle at
least, one approaches a given rhetorical performance or discursive whole
and pays close attention to what goes on in it while, at the same time,
playing that off against constructs that are more or less inductively
grounded, in order to come to some "understanding" of it. In this way,
the critical process continues, feeding off itself and on new material, thus
nourishing the appetites of scientific curiosity.[30]

That saying from Heraclitus is a good one, and probably ought to be
taken more seriously than it has been. But if what is being suggested here
about the tendency of genre criticism to drift toward the deductive and a
priori is right, then a different citation is in order. Thelonious Monk,
paraphrasing another famous Heraclitean proverb, said it better: "The
problem is not whether you can put your foot into the same river twice,
but whether you can put it in once without blowing your mind."

The truth of The Monk's version should be evident from the fact that
a great deal of the work done so far along the lines of "Form and Genre"
on actual rhetoric (speeches, for the most part) has been formalistic
and—willy-nilly—rather a priori, sometimes in spite of otherwise com-

65

mendable critical objectives and careful readings. Some of the constructs that dominate that criticism are drawn from traditional rhetoric: Ryan's work, for instance, uses a rather prescriptive (and consequently muddled) version of "stasis theory."[31] By his account, speeches by Martin Luther and Franklin Delano Roosevelt come out looking good or bad by as much as they succeed or fail in addressing the *status* proper to their genre. Mohrmann and Leff[32] are quite blunt about their aim: "To focus the neo-classical taxonomy," they say, "we [establish] an *a priori* definition of the end of campaign oratory." The advantage of working that way, they explain elsewhere in the same paper, is "that it permits the creation of intrinsic standards for rhetorical discourse."[33]

In Ware and Linkugel's study we see another sort of construct applied to a group of speeches, one drawn not from traditional rhetoric but from research on psychological consistency. And we see the results that application yields. They claim that they have become convinced of the relevance of Abelson's factors on the basis of their careful examination of over a dozen apologies, including Socrates' *Apology* and Isocrates' *Antidosis*, along with the speeches by Darrow and Garvey. But in fact the speeches by Socrates and Isocrates do not, for various obvious literary reasons (for one thing, neither is really a speech), fit comfortably within the framework of Abelson's factors. And, as we saw, the success of Darrow's defense and the relative success of Garvey's[34] have far more to do with the presumption of innocence and the apparent failure, in both cases, of the prosecution to make a prima-facie case on all counts of the respective indictments than with any schema of psychological factors or with any generic demands imposed by "the genus *Apologia*."

Mohrmann and Leff make it very clear that what they want to do by means of the addition of genre criticism to the critic's repertoire is to "introduce formalism into rhetorical criticism."[35] Linkugel and Ware do exactly that, without being quite as explicit about it. In the former case, the result is—perhaps intentionally—a very mechanical reading of Lincoln's address at Cooper Union. In the latter case, we have a pair of systematically distorted readings. Both are inevitable, given the basic thrust of the genre approach, which, by its very nature, demands that conception rid itself of the irritations of perception.[36]

FROM LINNAEUS TO DARWIN

As is well known, Charles Darwin's major contribution to systematic biology was his theory of natural selection. This notion of a variational evolution, one in which the collection of individuals evolves by a sorting process in which some types persist and reproduce while others die out, made it possible to explain how Linnaeus's hierarchical (genus-species) classifications could be understood in regard to the origin and differentiation of species. Just as we have in the work of some genre critics echoes of Linnaeus, so too we find traces of this sort of Darwinian thinking.

In fact, we find in Kathleen Jamieson's "Generic Constraints and the Rhetorical Situation" an injunction that one should approach the study of genres "with a Darwinian rather than a Platonic perspective."[37] And indeed, here and elsewhere, we find Jamieson talking about "the chromosomal imprint of ancestral genes,"[38] a phrase that apparently drags Gregor Mendel into the picture, too; but which nonetheless preserves the biological idiom. Genres, like Darwin's species, come into being and survive by adapting to their social environments. The "genetic codes" within them constrain the ways in which they can respond to rhetorical situations. "Institutional genres" guarantee survival of the institution's "identity."[39] Instead of the sort of Linnaean *dispositio theoretica* that we noted in the Kruse article on "generic parameters" (see above, n. 36), we seem here to be confronted with the scenario of "the struggle for survival" and the necessity to adapt, familiar to us from the *Origin of Species*.

The spurious nature of the "Darwinian" perspective on literary development has, of course, been long recognized.[40] And it ought to be recognized—even in an age when the sociobiologists could presumably describe rhetorical adaptation as, to use the neo-Darwinian idiom, half of a positive feedback loop[41]—that rhetorical "genres" do not "behave" by Darwinian rules, either.

It should, in any event, be recognized that Jamieson's early work has very little to do, in fact, with anything "Darwinian." What Jamieson does in "Antecedent Genres" is show that certain features of encyclicals and early State of the Union addresses that might prove puzzling to scholars ought not to. Once we understand the evolutionary status of those genres, we are told, everything becomes clear. This is not an unimportant observation. But it is closer, as scholarship, to what Milman Parry did for Homer[42] or Michel Zink for medieval French vernacular preaching[43] than it is to anything that might be described as taking a "Darwinian perspective." It is, rather, good, old-fashioned philology of the sort that inquires into literary antecedents.

Quite aside from that problem, however, one might with some reason be uncomfortable with Jamieson's readings of the rhetorical situations confronting the subjects of her essays. Pope Paul VI was probably very aware that both the style and the diction of encyclicals derived, ultimately, from imperial Roman decrees, tempered by forces of artificiality that are, in such cases, inevitable.[44] But Paul's use of such diction and style, if he did know their origins, would hardly make him a "willing bearer of pagan forms."[45] Nor does the behavior of early Presidents, well aware of just where the protocols of their appeals had their origins, make them unconscious promoters of monarchy. It is far more likely—especially from a generic perspective—that a pope or a president would arouse suspicions of heterodoxy or self-aggrandizement in their audiences if they had *not* remained rather faithful to what their audiences expected to hear from Popes and Presidents.

Interestingly, Kathleen Jamieson and Karlyn Campbell drop the biological business in their introduction to *Form and Genre: Shaping Rhetorical Action*. They speak of "constellations" there, and of "fusion" and "internal dynamics."[46] But the shift is only superficial, for the basic stimulus-response mechanisms that "shape rhetorical action" remain the same. The model is still evolutionary, albeit in the sense in which one talks of the "evolution of a galaxy." More recently, the two sets of controlling analogies have actually been merged: the same authors' piece on rhetorical responses by ascendant Vice Presidents to the deaths of Presidents is entitled "Rhetorical Hybrids: Fusions of Generic Elements."[47] In this essay the situational element is even more confidently promoted than it was in *Form and Genre*. Their ardor for the kind of order that might be achieved by assimilating criticism to a quasi-scientific model has, evidently, not cooled.

"FORM" AND "GENRE"

The shifting use of biological and astronomical metaphors is worth noting because it signals some important confusions in the use—and consequently, in the understanding—of the very terms "genre" and "form." All genre critics evidently feel uncomfortable about attributing to "genre" the status of "Platonic form"—i.e., thinking of "genre" as an immutable universal exemplified in particular, less perfect, rhetorical performances. "A genre," Walter Fisher tells us, "is an Aristotelian, not a Platonic construct." Genres are "inductive generalizations," he adds; "they are made by humans out of the penchant for observing similarities in things, to provide order to understanding."[48] On the other hand, we have critics who want to make of "genre" something more than a "construct." "Genre" is the name we give to similiar responses to recurrent rhetorical situations. "Genre," then, is not a mere construct, but constitutes an objective historical reality. That reality, a "constella-

68

tion of elements," is there, in the texts of speeches given in recurrent situations.[49]

In their application, both notions of "genre" work the same way in the end. They are normative models in terms of which particular objects may be classified and evaluated. The difference is in the ontological status attributed to them. The problem is that it is often hard to tell, in a given example of the genre approach, which status is being attributed. Sometimes, I suspect, both notions are being employed at the same time.

Unfortunately, either understanding of "genre" leads back to the sorts of problems I referred to earlier. The "objective" school must depend on questionable analogies with systematic biology; and the "construct" school seems likewise fated to suffer acutely from the Linnaean Blues.

Compared to the uses of "form" that we see in genre criticism, "genre" is a piece of cake. In the introduction to *Form and Genre*,[50] Campbell and Jamieson use "form" in at least four distinct senses, trading on what seems to me an unsupportable chain of equivocations.

1. "Form" is a *constitutive element* of a genre: "A genre is a group of acts unified by a constellation of forms that recurs in each of its members" (p. 20, and recall what is said on p. 25 about constellations).
2. "Form" is a rule-governed mode of response to a situation: recurring situations elicit different "formal," that is, "*strategic*" responses that are, as it were, *de rigeur*.
3. "Form" is used as in "forms of argument," for example, the syllogism may be distinguished "formally" from the enthymeme.
4. "Form" also covers "lines of argument," that is, *loci*. Into this class of forms falls the concept of *stasis* (p. 20), which determines the appropriate issues that can be addressed in a given situation.

And we should probably add:

5. Stylistic "forms," for example, repetition, crescendo, parallelism.

The advantages of being able to work with this range of meanings for "form" should be obvious. The picture shown to us of the genre approach, where genres are defined as "constellations" of forms, allows all of the traditional concerns of modern rhetorical criticism—style, *topoi*, enthymematic reasoning, motive and intention, and situation—to be incorporated into a unified vision of the critical object and to be addressed with a unified critical goal in view. The result of attention to all of these aspects of a text would be a truly close reading and analysis of a given rhetorical performance, something for which rhetorical critics have not always been distinguished. In addition, the notion of "form" seems to have been purged of its Platonic overtones, and placed in a different relation to "genre" from that implied (or even asserted) in pre-*Form and Genre* criticism, where "form" and "genre" tended to be synonymous with one another. Even more, this play on the meanings of "form" allows genre criticism to co-opt Kenneth Burke's observations on "form" in *Counter-Statement*.[51] A very attractive picture indeed.

What we see in Campbell and Jamieson's usage of "form," however, is a conflation of several quite different meanings of the term, none of which gets us completely clear of the view of "form" usually associated with the Platonic version. The several meanings will become apparent if we note that "$form_1$" means "formative element (as in "a formation of geese")"; "$form_2$" is close to what we mean by a "formality" or by the sort of "form" implied by "formal dress"; "$form_3$" is tantamount to "formula"; "$form_4$" resembles the molds into which plaster is poured or the "forms" that concrete-workers use; and "$form_5$" seems to stand for the "formal" (as opposed to the substantive?) use of stylistic devices. In any dictionary, you will see that the editors distinguish, and number separately, up to a dozen quite different meanings of "form." The impression given by Campbell and Jamieson, however, is that a "form" is a "form" is a "form."

What I have just described is probably what Harrell and Linkugel had in mind when they complained of the "conceptual slippage" in much of the literature they surveyed in an article which after its publication in *Philosophy and Rhetoric* attracted a fair amount of attention.[52] I share their concern, but I think "conceptual slippage" is too grand a phrase to use. Instead of "conceptual slippage," I prefer to characterize what we have just seen as an instance of the Elephant, New York, Phenomenon.

The following is not a fable, but a *paradeigma*:

One day, a wino approached a ticket window in the Port Authority Bus Terminal, in New York City. "Gimme a ticket to Elephant, New York," he demanded.

"I'm sorry, sir," said the agent, "but I don't think Greyhound services Elephant directly."

"Don't give me that," the wino shouted. "I take the bus to Elephant every week!"

The agent took out a map, and the two of them pored over it, looking for Elephant, New York. Twenty minutes passed, and the line in front of the window grew longer.

70

Finally, the man behind the passenger for Elephant tapped him on the shoulder and said, "Say, man. Don't you mean *Buffalo*, New York?"

"Oh. Yeah!" answered the wino. "I knew it was *one* of them big animals!"

That sort of vagueness aside, the use of "form" to designate such diverse items as enthymemes, commonplaces, figures, and situations does not succeed, in the long run, in getting rid of the connotations of "Platonic" form. What is true of the classification of genres, or of "situations," is just as true of classifications of argumentative formulae, *topoi*, or *schemata lexeon*—or, for that matter, of motives and strategies and factors in the resolution of belief dilemmas. The problems that dog Linnaean classification, whether or not it is given a Darwinian twist, are built-in, permanent, and will not go away.[53]

CLASSIFICATION, CLARIFICATION, AND UNDERSTANDING

Unique as it is in comparison with all other beasts, the guanaco structure seems to leave little room for great individuality within the species—but probably they think the same of us. Even the difference between males and females is practically impossible to make out in the living animals, except that the males average a little larger and behave differently. There have, however, been famous individual guanacos that were widely known among the settlers.

George Gaylord Simpson[54]

The critic who ignores genre, Jamieson writes,[55] "risks clouding rather than clarifying the rhetoric he is attempting to explain." Up to a point, there is nothing much to argue with in that statement. If I pick up *Bleak House* thinking it is a romance or a *policier*, I will be disappointed; and if I persist in reading it as a *policier*, I will not read it rightly. But, as I have suggested elsewhere, the real question is whether the converse is true: does rigorous attention to the generic status of a given work becloud, rather than clarify, what goes on in the rhetoric the critic tries to explain or to evaluate?[56]

From what we have already seen, we should be able to conclude that sometimes *that* happens, too. One has only to look carefully at what Ware and Linkugel did in their study of "apologia" or what Ryan has been doing with Franklin D. Roosevelt's rhetoric to see that critical fixation on genre identity may, in fact, obfuscate more than it illuminates. The reason is quite simple. Making speeches fit into classificatory

71

schemes inevitably involves radical abridgment. The result is something like abridging *Gulliver's Travels* to make it into an adventure story for children. A great deal is lost, and for no particularly good reason except to make it easier for them to grasp.

In that respect, it might be argued that generic classification leads to clarification mainly by way of simplification of the object being looked at. Simplifications, like abridged versions of great books, can be helpful to certain audiences.[57] But when simplification results in distortion—as I believe it does, for instance, in the impression given by Ware and Linkugel of the basic strategy of "They Tried to Get Me"—then it cannot be strenuously defended, however much "clearer" the speech becomes.

Humans, of course, must generalize to survive psychologically. They have, as Morse Peckham put it, a "rage for order."[58] Claude Levi-Strauss shows us in *The Savage Mind*[59] that Indians in remote Amazonian regions have a system of classification of flora and fauna that rivals that of Linnaeus. Control of nature—survival—is the goal. The genre approach, a region "not of men but of laws," is "an-aesthetic" by as much as it "strives to generate theoretical constructs that assist the critic in making his assessment of specific instances of discourse."[60] It is, at base, an attempt to control, to order nature and art alike strictly by the dictates of a sort of reason. But constructs do not teach. They only measure and rank. And control is not understanding. Control, in criticism, as in behavior-modification technologies, is not understanding but the desperate last resort sought when the possibility of understanding is denied or abandoned.

What I have said here will probably not be enough to prompt any among those faithful to the form-and-genre approach to recant. Nor is it likely that postulants to that order will abandon their vocations. But for the uncommitted it might be worth adding, by way of concluding, some observations on some ways in which the problems with the generic approach might be avoided or, at least, made less likely to crop up.

In a symposium in the 1950s on the state of rhetorical criticism, Donald Bryant raised a question to which those who call themselves rhetoricians and scholars have never responded satisfactorily: Why is it, he asked, that style is so ignored? Style, after all, "makes discourse out of the materials of invention." The facts of the case become the facts of discourse when transformed by style. Style pervades all. And yet it is for the most part ignored.[61]

I do not intend here to try to make the case for style. That will have to be done on another occasion, one that I believe would involve not just a rethinking of form-and-genre criticism, but a rethinking of criticism itself—a rather thorough revision of critical priorities and, consequently, something rather less "theoretical" than many would find desirable.

I would, however, urge that style be accorded the close attention that is its due. Such attention, since it would involve a departure from the "an-aesthetic" concerns of the kind of criticism I have been discussing, might very well lead to a virtual repudiation of the form-and-genre approach altogether. But it need not. Concentration on style, I believe, could do at least three things to enhance the kind of criticism envisaged by the most prominent of the form-and-genre critics.

First, giving priority to style (by which I do not mean "verbal ornamentation" or "deviant choice") would ensure the close attention to the text/transcript that critics of almost every persuasion hold to be desirable, if not required, in good criticism. Second, such attention would tend to preserve the rhetorical idiom of the object of critical scrutiny. The main problem with invention-oriented critical approaches is that they abridge speeches to their "arguments" or "strategies," stating the speech, in effect, in ways not stated by the speech itself, throwing out everything but "motive" and "message content." Since audiences do not apprehend speeches in those terms, however, it would be useful to cultivate critical sensitivity that is as analogous as it can be to the sort of apprehension audiences do experience, an apprehension more "syntagmatic," so to speak, than "paradigmatic." Third, if indeed we want to take Burke seriously—and I read and hear much that inclines me to believe that many who do form-and-genre criticism would like to take him seriously—we can do it only by attending *first* to the style of any piece we examine as critics.

My views on recent and current research along form-and-genre lines are not much different today from what they were five or six years before this writing. I still see problems that I think are serious, some of them solvable in practice, some of them unsolvable in principle. The problems I see are not, it should be said, peculiar to form-and-genre criticism. They are problems that transcend literary criticism, for they concern the nature of our conscious life in the world and the connection between perception and understanding. Genre criticism in rhetoric must be seen, therefore, as an approach that has implications for larger questions of method and what method lets us see, and not just for smaller questions that arise when one tries to organize the genres of rhetorical practice.

Notes

1. Conley, in *Communication Quarterly* 26 (1978):71–75. See also Conley, "Ancient Rhetoric and Modern Genre Criticism," *Communication Quarterly* 27 (1979):47–53.

73

2. Benedetto Croce, *Aesthetic as Science of Expression and General Linguistic*, trans. Ainslie (London: Macmillan, 1922), pp. 36ff., 447ff.

3. See Ferdinand Brunetière, *L'Evolution des genres dans l'histoire litteraire* (Paris: Hachette, 1931 [10th ed.; 1st ed. 1882]). In English criticism, John Addington Symonds (heavily influenced by Herbert Spencer) attempted much the same thing. See his *Essays Speculative and Suggestive* (New York: Scribner, 1894).

4. Cf. Conley, "Ancient Rhetoric," pp. 50ff.

5. Definition *per genus et differentiam* works this way: the *genus* is divided into *species* in terms of the characteristics that the member-*species* shares with the *genus* and in terms of the characteristics that distinguish one *species* from another. Strictly speaking, defining characteristics will be either those that every member and only a member of the *genus* possesses, or those that only a given member-*species* possesses.

6. A good introduction to Linnaeus's contribution can be found in James L. Larson, *Reason and Experience* (Berkeley: University of California Press, 1971). In the discussion of the genus *Fulica* that follows, I am indebted to W. T. Stearns, "The Background of Linnaeus's Contributions to the Nomenclature and Methods of Systematic Biology," *Systematic Zoology* 8 (1959):4–22, esp. 16ff.

7. A translation is in order: "*Fulica* ('coot'): Convex bill: upper mandible extending a little beyond the lower; lower mandible arched a little behind; forehead smooth; feet with four toes, somewhat lobed."

8. The *differentiae* should be evident even to those who have no Latin. Nevertheless, translation may be in order here, too:
1. *atra* ("black"): forehead smooth; body black; *toes lobed.*
2. *chloropus* ("yellow-faced"): forehead smooth; body black; *toes smooth.*
3. *porphyrio* ("purple"): forehead smooth; body *violet*; toes smooth.
4. *spinosa* ("thorny"): forehead with a projecting piece of flesh; body mottled; spurs on wings; very long hind-claw.

9. This is apparent from his references to the creature in his *Fauna Suecica* (1746) and in his notes in *Systema* about *Fulica*'s habits. Modern biologists, incidentally, would not agree with Linnaeus's genus-species arrangement.

10. This is one of the issues raised by Herbert Simons in "Genre-alizing about Rhetoric," in Karlyn Kohrs Campbell and Kathleen Hall Jamieson, eds., *Form and Genre: Shaping Rhetorical Action* (Annandale, Va.: Speech Communication Association, 1978), pp. 33–50; see esp. pp. 37ff. Simons's perspective is quite different from my own, but his point is well taken. It is to Walter Fisher's credit that he was able to see, and resist, the biology analogy. See his article, cited below, n. 48.

11. "Predictability" is no small part of the genre-approach program. See e.g., Kathleen Jamieson, "Generic Constraints and the Rhetorical Situation," *Philosophy and Rhetoric* 6 (1973):163: "When one knows what characteristics will inform an inaugural not yet composed, one has isolated the generic membranes of the inaugural." See also Jackson Harrell and Wil A. Linkugel, "On Rhetorical Genre: An Organizing Perspective," *Philosophy and Rhetoric* 11 (1978):264f. Stephen Jay Gould's observation in the *New York Review of Books*, June 30, 1983 (p. 6), might be relevant if we substitute "rhetoric" for "culture" in what he says: "A culture held on a taut one-foot leash is a fundamentally different

thing from one suspended from a ten-foot cord that cannot specify a particular institution but only a broad range of possibilities."

12. B. L. Ware and Wil A. Linkugel, "They Spoke in Defense of Themselves: On the Generic Criticism of Apologia," *Quarterly Journal of Speech* 59 (1973):273–83.

13. Ibid., p. 273.

14. Ware and Linkugel refer us to Robert P. Abelson's "Modes of Resolution in Belief Dilemmas," *Journal of Conflict Resolution* 3 (1959):343–52.

15. Ware and Linkugel, "They Spoke," p. 282. "Usually" here is a recognition that there may be exceptions. See below, n. 19.

16. See Ware and Linkugel's observations, "They Spoke," p. 281. But one could argue that Darrow depends much more on commonplaces that would serve to support his denial of the prosecution's allegations (see "They Tried to Get Me," in A. Weinberg, ed., *Attorney for the Damned* [New York: Simon & Schuster, 1959], pp. 506–7); that bolster the jury's beliefs (see below, n. 18); and that differentiate acts (Darrow's own and McNamara's; see "They Tried to Get Me," pp. 512f.) than he does working out a strategy of "transcendence." The main line of argument in the body of the speech is designed to discredit the prosecution's witnesses (see, e.g., pp. 501f., 507f., 510f., 515f., attacking the credibility of Lockwood, Franklin, Harrington, and the rest). To argue this fully would require another essay. But I think any fair-minded reader would agree that Ware and Linkugel's interpretation of Darrow's speech is affected more by the *Chicago Tribune* story printed by Weinberg (pp. 491–93) than by the speech itself.

17. See Garvey, *Philosophy and Opinions of Marcus Garvey*, 2 vols., Amy Jacques-Garvey, ed. (New York: Atheneum, 1969), 2:186f. "Differentiation" is an important part of Garvey's appeal (cf. pp. 150ff.), both legally and rhetorically. It should be noted that Garvey's use of the strategy of "transcendence" occurs in the most inarticulate part of the speech (pp. 212 ff.).

18. See, e.g., Darrow, "They Tried to Get Me," pp. 502f., 504, 506f.; Garvey, *Philosophy*, pp. 185, 188f., 206.

19. In some cases, more than one strategy can be detected in a single passage. Darrow's argument to the effect that he is being tried for his political activity is not only "transcendence," but an attack on the motives of the prosecution designed to undermine their credibility. Ware and Linkugel concede (p. 282, n. 49) that apologia may "rely" on *two* "factors;" but if that is the case, could we not come up with as many as eleven "subgenres"? They assure us that the determination of generic identity is only partly based on frequency, but do not tell us what other factors might be involved.

20. See Darrow, "They Tried to Get Me." pp. 501f., 503f: ("Here comes another little bit of perjury . . ."); pp. 507f.:("Now, what about Bain?"); pp. 510f.: ("Gentlemen, there is one thing I can say in favor of Franklin; by comparison, Harrington has made a gentleman of him"). See also Garvey, *Philosophy*, pp. 187–200, 203–8, designed to discredit the motives and credibility of the prosecution's witnesses, one of whom (Watkis, see p. 207) is called a "white wife kicker."

21. See my observations in "Ancient Rhetoric," p. 49.

22. Noreen Kruse—a believer in the genre approach—makes some observa-

tions relevant to this issue in "Motivational Factors in Non-Denial Apologia," *Central States Speech Journal* 28 (1977):13–23.

23. See Carl Linnaeus, *Philosophia Botanica* (Stockholm, 1751), no. 152.

24. See Harrell and Linkugel, "On Rhetorical Genre," pp. 271, 276. Similar interest in using genre as a normative measure is exhibited in K. Ritter, "American Political Rhetoric and the Jeremiad Tradition," *Central States Speech Journal* 31 (1980):153–71; and C. Jack Orr, "Reporters Confront the President," *Quarterly Journal of Speech* 66 (1980):17–32. See also J. Harrell, B. Ware, and W. Linkugel, "Failure of Apology in American Politics: Nixon on Watergate," *Speech Monographs* 42 (1975):245–61.

25. On the influence of Herder, see Irvin Ehrenpreis, *The Types Approach to Literature* (New York: King's Crown Press, 1945), pp. 18–24.

26. Europeans in the later eighteenth century were rather suddenly alerted to the fact that vast literatures in, e.g., Sanskrit and Gaelic, were there to be studied by anyone who cared to learn the languages.

27. Johann Gottfried Herder, *Outlines of a Philosophy of the History of Man*, 2 vols., trans. T. Churchill (London: J. Johnson, 1803), 1:450ff.

28. Among the many critics influenced by Herder, we might mention for particular notice, Herbert Spencer and Hippolyte Taine. Taine was deeply influenced by Hegel and Comte, as well. Spencer's authority in the area of evolutionary theory may be formidable; but what do we make of the literary sensibility of a man who admitted that he seldom read serious books and who says in his autobiography that he would "rather give a large sum than finish the *Iliad*"?

29. On this general question, see the opening sections of Edwin Black, "A Note on Theory and Practice in Rhetorical Criticism," *Western Journal of Speech Communication* 44 (1980):331–36.

30. M. Leff, "Interpretation and the Art of the Rhetorical Critic," *Western Journal of Speech Communication* 44 (1980):337–49. The simile appears on pp. 347–48.

31. The article I have in mind is Halford Ross Ryan, "*Kategoria* and *Apologia*: On Their Rhetorical Criticism as a Speech Set," *Quarterly Journal of Speech* 68 (1982):254–61, esp. 256ff.

32. G. Mohrmann and M. Leff, "Lincoln at Cooper Union: A Rationale for Neo-Classical Criticism," *Quarterly Journal of Speech* 60 (1974):459–67.

33. Ibid., p. 464.

34. Darrow and Garvey "succeeded" variously in their respective cases. It could be argued that it actually was Darrow's reputation, not his rhetoric, that won him acquittal—notwithstanding the report that he moved the jurors to tears. Garvey was convicted on only one count—enough to send him to jail—of a two-count indictment.

35. Mohrmann and Leff, "Lincoln," p. 467.

36. This becomes starkly evident, it seems to me, in a more recent article by Noreen Kruse, "The Scope of Apologetic Discourse: Establishing Generic Parameters" (*Southern Speech Communication Journal* 46 [1981]:278–91), which came to my attention after the body of the present paper had been written. In it, Kruse attempts to follow the procedures laid down by Harrell and Linkugel in their 1978 article (cited above, n. 11) and "map" the combinations of situational, structural, and motivational features exhibited in apologias. By the end of the

article, Kruse has pretty well succeeded in specifying the characteristics of apologias so as to distinguish "apologia" proper from "justification," "defense," and speeches that are "apologetic" only in an equivocal sense. Having thus set the generic "parameters," she concludes: "I have attempted to put the horse back before the cart. For too many years we have been examining apologetic discourse . . . without *first determining* in some detail the criteria to which an apologetic discourse *must conform*" (italics added). The problem is that by thus putting "the horse back before the cart," Kruse imposes a definition, which, although it would undoubtedly allow us to "execute our critical tasks more precisely" (ibid.), defines a genre of which no examples are likely to be found in the literature of public address. It is not simple oversight, in other words, that explains the fact that she nowhere shows us an example of a speech that truly fits. The Monk was right.

37. See Jamieson, "Generic Constraints," p. 165.
38. Ibid., p. 163. The same phrase is used in "Antecedent Genre," p. 406.
39. Jamieson, "Generic Constraints," p. 165.
40. See, e.g., Ehrenpreis, *The Types Approach*, pp. 38ff., 43ff.
41. The other half of the "loop" would, of course, be social and cultural conditions that produce the sorts of exigencies Lloyd Bitzer sees as so central in his "The Rhetorical Situation."
42. See Milman Parry, "Studies in the Epic Technique of Oral Verse-Making, I: Homer and Homeric Style," *Harvard Studies in Classical Philology* 41 (1930):73–147. Parry revolutionized Homeric studies.
43. See Michel Zink, *La prédication en langue romane avant 1300.* Nouvelle Biblioteque du moyen âge, 4 (Paris: Éditions Champions, 1976).
44. Jamieson's comprehension of the relevant principles of decorum seems limited in both "Antecedent Genre" and "Generic Constraints." Every brief submitted to an appellate court contains language that goes back to the eighteenth century, and even to old Anglo-Norman formulae. Yet it would not be reasonable to accuse an American lawyer in 1983 of being a "willing bearer" of eleventh-century Norman values.
45. Jamieson, "Antecedent Genre," p. 414.
46. I should mention here that I think many of the stated aims found in the introduction to *Form and Genre* are admirable. Unfortunately, as we shall see, it is sometimes hard to see what Campbell and Jamieson are actually getting at.
47. Kathleen Hall Jamieson and Karlyn Kohrs Campbell, "Rhetorical Hybrids: Fusions of Generic Elements," *Quarterly Journal of Speech* 68 (1982):146–57.
48. Both statements can be found on p. 291 of Walter Fisher, "Genre: Concepts and Applications in Rhetorical Criticism," *Western Journal of Speech Communication* 44 (1980):288–99.
49. Theoretically there can be no reason to deny the possibility that a given "constellation of elements" could not occur once, and only once, such that the speech embodying those elements would share no significant characteristics with "specimens from other genres" (see Jamieson, "Generic Constraints," p. 162).
50. See Campbell and Jamieson, *Form and Genre*, pp. 18–25.
51. It should be noted that none of the three citations of Burke in Campbell and Jamieson's introduction to *Form and Genre* (see nn. 21, 41, and 43, printed on pp. 30 and 31) is germane to the points they are trying to make. What Burke

has to say about form in *Counter-Statement,* perhaps the most important discussion available on rhetorical form, is ignored. Comparison between what they say and what Burke says in *Counter-Statement* is most instructive; cf. Kenneth Burke, *Counter-Statement* (Berkeley: University of California Press, 1968), pp. 29–44 (the famous essay on "Psychology and Form") and pp. 123ff.

52. Harrell and Linkugel, "On Rhetorical Genre: An Organizing Perspective."

53. In some ways, I suspect, the very concentration on "form" is what makes such problems inevitable. In Roman writers, the most common, and perhaps closest, synonyms for *forma* are *facies*—"face" or "visage"—and *species,* whence, to be sure, the English "species," but in Latin a word that refers to outward appearances, exteriors, or contours.

54. George Gaylord Simpson, *Attending Marvels: A Patagonian Journal* (New York: Time Books, 1965; original ed.: New York: Macmillan, 1934), p. 187. Cf. Simpson's discussion of ostriches and rheas on pp. 193ff.

55. Jamieson, "Generic Constraints," p. 169; a remark repeated in "Antecedent Genre," p. 415.

56. See my comments in "Ancient Rhetoric," pp. 49f.

57. I sometimes wonder whether or not we are victims of our own pedagogy in rhetorical criticism. Think of how students are compelled to approach the texts of speeches in a criticism course. They don't know a great deal. The texts are new to them. So we give them things to look for, which they dutifully do and—*mirabile dictu*—find. We teach them neutral "methods," which they can apply to any text set before them. If the method produces few "results," the fault is usually found in the poor speech, not in the method.

58. Cf. Morse Peckham, *Man's Rage for Chaos: Biology, Behavior, and the Arts* (Radnor, Pa.: Chilton Books, 1965), pp. 3–40 (a summary of his argument on the relationship between the "rage for order" and art can be found on p. ix, in his preface).

59. Claude Lévi-Strauss, *The Savage Mind* (Chicago: University of Chicago Press, 1969), pp. 35–75 esp.

60. Harrell and Linkugel, "On Rhetorical Genre," p. 275. By "an-aesthetic" I mean both "nonaesthetic" and "unfeeling." Cf. John Dewey, *Art as Experience* (New York: Capricorn Books, 1958), pp. 39ff.

61. Donald C. Bryant, "Of Style," *Western Speech Communication Journal* 21 (1957), 103ff.

4

Michael Osborn

RHETORICAL DEPICTION

There is a moment of rhetorical transport, Longinus noted, "when you think you see what you describe, and you place it before the eyes of your hearers."[1] In later centuries Francis Bacon rediscovered the importance of such shared illusion, finding hope for humankind in graphic images of good and evil that in effect telescope remote and abstract antecedents and consequences into the present.[2] The result is to remind us of our three-dimensional existence in time, and to strengthen reason in its everlasting war with the passions. The Port-Royalists in their turn placed such picture-making at the very center of the quest for eloquence. Antoine Arnauld wrote: "The principal design [of eloquence] consists in conceiving things strongly and in expressing them so that one carries over to the minds of the auditors a lively and shining image of them, an image which does not stop at picturing things in a naked way but which also pictures the impulses which one conceives them as having.[3] Fénelon added: "Since the time of the original sin, man has been entirely enmeshed in palpable things . . . he cannot for long be attentive to that which is abstract." He concluded that "lively portraiture of things is as it were the soul of eloquence."[4]

This "soul of eloquence" is the subject of the present essay, for the conditions and technology of our time have combined to project what I shall call "depiction" into even greater prominence in the workaday rhetoric of our world. Contemporary rhetoric seems dominated by strategic pictures, verbal or nonverbal visualizations that linger in the collective memory of audiences as representative of their subjects when rhetoric has been successful. Depiction, however, is characteristically more a compression than a reflection. The portrait it offers may express

The author thanks his wife, Dr. Suzanne Osborn, for her research and editorial assistance in the preparation of this paper. An earlier version was first presented as an A. Craig Baird Lecture for the Ph.D. seminar series at the University of Iowa.

implicitly and simultaneously an assertion concerning the origins of a subject, a prediction of that subject's fate, and the moral stance of the speaker. Therefore depiction may function as "an allegory in miniature," to borrow George Campbell's happy description of significant metaphor.[5] Its full rhetorical implications wait to be articulated in the ongoing text of discourse that preoccupies humankind. Yet its reverberating meanings can be influential even before they have been fully realized by either speaker or audience. Thus depiction is a key to synchronic, multiple, simultaneous meanings in rhetoric, just as enthymeme is the elemental model for diachronic or linear demonstrations.[6] The reason for the peculiar power of depiction is that it often possesses its audience at the moment of perceptual encounter, just as they are being introduced to a subject, and when they may be especially vulnerable. Depiction may provide a benign moment of sharing, as rhetors overcome abstraction to disclose the world as it is revealed to them. Or depiction can be a cynical hoax, a manipulative vision that poses as disclosure for the sake of exploitation. It can insinuate itself into our consciousness, where it becomes difficult to dislodge. Its forms and forces are the subject of this essay.

Rhetorical depiction typically does not arise from any single technique or moment in discourse. More often it is a controlled gestalt, a cumulative impact. The master rhetorician will build rhetorical depictions carefully, citing evidence that lends substance and authenticity to an image, using stylistic techniques that provide its sense of living presence.[7] The depiction might be projected from some contrast or juxtaposition of visual or sensual opposites, intended to represent moral opposites. Or a speaker's or writer's radical metaphor might invite us to visualize a remarkable tenor-vehicle relationship.[8] Or synecdoche might focus upon and enlarge some part of the subject while disguising perhaps its moral wholeness. Within a single work that conveys these impressions, or within the many discourses that make up the ongoing text of society, there is the constant work of relating and adjusting so that comprehensive depictions emerge or are sustained with coherence and vitality. Just as depiction is cumulative, emerging often from the application of many rhetorical techniques, it can also be ephemeral, unless the priests of social rhetoric faithfully tend its fire. Depiction must be constantly renewed in a larger social application of the ancient art of amplification. Thus much of public rhetoric must be repetitive and ceremonial, impressing constantly upon us the pictures that are vital to social vision.

These thoughts suggest why "depiction" may be considered a master-term of modern rhetoric—a significant, recurring form of address. In our time great masses of people, often having much political power and therefore increased recalcitrance, must be joined in megacommunities. Such communities can be sustained by simple but mythic pictures that embody common values and goals. To partake of these pictures through communication is to celebrate and participate in a social communion. Communicants may be semiliterate or preoccupied with daily problems of survival; they may have little patience for abstraction, and their short and unsophisticated spans of attention may tolerate only a few broadly painted symbols that express their common history and purpose, creating a shared sense of time and cultural context. Accordingly, much of the most important communication of our times is conducted slightly above the level of the cave paintings at Altamira. We have developed a radically simplified hieroglyphics to serve our most vital rhetorical commerce.[9] Then again, because no Tower of Babel has confused and nationalized the visual or sensual apparatus of humankind, nonverbal depictions can join us in cross-cultural recognitions of our condition and of possible destinations in the human adventure. Finally—perhaps in response to pressures for maintaining mass culture—film, television, and large-circulation magazines and newspapers have become mechanisms for imprinting depictions upon limitless audiences, and by their very availability they increase the salience of strategic pictures in modern rhetoric.

This essay will examine five functions that rhetorical depiction can serve in public communication.[10] The vehicles for such communication range from fictional novels to propaganda films, wherever discourse addresses itself to an immediate audience in hopes of affecting attitudes and actions on specific issues of the moment. None of the examples cited is especially subtle, for this exploratory essay must be concerned with the more obvious manifestations of rhetoric before we can deal with the more elusive. The final section will offer hypotheses suggesting how investigation of depiction might be extended, applied, and refined.

FUNCTIONS OF DEPICTION

DEPICTION AS PRESENTATION

The first and arguably the most important function of depiction is *presentation*. We experience the world either directly or through depiction, and even direct experience can be mediated and predisposed by previous depictions that prepare us for the experience. Depictions can range from the highly reflective, in which the rhetorical presence appears minimal or at most fugitive, to the highly symbolic, in which implicit judgments, predictions, and professions of a communicator's character

81

combine conspicuously to color and shape the perspective offered. Such rhetorical presentations can be effective even when crude and obvious, especially when depictions satisfy some compelling will-to-believe in an audience.

Significant rhetorical presentations are of two kinds, repetitive and innovative. Repetitive presentations show us what we already know and accept, but in a manner that attempts to reinforce our acceptance. The cumulative effect of repetitive presentation is to imprint certain symbolic configurations upon our minds, to charge such formulations with an especially intense cultural energy. These presentations may come to represent ultimate oppositions of virtue and depravity in the social order. One name for these special symbols is "culturetypes." The term signifies the timeliness and specificity of their power in contrast with the timelessness and cross-cultural power of archetypal symbols.[11] Other names, suggesting other rhetorical dimensions of repetitive presentation, are: (1) *icons*, a name that suggests the secular sacredness such symbols can acquire, the awe and reverence they can inspire when employed in the communicative commerce of a people;[12] (2) *God-and-devil terms*, which suggests both the sacredness and the sense of dialectical order carried by such symbols;[13] and (3) *ideographs*, which suggests that at least some of these terms express an underlying ideology in which they are grounded and which they constantly express and promote.[14] It is possible also to consider rhetorical fantasies and narratives as very much related to the work of repetitive presentation.[15] The folk dramas in which significant presentational symbols are often embedded can both revitalize and perpetuate their power.

The importance of such symbols is that they imply shared evaluative outlooks, which are a necessary condition to mass cooperative action. We may think of culturetypes also as sources of rhetorical energy from which one can draw to activate processes of rhetorical demonstration. They are potent with possible judgment and deliberation. Such symbols will sanction or *premise* certain behaviors and repudiate others. Therefore, while depiction enjoys coordinate importance with the enthymeme in accounting for synchronic as opposed to diachronic processes, there is another sense in which depiction is even more basic to the workings of rhetoric. Repetitive depiction can account for the formation of premises that initiate enthymematic reasoning.

These thoughts should lead us to reevaluate the stereotype, which—if one can repress one's stereotype of stereotypes—functions simply to establish and acknowledge personal and institutional roles within a society. Stereotypes are prearranged *ethos* that performs vital culturetypal work. Most often, stereotypes are accepted without question and without awareness of their service as anchors of the social order. They become notorious only when individuals chafe within the limitations on action and becoming that stereotypes can impose.

When we do become aware of the limiting nature of culturetypes and stereotypes, of what they *deny* us, there dawns a revolutionary consciousness that may seek expression through innovative presentation. Metaphor is a form of consciousness that actually bridges the two forms of presentation. By definition, metaphor crosses and disturbs patterns of expectation established by repetitive presentation. But such disturbance can actually serve to vitalize such patterns, correcting their drift toward dullness. Metaphor also has the power to extend the range and competency of such expectations, an additive function identified by Philip Wheelwright as "epiphor."[16] But when a flawed mode of vision can no longer be sustained and vitalized, metaphor has the power to explode the failed presentation in a new perspective-by-incongruity that cleanses and reorients the public mind with its verbal shock treatment.[17] As Edwin Black has said, "Truly revolutionary literature proves its character by bringing an audience to some new form of sensibility, to some novel and pervasive and fateful perspective that was not there before."[18] Such moments of attempted change in perspective, because they are often so crucial, so *conversionary* in what they require of audiences, provide ideal studies of repetitive and innovative presentation and of the struggle that is always potential between them.

Such a study is John Steinbeck's *The Grapes of Wrath*, "perhaps the most popular reform work of the New Deal period."[19] The novel records the passing of a social order based upon the primary family and celebrates the birth of a consciousness based upon the archetypal metaphor of the Family of Man.[20] We watch the progressive disintegration of the Joad family under the grinding heel of a capitalist system that cannot see beyond a "what's in it for me" preoccupation. But through the redemptive death of the preacher Casy, who is crucified at the hands of the exploiters,[21] the Joad family redefines itself within the larger community of the dispossessed. Concern for self is transcended in a "what's in it for us" orientation.[22] In the celebrated closing scene, criticized by literary critics often for the obviousness of its symbolism,[23] the daughter Rosasharn, who has given birth to a stillborn infant, offers her breast to a starving man, a stranger in a boxcar.[24] The scene is merely the striking peroration of Steinbeck's presentational rhetoric. These innovative, synthesizing depictions of death and rebirth are what remain with the reader, just as Steinbeck wished them to.[25] Thus Steinbeck's novel functions as a judgment upon established modes of thinking, which he presents as corrupt and moribund. The metaphor of rebirth is topical in such rhetoric, as the radiance and promise of a new vision opens in the novel.

Another such instance of radical innovation in presentation was Harriet Beecher Stowe's *Uncle Tom's Cabin*, which in its own time challenged the established view of black people as something less or other than human. Stowe's intention, she tells us in all frankness in the preface to her novel, was "to awaken sympathy and feeling for the African race . . . and to show their wrongs and sorrows."[26] For her time such depiction was bound to be sensational and incendiary.[27] Slavery could not abide a view of black people as fully human, for that admission would open an impossible moral contradiction between Christian precepts, on the one hand, and prevailing economic and social practices, on the other. As she grapples with this entrenched negative image of black people in the minds of her readers, Stowe uses all the means of persuasion available to her considerable ability as a dramatic writer. She introduces personae who embody black pride and talent and presents denigrative pictures of whites to emphasize by contrast the greater humanity of blacks. Her proud runaways invite consubstantiality by paraphrasing white ideographic slogans, such as George Harris's defiant "I'll be free or I'll die!" Stowe uses the white blood in quadroons and mulattoes to invite further the sense of identification, and to make credible the threat of a slave uprising: "There are plenty among them who have only enough of the African to give a sort of tropical warmth and fervor to our calculating firmness and foresight . . . , sons of white fathers, with all our haughty feelings burning in their veins, will not always be bought and sold and traded. They will rise, and raise with them their mother's race."[28]

Finally, to seal her argument concerning the humanity of blacks, Stowe presents Uncle Tom himself, not widely recognized now for the revolutionary figure he constituted for the audiences of Stowe's day.[29] Tom had to be destroyed by the slaveholding interests represented in the novel, because even less than black talent and pride, slavery could not abide black people with souls who would take Christianity seriously on its own terms and be obedient to God rather than to man. Such commitment makes the character of Uncle Tom "one of the strongest things in the book," wrote Edmund Wilson. "It is only the black Uncle Tom who has taken the white man's religion seriously and who attempts to live up to it literally."[30] For his final trial as a Christian, Tom is dragged off to Simon Legree's plantation. Stowe was not above using the racism in her readers as well as excoriating it, for in Tom's last agony he

84

denies Legree his soul, and is whipped and beaten by Legree's black overseers, who have been brutalized by the slave experience into true beasts. They take to their task with what she describes as "fiendish exultation," and are associated with "powers of darkness." Thus the crucifixion of Tom proceeds. Like Steinbeck's revolutionary, he dies as a Christ archetype, except that here the rhetorical purpose is not so much the promise of redemption as it is to present Stowe's readers with a remarkable perspective-by-incongruity: a black man not just human but beyond human, dying the death of a Christ.[31] To the extent that they were persuaded by the vivid images and arguments of the novel, readers of Stowe's time had to accept responsibility for this crucifixion, for it was their moral contradictions that had fashioned Tom's cross.

Often, it appears, the protagonists of reform literature are portrayed as victims of society in metonymical association with the Christ-figure. Their sacrifice calls usually for redemption, profound change within the social order, so that harmony and balance may return to the moral universe. Their individuality becomes finally only an artistic challenge to be overcome, as the writer develops the archetypal association. Thus the illiteracy of Steinbeck's Jim Casy and the blackness of Stowe's Uncle Tom functioned only to make their contemporary readers marvel the more at the deeper association with Christ's crucifixion. Like radical metaphor, radical metonymy makes its innovative meaning all the more impressive.

This discussion of two cases of presentational depiction in fiction suggests that art can be instrumental in the cause of rhetoric, especially in those moments of collision when culturetypes are first confronted by innovative presentation. In such times rhetoric may have to pose as art in order to find a public. The novel should be especially interesting in this regard to the historian of rhetorical movements. The extended and leisurely symbolic experience implied in reading a novel gives the artist/rhetorician an opportunity to introduce and develop depictions that can finally seem monumental. Such rhetoric can have a trickle-charge effect, building innovative images gradually and powerfully, perhaps even without a reader's awareness. Novelists are often regarded as outriders who are not blinded by the fog of self-serving rhetoric that social structures may generate to protect themselves from doubt and change. We may even think of such artists as prophets, as the lookouts of history who signal that change is coming. Their readers may at first seem few though fit, to reverse the Miltonian emphasis, but their novels nonetheless may establish an important beachhead in the public mind.

Not only does a novel make extended symbolic experience possible for readers and create powerful ethos for the artist. It can also constitute an enduring message, available for proselytizing, becoming itself a rite of entry for all who would join the cause it promotes. Such art does not die like the spoken word upon the wind. Finally, its audience may be inclined to "suspend disbelief" in order to enjoy the fiction it presents. Reassured by the notion that make-believe is nothing more than the harmless play of the mind, readers may entertain depictions that are quite revolutionary, and which they might reject out-of-hand if offered in "serious" persuasion.

The many memorable scenes of successful rhetorical novels serve to authenticate the author's message by their sheer quantity and vividness. What the author works to accomplish by such "proofs" is not so much verification as verisimilitude, the sense of closeness of the world modeled in the novel to that already experienced by the reader.[32] To the degree that versimilitude is established, the rhetoric in the one can be transferred and transformed readily into action in the other. Moreover, when readers are naïve concerning the world depicted in the novel, as many of Stowe's audience were ill-informed concerning an actual world of slavery, they may be especially vulnerable. If the novel seems plausible, they may accept it as a substitute for actual experience. And, according to its moral urgency, they may march to battle to the militant beat of a myth. For such readers, participation is first vicarious, then actual, as they get caught up in some dramatic narrative that interprets for them the reality of their time.

Thus the presentations of art can have profound importance in rhetorical history. Despite disclaimers of those artists who would still seek refuge in a doctrine of self-proclaimed irrelevance, art can form life after its own images.

DEPICTION AS INTENSIFICATION

A second major function of depiction is intensification of feeling. Depictions are lenses that can color what we see and make our reactions smolder. Depiction thus corrects a certain ironically self-enervating tendency of human reason, which, Francis Bacon observed, deals typically in abstraction. In lending form to formless subjects through metaphorical speech, depiction makes it possible for us to transfer feeling to such subjects. Depiction also intensifies by reducing vast numbers of a subject to a few synecdochal instances or examples for which it is possible to develop human recognition. As Steinbeck observed, "It means very little to know that a million Chinese are starving unless you know one Chinese who is starving."[33] His own use of the Joad family in *The Grapes of Wrath* had this significant synecdochal quality.

In developing such synecdoche, the choice of personae, the manner of their introduction, and the order and orchestration of images are all significant to intensification. Stowe obviously understood these rhetorical arts of character selection and portrayal. Her characters are flat, two-dimensional, but vivid: one never forgets the arguments they embody for the sake of some larger aesthetic consideration. Rhetoricians traditionally have addressed the problem of order in messages with a rational bias; they have thought of *dispositio* as an intellectual challenge: What is the best *logical* order for the presentation of *arguments*? But order is also critical in intensification, as a speaker or writer arranges rhetorical montage or narrative. For such purposes the first and last glimpses of a subject remain vital, but the issue changes considerably. Rather than asking where to place the strongest arguments in a sequence, one now considers how to build powerful, overall impressions by the end of the presentation. Each image in the sequence must be assessed for its contribution to or interference with development of consummate impressions.

Television and film are surely the preeminent media of intensification in our time, and the documentary has emerged as an especially polemical form in these media. In 1975 CBS offered a documentary on hunting in America, *The Guns of Autumn*. The program disclaimed propagandistic intent, promising, in the words of Bill Leonard, CBS News vice president, "a graphic look at what hunting is all about, with 50% from the animals' point of view."[34] The opening episode in this interesting application of the Fairness Doctrine depicted a hunt for black bears in a garbage dump. Bears of course enjoy a favorable persona by virtue of previous portrayals as teddy bears, Smokey the environmentalist bear, Yogi bear, and so on. We learn from the opening scenes that the bears who become victims in *The Guns of Autumn* deserve such a sympathetic presumption. They are shown as innocent, half-tame, somewhat lovable creatures who might be fed by hand. The hunters who dishonor themselves in the subsequent slaughter are depicted as beer-swilling, urban-outdoorsmen in search of an easy mount for the den wall. Their credibility is suggested in an interview when one of their number defends himself, saying, "If the bears are supposedly so tame, and everybody feeds 'em and you can go up and pet 'em, I don't see anybody steppin' out. They're strictly all locked up in the cars." Of course, the viewer enjoys superior knowledge, having already seen the hand-feeding in a previous scene. This technique, which seems unique to filmic rhetoric, works by juxtaposing the lie of the word with the truth of the picture, suggesting the rhetorical preeminence of the one form over the other. Perhaps it is a species of irony, but the technique's special use seems to be that of naïve subversion of one's own ethos by one's own words, artfully arranged, of course, by the film-maker posing as objective journalist.[35]

Guns goes on to create "parodies of hunts,"[36] piling "carnage upon atrocity."[37] The final scene depicts the bloody and prolonged butchering of a white deer in a hunting preserve. This scene balances the opening scene in several interesting ways. First, the final scene, like the opening scene, presents a sympathetic victim, appealing, observed the *New York Times*, to the "Bambi syndrome."[38] Second, the contrast in color between the black bear and the white deer resonates effectively in the film. The arrangement of this contrast seems fortuitous, for the white deer is especially well suited to the martyrdom arranged for it in the film's conclusion. In its terrible agony the deer seems to represent all the slain and pursued animals who are targets of hunters. Finally, the setting for this final scene itself diminishes both hunter and the hunt. Just as the garbage dump suggests the degradation of hunting, the prearranged butchery in the hunting preserve, which removes all elements of chance or sport or surprise or woodlands enchantment from the hunt, under-scores an implied indictment of unfairness and inhumanity. Indeed, by the film's end a profound role reversal has occurred, in which the animals seem almost human in their victimage, and the hunters have degenerated into beasts who roam the woods intent on senseless destruction. As the beginning and ending balance and affirm each other, they magnify the intensity of this film's depictions.

The Guns of Autumn did not convene any groups that might change or abolish hunting, nor did it deliberate any programs of reform. It seemed content to provoke and arouse its audience. In its "purity" as intensifying rhetoric, it provides an ideal study of how depiction can work to engage us in objects of portrayal. We may raise ethical questions concerning some of the procedures of this particular film, but not about the necessity and even desirability of our feeling relationships with the world of our perceptions. By engaging us in our perceptions, intensifica-tion counters a certain tendency of our rationality to establish distance between ourselves and objects of perception. Thus through its intensify-ing function, rhetorical depiction invites action and discourages us from becoming detached onlookers of life.

DEPICTION AS IDENTIFICATION

Another great resource of depiction is its capacity to facilitate identification, the sense of closeness or oneness that can develop among those who participate in social communication. Depiction generates pictures for sharing that can be transmitted quickly and precisely by mass media and possessed easily by mass audiences. Certain of these pictures will come to facilitate daily commerce in communication. We have already encountered the deep usefulness of culturetypes in authorizing arguments and social practices. For example, the widely shared and constantly reinforced image of the black person as subhuman was the ultimate justification for an elaborate system of economic, social, and political injustice. A change in that image to one of martyred and wronged humanity would trigger a process of social transformation that continues even today. But beyond such practical importance, I am now suggesting that the very sharing of symbols can itself be significant in the appeal of rhetoric. If humans are imprinted as cooperative, sharing beings,[39] then the sharing of symbols must be a profoundly satisfying experience, a terminal as well as instrumental function of depiction. Just to merge in the use of certain symbols is deeply reassuring.

Identification clearly does not function apart from presentation and intensification; rather, it depends upon their accomplishment. Certain presentations become authorized as legitimate group perspectives. Intensified feeling must be converted into group emotion: we discover together that we share feelings. In that discovery we affirm our identification in a community. These feelings are then sanctioned as patriotic and worthy of further intensification. It is also clear that culturetypes produced during repetitive presentation do their most important work in identification. Stereotypes discipline perceptions into common patterns. Icons provide gathering points for secular worship. God-and-devil terms offer hierarchy and symbolic structure for the developing group identity. Ideographs, which in McGee's discussion tend to be more abstract and less pictorial than other species of culturetype, compensate for whatever unifying power they lack by their flexibility for use in various contexts. Thus "liberty" can sanction activities as disparate as weapons-building or protests against the arms race. Ideographs can thereby sustain illusions (and delusions) important to identification, the oft-heard faith that different sides in disputes nevertheless share common goals and values. Moreover, ideographs are usually presented in combination with more concrete culturetypes or archetypes; these symbolic clusters can become all the more powerful as identifying devices. For example, liberty may be depicted as that dawn first seen by visionaries from the tops of symbolic mountains. Or liberty may be imaged as the tranquil destination for the storm-tossed ship-of-society. Such archetypal figuration connects ideographs and other culturetypes with experiences that we share by virtue of our humanity. This connection with human identity helps to justify the social identity offered in the rhetoric.

Archetypes may also strengthen identification by providing patterns for narrative development. The crucifixion motif observed in the Stowe and Steinbeck examples is one such pattern. Archetypal narration can be especially important as it dramatizes the major identification themes of heroism, martyrdom, and villainy. As such narratives develop they generate new culture-specific symbols. Culturetypes, we have observed, often derive their power from fantasies and folk tales in which they are embedded, fiction which often passes for history. To the extent that they compress and resonate stories that explain the origins and purposes of a society, culturetypes may come to function as implicit myths. As expressions of *mythos*,[40] they may constitute a source of proof in rhetoric that rivals *logos, ethos*, and *pathos*. Thus culturetypes in argument may be seen as efforts to appropriate the faith of a people for the sake of some specific demonstration. Such appeals presume and reinforce identification in the social order.

The rhetoric of identification can be conveniently studied when some established order has been discredited and a new system or social and political relationships is struggling to come into being. The first task of such a system will be to build just such a symbolic vocabulary as we have been discussing. A special identity requires a special language. In this light the classic German propaganda film, *Triumph of the Will*, remains an excellent illustration of depiction-as-identification.[41] Within this film "Führer," "youth," "obedience," "future," and "racial purity" are advanced as culturetypes that focus the new social values. The new regime is legitimated by archetypal metaphors of fire that cleanses and dedicates, and by a vertical spatial preoccupation that reinforces authoritarian order. (It is significant that Hitler descends from the clouds in the first scenes of the film, and that the marching masses who are touched by his Promethean words seem to ascend to the clouds in the closing scenes of the film.)[42] Another interesting symbol emphasized by the film, the shovels held by workers as though they are guns, blends construction and war archetypes and combines also the principles of metonymy and metaphor, suggesting both the building of the new Germany and the martial spirit with which that construction will be undertaken. These various symbols accumulate into the vocabulary of Hitler's new order and articulate the nature of the rebirth he promised Germany.

Rebirth, indeed, is the archetype perhaps most functional in depiction-as-identification. Any new order rises out of the exhausted structures of the old. In the symbolic geometry of social rhetoric, to the extent that the old order seems moribund, the new must promise hope and vitality. To the extent that an earlier identity is decayed, people will be more vulnerable to the extraordinary visions of the prophets of the new. Indeed, it may require a superhero, depicted in the self-serving rhetoric of the new regime as beyond human, to redeem the past and lead the people to a triumphant new identity. The rhetoric of identification often possesses then the qualities of epic poetry, becomes lyrical and transcendent as it trumpets the death of the old and the birth of the new. In *Triumph* Hitler is portrayed as the very personification of the social order, that from which all else emanates. He speaks in what now seem brazen possessives: "My German Youth," "My Order." He is depicted as the fulfillment of the German national legend, the superman who redefines good and evil. The camera angles show him repeatedly in the vertical power position, superimposed against a backdrop of massive architectural forms, accompanied by martial music suggestive of German culture and strength. Such metonymy reemphasizes the central identification of Hitler with the German state. It invites the audience to join the adoring multitudes shown in the film in transcending the old Germanic geographical, political, and spiritual subdivisions, in a new vision of "One Führer, One Germany, One People."

If heroes are thematic in the rhetoric of identification, so also are images of martyrs. Indeed, the two often blend together. The martyr is a kind of symbolic argument that serves to validate the new order by blood sacrifice. Thus we seem to follow some Mayan impulse in our rhetorical nature. The martyr can serve simply as a model for emulation, or, as in *Triumph*, can function even more darkly as a symbol of shame and betrayal, requiring eventual redemption through new wars of honor. Such wars will be directed toward enemies both without and within, but especially toward the latter, who have had the opportunity to affiliate. They have chosen to reject the new identity, and to remain symbols of contamination that repudiate by their presence the radiance of the new vision. *Triumph* identifies such enemies as "reds and reactionaries," but eventually Hitler found his arch-villain in the more compelling culturetype of the International Jew.

From the interplay of hero, martyr, and enemy themes can arise finally a picture of the people themselves. In *Triumph* that depiction is unmistakable and ominous. Erik Erikson, writing in 1942, observed: "The German soldier is and remains today more than ever a collective expression of everything that makes for synthesis in the German national character ... ; the German soldier is ... a personification, nay, the spiritualization of what is German."[43] "Whenever isolated German soldier faces are picked out in the campaign films," Siegfried Kracauer agrees, "their function is to denote the face of the third Reich."[44] So it is that in *Triumph* the face of the young Nordic warrior, cold and ruthless, possessed of only one passion, that of absolute devotion to the Führer, fills the screen as emblematic of the people.

Much of the rest of the film reinforces this identity by suggesting participation rituals and badges of affiliation. Marching together becomes a ritual of discipline and aggression, which sets the new order apart from the old. Singing together is a ritual of sharing and partaking, and emphasizes the happiness of the new common purpose.[45] Saluting and pledging constitute rituals of submission and obedience. Badges of affiliation include the wearing of uniforms and the waving of flags,[46] but in Hitler's Germany they eventually would include one especially ingenious device: the myth of pure Aryan blood. This myth reinforced the larger metaphor of the state as organism, which transcended those in whom its blood circulated, but which also filled their lives with its spirituality. These Aryans were, by the grace of Hitler, its embodiment. The blood-membership principle proved vague enough to include all who needed to belong, and specific enough to define and exclude enemies and inferiors. In its international aspect the principle provided a rationalization for Hitler's invasion of neighboring countries, whose expatriated Aryans had to be restored to the Fatherland in order to complete its being.

Fortunately, not all efforts at identification prove so monstrous, because the search for identification among humans is a powerful impulse. Much of our most important rhetoric should be studied as symbols in quest of society.

DEPICTION AS IMPLEMENTATION

Identification is consummatory, as it uses and transforms the processes of presentation and intensification. Implementation, on the other hand, is instrumental, depiction's time of action. Indeed, the linkage among functions appears all the more striking, for implementation can be defined as applied identification. What we are determines what we shall do, or at least what we shall attempt.

Implementation includes the classical idea of deliberative rhetoric, for it has to do with designs for the future. Depiction becomes involved in implementation in a manner suggested by Aristotle, who identified example as the technique most characteristic of deliberation. An example can be offered as an illustration of a principle or general rule, or as the embodied consequence of following or not following some potential course of action. Using its resources, rhetors scan the past for graphic lessons that can influence and lend urgency to present decisions. Often these examples will be drawn from myths accepted as serious interpretations of reality. The designs themselves will be offered as ways to actuate the promise of culturetypes.

Beyond deliberating and resolving plans of action, implementation must sustain action to its conclusion. Often the way is weary and perilous, and the faint of heart begin to falter. At that moment the fate of a program may depend upon symbols of sustenance, upon the depictive powers of communicators to show what is at stake, to renew hope, and to remind audiences of the dedication required of them. All may depend upon the personal and leadership power of a speaker. And "speaker" is rightly used, because at no other moment is the public oration—in its directness, its immediacy, its *personal* relationship between rhetor and audience—more crucial. In great speeches of implementation we encounter the urgency of a situation, and partake of words that, pressed to the very limits of meaning by the risk of the moment, burn with a peculiar power. In such speeches we share the soul of the speaker, are kindled into a larger realization of ourselves and our purpose, and are lifted again to the challenge that confronts us.

Martin Luther King's final speech in Memphis, delivered the night before his assassination, exemplifies such rhetoric. At this grim moment in a strike that had convulsed the city for several months, and that now threatened his own somewhat beleaguered leadership in the black movement, King came before thousands of supporters packed into Mason Temple in a decayed slum area not far from the Mississippi River. With a storm thundering outside, adding to the depression of a rather low moment in that confrontation over black economic rights, King stood to renew once again the spirit of resolution in his followers. He found hope even in the turbulent night, for, as he said, "Only when it is dark enough can you see the stars." So he first provided a historical panorama of great moments in the quest for freedom, beginning significantly with the flight of the children of Israel from Egypt. His account gradually came to focus upon Memphis, Tennessee, and the struggle at hand; this grand moral context seemed to enlarge the present moment, and to lift all within it to historical prominence. Moreover, King's rhetorical history established the essential dramatic outlines of the speech that would cast the Memphis mayor as Pharaoh, those present as the children of Israel, and King himself as Moses.[47] The speaker then turned to the contemporary social meaning of the struggle, and settled it within the larger frame of revolution among the rising masses of the world. Within these historical and social, and diachronic and synchronic frames of meaning he found a new, transcendent identity for his listeners: in their spiritual exodus they had passed from children in the racist sense of that term to "men and people," and now they were emerging into a triumphant new identity as "God's children."[48] They were in God's hands, and they must do God's work.

After refocusing the immediate issues and objectives of the strike and recalling great and similar struggles that had been successful, King returned to the task at hand. His listeners must develop a "dangerous unselfishness," a passage from the "I" to the "thou." Cast in roles now within the parable of the Good Samaritan, they must stop on this dangerous road and help their brothers, the sanitation workers, striking, and restore them and their families to human dignity. In that spirit they would move on together, and with him or without him, they would find the Promised Land.[49]

Beyond depicting images of sustenance for strike partisans, King's strategy was to raise doubt and confusion among opponents by preempting the moral ground in the dispute. He pictured the Memphis situation as one more instance of contradiction between the national reality and the national dream, between the lives people led and the religious and social ideals they professed. On the one hand, he wished to divide the ranks of opposition by reminding them of the moral dilemma they must confront. But his aim was not just to confound them, but to make possible their salvation and the survival of the society they enjoyed. His intent therefore was not so much to defeat his opponents as to save them from repudiating their own high principles. As Richard Neuhaus observed, "A strategy for change that confronts a people with the choice of either accommodating the change or of consciously surrendering the values by which they think they live is a most realistic strategy, striking at the heart of society."[50] One begins to understand why King was regarded by so many as a dangerous man, and why his life was constantly surrounded by threats of death.[51]

One also understands how depiction that sustains and implements action can play a prominent role in social rhetoric and in the fate of a people.

94

DEPICTION AS REAFFIRMATION

The final function of depiction is to *reaffirm* identity, often in ceremonies during which heroes, martyrs, villains, and the role of the people are recalled and renewed in common appreciation. Such rhetoric serves what Aristotle identified as an "epideictic" function: It "magnifies" deeds to reveal their honor or shame, showing especially "the luminosity of noble acts and thoughts."[52] Successful epideictic often invites us to contemplate in concrete embodiment the great moral truths that continue to offer meaning and direction to our lives. Such rhetoric awakens these moral markers so that they fill our minds again with their radiance and power, and coronates them as basic premises that ought to govern moral reasoning. Thus the effect if not the duty of reaffirmative rhetoric is to strengthen the grounding of those enthymemes vital to social judgment and deliberation.[53]

Reaffirmative depiction attempts to maintain the structures of society against the ravages of time, the erosion of memory, and the decay of commitment. Typically such rhetoric is a ritual celebration, which follows highly constrained patterns of feeling and reflection. There is something satisfying in the very redundancy, even the triteness, of such rhetoric. Its "second sophistic" quality need not be effete; rather, reaffirmative rhetoric seeks to regenerate vital culturetypes and appropriated archetypes through stylistic innovation. It is novelty engaged in the cause of continuity that distinguishes the art of reaffirmation. Reaffirmative depiction guards the sacred fire around which a nation or a subculture gathers periodically to warm itself in recognition of its being.

In times of war such rhetoric can be especially vital and crucial, producing documents such as Frank Capra's *War Comes to America* in the "Why We Fight" series of American propaganda films made during World War II. In the crisis of war, epideictic praise of one's own society often swells to apotheosis, while blame of the enemy rises to shrill denunciation. Capra used the entire encyclopedia of American stereotypes, culturetypes, rites of participation, and badges of affiliation to reaffirm a vision of America the Beautiful, built upon the central moral principle of "We the People." The very music "was designed to help celebrate national traditions," wrote Charles J. Maland. The vision was further intensified by appropriations of the archetypal metaphor of light and darkness. Maland has observed concerning other films in the series, "In one shot in *Prelude to War*, a globe of the world separates into two:

one light (the Western Hemisphere), the other dark. A superimposed title quotes Henry Wallace: 'This is a fight between a free world and a slave world.' . . . In *The Battle of Britain* an animated map of Europe begins white, but gradually black spreads over all of it to convey the German occupation." Maland credits these Disney animations as "some of the most powerful rhetorical images" of the series.[54] It is interesting how the authenticity of such melodrama seems confirmed here by nature itself. A depiction of two and only two options induces choice and commitment. Moreover we see again how the archetype, especially in times of crisis and great cultural upheaval, can reassure by anchoring events of the moment in the deeper symbols of human continuity.[55]

In its overall strategy, *War Comes to America* developed a central thesis: if the country and its ideals are so magnificent, then any significant threat to it must be answered at any personal and social cost. In picturing this threat, the Capra film performed a war dance of words and images. For those who had been taught to respect human life, it reduced the enemy to a subhuman or other-than-human level. The images of the German and especially the Japanese are so loathsome that one could kill them without confusing the act with the taking of human life. As Richard Barsam noted, "They make a beast out of Hitler and heroes out of the ordinary citizens who were his victims."[56] Other films in the series built up the courage and bravery of allied nations, inducing trust and respect in the place of previous suspicion and even contempt. There were, for example, rather useful panegyrics in honor of the Russian and Chinese people, a convenient epideictic of brotherhood in the face of the common peril.

The intensity of such rhetoric makes it clear that war can invigorate as well as strain a social system. The dangers of war can be made to bring fresh enthusiasm and a sense of mission to the national identity. Of course, reaffirmative depiction is normally less intense, performing its regular duty of keeping vital as well as stable the authorized images of a society. This observation suggests again a certain interplay among the functions in depiction. As it reaffirms, rhetoric also continues the processes of repetitive presentation and intensification, maintaining the preeminence of certain ways of seeing and feeling. This linkage of reaffirmation with other elemental functions suggests a circular relationship among the functions of depiction. This dynamic circle, which energizes and is itself constantly reenergized in public rhetoric, may be that centripetal force in social communication that holds society itself in place across time.

CONCLUSIONS

The approach to rhetoric represented by this essay, while as ancient as Longinus, is also radical. It challenges rhetoric's own depiction as a study primarily of rational calculations, and emphasizes instead the symbolic moorings of human consciousness. This approach shifts the emphasis in rhetorical studies from that advanced state of awareness in which speakers devise complex arguments and proofs to defend well-considered positions. Instead it seeks those moments in which audiences encounter significant presentations of reality, and it strives to illuminate the rhetorical implications of such encounters. This shift in focus suggests not a different but a more inclusive study that expands rhetorical theory into a quest for the roots of public rationality itself. Such study aims at describing diastrophic processes in group orientation by which premises rise into consciousness to predetermine the course of rational demonstration.

But depictive rhetoric can also play an important role in the process of demonstration. The strategic pictures it builds may have proof implications beyond the pathos traditionally associated with the work of rhetorical imagery. As I have noted, certain depictions may seem to condense vital folk dramas and narratives in which they are often found embedded. When invoked in discourse these powerful depictions may seem to resonate such stories, and to enjoy that peculiar authority we have ascribed to mythos. Moreover, such depictions enjoy the intrinsic credibility we assign to the tangible within any configuration of abstractions. "Seeing is believing" may well be a principle of preeminence among rhetorical techniques, even when the seeing is vicarious. Thus depiction enjoys a kind of ethos intrinsic to discourse itself.

Depictions may also do the work of enthymemes and perform a logos function. Often a depiction appears as the minor premise in an otherwise submerged syllogistic structure. In pointing to the "impulses" in what they portray, to follow Arnauld's acute observation, depictions may suggest the basic premises they engage and point to the conclusions they would have enacted in audience response. Consider again the portrait of the hunter drawn in *The Guns of Autumn*. The hunter is depicted as a cruel celebrant of death and as an assassin of innocence. This vivid picture, especially in light of the engaging personification of the victims, tends to activate religious proscriptions against killing. The conclusion, that we ought to condemn the wanton act of hunting, is insistent even if left unstated. The example suggests that rhetorical depiction can be a powerful form of enthymeme.

Such proof potentials in cinematic depiction may not reveal themselves to casual inspection. Even more crudely rhetorical portraits, such as those painted in *The Guns of Autumn*, can exhibit considerable complexity of appeal. There is, for example, the presumption of representation enjoyed by any specific, graphic presentation. Our tendency, especially as naïve observers, is to presume that the hunters we see in *Guns* fairly represent hunters as a class and that the actions we observe typify the activity of hunting. The feelings aroused by such presentations can be augmented by background music, which Susanne Langer has defined as the language of emotion.[57] Again, the audience can be guided through these visual and aural experiences by a narrator who by both word and inflection assures that auditors draw the intended inferences.

Modern, mass-mediated depiction has become more elusive even as it appears to have become more powerful. The traditional image of which Longinus wrote had to be induced through the abstract medium of language alone. The virtuoso performance that is required to transform abstract words into pictorial illusions makes the rhetorical intention of the effort more obvious. Electronic images now come to us more easily, directly, with disarming innocence and a presumptuousness that may bluff us into accepting them as clear and favored windows upon reality. They may even hide and deny the enchantment in their own "enchanted glass." We have no tradition of theory that deals directly with this often complex and subtle form of rhetoric. The theory we do possess equips us primarily to detect the sound and the spurious in arguments that display their proofs and inferences in linear development from proposition to conclusion. Attempting to apply this quasi-logical theoretical equipment to powerful new synchronic forms of communication is likely to produce a quaint and curious criticism that baffles at least as much as it enlightens.

How then can we lay foundations for a criticism better able to cope with the work of depiction in contemporary rhetoric? As Conley has hinted elsewhere in this book, we surely must reconsider and reconstruct the theory of style to account for nonverbal as well as verbal resources of expression. Certainly the theory of figuration will require renovation. As I have indicated in my *Orientations to Rhetorical Style*, it is clearly possible and perhaps profitable to reinterpret many of the traditional figures according to how they advance the various depictive functions identified here. Newly identified forms of figuration, such as the culturetype and the ideograph, must be assimilated within this new conception. As an elaboration of the many resources of depiction, this renewed concept of style should be free from the preciousness and pedantry that have often enfeebled stylistic analysis. More than a study of language forms, the theory of rhetorical style needs to center on the relationships among symbols and social control.

It is not yet clear how the inclusion of nonverbal rhetoric in the study of style will affect conceptions of figuration.[58] One possibility is that synecdoche and metonymy, as extremely flexible forms of focus, may emerge along with juxtaposition and contrast as dominant techniques in nonverbal depiction. As knowledge grows more complicated and remote, and as more people become responsible for informed judgments and decisions, synecdoche, which makes the world accessible through concrete representation, seems likely to become increasingly vital. It would be remarkable if nonverbal metaphors did not also possess distinctive features, but the metonymic symbol that reverberates rather than changes meaning may yet prove more significant in visual rhetoric. Color and music, which among other uses multiply the resources of irony in nonverbal communication, should also become subjects for rhetorical inquiry. Obviously these possibilities will require much additional work before the revised rhetorical criticism they envision emerges in clear outline.

Depiction may eventually prove to be one of those architectonic concepts that can reorder our conception of rhetoric itself. In this essay we have glimpsed the extensive range of depiction. At one point depiction emerged as a possible key to synchronic meaning, coordinate in importance with enthymeme. In this sense depiction could be seen as the modern equivalent of example, identified by Aristotle along with enthymeme as techniques basic to persuasion. But example was connected by Aristotle primarily with deliberative rhetoric, related here to implementation. We encounter depiction again in Aristotle's concept of magnification, which he describes as a technique characteristic of epideictic. That genre is associated with reaffirmative depiction. Even forensic rhetoric, which depends more on enthymeme, connects ultimately if indirectly with the theory of depiction. Depiction, I have argued, can be instrumental in the formation and maintenance of basic premises that ground enthymemic demonstration.[59] Thus forensic discourse may depend finally upon the elemental depictive functions of presentation and intensification. But the work of forensic rhetoric, which attempts to arrange and rearrange our evaluations of the past, can also be vital to identification, which seeks to build collective memories of the past as well as anticipations of the future. Thus forensic discourse may both draw upon and contribute to basic depictive functions.

Therefore, if depiction connects closely with example, magnification, and enthymeme, we have established central relationships with the three forms that exhaust the range of rhetoric for Aristotle. And we may have excavated in classical rhetoric the implicit foundations for our modern theory of rhetorical depiction.

At the moment it may be enough to consider depiction as a term that can interrelate five of the more significant rhetorical functions. Even in this more conservative assessment, the term remains problematic. Does depiction *include* the major functions we have identified, as a master-term for its components, or does it only relate these functions as the nexus for their eccentric spheres? Can, for example, all the rhetorical behaviors attendant to implementation be comprehended in terms of depiction? It seems probable that depiction is at least central to these various functions, but again the theoretical work is incomplete.

However, if problems remain with even this more limited assessment, so also do exciting possibilities. Throughout this essay the interplay among the major functions has seemed compelling, impossible to ignore. The image that emerges is that of a pulsating circle at the center of social discourse, visible through its presenting, intensifying, identifying, implementing, and reaffirming functions. But such an interactive metaphor, stripped of any intrinsic appeal it may itself possess, remains an as yet unproved assumption. Is there, for example, a kind of process in the history of a social movement in which emphasis moves gradually about the suggested circle from presentation through reaffirmation as the movement matures rhetorically? How long can a society sustain reaffirmation without the need for innovative presentation? Are we simply creatures who live within the vast unfoldings of social-historical depictions, with little control over their remote origins or distant destinations? The theory outlined here, it seems, may finally only deepen the mysteries of human rhetorical behavior.

Notes

1. Longinus, *On the Sublime*, trans. W. Rhys Roberts, in James Harry Smith and Edd Winfield Parks, eds., *The Great Critics: An Anthology of Literary Criticism* (3rd ed. rev., New York: Norton, 1951), p. 82 (sec. 15. 1).

2. Francis Bacon, *Advancement of Learning*, in *Great Books of the Western World*, 54 vols. (Chicago: Benton, 1952), 30:66–67 (Bk. 2, 18. 2–5). Also see the discussion in Marc Cogan, "Rhetoric and Action in Francis Bacon," *Philosophy and Rhetoric* 14 (1981):212–33; James Stephens, "Bacon's New English Rhetoric and the Debt to Aristotle," *Speech Monographs* 39 (1972):248–59; and Karl R. Wallace, "The English Renaissance Mind and English Rhetorical Theory," *Western Speech* 28 (1964):70–83, and "Aspects of Modern Rhetoric in Francis Bacon," *Quarterly Journal of Speech* 42 (1956):404–6.

3. *Œuvres de Messire Antoine Arnauld* (Paris, 1775–81), 41:341, as quoted

in Wilbur Samuel Howell, "Introduction," *Dialogues on Eloquence* (by Fénelon), trans. Howell (Princeton, N.J.: Princeton University Press, 1951), p. 42.

4. Fénelon, *Dialogues*, pp. 92–93.

5. Lloyd F. Bitzer, ed., *The Philosophy of Rhetoric* (Carbondale, Ill.: Southern Illinois University Press, 1963), p. 75 (Bk. 1, ch. 7, sec. 2).

6. The observations here concerning diachronic and synchronic structures of meaning owe much to Michael Leff, "Topical Invention and Metaphoric Interaction," in "A Symposium: The Power of the Symbol," Michael Osborn, comp., *Southern Speech Communication Journal* 48 (1983):214–29.

7. "Presence" becomes a master-term "of paramount importance for the technique of argumentation" in the work of Ch. Perelman and L. Olbrechts-Tyteca. Their account of "presence" anticipates to some extent the concept of depiction developed here. See *The New Rhetoric: A Treatise on Argumentation*, trans. John Wilkinson and Purcell Weaver (Notre Dame, Ind.: University of Notre Dame Press, 1969), pp. 115–20, 174–76, et passim.

8. Michael Osborn and Douglas Ehninger, "The Metaphor in Public Address," *Speech Monographs* 29(1962):223–34.

9. Some writers find this simplicity distressing. One can almost feel the shudder in Daniel Boorstin's observation: "Man's power to produce graven images [has] exceeded the most diabolical imagination of Biblical times." He adds that the "vivid image . . . [has come] to overshadow pale reality." See his *The Image: A Guide to Pseudo-Events in America* (New York: Atheneum, 1980), p. 13. In his call for a return to a reality that lies somewhere out beyond the symbol, presumably uncontaminated by it, one hears an echo of Platonic rejection of public communication and popular culture.

10. I first discovered this cluster of functions in attempting to answer Herbert Spencer's complaint that humankind had yet to articulate a comprehensive theory of style (*Philosophy of Style: An Essay* [New York: Appleton, 1892], p. 10). My initial description of them appears in *Orientations to Rhetorical Style* (Chicago: SRA, 1976), and I have further explored their usefulness in *Speaking in Public* (Boston: Houghton-Mifflin, 1982).

11. The discussion of communal and archetypal qualification in the Osborn and Ehninger essay began lines of thinking realized in the above contrast. I developed the concept of archetypal metaphor in rhetoric in "Archetypal Metaphor in Rhetoric: The Light-Dark Family," *Quarterly Journal of Speech* 53 (1967):115–26, and further explored its possibilities in "The Evolution of the Archetypal Sea in Rhetoric and Poetic," *Quarterly Journal of Speech* 63 (1977):347–63. The term "culturetype" was first introduced in *Orientations to Rhetorical Style*.

12. The icon is the subject of an ongoing program of research by Suzanne Osborn. See her initial statements in "Inaugural Imagery: The Icon of a Nation," paper read at the Speech Communication Association convention, Chicago, Nov. 3, 1984.

13. This concept is developed in Richard M. Weaver, "Ultimate Terms in Contemporary Rhetoric," in *Language Is Sermonic: Richard M. Weaver on the Nature of Rhetoric*, Richard L. Johannesen, Rennard Strickland, and Ralph T. Eubanks, eds. (Baton Rouge: Louisiana State University Press, 1970), pp. 87–114.

14. Michael Calvin McGee, "The 'Ideograph': A Link between Rhetoric and

Ideology," *Quarterly Journal of Speech* 66 (1980):1–16. See also the concept of *ideogeme* developed in Fredric Jameson, *The Political Unconscious: Narrative as a Socially Symbolic Act* (Ithaca, N.Y.: Cornell University Press, 1981).

15. Ernest G. Bormann, "Fantasy and Rhetorical Vision: The Rhetorical Criticism of Social Reality," *Quarterly Journal of Speech* 58 (1972):396–407; and Walter R. Fisher, "Narration as a Human Communication Paradigm: The Case of Public Moral Argument," *Communication Monographs* 51 (1984):1–22.

16. Philip Wheelwright, *Metaphor and Reality* (Bloomington: Indiana University Press, 1962), pp. 70–91. Although Wheelwright's discussion is concerned solely with poetic analysis, he accounts also for social, rhetorical processes. The complementary function he discusses, that of "diaphor" (the creation of new meaning by radical juxtaposition), corresponds to the revolutionary potential in metaphor, just as epiphor does to the work of reform.

17. The rich idea of perspective-by-incongruity is developed in Kenneth Burke, *Permanence and Change: An Anatomy of Purpose* (New York: New Republic, 1935), pp. 118–64.

18. Edwin Black, "The 'Vision' of Martin Luther King," *Literature as Revolt and Revolt as Literature: Three Studies in the Rhetoric of Non-Oratorical Forms* (Minneapolis: University of Minnesota Press, 1970), p. 7.

19. Charles L. Sanford, "Classics of American Reform Literature," *American Quarterly* 10 (1958):308.

20. Warren French, *Filmguide to The Grapes of Wrath* (Bloomington: Indiana University Press, 1973), p. 27.

21. Martin Shockley develops numerous parallels that indicate Steinbeck's consciousness of Jim Casy as Christ-figure, not the least of which are the initials of his name ("Christian Symbolism in *The Grapes of Wrath*," *College English* 18[1956]:87–90). Charles T. Dougherty argues less convincingly that it is actually Tom Joad who emerges as the novel's Christ-figure ("The Christ-Figure in *The Grapes of Wrath*," *College English* 24 [1962]:224–26). It is not necessary, of course, that the Christ-persona be confined to one character in the novel, although it seems undeniable that Casy is the predominant embodiment. Such a fused or composite image is suggested by H. Kelly Crockett in "The Bible and *The Grapes of Wrath*" (*College English* 24 [1962]:198).

22. This coming to a larger consciousness is discussed by Jules Chametzky in "The Ambivalent Endings of *The Grapes of Wrath*," *Modern Fiction Studies*, 11 (1965):34–44, and by Warren French, *John Steinbeck* (New York: Twayne, 1961), pp. 100–01.

23. Clifton Fadiman, for example, denounced this scene as "the tawdriest kind of fake symbolism," in *The New Yorker*, Apr. 15, 1939, p. 81. Barker Fairley agreed that the ending is faulty, but at least acknowledged that "the force of argument has drawn Steinbeck the writer into this artistic error." See Fairley, "John Steinbeck and the Coming Literature," *Sewanee Review* 50 [1942]:155. A more rhetorically sensitive analysis is Theodore Pollock, "On the Ending of *The Grapes of Wrath*," *Modern Fiction Studies* 4 (1958):177–78. Celeste Turner Wright identified precedents for the closing scene, in "Ancient Analogues of an Incident in John Steinbeck," *Western Folklore* 14 (1955):50–51.

24. As Peter Lisca has noted, "The ending of the novel becomes truly organic because it is Rosasharn, who had been the most self-centered, who now, out of necessity, adopts the human race as her family." (See Lisca, "The Pattern of

Criticism," *The Grapes of Wrath: Text and Criticism* [New York: Penguin, 1977], p. 704).

25. Linda Ray Pratt, "Imagining Existence: Form and History in Steinbeck and Agee," *Southern Review* 11 (1975):84–98.

26. Stowe, *Uncle Tom's Cabin: or, Life among the Lowly* (Garden City N.Y.: Doubleday, 1960), p. 6.

27. In 1852, its first year of publication, *Uncle Tom's Cabin* sold over 300,000 copies in the United States alone. In its first five years it sold over a million copies in Great Britain, and may well have restrained that country's pro-Confederate enthusiasms. "In the North it indoctrinated a whole generation with the anti-slavery viewpoint," while in the South it excited both outrage and fear, says Jane Gardiner in "The Assault upon Uncle Tom: Attempts of Pro-Slavery Novelists to Answer *Uncle Tom's Cabin*, 1852–1860," *Southern Humanities Review* 12 (1978):313. Lincoln must have been at least half-serious when he reportedly described Harriet Beecher Stowe as "the little woman who wrote the book that made this big war"; quoted in Thomas P. Riggio, "*Uncle Tom* Reconstructed: A Neglected Chapter in the History of a Book," *American Quarterly* 28 (1976):56.

28. George M. Frederickson, *The Black Image in the White Mind* (New York: Harper & Row, 1971), pp. 117–18, notes caustically that the virtues of refinement and rebellion are always reserved for mulattoes in such "protest" novels. His point is reinforced by David W. Levy, "Racial Stereotypes in Anti-Slavery Fiction," *Phylon* 31 (1970):275–77; and by James Baldwin, "Everybody's Protest Novel," *Partisan Review* 16 (1949):578–85. What these critics fail to observe is the rhetorical value, the invitation to identification, in such images of mixed race. As Cushing Strout observed, "The relative whiteness of her blacks . . . dramatizes Mrs. Stowe's sense of the great horror of slavery—the breaking up of families for exploitative reasons." (See Strout, "*Uncle Tom's Cabin* and the Portent of Millennium," *Yale Review* 57 [1968]:376.) Moreover, the Uncle Tom depicted in Stowe's novel is indeed a revolutionary figure by the argument developed above. His grace and his rebellion are those of the ideal Christian who accepts his faith with full innocence and commitment in a world that is often cynical and even bestial.

29. Literary critics are often quite awkward in dealing with the rhetorical presence in fiction. The more predominant that presence, the greater the awkwardness, especially when the fiction seems all the more compelling for the passion of its rhetoric. In the case of Uncle Tom, this problem was compounded by the popular "Tom plays," which would follow and exploit the novel into later generations. In these plays the persona of Uncle Tom was debased into the stereotype that lingers even now in our culture. Many critics have simply overlooked the distinction between the original and derivative characters, and have chosen to blame Stowe for the derivative legacy. The difference and such confusion are profound, for the original Tom challenged racist practices in one time while the derivative Tom reinforced racism in another. Thus James Baldwin finds that in Stowe's novel Tom "has been robbed of his humanity and divested of his sex" ("Everybody's Protest Novel," p. 581). But Howard Mumford Jones describes him as a "splendid black Christian Prometheus, epic in his grandeur and simplicity, whose attitude towards injustice anticipates by more than

three-quarters of a century the Christianity of Dr. Martin Luther King, Jr" (Introduction, *Uncle Tom's Cabin* [Columbus, Ohio: Merrill, 1969], p. vii.

I would argue in agreement with Jones that the Uncle Tom of the novel is not less but more than human. In her rhetorical zeal Stowe depicted a larger-than-life character, an ideal or perfect Christian, as the peroration of her argument. It may be that such moments of rhetorical apotheosis eventually dwindle into subhuman images by the ironies of time and changing circumstance. But rhetoricians cannot be blessed with prophecy concerning the possible debasements of a later age. Neither should they be held responsible for how their rhetoric may be perverted to serve less than honorable ends. In judging the ethics of rhetoric and the responsibility of rhetoricians, directness and remoteness of consequence in both time and place are great variables in the calculation.

30. Wilson, review of *Uncle Tom's Cabin,* in *The New Yorker,* Nov. 27, 1948, p. 138.

31. The evidence supporting the identification with Christ's agony is summarized by Moody E. Prior in "Mrs. Stowe's Uncle Tom," *Critical Inquiry* 5(1979):635–50. Prior, however, misses the rhetorical significance of Tom's death as the consummation of a line of argument.

32. See also Walter R. Fisher and Richard A. Filloy, "Argument in Drama and Literature: An Exploration," in J. R. Cox and C. A. Willard, eds., *Advances in Argumentation Theory and Research* (Carbondale, Ill.: Southern Illinois University Press, 1982), pp. 343–62.

33. Steinbeck, Preface to *The Forgotten Village,* as quoted in Peter Lisca, "*The Grapes of Wrath* as Fiction," *The Grapes of Wrath: Text and Criticism* (New York: Viking, 1977), p. 736.

34. Cited in the Memphis *Commercial Appeal,* Sept. 5, 1975, p. 32.

35. To the very end Irv Drasnin, the show's producer, insisted on its innocence of any persuasive intent. He had only filmed what he had found, and his had been "a calm, dispassionate view," a reflection of reality (see "A Producer's View of *Guns of Autumn,*" *New York Times,* Sept. 14, 1975, sec. 5, p. 2; and "*The Guns of Autumn*: The Producer Replies," *Columbia Journalism Review* 14 [January 1976]:48–49). Many hunters, however, thought themselves the targets rather than the subjects of the documentary. As Bill Cochran, editor for the *Roanoke Times,* put it: "Most of the so-called hunting on the show was done by one Irv Drasnin, whose prey was the hunter himself" (quoted in "A Pot-shot Angers Its Quarry," *Sports Illustrated,* Sept. 22, 1975, pp. 20–22, 27). First describing the documentary as a "cheap shot," *Sports Illustrated* went on to charge that Drasnin's depictions of hunting were "a series of bizarre scenes, most of them far out on the freakish periphery where no self- or game-respecting hunter would be found" (p. 21). The technique of juxtaposing word with picture in order to discredit a spoken claim is described by the magazine as "an invidious kind of editing" and as "weighted montage" (pp. 21–22). Indeed, it could be that the greatest value of *Guns* was to raise consciousness of rhetorical technique in film-making among those who felt themselves abused by unfair depiction.

36. *Columbia Journalism Review* 14(November/December 1975):4.

37. *Time,* Sept. 22, 1975, p. 73.

38. *New York Times,* Sept. 14, 1975, sec 2, p. 25.

39. Richard Leakey and Roger Lewin, *Origins: What New Discoveries Reveal about the Emergence of Our Species and Its Possible Future* (New York:

Dutton, 1977), pp. 117, 190, et passim; Morris Swadesh, *The Origin and Diversification of Language*, Joel Sherzer, ed. (New York: Aldine, 1971); Donald Johanson, "Ethiopia Yields First 'Family' of the Early Man," *National Geographic* 150 (1976):811; and Michael Osborn, "Our Communication Heritage: The Genetic Tie That Binds," *Southern Speech Communication Journal* 44 (1979):147–58.

40. Here I borrow a word that, for Aristotle, identified plot-line or narrative structure. I use the term in later senses of its meaning.

41. In the words of one critic, the film was intended to promote "ecstatic acceptance" of Hitler's New Order (see Marshall Lewis, "Program Notes: *Triumph of the Will*," *Film Comment* 3 [1965]:23).

42. David B. Hinton observes, "The descent of Hitler from the clouds in the first and the S.A. marching against a background of clouds in the last suggest a super worldly aura. . . . The first sequence looks from the clouds at the earth, while the last sequence looks from the earth to the clouds" (see "*Triumph of the Will*: Document or Artifice?" *Cinema Journal* 15 [1975]:56). Kelman confirms on this final scene: "The marchers themselves are shot from an angle to show them not merely against the sky, but headed up into it . . . a subtle, even subliminal ascension of the German nation to the heavens . . ." (Ken Kelman, "Propaganda as Vision—*Triumph of the Will*," *Film Culture* 56–57 [1973]:65).

43. Erik Erikson, "Hitler's Imagery and German Youth," *Psychiatry* 5 (1942):489.

44. Siegfried Kracauer, *From Caligari to Hitler: A Psychological History of German Film* (Princeton, N.J.: Princeton University Press, 1947), p. 301.

45. Cheryl Irwin Thomas says that "songs emphasize a strength-in-unity pattern of a movement," and can connect singers with tradition that authenticates their group identity; see her "Look What They've Done to My Song, Ma: The Persuasiveness of Song," *Southern Speech Communicational Journal* 39 (1974):260–68.

46. Susan Sontag writes, "Uniforms suggest fantasies of community, order, identity (through ranks, badges, medals which 'say' who the wearer is and what he has done: his worth is recognized), competence, legitimate authority, the legitimate exercise of violence" ("Fascinating Facism," *New York Review of Books*, Feb. 6, 1975, p. 28).

47. The biblical theme of exodus out of bondage was an "archetypal experience" for King, useful on many fronts during the civil and human rights struggle. (See James H. Smylie, "On Jesus, Pharaohs, and the Chosen People," *Interpretation: A Journal of Bible and Theology* 24 [1970]:74–91; and John W. Rathbun, "Martin Luther King: The Theology of Social Action," *American Quarterly* 20 (1968):42.)

48. I would argue that such fundamental changes in human perspective confirm the revolutionary character of King's discourse more than his development of new forms of communication; but see the perceptive argument in Edwin Black, "The 'Vision' of Martin Luther King," pp. 7–16.

49. Wesley T. Mott argues that King's great technical achievement in rhetoric was to convert the old-time sermon form into effective polemic for social reform ("The Rhetoric of Martin Luther King, Jr: 'Letter from Birmingham Jail,' " *Phylon* 36 [1975]:411–21). For a superb analysis of this form and of King's use

of it, see Garry Wills, "Martin Luther King is Still on the Case," in Tom Wolfe, ed., *The New Journalism* (New York: Harper & Row, 1973), pp. 356–76.

50. Richard John Neuhaus, Letter, *Commonweal* 88 (1968):342.

51. Black concludes that King's death was an aesthetic failure, because he was "shot from the shadows by a petty thief" ("Vision," p. 15). It is a mistake, however, to think of King as simply the victim of an obscure criminal. King was caught in the collision between old racism and the rising level of black expectations, a consciousness that he himself did much to elevate and articulate. Therefore, he willed the conditions of his own destruction, and, driven by the imperatives of his character, came to his destiny in Memphis. Such a death was surely tragic, both in the aesthetic sense and in its larger impact upon moral life.

52. Lawrence Rosenfield, "The Practical Celebration of Epideictic," in Eugene E. White, ed., *Rhetoric in Transition: Studies in the Nature and Uses of Rhetoric* (University Park: Pennsylvania State University Press, 1980), p. 134.

53. The status of epideictic is a false argument that has preoccupied commentators from Cope, who calls it an "inferior" form, to Duffy, who contends "it is at least the equal of forensic and deliberative." (See E. M. Cope, *An Introduction to Aristotle's Rhetoric* [London: Macmillan, 1867], pp. 121–22; and Bernard K. Duffy, "The Platonic Functions of Epideictic Rhetoric," *Philosophy and Rhetoric* 16 [1983]:92). The real though neglected issue is how epideictic functions in relation to other forms, and how all work together to enable human communication. Perelman and Olbrechts-Tyteca are quite aware of this dynamic relationship, but their observations in *The New Rhetoric* are not altogether consistent. After observing that "epideictic oratory forms a central part of the art of persuasion" (p. 49), they position the epideictic function between acceptance of a course of action, which is the product of successful deliberative rhetoric, and the enactment of that commitment (pp. 49–50). Thus epideictic would become the actualizer of deliberative rhetoric by intensifying commitment and overcoming inertia. In the sequence of functions, epideictic would follow deliberative. At another point, however, they suggest that epideictic works to intensify adherence to values themselves, thus providing the "foundation" for "deliberative and legal speeches" (pp. 52–53). This position, which agrees with the argument I make above, sees epideictic as operating logically prior to and sanctioning both deliberation and judgment.

54. Charles J. Maland, *Frank Capra* (Boston: Twayne, 1980), pp. 12, 126.

55. Osborn, *Orientations,* pp. 10–11, and "Archetypal Metaphor in Rhetoric," pp. 119–20.

56. Richard Barsam, "Why We Fight," in Richard Glatzer and John Raeburn, eds., *Frank Capra: The Man and His Films* (Ann Arbor: University of Michigan Press, 1975), p. 154.

57. Langer, *Philosophy in a New Key: A Study in the Symbolism of Reason, Rite, and Art* (New York: New American Library, 1951), pp. 174–208.

58. Sergei Eisenstein's account of montage imagery in film parallels in many respects the treatment of rhetorical figuration by language scholars (see Eisenstein's *The Film Sense,* trans. Jay Leyda [New York: Harcourt, 1942], pp. 3–68). A more recent work that attempts to develop a theory of figuration for film is N. Roy Clifton, *The Figure in Film* (Newark: University of Delaware Press, 1983). However, the systematic integration of verbal and nonverbal theories of imagery remains a challenge to theorists.

59. In this view I am joined essentially by Ernesto Grassi, who has written that the first premises for ratiocination are themselves evoked by nonrational, figurative, imaginative discourse. This nonrational or, as I have preferred, prerational origin of basic premises, if not the "tragedy of the rationalistic process," is surely one of its more interesting ironies. (See Grassi, "Rhetoric and Philosophy," *Philosophy and Rhetoric* 9 [1976]:200–216.)

5

Michael Calvin McGee

AGAINST
TRANSCENDENTALISM:
Prologue to a Functional Theory
of Communicative Praxis

Only the *Enuma Elish* or the Torah can begin in the beginning. I have
no such pretensions. I begin somewhere in the middle with an interest in
understanding the relationship between communicative praxis and tran-
scendental conceptions of form. I need to define these two key terms; but
first, I want to tell the story of what comes before my argument. Both the
idea of communicative praxis and the perspective in which formalism is
problematic emerge from the postmodern critique of scientism.

THE STARTING POINTS OF AN ACADEMIC MOVEMENT

At least since the appearance of Michael Polanyi's *Personal Knowledge* and Thomas Kuhn's *Structure of Scientific Revolutions*, scholars
have been toying with alternatives to "science" in explaining how human
beings come to know things.[1] From as many perspectives as there are
disciplines, the assumptions and practices of abstract empiricism are
being challenged.[2] Something resembling a political movement is afoot,
in other words, and that makes for a problem because science is not
supposed to be political. In fact, the suggestion that there is a political
dimension to new fashions in science is enough to interest Edwin Boring
in making some stark distinctions between creating a new science and
getting caught up in an academic movement:

Science can actually . . . lift itself by its own boot straps, but the result is
not what we call a "movement" because motion can be defined only with
respect to something, and progress must move away from something. . . .
It is therefore the business of the founders of new schools, the promoters
and propagandists, to call persistent attention to what they are not, just
as one political party is forever emphasizing the shortcomings of the
other. . . . A school may be flexible and disposed toward change and
growth in all directions except those against which it has set itself. Here
it is hardened by its own drive.[3]

108

Notice that there is a sneer in this passage, partly derived from the general bad taste of politics common among truth-seekers, and partly derived from an almost Mosaic faith in science. People who intend to acquire power and money by influencing decisions about what counts as knowledge might compromise their integrity as well as the truth. So one might be alienated from the new movement if it were only a competition between "scientists" and "humanists," with the right to dominate academic resources and research agendas as the prize. But there is another kind of politics in Boring's disembodied and disenacted vision of science. Other poor mortals are fooled by propagandists; but Horatio Alger, with a pure heart and the sacred commandments of scientism, has the strength of ten! He patiently shines shoes and slowly pulls himself up out of power politics, only to disappear inside Boring's allusion to one of the more popular romances of "the Gilded Age" of monopoly capitalism. Scientism has been the Standard Oil of the intellectual's world, claiming a "monopoly" on the production of knowledge. In part, at least, scientism has been funded by nakedly political claims to be apolitical, the very sort of sneer at promoters and propagandists that Boring indulged. The political actor who hides his politics is no more trustworthy than the truth-seeker who profits from publicity.

Science is not *supposed* to be political, but like every other human social activity, it *is* political. The new movement may be simply a new arena for an old war between poets and scientists, or it may be a positive response to the political antipolitics of scientism. The problem is understanding its meanings and motives. Understanding requires that the new orientation be dwelled-within for a time, surrendering to the terms and resources of "promoters and propagandists" long enough to permit assessing the movement's potential. I will thus commit myself to three interpretations, which I believe constitute the driving force of the new movement. Note well that I regard these commitments not as assumptions, nor as perspectives still bracketed and subject to dispute, but as declarations of a hardened attitude, beginnings to be worked from rather than toward or against.

1. PHILOSOPHY HAS ENDED

This is as provocative a phrasing of the first commitment as I can manage, and one that preserves association with the archetypal postmodern argument that "God is dead." To say that "God is dead" is hyperbole, provocation to think about the disorientation of values that resulted in the transition from a religious culture in Europe to an

109

industrial culture. It is a religious plaint in many ways, for it mourns even as it celebrates, much in the manner of the English lament, "The King is dead, long live the King." In like manner, declaring the "end of philosophy" is a philosophical hyperbole. It provokes new, less teleological readings of the history of philosophy so that we understand the disorientation of values attendant upon seeing all knowledge flow inexorably into the impenetrable troughs of a philosophy of science.[4] To say that philosophy has ended is not to mean that philosophers are an endangered species, but rather, that the philosophy of the future will have increasingly less to do with abstractly empirical epistemology and the ontology that supports it.[5]

As one hostile reviewer of Richard Rorty's *Philosophy and the Mirror of Nature* illustrates, the disquietude about old problems can be portrayed as technical, a squabble in the philosopher's guild to be resolved with regard to one's conception of philosophy as a profession. When Rorty points out the difficulties inherent in any teleology and begins to explore alternative constructions, his reviewer sees only a "historical argument" to be judged by someone's understanding about what *really happened* in the history of the profession. When Rorty discusses the wrongheadedness even of conceiving that mind and body might be analytically distinct, his reviewer sees a second-guessed televisual sporting event, an "instant replay of major contemporary strategies with respect to the mind/body problem." *Philosophy and the Mirror of Nature* is misrepresented when it is read in the context it attacks. Rorty should not be portrayed as responding to the very questions he says are poorly framed and irrelevant to what he wants philosophy to be.[6]

More is at stake than mistaking the logical apparatus of the profession for the integrity of living philosophy. What bothers participants in the new movement is a general malaise, a feeling that epistemology (perhaps the whole enterprise of professional philosophy) has become irrelevant to the problems of knowledge and understanding. "Cartesianism" (a somewhat misleading label for the "mirror-of-nature" figure Rorty discussed) can lead to uncomfortable and simply wrong attitudes:

[D]uring the last century, . . . under the influence of mathematical logicians, logic has been limited to . . . the study of the methods of proof used in the mathematical sciences. The result is that reasonings extraneous to the domain of the purely formal elude logic altogether, and, as a consequence, they also elude reason. . . . Must we draw from this evolution of logic, and from the very real advances it has made, the conclusion that reason is entirely incompetent in those areas which elude calculation and that, where neither experiment nor logical deduction is in a position to furnish the solution of a problem, we can but abandon ourselves to irrational forces, instincts, suggestion, or even violence?[7]

Much of philosophy seems to be minding its *p*'s and *q*'s, perhaps forgetting that human interest in such things as nuclear devices is not confined to the method or logic used in their creation and manufacture.

2. UNDERSTANDING IS THE SINE QUA NON OF KNOWLEDGE

One must be careful always to distinguish "science," the practice usually credited with producing the largesse of technology, from "scientism," the abstract theory that insists that the only knowledge we can possess is actually or potentially verified through application of the scientific method. The proof that science offers is its product. The proof that scientism offers has less to do with practice than with a stultifying reading of the history of human knowledge. As Kenneth Burke observed, the theorists of scientism argued their case much less "positively" than they led us to believe. They held their vision of science over and against what they portrayed as primitive magic, saying that the miseries of the world could be explained in humankind's insane preoccupation with the irrational.[8] They offered as a clear alternative to religion, magic, and superstition the procedures of the scientific method, suggesting that this method applied in principle in any domain of inquiry where knowledge is possible.

There is, of course, another way to tell the story. Alasdair MacIntyre's *After Virtue*, for example, begins with an interesting fable designed to provoke thought about what was *lost* in the great scientific revolution of the nineteenth century. He asks that we imagine science lost in some catastrophe, a nuclear holocaust perhaps. Not all humans die, nor is all knowledge lost. But we retain "the simulacra of knowledge," the words of a dusty text when no one of experience remains to demonstrate the practices of chemistry, for example. There are clear instructions for the building of a storage battery, but no one understands what these strange words might have indexed—what might a "nickle plate" be, one wonders? Such a world is as improbable in imagination as it is entertaining, until one remembers that the story really is more about our past than our future. MacIntyre observes that for two millennia human beings concentrated on accumulating moral knowledge. If they were as intelligent and diligent as modern scientists, we must suppose that they learned something. But in our haste to embrace the dogma of scientism, we have forgotten what they knew. Their texts are still available, and we can parse out the words, but the experience these terms once indexed is gone,

111

all but irretrievable. For moral knowledge, the great industrial/scientific revolution of the nineteenth century was a real catastrophe, MacIntyre suggests: "We have—very largely, if not entirely—lost our comprehension, both theoretical and practical, of morality."[9]

Though we have long since abandoned the notion that reason is a reflection of the "Divine Mind," we have retained metaphors of religious understanding in the notion that the "direction" of truth is always *up* as opposed to the *down* of ordinary experience. "Higher" mathematics is more sophisticated and more abstract, empty even of rudimentary sense content from living in the everyday world. "We "climb up" the ladder of abstraction to express generalizations that, curiously, apply to no particular at all and to all particulars. We have "higher," and presumably "lower," truths. Science, Boring observed, pulls itself *up* by its bootstraps when it creates knowledge.

"Order" is thus an important term in accounts of knowledge. In the physical world, only gravity lets us know which way is "up." In the world of ideas, sets of predispositions and presuppositions establish directional coordinates separating "higher" from "lower," the "ideal" from the "merely expedient" or, the other way around, the "useful" from "mere theory." For a time, religion was a center of gravity as academics oriented their knowing to the heavens. More recently, science has been a center of gravity as academics oriented knowing to descriptions of the physical world. In addition to collections of facts and arguments, such orientations produced *understanding* of the relationship between particulars and whichever way was "up" at the time. Knowledge, in other words, had understanding built into it by virtue of common cultural agreement as to coordinates of what constituted the "up" and "down" of ideas that purported to be knowledge. But the "gravity" of the world of ideas is not so constant as gravity in the physical world. Reorientations occur. And in the gaps created by reorientation, there is free-fall space, thinking *without* a center of gravity.

Scientism is still caught in its Cartesian rhetoric, but science has become "pluralistic" in contemporary times. We continue to gather facts, we continue to process them methodically, and our language indicates that we believe we have produced knowledge. What distinguishes knowledge, however, has to do with standards derived from the labor itself—with the techniques of survey research, for example. The word "method" is frequently invoked, but it indexes *strategy of thought* more than the "universal method" of scientism. Indeed, as John Nelson has argued, procedural concerns can come to dominate some disciplines so thoroughly that *argument itself disappears*.[10] The dream of unified

112

science has been diluted by a pluralism that makes each field of academic labor into a community of judges who determine what constitutes knowledge within a special field.[11] From the viewpoint of scientism, this situation is confusion that results in inability to organize particulars into a body of "verifiable facts." The new orientation views pluralism more favorably, for the emphasis on community locates the center of gravity for human understanding where it should be—in the hands and minds of practicing scientists and artists.[12]

3. DISSEMINATION IS THE UNEXPLORED PROBLEM OF KNOWLEDGE

Students of the philosophy of knowledge have been enamored of the idea of method because they want *certainty*, "to know that they know about knowing." Their understanding of certainty makes it a very personal goal for intellectual labor: a teacher would ask that a student be able to re-present knowledge, and an engineer would ask that the finished bridge be sturdy enough to bear its weight; but in scientistic discourse, the proof lies in the recipe, not in the pudding. Knowledge, in other words, is thought to be determined by the conventions and rules used to *produce* it. Another version of the story might concentrate more on the dissemination of knowledge, on the conventions and rules used to *market* and *consume* it.

The marketplace metaphor grates against the ear of one who is accustomed to think that knowledge is "high above" a prevailing center of gravity. Since sophists were degraded for accepting money for teaching, and since money changers were cast from the temple, both philosophy and religion have been dead set against treating knowledge as a medium or an object of exchange. This may be the decisive factor that gives knowledge its otherworldly aura. It certainly is the source of scientism's most celebrated contradiction: from one direction, scientism argues against the superstition, religion, and magic of earlier times by suggesting that the connection between knowledge and the world of political economy is purely technical—whatever happens in the world can be explained without reference to extrasensory perceptions. But from another direction, scientism follows its ancestors in withdrawing from the workaday world, denying responsibility for the use of knowledge in the political economy, and holding itself above the fray of decisionmaking. Proponents of scientism have claimed that "if the appropriate general laws are known and the relevant initial conditions are manipulable, we can produce a desired state of affairs, natural or social. But the question as to which states of affairs are to be produced cannot itself be scientifically resolved. It is ultimately a matter of decision, for no 'ought' can be derived from an 'is,' no 'value' from a 'fact.' Scientific inquiry is itself *'value free'*; it strives only for objective (that is, intersubjectively testable, value-neutral) results."[13]

However grating they may be, metaphors of the marketplace have a distinguished history. They appear in intellectual history when it seems necessary, for one reason or another, to call producers of knowledge back "down" to the social world in which they work. Aristophanes bankrupted Strepsiades to bring Socrates down from *The Clouds*. Francis Bacon rudely decentered Scholasticism by injecting images of pagan worship and the marketplace into a critique of peripatetic logic. And, of course, Karl Marx nearly threw the figure out of joint. One of the more interesting uses in recent years is Alvin Gouldner's suggestion that the theories of scientism could be anthropologically determined.

We speak of knowledge as if it were disembodied, existing apart from the human beings who possess it. In truth, only *facts* could possibly be disembodied. "Knowledge" is a formation of represented facts, a text accorded its grand name because it conforms to the conventions of a peculiar kind of discourse. A text purporting to be knowledge is peculiar, Gouldner suggests, because of its internal features and because of certain values of the people who produce it. In itself, a "knowledge-text" is a series of claims written in anticipation of their denial. It is thus intended to justify beliefs, and it is conscious of being critical. Knowledge-texts are wrought by people who value them in the same way most of humanity values wealth. The society of intellectuals is a "culture of critical discourse" devoted to allocating what money usually acquires (status, security, etc.) according to the quality of knowledge-texts. On this view, knowledge is determined by a grammar and a rhetoric of polite communication—which is to say, by the skillful use of a set of rules that privilege the speech act of justification.[14]

Gouldner's description of the "culture of critical discourse" is thus a restatement of the problem of knowledge. The old way of thinking insisted upon *one* understanding of theory, but embraced at least *two* conceptions of practice:

Practice [A]: What scholars do in particular disciplines to discover facts and arguments is a practice because it is the business and daily labor of scholars to produce knowledge. The practice of research ought to be governed by rules derived from and applicable to the *production* of knowledge. But in fact, academics typically pay more attention to rules derived from and applicable to the *dissemination* of knowledge.[15] Either they are unaware of the contradiction or they accept it as a necessary consequence of "marketing" the results of research.

Practice [B]: The use to which people in general put facts is also a practice, but not in the same sense. People *ought* to use facts just as practitioners of special sciences and arts are supposed to use the theory of scientism; that is, according to rules derived from and applicable to the production of facts. But people actually condition knowledge with unscientific values and hold these "value-polluted" beliefs as if they were factual. They make unscientific, and hence irrational, judgments; and they consult scholars only in the interest of finding a way to implement their commitments technically.

Gouldner wants to understand the problem of knowledge as a need to work through these two contradictions, exploring them for an insight into the texture of technological society and finding a way to eliminate their more negative features.

SCIENTISM AND DISCOURSE THEORY

This formulation is interesting to discourse theorists because it forces a more precise understanding of the connection between knowledge and its communication. The commitment to scientism is not simply a bad idea, an ill-advised policy of academics, or an error in reason—it is ideology, in the old-fashioned sense of "false consciousness." Academics are conditioned to believe that questions of deciding what is to count as knowledge can be resolved in principle with the aid of formal methods and logics. Such questions are really settled in practice, however, with the aid of historically evolved rules of discourse production. This basic contradiction is complicated by the intrusion of scientism into the rhetoric of the culture of critical discourse, and by the increasing gap between the two senses of practical knowledge discussed above.

Scientism, of course, has had great impact on our understanding of how discourse produces agreements in practice—indeed, much of the rhetoric of scientism has been aimed at reforming corrupt discourse practices, both in and out of the academy, to make our talk "more rational."[16] Academics especially have been urged to remove "value judgments" from what they count as knowledge, to regard ambiguity of language and figuration as impediments to knowledge, to produce discourse according to such conventions as those of the American Psychological Association, and to express knowledge "quantitatively."[17] These reforms now have historical standing and thus seem to be identical with the rules of discourse production in the culture of critical discourse.

A too hasty conclusion might leave one believing that the mistake of scientism is no more serious than failing to acknowledge its own textuality, for if the visions of scientism have taken root in the culture of critical discourse, the new grammar and rhetoric of knowledge production would make Gouldner's critique of scientism moot: whether formal criteria of knowledge are funded by rationality and empirical relevance or by the agreement of scholarly communities, the result is the same—knowledge is determined by its mode of production in both cases. In one case, scientism justifies a bundle of research methods privileged because they can produce truth; in the other case, scientism justifies a style of argument privileged because it is the most effective or most ethical means of persuasion.

The difficulty with this interpretation is that the impact of scientism on discourse practices, though pervasive, has been superficial. The ideology has produced a *style* of discourse that dominates academic publication, but evidence multiplies to support the claim that scientists and artists actually persuade each other by following older rules of discourse production. In economics, for example, a rhetoric of inquiry appears to be most important in determining knowledge—the discourse practices envisioned by scientism are not quite cosmetic, but they seem to be merely conventional, a sort of lingua franca used more to codify than to determine knowledge.[18] Similar situations have been reported in anthropology, history, language arts and sciences, law, mathematics, politics, psychology, and sociology.

Some suggest that beneath the veneer of scientism lies a hidden "narrative paradigm," which in fact determines what gets counted as knowledge.[19] This notion is attractive because it accords with evidence that scientistic theories of discourse have occluded understanding of rationality in everyday practice (*Practice [B]*, above). Studies of jury deliberations, for example, suggest that jurors decide the questions of guilt and innocence by asking whether or not an act is narratively probable within the frame of the "story" told by witnesses and opposing attorneys.[20] This despite an intimidating array of expert witnesses imported from the academy to testify in the lingua franca of scientistic discourse.[21] Studies of such political-economic crises as the failure of the Three Mile Island nuclear facility suggest that there is a tension between "technical reason" and "social reason." The former is promoted by academics, writers in the popular press, and government officials, and is funded by the scientistic ideology. The latter is implicit in the fact of social organization and is funded by the history and structure of social practices.[22]

116

The ideological nature of scientism, then, is evident in what it occludes more than in what it promotes. In *Practice [A]*, the rigidity and orthodoxy of scientism make it difficult to see how scholars persuade one another and thus determine knowledge. In *Practice [B]*, the pervasiveness of scientism and the complexity of postindustrial society combine to motivate the repression of social reason in people who wish to be reasonable.[23] The agenda is clear for discourse theorists who would add a line to the argument that seems to be producing an alternative to the ideology of scientism: What general theory of discourse permits description, simultaneously, of practical persuasion in science, of social reason in everyday practice, and of the relationships that exist between each and the ideology of scientism?

THE GENERAL THEORY OF COMMUNICATIVE PRAXIS

Knowledge in theory is said to be the "highest knowledge," and it is that to which students of discourse aspire. Conceived as in scientism, however, "discourse theory" is a curious ambition. Writers with a practice (the study of texts) look to an idea of knowledge that ostentatiously refuses to recognize any special practice as its context, object, and motive. Calvin Schrag has called attention to this odd situation by comparing scientistic philosophy with recent advertisements urging travel on Greyhound buses. Rhetoricians, literary historians, and critics of every stripe are paid to produce what most would count as "knowledge." For the most part they are left alone to settle among themselves what will be presented to the next generation as the knowledge of their field. When scientism is appealed to for criteria of judgment, however, either from within the field or from outside it, there is an attempt to settle the dispute *in principle*, without reference to the particulars of the field. This feat is accomplished by people "trained in philosophy." Such training emphasizes "formal thought" based on "symbolic logics"— every effort is made to evacuate thinking, to drain concepts of their particular, radically empirical meaning. Professionalism in philosophy consists of a community-based claim to specialize in thinking-as-such, and a consequent insistence on the prerogative and responsibility of expertise: "When you ride in our bus," quips Schrag, exposing the deceptive rhetoric of philosophy for an audience of nonspecialists, "you can leave the thinking to us!"[24]

Schrag's point is not that practitioners of the special arts and sciences should so valorize the idea of "practice" that interest in speculative reflection is lost. Like Hans-Georg Gadamer, he wants more productive understandings of "theory":

117

Today practice tends to be defined by a kind of opposition to theory. There is an antidogmatic tone to the word *practice*, a suspicion against the merely theoretic, rote knowledge of something of which one has no experience whatsoever. To be sure this polarity has been constantly present; and antiquity was also familiar with it. But the opposed concept, the concept of theory, has become something different in our time and has lost its dignity. It suggests nothing of what *theoria* was to the eye disciplined enough to discern the visibly structured order of the heavens and the order of the world and of human society. Theory has become a notion instrumental to the investigation of truth and the garnering of new pieces of knowledge. That is the basic situation in terms of which our question, What is practice? is first motivated. But we are no longer aware of this because in starting from the modern notion of science when we talk about practice, we have been forced in the direction of thinking of the application of science.[25]

Gadamer's recovery of the Greek terms *theoria* and *praxis* captures the sense in which *Practice [A]* and *Practice [B]* must be integrated, conflated in a whole understanding that defies their separation on any other terms than simple analytic convenience.

The difficulty, then, is not that students of discourse want to regard theory as their "highest knowledge," but that they chose a poor compass whereby to guide their upward course. *A critic's own practice is already theoretical.* That is, the understanding of discourse in *Practice [B]*, in the halls of Congress, for example, requires knowledge of "how to" communicate politically. One can leave it at that, simply "going through the motions" of a career in politics, or one can reflect critically on what it might mean to "know how to" communicate politically, fabricating knowledge-texts on the basis of such speculation. From another angle, the critic who intends in the first place to produce knowledge-texts must have something to think about, in this case a politician's communication. One can "go through the motions" of fabricating a criticism, using the conventions of interpretation vogue among critics, or one can make the attempt to understand what it might mean for a politician to "know how to" communicate politically. Politician and critic meet on common ground, in a public "space" where knowledge consists of indexing an other's vital experience while reflecting on one's own in an attempt to realize a common aspiration to *theoria*. Their goal is neither being certain with regard to the "how to" of political communication nor being "right" with regard to conventional theories of criticism. The prize is what the Greeks called *phronesis*, the same practical wisdom and prudence that has been a valuable commodity in Western thought at least since Ulysses used Agamemnon's royal staff to whip the coward Thersites out of the Achaean's camp.[26]

Schrag wants to emphasize that this "space of subjectivity" is a *communicative praxis*, because knowledge is manufactured in the act of contributing to conversations about the meaning of praxis. Scholars act in and on the world by making manifest their participation in the "culture of critical discourse" and, by implication, the larger culture of *Practice [B]*. The vehicle and product of such participation is speaking and writing, texts that seek to determine knowledge even as they legitimize claims to be knowledgeable, persuasively displaying evidence of thought and reflection as demanded by the culture of critical discourse. The space of communicative praxis is *subjective*, because it is not possible for the scholar ever to "be objective." As I have already argued, the scholar's feeling that he or she might, in principle, rise above *Practice [B]* is part of the ideology of scientism in three respects: (*a*) because they are not cloistered, scholars are subject to the nonacademic pressures of life in the workaday world; (*b*) in fact, it is often the case that scholars' research agendas are set by powers-that-be within the political economy; and (*c*) whether or not research is placed on the agenda for nonacademic reasons, it will be used in *Practice [B]* as if it had been bought and paid for, without regard for scholarly values and aspirations.

Everyone who participates in the political economy shares a like circumstance: each must act in and on the world by creating and responding to conversations about *right action*—action that presupposes prudence, wisdom, and knowledge of facts. A banker, for example, acts in and on the world by making manifest his or her knowledgeability—which is to say, by claiming to "know what to do" with money, and having the ability to manage the doing of it. Knowledgeability is vital to the business of accumulating and preserving wealth. Specifically, bankers must be educated, and so be skilled enough in intellectual labor to interpret what academic economists, for example, say to them. Further, bankers commonly adhere to an agenda set for them by the academics who supervise their education. And, whether or not the action of a banker is responsive to items on an academic agenda, it will be criticized and evaluated as if it were—academics determine what will be counted as knowledge in the next generation and, with or without permission, they will pass judgment on the work even of the wealthiest and most powerful capitalist.

The concept of communicative praxis is thus a wide net meant to collect the interpretations needed to reorient discourse theory toward the larger project of finding a discourse-based alternative to scientism. Of

119

course, I need to elaborate—to describe the particular dimensions of communicative praxis, and to say something about how they relate to one another. I shall amplify by interpreting some key words and phrases used by Schrag in a series of propositions designed to sketch the concept for a group of rhetoricians.[27]

1. COMMUNICATIVE PRAXIS IS AN *AMALGAM* OF DISCOURSE AND ACTION

1.1. The relational term "amalgam" suggests integration of sorts, a conflation, as two essays are read together in light of a common interpretation that would not be possible with just one or the other. The logic of perspective should be invoked by this term: each nuance of communicative praxis must be seen and collected in the mind as we collect different views of three-dimensional objects in space. Our view of the whole is properly a *rational construction* accomplished through *selection, coordination, interpretation*, and *application* of "present" and "compresent" data.[28]

1.2. None of the nuances of communicative praxis, in other words, can be thought of as a "discrete part" that might be interpreted and analyzed separately. As Kenneth Burke suggested, discourse can be a kind of action in itself, and there is a sense in which "all the world's a stage." Language itself is in part a social practice, and most social practices are "textualized" in one or another language usage. The "history and structure of language" is in a sense identical to the "history and structure of social practice." In short, the elements of communicative praxis are properly *dimensions* and not *elements* of it. One may dwell for a moment on the performative aspect of discourse, for example, in the same way that one would ponder the nuances of a colorful word ensconced in a poem; but communicative praxis, like the poem, is an amalgam of its dimensions, which resists atomization. That communicative praxis has dimensions must be acknowledged, but it makes no more sense to focus exclusively on one of them than it would to reduce Eliot's *Prufrock* to the marvelously ambiguous word "etherized."

2. *DISCOURSE* IS AN AMALGAM OF *THE EVENT OF SPEAKING* AND THE *HISTORY AND STRUCTURE OF LANGUAGE*

2.1. *Discourse* is the product of language put to use by human beings for the purpose of communing, with themselves, with other people, with gods and animals. That which must be understood in communication is not an *idea*, but a *meaning*—the meaning of discourse. One cannot reveal

120

ideas apart from language, even if it is possible to imagine thought without symbols. In truth, one can do no better than *represent meanings* as discourse in discourse. One may verbalize in empty gibberish, but one cannot *communicate* "out of context." Every speech and every essay contributes to an ongoing conversation. Reference must be made to discourse produced by others, or one's utterance will have little or no meaning, and therefore little or no thought. But, on the other hand, one has a *space* within community, a view on life unlike any other. Meanings are, as they must be, vague and ambiguous enough to bear the nuances of individual autonomy.

2.2. The *event of speaking* is a "live" performance, occurring at *this* moment and in *this* place. Two implications require comment. First, the term indexes an argument about the function of speaking and writing that has gone on throughout the history of Western thought, from Plato to Derrida.[29] Speech has presence that writing does not, and writing has a permanence that speech does not. Arguments abound as to which should model for discourse theory, but in truth discourse consists of writing *and* speaking. One can prefer one over the other, but one must account for the relationship of the two. Here it is argued that speaking is an *event*, a materially present dimension of communicative praxis. It thus is like *action*, but it is properly only analogous, as the words of an actor in the theater help to "play a part", but do not "take part" in whatever we define as the "not-play" world. Stage actors are presented with formed discourse—a script—and are charged to "per-form" it, to embody it and make it come alive. In like fashion, the engagement of a community in discourse supposes that one has pre-formed meanings and now is involved in per-forming them, making them manifest to others. In this situation lies the possibility of realizing the theoretical autonomy of individuals: we can sometimes pre-form our own meaning; but if we are willing to accept the consequence of community disapproval, we are always able to per-form meaning with our own nuance and flair.

2.3. The *history and structure of language* has to do with writing and not speaking. It is abiding, permanent; it determines human belief and sits against the theoretical autonomy of individuals. *Language* must be construed broadly to include words, terms, conventions, stock arguments, and "classic" literature canonized by particular groups—in short, all the various usages that are characteristic and constitutive of a "language community." One must "speak their language" just to participate in a community's patter. This is to say, one must work from a complex pattern of usage that is filled with already present meanings. Language and meaning are both historically material. By this I mean that the usages are presented to each human being as a condition of one's Being-in-the-World, without permission, beyond the capacity of a person's intent to alter. Every repetition of a usage seals it deeper in the practice of the community, makes it more resistant to change, more abiding and material. Even should one intend to alter established usages, still they must be taken into account. What one can say is thus in part determined by usages. Fredric Jameson made much of the observation that the history and structure of language is a "prison house."[30]

3. *ACTION* IS AN AMALGAM OF *INDIVIDUAL INTENTIONS* AND THE *HISTORY AND STRUCTURE OF SOCIAL PRACTICE*

3.1. *Action* is doing-to the world, the chopping of trees, their shaping for use, and the being-within an environment human beings have altered. There is a tremendous gulf between action and discourse, the distance between murder, for example, and the "symbolic killing" of name-calling. The line can be made fuzzy, however, sometimes from strategic intention: The passage of law such as the Civil Rights Act of 1964, for example, can be taken as itself a solution to the problem of racism. The declaration of fond hope and fervent desire can blind one to the truth that "freedom is as freedom does." Such confusion indicates that the difficulty with understanding action has to do with the capacity of discourse to emulate it. In truth, *the only actions that consist in discourse are performed on discourse itself.* Speech will not fell a tree, and one cannot write a house to dwell in. One can act through discourse on discourse to guide or control the meaning people see in selected representations of the world. Discursive action, however, always stands in anticipation of its consequences, an act that requires additional acts before one is clear that it ever was more than "mere talk."

3.2. *Individual intentions* are not always manifest in discourse, and it isn't clear that they matter much in understanding texts. Poets and other creative writers manufacture discourse primarily as a means of venting the creative urge—they make art for art's sake, or more radically, art for self's sake. A whole class of professionals is charged to find meanings in works of art; their interpretations are not about "what texts communicate," however. Meanings are *made*, in and from "metatexts" about similar artistic expression. Even recalling that the text was authored is not essential to its interpretation. From the viewpoint of action, however, all discourse presents itself as *intended*. We may not know what the intentions were, and knowing intentions may have no bearing on understanding meanings in discourse; but one cannot look at anything human beings created as if it were accidental. Discoveries may be the fortuitous result of happy circumstances, but things that are *created* evince individual autonomy and willfulness. Further, as Burke is fond of saying, the presence of such intention is required to distinguish action from behavior. Behavior is merely motion, a "doing" that has no clear meaning apart from being. Action is "doing-to" the world, *on purpose!*[31]

3.3. The *history and structure of social practice* is historically material. We construct a history of traditions and institutions in such texts as articles of incorporation. Though individuals will be called upon to embody and enact scripted roles, they are irrelevant to the structure of the social practice—the order of things exists in the text, not in the creatures who momentarily play its parts. In spite of the clear textuality of the history and structure of social practices, we regard them *as if* they were physically substantial, as inert as a mountain even in tiny words and phrases. One doesn't "see" a social practice so much as one conjures it in apparently innocent interactions: When I greet a person, and receive a polite response, the "community" existing between us is wholly concrete and fleeting—except as it is contextualized in the history of our relationship. I have many friends, the other has many friends; I occupy space in the social order, the other occupies space; I have a biography, and so does the other. If my companion is a total stranger, I will inject her or him into the history and structure of what I know already, perhaps in the space of a friend, perhaps in the space of an enemy.

The space of communicative praxis permits one to understand what others have called "public knowledge."[32] In the argument that such knowledge occurs *in discursive space*, we get the view that it differs from the kind of knowledge promoted by scientism because it is understood according to the rules of its dissemination rather than the rules of its production. This ties the problem of knowledge firmly to discourse theory, making knowledge itself as much a topic of discourse theory as rhetoric or narrative. Arguments made thus far, however, do not speak to the need for a general theory of communicative praxis. More than anywhere in academic circles, discourse theorists resisted scientism, preserving the great traditions of antiquity—poetic, rhetoric, and dialectic—against the mad rush to methodize human knowledge. Treated as general perspectives on human life, these traditions have already funded such discourse-based alternatives to scientism as Burke's theory of dramatism, various theories of narrativity, and the evolving theory of rhetoric as "epistemic," a practical account of human inquiry. What is to be gained from reorienting contemporary discourse theories toward communicative praxis?

123

The need to reorient discourse theory comes clear in following Rorty's statement of the case against philosophy conceived as a "mirror of nature." In his view, scientism is not *merely* an accouterment of the Enlightenment or of the industrialization of the West. It is the eventual consequence of insisting that problems of ontology and epistemology be framed in a particular way. Rorty traces this commitment back to Plato's invention of a disembodied and disenacted way of thinking about thinking. He suggests that we need to recover the perspective, the *space*, occupied by philosophy before Plato gave knowledge a mystic aura of otherworldliness. In this space, he says, we shall "be where the Sophists were before Plato brought his principle to bear and invented 'philosophical thinking': we shall be looking for an airtight case rather than an unshakable foundation."[33] If the objectionable characteristics of philosophy are traceable to Platonic idealism, discourse theories traceable to Plato will be deficient in parallel ways, despite an appearance of alterity to scientism. The deficiency should be evident in theories that are presented as *formal*.

THE PROBLEM OF FORM

Though it is not a space to be staked out as the substance of a new discipline, one cannot ignore the fact that critics of every sort have made the study of communicative praxis a special art and science. All critics, from realistic scientists of the Frankfurt School of *Ideologiekritik* to metaphysically inclined interpreters of literature, are alike in their attempt to tease knowledge out of discourse manufactured in the world of everyday practice. Criticism, in other words, is an established intellectual project that has always functioned by amalgamating what I have called *Practice [A]* and *Practice [B]*, considering the dimensions of communicative praxis as *topoi* of critical analysis. If I am to be consistent with my own argument—that theoretical questions should be settled with reference to the conversation of those who produce practical knowledge—I should understand "formal theories of discourse" as they are presented and appropriated among critics.

The deficiencies of Platonic idealism are most clearly revealed in the conversation among literary and rhetorical critics on the subject of "form and genre." In part because it is detailed in an earlier chapter, I shall not rehearse the history of the idea of literary formalism. Perhaps more importantly, literary formalism is not a "live" issue in the scholar's communicative praxis when it is conceived strictly as the history of an idea. It is no more than a moment in the history and structure of critical

124

practice. For a full view of the matter, we need to see that scholars talk to one another as well as publish essays. Further, scholarly talk and writing is fully embodied and enacted: though it is polite, and thus focused on meanings rather than personalities, academic communication occurs among people who target each other as well as arguments. There is a spirit of excitement and discovery in scholarly talk and writing, the feeling that high stakes lie on the table to reward the one who holds the "best hand," the next and most elegant bit of knowledge.

Though the ordinary path toward agreement is more circuitous, one excellent model of the scholar's communicative praxis is the research conference like that which inspired this book. Scholars read bits and pieces of arguments in their professional journals, getting the idea that "something new" is in the wind. There is a moment of indecision as the history and structure of the field is consulted in an effort to discover what counts as "new." When a sufficient number of scholars are convinced to take a closer look at "something new," a research conference may be organized, as a vehicle for distributing informal essays too speculative for an established journal, and as an occasion for talk about the new meanings. After several days of chatter and argument, in the spirit of inquiry, a decision is made to textualize what was said. Participants are asked to conventionalize their essays for formal distribution, and a book is edited. In conjunction with the book, and in its wake, other books and scholarly essays on the subject appear, indexing previous writing and encouraging more. At some point, the weight of the talking and writing leads someone to include the new literature in educational materials as a part of "what we know" that deserves to be passed on to future generations of scholars.

The spirit of reflex invites me to continue indexing this book as I seek to understand the problem of form. But I cannot know that any of what we say here will one day be counted as knowledge. I shall therefore work with one antecedent to this book, a relatively small storm in the long history of "form-and-genre" criticism, but an instructive one nonetheless. Specifically, I shall analyze the conversation about a new understanding of the concept "genre" in the community of rhetorical critics. The interesting part of the conversation began in 1965 and reached its highest intensity with the publication in 1978 of *Form and Genre: Shaping Rhetorical Action*.[34]

Critics in rhetorical studies have always relied upon the idea of "genre" in two ways: (1) Rhetoricians have thought it important to argue that "rhetorical criticism" is unique, not because of its methods or its rationale, but because of the *kind* of discourse it studies. Critics have

125

therefore been at pains to establish that "rhetoric" is a *form* of speaking and writing distinct from "poetic" (literature) and "dialectic" (philosophy). (2) Within the domain of "rhetoric," as Jamieson has argued, the idea of "genre" was "a trusted friend whose identity is known, whose function is clear, and whose utility is established."[35] This feeling of surety was funded by the community's wholehearted acceptance of Aristotle's classification of rhetorical discourse as deliberative, forensic, or epideictic. Aristotle's categories became standard *topoi* of rhetorical criticism.[36]

In an influential 1965 book, Edwin Black altered the terms of the conversation by arguing that the appropriation of Aristotle's theory of rhetoric as a sort of cookbook of *topoi* for criticism resulted both in a misrepresentation of Aristotle and in uninformative criticism. He called for attention to the idea of genre conceived in an "alternative frame of reference," which would take the existence of rhetorical genres as something to be discovered rather than recognized. Generic categories would be a conclusion of argument rather than a privileged first premise "authorized" by Aristotle.[37]

In an equally influential 1968 essay, Black's colleague Lloyd F. Bitzer contributed to this conversation about "something new" by providing a theoretical rationale for the existence of common and recurring themes in rhetorical discourse. Bitzer suggested that rhetorical discourse was distinct from other types of discourse because it responded to a unique kind of *situation* in human experience. The "rhetorical situation" invites human beings to use discourse as a means of mobilizing themselves to remove an "exigence" in their environment. Such situations can be recurrent. Strategies to deal effectively with them become conventionalized. And finally, "rhetorical forms are born and a special vocabulary, grammar, and style are established."[38]

Kathleen Hall Jamieson articulated the logic of "genre studies" in rhetorical criticism in 1973:

Isolation of genres implies that significantly similar characteristics inhere in works of the same type regardless of author and period of production. A genre of rhetoric contains specimens of other rhetorical genres. If there is an apologic genre then the apology of Socrates and the Checkers Speech of Richard Nixon, if members of that genre, should be similar in significant respects. Moreover, these two specimens should be more comparable than either is to a Speech of another genre produced by the same speaker. The Checkers Speech should in salient respects more closely resemble Socrates' *Apology* than it resembles Nixon's *First Inaugural*. If rhetorical specimens are more different than similar in

126

significant respects, we would not properly class them as parties to the same genre. When one knows what makes an inaugural and not an apology, one has isolated generic characteristics. When one knows what characteristics will inform an inaugural not yet composed, one has isolated the generic membranes of the inaugural.[39]

In a short while, the new orientation came to dominate talking and writing about rhetorical criticism, almost as a new fashion sweeps the clothing industry when "nothing new" has been tried for a number of years. In 1976, a research conference was held at the University of Kansas to study " 'Significant Form' in Rhetorical Criticism." This conference is interesting for its anomalies.

THE FORBIDDEN TERM

I was not privileged to attend the Kansas conference, so I must try to reconstruct the feeling of *talk* about the problem of form and genre from its published proceedings. People at Kansas apparently were ready to consider thoroughgoing change in their academic practice, but the problem put to them strained at their vocabulary because the term "genre" was all but forbidden at the outset of their thinking. The point of the new perspective, after all, was to give up apparently a priori meanings of "genre" for disciplined understandings that follow close analysis of artifacts. The question in dispute was deciding when it was proper to use the word "genre," and until one had earned a right, one had to avoid it altogether. The conference directors decided that the widest net could be cast with the term "significant form":

The phrase "significant form" is intended to refer to recurring patterns in discourse or action including, among others, the repeated use of images, metaphors, arguments, structural arrangements, configurations of language or a combination of such elements into what critics have termed "genres" or rhetorics.[40]

Nearly every order-term in the language is conjured in this brief statement of purpose. "Form" and "genres" are in quotation marks, one supposes, to indicate that they are the target-terms, problematics of the conference. Other order-terms are listed as apparently unproblematic: "Recurrence," "patterns," "repetition," "structure," "arrangement," "configuration," and "combination" are *topoi* for brainstorming and not objects of thought.

127

THE BAGGAGE OF *SYNONYMIA*

Rhetoricians are, or ought to be, more sensitive than most people to the power of figuration, particularly to the ways in which such devices as *synonymia* alter the meaning of premises underlying arguments. As a rule, synonyms actually *contain* important and usually unstated assumptions.[41] When the subject is one's own academic practice, however, and when the priority is creative thinking about an alternative agenda for scholarship in one's own discipline, synonyms come into the conversation haphazardly. Each contributor to *Form and Genre*, for example, developed distinct conceptions of "genre," whether intentionally or not, because of the necessity to find synonyms to stand in momentarily for the forbidden term. Each synonym carried with it a general attitude toward "order" that reflects differences of opinion about the way reason functions to produce knowledge.

That is, we have a number of order-terms to index the *kind* of "order" created when reason functions in different ways. So, for example, the following order-terms are associated in common usage with function-terms that suggest an attitude about what "reason" produces, or should produce, in the way of "knowledge":

1. *Regularity* is more and less "probable," or it is "lawful," that which makes "prediction" possible.
2. *Patterns* are more and less "meaningful," "interesting," or "suggestive" of a particular "interpretation."
3. *Structures* are more and less "material," "constraints" on human agency, which "determine" the realistic possibilities of behavior and belief.
4. *Forms* are more and less "timeless," "recurrent" human responses that signal "mythic," "archetypal," or "permanent" features of the human condition.

The "order" supposed by the concept of communicative praxis that I propose here is different from that supposed by the concept of "scientific method," for example, and from most of the concepts implied by the terms used in *Form and Genre*. The concept asks nothing about "lawfulness." Instead, it asks how knowledge claims are made manifest in two amalgamated "structures," of the history of language and of the history of social practice. The conceptual choice to think of "order" as *historical structure* rather than as "regularity," "pattern," or "form" carries with it an attitude about how reason functions. Let me illustrate, again from essays published in *Form and Genre*.

128

Simons, in "Genre-alizing about Rhetoric," has a very clear idea of what should be counted as knowledge. He seems self-conscious and self-assured about associating "genre" with theories of lawful, or lawlike regularity:

The new scholarship [on "genre"] bids fair to producing a social science of rhetorical choice, one that delimits strategies and stylistic options in the face of situational and purposive constraints. . . . I should like here to point the way toward a science of rhetorical genres, one that might give theoretical coherence to the speculative generalizations of individual critics, help verify (or disprove) their claims by subjecting them to controlled tests, and ultimately guide the interpretation and evaluation of particular artifacts.[42]

At the other end of a continuum of confidence is Bruce Gronbeck's tentative, reflexively operational, commitment to conceptions of order-as-pattern, in "Celluloid Rhetoric": "By 'form' I mean to imply nothing more complicated than patterns of arrangement which are given rhetorical force by their habitual use and codifiability."[43] In between is Black's subtle masking of the themes of *marxissant* theories of the relationship between "structure" and consciousness in the "dialectical complementarity" of the terms "form" and "genre":

Groups of people become distinctive as groups sometimes by their habitual patterns of commitment—not by the beliefs they hold, but by the manner in which they hold them and give them expression. Such people do not necessarily share ideas; they share rather stylistic proclivities and the qualities of mental life of which those proclivities are tokens. Below the continuously mutable dialectic that shapes and reshapes our social actions, there are deeper constancies of consciousness. Their explication is essential to understanding the varieties of rhetorical experience.[44]

Though coherent meaning is found for "genre" in each of these essays, the meanings are incompatible because each presupposes a criterion of knowledge unacceptable as the precondition of others. Simons's vision of knowledge being verifiable challenges Gronbeck's vision of knowledge being codifiable, and neither of these visions fits with Black's of knowledge being oppositional (i.e., located in critical explication of dialectical complementarity). Further, though there is an implicit recognition of tension between wholly general meanings of "science" and "humanism,"[45] it appears that each contributor to *Form and Genre* attributed his or her vision of the preconditions of knowledge to all competent readers. This could have resulted from error in assessing the community's homogeneity, or it could have resulted from political commitment to an intellectual version of liberalism.

AN IDEOLOGY OF TRANSCENDENCE

Despite the implication of other order-terms, and despite Hamletic protestations, contributors to *Form and Genre* seem comfortable with what I shall call an "ideology of transcendence." With this phrase, I mean to imply that each author appears to argue actively for, or passively to accept, a raison d'être of form-and-genre study that posits the need for allegedly timeless generalization. The supposition seems to be that scholarship is a movement toward universals. The critics do not see themselves as manufacturers of knowledge in more than a technical sense; and when matters of the utmost importance are taken up, they truncate productive lines of argument rather than make knowledge claims. In consequence, many of the issues raised by knowledge claims regarding form and genre are never even framed, let alone resolved.

Ernest Bormann's essay on "Rhetorical Criticism and Significant Form" is direct evidence of the presence and predominance of an ideology of transcendence. He claims that a "strong impulse towards studying enduring features of rhetorical discourse" superintended the talk of the Kansas conference. Other conceptions of criticism had been "ephemeral" because they were tied too closely to the technology of communicative praxis—to teaching *techne* of producing discourse—or tied too closely to particular political interests masquerading as "criticism." Bormann envisions a number of ways scholars might transcend communicative praxis, and concludes with a romantic sermon about what follows from such an exercise: "The prospect of meta-criticism which seeks to provide explanations of human symbol-using which transcends particular times and places and styles of communication is an attractive one. To the function and purpose of such criticism the humanistic perspective on scholarship is most appropriate and the illumination of the human condition which can follow from perceptive and talented critics applying such a perspective to human discourse is well worth the time and effort."[46]

The general spirit of commitment to an ideology of transcendence at the Kansas conference seems to have been prompted, or at least exacerbated, by the fact that everyone at the conference was in favor of "pluralism." Bormann and Simons might be exceptions to this rule, for one senses that nods toward pluralism are somewhat ingenuine among writers who seem intent on replaying the game that pits humanism

130

against science. All contributors to *Form and Genre*, however, presupposed a politically neutral meaning in "pluralism." In truth, the concept, as used, translates into what Marcuse, Moore, and Wolff have called "pure tolerance." Pure tolerance in the academy, Barrington Moore suggests, consists of belief that standards of professionalism authorize all properly credentialed experts to make disagreeable knowledge claims. The commitment is warranted politically and not through principles of justification normally insisted upon within the culture of critical discourse: an academic version of "free speech" suggests that "good citizens" are entitled to be as wrongheaded as they please, even when their claims threaten the next generation's inheritance.[47]

Michael Halloran, for example, argues that such public proceedings as the televised debate about whether or not to impeach Richard Nixon are better understood if conceived as constituting a rhetorical genre. "Doing Public Business in Public" is an excellent essay that could have provided useful insights into the problem of deciding what we know about the concept "public." The essay is argued toward the forbidden term, however, and as soon as he is confident that he is entitled to use the word "genre" as he proposes, Halloran quits! It might be premature to expect tautly argued knowledge claims in what is advertised as "an essay, in the old sense of a tentative effort or a probing." But Halloran isn't even clear as to what he will accept as constituting a knowledge claim—or, put more to the point, he's unsure about what he would *not* accept:

Certain aspects of the critical perspective developed in this paper suggest hypotheses that could be submitted to empirical testing, either in field studies or in experimental settings. . . . With respect to the impeachment debate, any number of alternative critical perspectives might be brought to bear on the event. One could, for example, analyze politically the behind-the-scenes bargaining among members of the committee; perform a Toulmin-based analysis of the argumentative structure of the debate; examine audience response as evidenced in press accounts, correspondence with congressmen, public opinion polls, and the like; or do a fantasy-theme analysis of the discussion of Nixon's conduct in the debate. The general point is that criticism is and ought to be pluralistic. There is no one correct perspective on the impeachment debate, or for that matter on any public proceeding or any other rhetorical event.[48]

"Genre" is thus appealed to as a space where someone else, using tools from nearly any system of knowledge production, might find a useful knowledge claim to make. It does not itself constitute the knowledge we need about public business, nor is it by itself a way to achieve knowledge. We know that critics produce knowledge, and it is clear that Halloran produced knowledge. The problem is that he does not evince awareness of having done so. The argument may say that "genre critics" should tolerate anything in the way of a systematic knowledge claim, but they should claim nothing on their own, lest the ringing cry of "Balderdash!" be heard as illiberally intolerant.

Consider as another example the problem of history confronted by the contributors to *Form and Genre*. The imperative that genre must be argued toward can mix unproductively with the notion that "genre" exists only over and in time. My primary resource when I make what Campbell and Jamieson call a "generic claim" must be the *history* of public address.[49] This means that my attention is oriented *to the past*. I am engaged in a line of thinking that relates past to present possibilities of discourse, but I am thinking more about the past than the present because I have to establish that "genre" exists before I can do anything with it. The question is, do I ever really leave the past? What knowledge do I attain by arguing successfully that thus-and-such discourse practice constitutes a genre? Campbell and Jamieson offer one answer in their description of the aims and functions of generic criticism:

The critic who classifies a rhetorical artifact as generically akin to a class of similar artifacts has identified an undercurrent of history rather than comprehended an act isolated in time. Recurrence of a combination of forms into a generically identifiable form over time suggests that certain constants in human action are manifest rhetorically. One may argue that recurrence arises out of comparable rhetorical situation, out of the influence of conventions on the responses of rhetors, out of universal and cultural archetypes ingrained in human consciousness, out of fundamental human needs, or out of a finite number of rhetorical options or commonplaces. Whatever the explanation, the existence of the recurrent provides insight into the human condition.[50]

Campbell and Jamieson thus forswear interest in knowledge or in the issues raised by knowledge claims. They profess to want only "insight," whatever that may be or mean, and care not to commit to or even to speculate about the truth of competing explanations of "genre." We are not even sure *what* is at stake when one's "insight" gives vision of something so ill-defined as "the human condition." The problem raised by the history and structure of discourse and the history and structure of social practice has to do with freedom and constraint, not just on the part of public speakers who choose this strategy of persuasion over another, but with the *very principle* of liberty. The only game worth the candle in Campbell and Jamieson's account of "form and genre" is precisely the question of deciding *how* and *why* recurrences embed themselves in the lives of the living, either as limitations of liberty and subversions of the theoretical autonomy of the individual,[51] or as "enabling prejudices" that create and maintain conditions conducive to liberty and to the theoretical autonomy of the individual.[52] When such stakes as these are on the table, it seems wrong to quit the game with nothing more exciting than an insight.

FORMALIZING THE ALTERNATIVE TO FORM

I have discussed generally and by reference to specific usages such terms as "lawful regularity," "meaningful pattern," "material structure," and "timeless form." I have done so to show how attitudes toward knowledge are manifest in the terms we use to describe the arrangement of facts. In part to illustrate how conversations in a community of academics constitute theory, I showed how formalism becomes problematic even within a community of like-minded authors who try to make communicative praxis their special art and science.

The critics whose work I have been examining were involved directly in the production of knowledge, but they were unaware of it, or at least unaware of the importance of their activity. They created and participated in a communicative praxis wherein our knowledge about such ideas as "public," "currents of history," "liberty," and "constraint" is established. These topics are signally important in contemporary intellectual life, for they are part of the texture of communicative praxis generally, topics that inform conversation in every human science and thus bear upon determinations of knowledge. But the contributors to *Form and Genre* had a very narrow view of their practice, an understanding of their "place" in the scheme of knowledge production which made them timid and overly deferent. Their talking at Kansas and their subsequent writing both seem to anticipate "formal" knowledge that exists "out there" somewhere apart from their talking and writing.

If the subject were not so important, the ironies of the situation would be amusing: a group of writers who have made communicative praxis into a special art and science operate as if there were nothing substantive in the way of truth and knowledge at stake in their own speaking and writing. Further, these are *rhetorical* critics, attenuated by their tradition and by their own discourse to the "epistemic" power of talking and writing[53]—but in characterizing knowledge about discourse, they seek transcendence. And the final irony, the very topic of their conversation invited a critique of transcendence; but such a critique has never emerged because those in a position to mount it appeal to "form and genre" such as Cartesian epistemologists appealed to neat regularities in geometry and calculus—to make knowledge claims seem technically formulary rather than persuasively argumentative.

I think my argument establishes that discourse theory is not safe from recent attacks on scientism. I have thus demonstrated a need for the concept of communicative praxis in discourse theories. But I have not finished with the ideology of transcendence, for I have discussed it only as the smokescreen that has prevented even critics from realizing the theoretical nature and power of their own practice. What we determine as knowledge should depend on lived, subjective truths, carefully and fully argued in the space of communicative praxis. The ideology of transcendence, I believe, corrupts and distorts communicative praxis generally. The ideology has its effects not only among discourse theorists, but among scholars throughout the human sciences, and in everyday *Practice [B]*.

AMBIGUITIES OF FORM AND FUNCTION

An ideology of transcendence can distort communicative praxis in any dimension of discourse or action where an ambiguous order term invites one to extract and idealize the "form" of knowledge. Assume that the topic is political economy. In academic writing, a scholar claims that one way of organizing facts should guide a community of scholars on the question of determining knowledge about political economy. In a political speech, an advocate asks that one of many possible political economic policies be pursued. The two are, of course, interpenetrating, involving both discursive and active dimensions of communicative praxis: scholars act in organizing knowledge-texts one way as opposed to another, and politicians must appear to be familiar with knowledge-texts before their policy recommendations will be persuasive. Further, each of the two dimensions of communicative praxis contains a formal element. In the discursive dimension, the history and structure of language, broadly construed, constrains the scholar's argument directly, the politician's indirectly. In the active dimension, the history and structure of social practice limits the politician directly, the scholar indirectly. The concept of "structure" is thus ambiguous in four ways, and a problem of form arises when it is necessary to eliminate the ambiguity. In talking and writing aimed at clarifying "structure," an ideology of transcendence can corrupt an inquiry into political economy in any one of four ways. I shall state these in general terms.

THE SCHOLAR CAN IDEALIZE THE HISTORY AND
STRUCTURE OF LANGUAGE

Sometimes this occurs as it does in Francis Bacon's "Idols of the Market Place," where a term of ordinary usage (usually a figuration) is given an arbitrary "technical" significance within an intellectual community and then is treated as if it mirrored some phenomenon in the political economy itself. In rhetorical studies, "movement" has become such a term. The term is idealized because it is used with a technical signification, indexing the history and structure of rhetoricians' discourse about strategies of agitation. Indexes of the history and structure of social practice can be lost in the scholar's general prejudice, regarding social change, for example: a social movement, from the viewpoint of the history and structure of social practice, can also be *criminal*, a nuance missed when the meaning of "movement" is taken from the discourse of scholars who tend to value social change over social stability.[54]

More frequently, scholars idealize the structure of language as in Bacon's depiction of the "Idols of the Theater." A bevy of texts is said to be *"the* literature" that contextualizes a problem, perhaps an entire "discipline." It then is argued that legitimate responses to a problem must be developed within the meanings and intentions of that "literature." If such discourse is thought to be a starting point, and if it is understood that scholars should *argue* with meanings it contains—even to the point of opposing initial assumptions, usages, and significations—no intellectual constraints arise. But if "the literature" is conceived to "have weight" because it constitutes a revered tradition, or if it is thought to be authoritative in any way apart from the power of its arguments, a very serious problem of form arises.

THE SCHOLAR CAN IDEALIZE THE HISTORY AND
STRUCTURE OF SOCIAL PRACTICE

Bacon's "Idols of the Tribe" illustrate. An account of human practice (usually some historical narrative) is taken to be the "frame" or "ground" in the context of which all knowledge of any kind should be understood. The history of social practice, for example, is thought to reveal "purpose" in human life. Where we are now is "progress" from barbarism, but only antecedent to what we may become. Current social practice is then conceived to be a point on a continuum of "final causes." Present institutions of "law," for example, are the *telos* of experience with trying to be "just," but only a step along the way to an "ideal" *telos* of "perfect justice." Any line of argument that can be portrayed as

135

"historicist" is such an idealization of social practices, a location of "purpose" or "destiny" in the "direction" of change.

THE POLITICIAN CAN IDEALIZE THE HISTORY AND STRUCTURE OF LANGUAGE

One can assume that what experts take to be knowledge "speaks for itself" and invites or determines particular actions. Sometimes this way of thinking is manifest in people's awe of the rhetoric of science. When nuclear experts suggest that we have nothing to fear from the proliferation of nuclear power, for example, some politicians take their words at face value, and they therefore pursue pro-nuclear policies. People forget that the arguments of scientism insist upon distance between what is taken as fact and acts of political and moral judgment. Scientists who argue for evaluative policy claims, or who allow others to claim that a set of facts "speaks for itself," cease being scientists in that act. That is, they contradict their practice as scientists and offer an opinion out of ignorance—indeed, an opinion from *self-imposed* ignorance of political and moral judgment that is insisted upon as a matter of professional ethics.

At other times, idealization of the history and structure of language is manifest in politicians' attitudes toward their own actions. It was so in the feeling of Richard Nixon that secret tape recordings should be made so that historians of the future would be able to "set the record straight." It was present in more general form in Lyndon Johnson's opinion that "History will make its judgments of the decisions made and the actions taken" during his Presidency.[55]

More technically, this way of thinking can be manifest in the politician's way of coping with the distance between principle and expedience. He or she may argue, for example, that we need not be concerned with the problem of conscription or with the condition of the poor because this *is* the "land of the free" by virtue of our fond hope and fervent declaration. The caveat that freedom is as freedom does gets lost in such idealization.

THE POLITICIAN CAN IDEALIZE THE HISTORY AND STRUCTURE OF SOCIAL PRACTICE

Such thinking is manifest in the "anti-intellectualism" of much American life.[56] Politicians conjure up some historically presentist idea of "public knowledge" and hold this "common sense," as the kind of

136

knowledge most useful in politics. Sometimes this "public knowledge" is understood in opposition to what "eggheads" have to say. At other times, it is understood as a check-rein on intellectuals who may be inclined to undervalue the historically conditioned trial-and-error experience of *Practice [B]*. In extreme form, this idealization can become the sort of cultural chauvinism which has been characteristic of phalange movements, syndicalism, and other variations of twentieth-century fascism.[57]

The ideology of transcendence is manifested differently in each of these four places, but it arises with the same consequence. The *particular* arrangement of facts and arguments is regarded as constituting "knowledge," when in truth any single arrangement is actually *one* of *many* conceivable orderings of facts. Any one ordering is only *taken* to be "knowledge" within a particularly situated community. The ideology of transcendence masks the fact that *knowledge is itself a "function."* This is true in two of the three senses of "function":

1. In the mathematical sense, knowledge is a "function," a "dependent variable," of the community's conception of and attitude toward reason and what reason can be expected to produce. Knowledge itself changes when we think of it as "regularity," "pattern," or "structure," rather than "form."
2. In the rhetorical sense, knowledge "functions," is useful, has consequences in action, differently in particular contexts. In consequence, "knowledge" is changed even in substance by its uses. So, for example, Altimore's analysis of research on recombinant DNA suggested that the knowledge claims of scientists differed dramatically depending on the audience being addressed. Claims were bolder in journals devoted to genetic engineering. Claims were less bold in microbiology generally, and measured by what was apparently believed "scientifically," they were boldly "misrepresented" in congressional hearings and in the press. In short, what "we knew" about DNA was a "function" of who "we" were when experts let us in on their secrets.[58]

I mention a third meaning, parenthetically, to dissociate my view from "functionalism" in social theory. The suggestion there is that social institutions "have a life of their own" and, hence, a set of tasks to perform in human community analogous to the way an organ of the human body "functions." Anthony Giddens is the latest in a long line of writers to explode this analogy, in his critique of traditional versions of historical materialism.[59] Legal institutions, for example, are public manifestations of what we think we know about "justice." They are instances of knowledge, "functions" of "order" in a mathematical sense.

The multiple possibilities for idealizing structure, and uncertain understandings of the relationship between "function" and "form," incline me to argue further in the context of a specific example. I want to choose a problematic knowledge claim that is significant in any dimension of communicative praxis and in any community, for I want it clear beyond doubt that "truth claims" are called for and needed. Suppose that we treat the following passage from George Steiner as a claim to knowledge about Adolf Hitler in a community of scholars located in a larger general community of Americans:

I'm haunted by a photograph in the New York Public Library archives that shows Hitler standing like a beggar, with a torn raincoat, his hat in front of him, and no one is listening to him. But then ten people listened, and then a million. . . . My whole work is devoted to language, to the central fact that we can use words to pray, to bless, to heal, to kill, to cripple, to torture. Man creates—and he uncreates—by language. And I have never seen a satisfactory explanation of why there is no brake inside us, nothing which says you can't say the next thing. This absolutely fascinates me, that there is no limit to the autonomous power of human speech.[60]

Steiner is an accredited scholar, accustomed to operating within a culture of critical discourse, who also published a best-selling novel about the fantasy that Adolf Hitler may have survived World War II by fleeing to South America.[61] He is here addressing the general public directly, as an "interested" writer, one who stands to gain financially, in status, and in influence as a result of the quality of his speech and writing. Let us assume that he is being read at this moment, as I have quoted his speech, in an academic community. Popular and academic audiences are both asked to confront the hard problem of understanding Adolf Hitler, National Socialism, and the Holocaust. Steiner specifically calls attention to the appearance of power in Hitler's public speech and to the problem that such an example poses for all speech users. A knowledge claim is made with our experience of Hitler as warrant: "There is no limit to the autonomous power of human speech." If I were afflicted with a tendency to idealize "form," and to confound function with form, how would my capacity to understand Steiner's claim be limited, and my ability to evaluate it disrupted?

In an ideology of transcendence, order "comes first." "Function" is something that one considers after settling the question of "form." Explanations of how and why "there is no limit to the autonomous power of human speech" would be proferred in one of two lines of reasoning: (1) "Function" would be taken as synonymous with "effect" if Hitler's speaking is considered as a "cause" for the development of a set of common opinions in his various audiences, including the one I conjured for him by referring to Steiner, and the much larger one created by Steiner's book and interview. (2) In a second line of thinking, "function" would be taken as a synonym for "meaning." Hitler's speaking would be considered as a "text" containing all the possible opinions his audience could come to have in common. The argument, in other words, would go directly to the connection between Steiner's warrant (experience of Hitler) and his claim (the autonomous power of speech).

In both these cases there would be an interaction between suppositions about the relationship between a category of discourse and an item that "fits" the category. At times analysis of a particular item (Hitler's speech) will influence what is known about the category (political speech in general). At other times, what we know about the category will influence a reading of particular items it seems to "contain." If the particular item is such a powerful exemplar that accounting for it could alter the history and structure of an entire category, one is never sure *what* is being studied. Are we learning about *Hitler*, the particularly situated butcher of Germany, when we analyze Steiner's claim? Or are we learning about the power and significance of *political speech*? Clearly, the answer is that we are learning about both simultaneously, in some proportion. We know about Hitler largely from analysis of texts, and we know about demagogic public speaking largely from traumatic experience with Hitler. We do not properly study *just* speech when Hitler is involved or *just* Hitler when the object is to explain his power—the object is *(Hitler's)speech*, a collapse of category into item best indexed by a single term.

The ideology of transcendence makes managing the collapse of item and category problematic. If we begin with an a priori notion that knowledge is of "form", and if we also have the prejudice that discourse functions are clear entailments of discourse forms, our opinion of Hitler, of demagogic speech, and of Steiner's claim is a settled matter. Judgments would derive from an understanding of (Hitler's)speech as cause-of-effects or text-with-meaning. The former conception disrupts communicative praxis by collapsing discourse into action; the latter disrupts by collapsing action into discourse. I will close this essay by showing how these things happen.

139

(HITLER'S)SPEECH AS CAUSE-OF-EFFECTS

The translation of "function" into a field-dependent problem of "effect" is most common in America, among rhetorical critics and communication theorists. A piece of discourse is usually seen as a response to one or another structured situation. Should I find myself addressing an audience or deliberating in a group and need the cooperation of others to accomplish a goal, it is said that I can pursue more and less successful strategies of persuasion. The logic of this portrait requires that the situation be conceived as simultaneously motivating and containing communication. That is, speakers are asked to consider the goal to be accomplished, the personality characteristics and commitments of others in the group or audience, and the total circumstance shared by everyone there. In this context, special theories of discourse provide a series of "rules" to follow in fabricating speech and writing fitted to the situation and to the communicator's purposes. (Hitler's)speech in this view would "function" as it "causes effects," and it would be judged "functional" to the degree that it accomplishes a speaker's purposes.

Such a portrait collapses communicative praxis into the single (or at least dominant) dimension of action. The event of speaking is seen as commensurable with a speaker's individual intentions. The participation of the immediate audience, their presence and conviction, gets buried in preoccupation with what a speaker wants from them. Even due attention to such factors as audience adaptation subverts the theoretical autonomy of audience members, because all that matters about people in the audience is the possibility that they might resist persuasion. Further, when it comes time to judge a particular communication situation, the history and structure of language is collapsed into the history and structure of social practices. Hitler is said to have "fabricated" a horrible anti-Semitism as he fabricated a set of social/political practices. He is portrayed as the only villain, or at least the arch-villain, of the Holocaust. All the guilty were Nazi thugs, the story goes, and the German people who sucked up the language of anti-Semitism with mother's milk are but dupes of artful speech.

The difficulty is that no situation has an objective existence, not even when it is conceived "formally." People commonly say that they are "in the same room," for example, and their claim is so obvious that few see the oversimplification involved. From one direction, we must, by virtue of being in "the same" room, also be in "the same" building, campus, city, state, country, continent, etc. From the other direction, though we are in "the same" room, we do not occupy the same position, chair, space, etc. Sameness and difference is a *rhetorical* topic. Settling upon "room" as one of many possible situations by virtue of which we are "the same" means that a rhetoric has already operated to produce tacit agreement about the frame of our interaction.

An integral component of circumstances in which I find myself as I compose this essay is the general history of my dealing with life and the special history of this particular moment of Being. Among other features, there is the tale of my coming-to-be in Iowa City, Iowa, though I formerly lived in Madison, Wisconsin. If there are twelve people reading my essay, there are twelve situations to be considered, twelve "forms" to contain action, twelve subjects upon whom my writing will have effect. For one of us (Hitler's)speech is but the background for beer-hall carousing; for another, it is comic; for another, it is serious politics, a search for fugitive truths. The key to understanding how a sense of "sharing" emerges from this multiplicity of "situations" is *perspective*.

Hitler *says* the same thing standing alone in a torn raincoat as before a screaming crowd of thousands in a glittering uniform. As Steiner portrays him, however, he is *heard* differently as more human beings are progressively persuaded to view his speech in a similar way. That is, as more and more listeners adopt the same general view of (Hitler's)speech, they discard idiosyncratic perspectives. We must inquire which of their options they elect in choosing *one* of the many possible ways of interpreting the (Hitler's)speech. It could have had the "effect" of a joke, of a political seduction, of an entertainment, perhaps of a truth. In "sharing" any of these possible perspectives, individuals do not become "the same" as their colleagues. The only sameness they have is sharing a fictionalized reconstruction of circumstances. That reconstruction is based on (1) a tacit agreement to reduce a complex situation in a certain way, and (2) consequent compromise of the absolute uniqueness of each individual's own experience. If we want to understand communicative praxis, the decisive problem to be solved is not the special question of determining which set of "rules" comes into play once circumstances have been constructed, but the more general question of how the situations come to be in the first place.

For the person trying to gain an understanding of communicative praxis, then, the important issue is not Steiner's issue—that we have no brake inside us to prevent saying things. What matters for an analyst of communication is that we do have inside us an impulse to conceive that we are all in "the same" circumstance, whether in the same room or sharing the same perspective toward a rhetorical event. This impulse to be "the same" puts the brake on what potential there might be in the theoretical autonomy of the individual. It also funds the belief that (Hitler's)speech "has the same effect" on an audience. Theorists of form and genre are thus on the right track in pursuing what is recurrent in human communication, but they need to concentrate on the *function* of reason in producing the "orderings" that simultaneously frame our thought and action rhetorically.

(HITLER'S)SPEECH AS TEXT-WITH-MEANING

The translation of "function" into a problem of "meaning" is most common among American literary scholars. The argument begins in the observation that all human practices (politics, architecture, medicine, geopolitics—literally everything) are constituted by and represented in "discourse." Language is required to know what to make of the curious lines and figures in an architect's blueprints, or the organizational structure of the government, or the workings of the Congress of the United States or of Standard Oil Corporation. These entities are thought to be nothing more than "instantiations of meaning" drawn out of the texts that envision and describe them. A group of similar texts make up a "world of discourse," the argument goes. So, for example, putting together all the texts that describe the earth's buildings results in the architect's "world of discourse." This world of discourse is the set of possible "meanings" from which a particular text, such as the World Trade Center, will be developed and actualized in the material environment. It follows from this reasoning that any human practice that exhibits order may be "read" as if it were a book. The problem of "function" is interpretive. The task is to settle upon one of many possible "readings." The human life-world is "textual," and each individual must adjust herself or himself to that set of special "meanings" that is most comfortable and productive, much as one creates a lifestyle from choosing which kind of book to read, which opera to attend, which game to play.

This is a very deceptive line of argument. Though it appears to respond to the discourse theorist's need to account for audience perspective on (Hitler's)speech, a close examination will reveal that thoughts on the "text/meaning relationship" are masks of the "cause/effect" relationship I just considered. The language is a bit different: (Hitler's)speech is said to be fabricated from the history of German political-economic texts. Because it orders and interprets the texts it uses as proofs, (Hitler's)speech positions audiences within two modes of Being. People are located in time, which is to say in the history and structure of German discourse, and in space, at Nuremberg participating in an event of speaking that features *der Fürher*. Hitler's(speech's) reference to Being-in-Time is presented to audience members as a condition of their socialization or acculturation. Hitler's(speech's) indexing of Being-in-Space is presented as a powerful threat to an audience member's physical safety, political and economic well-being. Any "reading" given to (Hitler's)speech, any "meaning" people find in it, is said to "form" (synonymous with "cause"?) consciousness and imprison individuals as "objects" ("effects"?) of discourse. "Discourse" is (Hitler's)speech + the "readings" from which it is constructed.

The reading of choice, a critic's reading, should be "liberating" or "enabling," designed to recover as much theoretical autonomy as possible. Though writers waffle here, wanting not to conceive of "method" or "rules" in the same way these terms are discussed in a logic of cause and effect, occluded "rules" of interpretation are nonetheless presented. Some think that it is possible to look for a kind of "validity."[62] Others look for "contradiction" in texts, believing that in the act of discovering contradiction lies a motive for rejecting oppressive practice.[63] Some promote a "dialogical" historical analysis, which holds a text over and against a received tradition that teaches "lessons."[64] Some argue for a thoroughgoing "deconstruction" of all texts, not just a present object such as (Hitler's)speech, but of all lines of thinking and writing that lead into it.[65] Whatever the approach, the claim is clear that in the act of interpretation a person has some hope of restoring his or her theoretical autonomy: the discourse created to interpret the world-as-text, the critic's own writing, "functions" as it "causes effects," and it is more and less "functional" (better and worse interpretation) as it is more and less "effective" in the job of knowing truth and/or resisting ideology.

Insofar as there is a motif in these arguments, I think it is the tendency to collapse communicative praxis into the single (or at least dominant) dimension of discourse. "Discourse" and "action" are structurally similar in that each is an amalgam of "individuality" and the history and structure of human practices. Structural similarity is a far cry from "identity," however. If I think of an architect's plans as an event of speaking that draws specific meaning from the history and structure of discourse about erecting buildings, my attention is drawn away from the creative energy and active intelligence of the architect. The World Trade Center is the materialized intention of those who created it. Further, all the talk about manufacturing realities that ever was uttered cannot alter the physical conditions in which people are forced to live. Buildings cannot be made from styrofoam; ceilings cannot be three feet high;

gravity cannot be ignored as a fact of existence; chemistry, biology, and physics do index material and are physical limitations on human "action" that are independent from the limitations of "discourse." The world is not a "text," in other words, nor will it do to try to "read" it as if it were. No sophistic word game, no eristic mental gymnastic can alter the inescapable fact that life is *lived* and not *read*.[66]

In a sense, my judgment of the "life-is-a-text" metaphor stands as a confession of faith more than as a reasoned conclusion. I am not content to leave it at that. I wish to discuss two significant problems that arise from distorting communicative praxis by collapsing action into discourse. (1) The problem of understanding is merely shifted in consequence of seeing life as a text, from difficulty in deciding what to make of an artifact to difficulty in deciding what to make of a critic's interpretation. (2) Further, collapsing action into discourse makes it difficult to understand that texts are significant in their actual power and not in their structural potentials.

1. FROM ARTIFACT TO INTERPRETATION

I began with George Steiner's frightened speculation that human speech is an autonomous power. I took Steiner's fearful memory of Adolf Hitler as a historical example of the consequences, not of the autonomous power of speech, but of the insidious power of an audience's desire to be "the same" in their hearing (reading) of discourse. I envisioned an audience of particular German people, alive in 1934, and listening to (Hitler's)speech. I supposed that they doubted the uniqueness and the trustworthiness of their own personal experience by inventing a situation that they "shared" together, through the terms and with the resources provided for them in (Hitler's)speech.

If I rethink the event following poststructuralist arguments, my first task is to reify (Hitler's)speech to the concept "text." When I do this, I am reducing communicative praxis to simple linguistic form. I would then reify people in (Hitler's)audience by thinking of them as "the same," as a collective persona to be understood by attributions in (Hitler's)text. I would thus be trying to link the metaphor "text" with a personification and animation of "audience" (a figure that expects human groups to exhibit all the capacities and qualities of individuals). Such a link can be forged only with the agency of another figure, a metonymy that substitutes my own critical consciousness and ability for that of the living (in 1934) audience who "read" the (Hitler's)speech. The point I wish to emphasize, in my own right, is that these figurations work together to

144

collapse history into a single dimension, either of the past, where I see no important difference between my own situation and that in which Germans were forced to live their lives in 1934; or of the present, where I see Hitler participating actively, as a threat, in *my* living experience.

I have no objection to this rather elegant way of describing the task of historical criticism, as long as the limits of such thinking are clearly recognized. I do not solve the problem of "function" in communicative praxis with such alchemy, however. In fact, my poststructuralist statement of the case merely shifts the ground on which the problem of "function" must be considered. From the perspective of communication studies, I had to explain how Hitler's discourse "functioned" to "cause effects." Now, as a post structuralist, I must be aware that my interpretation of Hitler, *my own critical discourse*, is itself a "text" with "meaning," the logical equivalent of a cause that produces certain effects. When I collapse history into a single dimension either of the past or of the present, I inject myself and all who read my prose into the communicative praxis of Germany in 1934. This can even have moral consequences, for I must be sensitive to what may result from keeping Hitler and his ilk "alive" by writing about them. Historians and critics can tell the dead villain's story and thereby become the witting or unwitting accomplices of evil. Accordingly, such critics as Walter Benjamin fret about the authenticity of their own writing:

Historical materialism wishes to retain that image of the past which unexpectedly appears to man singled out by history at a moment of danger. The danger affects both the content of the tradition and its receivers. The same threat hangs over both: that of becoming a tool of the ruling classes. In every era the attempt must be made anew to wrest tradition away from a conformism that is about to overpower it. The Messiah comes not only as the redeemer, he comes as the subduer of the Antichrist. Only that historian will have the gift of fanning the spark of hope in the past who is firmly convinced that *even the dead* will not be safe from the enemy if he wins. And this enemy has not ceased to be victorious.[67]

Positive constructions of the past must be protected from Hitler, and, conversely, present communicative praxis must be insulated from the possibility that Hitler could be constructed positively as an authentic hero of the received tradition.

The moral reflex of such as Benjamin is necessary to avoid contradiction in collapsing the past and the present. But it has the effect of making the critic and the critic's audience *self*-conscious. In the process of not "becoming a tool of the ruling classes," critics pretend that *their* writing and *their* audience are as important as Hitler's writing and Hitler's audience. The academic sees himself or herself operating in a world where people pay as much attention to a dusty book or journal article as to Hitler and his gangsters. Put another way, in terms Habermas is promoting, critics keep their distance from Hitler by manufacturing in their imaginations an "ideal speech situation" where their writing "functions" to "cause the effect" of persuading a fictionalized audience of disembodied and disenacted others to hear Hitler as he "should have been heard" by Germans in 1934.

The "ideal speech situation" is a utopia where every individual who heard Hitler, then or now, is held responsible for finding a way to reconcile his or her subjectivity with Hitler's suggestion that we are all objects, important only as "we" exist in "shared" time and space. Habermas has portrayed such reconciliation as a personal transaction between audience member as critic/consumer and the speaker as truth purveyor/merchant.[68] This is a utopian reduction because it portrays as *inter*subjective a phenomenon that is really *poly*subjective. When historical hindsight is used to inject *self* into Hitler's communicative praxis, speech situations are distorted in the imagination that one can negotiate directly with Hitler as a person converses with another person. In fact, people do not have such luxury, for they are in the presence of as many other subjects as there are fellow audience members, each with a stake in any transaction. Human society simply cannot be reduced to the neat symmetry of interpersonal dyads, particularly when such dyads are the product of figurational construction pitting a "text" against interpretive skills attributed to a metonymically collapsed "audience/critic." In the end, it is the perspective of (Hitler's)audience *as such*, set in its concrete lifetime of 1934, that determined the "function" of (Hitler's)speech. And there was nothing remotely "ideal" about the "speech situation" these people were forced to confront. If, of course, I wish to explore (Hitler's)speech as circulated in text form, or the circulation of reports about the speech, I must consider the new sources, new audiences, and new situations involved; but once more, each specific audience's perspective, in its concrete lifetime, will determine the "function" of the rhetoric.

2. THE POWER OF DISCOURSE

That all of us are born into a world of more or less organized practices is beyond question. The difficulty is explaining what it is about structures that binds people into this view of life rather than another. History

146

constrains. How? An increasingly common argument is that history itself is but a privileged story ("text") about the past, that its most prominent feature is its presentation in language, and that its "structure" parallels the "structure" of language.[69] Social usages (*action*) and linguistic usages (*discourse*) are "the same" by measure of their structure. History constrains, therefore, by inclining people to interpret usages as others before them have interpreted *action/discourse*. Thus, when Hitler says what people recognize from their own experience, he binds them by striking a chord in the corpus of their knowledge. At first glance, this seems to have been Hitler's view of his own discursive practice:

By "people" I mean all those hundreds of thousands who fundamentally long for the same thing without finding the words in detail to describe the outward appearance of what is before the inner eye. For with all great reforms the remarkable thing is that at first they have as their champion only a single individual, but as their supporters many millions. For centuries their goal is often the inner ardent wish of hundreds of thousands, till one man stands up as the proclaimer of such a general will and as the flag-bearer of an old longing he helps it to victory in the form of a new idea.[70]

If I try to understand how "chords" are struck rhetorically, and if I do so through the glaze of an ideology of transcendence, I look for the structures of articulation. I ask what Hitler's words in one order or another mean in relation to a tradition of usage, perhaps the "inner ardent wish" of a "people" that may lie repressed in memory for centuries. But how do I think of the (Hitler's) speech that "describes the outward appearance of what is before the inner eye"? Do I think of it as merely linquistic, "structured" by the "formal" semantic and syntactic possibilities of language as such? Or do I think of it rhetorically, as a *force* "structured" by the functional and pragmatic possibilities of language in action?

The study of linguistic structures as such is nothing but grammar, and grammar by any name cannot account for Hitler nearly so well as rhetoric. What matters in the end is the *power of speech*. One sees in Hitler's theory and practice an emphasis on the Leader, the orator who makes "old longings" come alive in the terms of present action:

The power which set the greatest historical avalanches of political and religious nature sliding was, from the beginning of time, the magic force of the spoken word alone. The great masses of a nation will always and only succumb to the force of the spoken word. But all great movements are movements of the people, are volcanic eruptions of human passions and spiritual sensations, stirred either by the cruel Goddess of Misery or by the torch of the word thrown into the masses, and are not the lemonade-like outpourings of aestheticizing literati and drawing-room heroes.[71]

To think of the "structure" of discourse grammatically (as syntactic, semantic, semiotic) is to think of usage as if it were a photograph of communicating, a stop-action snapshot of people living in their world. A photograph can only represent, however. Language does more than re-present. Language-in-action, rhetoric, regularly alters and establishes signifying practices, perhaps even establishing what will be taken as "knowledge" in particular communities. Nor is this "magic," as Hitler said—it is between science and magic. Language-in-action is what Kenneth Burke called "hortatory."[72] If I begin with no more than the family photographs of a particular language community, the end product of an attempt critically to recover experience of Adolf Hitler can only be a semblance of action, the sort of optical illusion, Ortega argues, that makes cinema:

Saussure's famous distinction between "synchronic linguistics" . . . and "diachronic linguistics" . . . is utopian and inadequate. It is utopian because the body of language does not remain still even for a moment—strictly speaking there is no synchronism of all its components. . . . [Further], all that diachronism accomplishes is to reconstruct other comparative "presents" of the language as they existed in the past. All that it shows us, then, is changes; it enables us to witness one present being replaced by another, the succession of static figures of the language, as the "film," with its motionless images, engenders the visual fiction of a movement. At best, it offers us a cinematic view of language, but not a *dynamic* understanding of how the changes were, and came to be, *made*. The changes are merely results of the making and unmaking process, they are the externality of language, and there is need for an internal conception of it in which we discover not resultant forms, but the operating forces themselves.[73]

Even if my only goal were understanding discourse, in other words, if I had no ambitions beyond explaining the history and structure of language as it is presented to me, I could not do my job without full accounting, not just of action, but of the "function" of discourse in action and of action in discourse. From one perspective, collapsing action into discourse creates an unsolvable problem. From another perspective, it begs the only question worth asking.

148

GETTING THROUGH THE MIRROR OF NATURE

Let me conclude by recalling some of the questions that are begged by collapsing action into discourse, for that will provide closure of sorts, even if it is only the technical unity of ending with reference to my beginning. The problem has to do with connections between theory and practice, so it can be mainly a summary, as any conclusion should be. Concluding the essay from this more general perspective has the additional virtue of emphasizing that issues raised here go beyond discourse theory as such, to the question of deciding what counts as knowledge everywhere in human experience. I shall discuss the problem of transcendence as it might be posed in response to a paper by the mathematicians Philip Davis and Reuben Hersh on "Rhetoric and Mathematics."[74]

Formal theories of discourse are problematic because we understand the word "form" as it has been used in geometry and mathematics. In a formula, things are signified in ambiguous terms that have no empirical content—the number "2" refers to two of anything. A mathematical theory is not about things, but about quantity, which is a *relationship among things*. Unless a phenomenon is unique, indivisible, and independent of other things, mathematical theories regarding it or its parts can always be generated. The ubiquity of quantity interacts with academic politics to make what Davis and Hersh call "mathematization" a common practice:

The level of advancement of a science has come to be judged by the extent to which it is mathematical. First came astronomy, mechanics, and the rest of theoretical physics. Of the biological sciences, genetics is top dog, because it has theorems and calculations. Among the so-called social sciences, it is economics that is most mathematical, that offers its practitioners the best job market, as well as the possibility of a Nobel prize. Mathematization is offered as the only way for a field of study to attain the rank of a science. Mathematization means formalization, casting the field of study into the axiomatic mode, and thereby, it is supposed, purging it of the taint of rhetoric, of the lawyerly tricks used by those who are unable to let facts and logic speak for themselves.[75]

Mathematization raises two related problems, involving different conceptions of rhetoric. First, the reputation of mathematics as an archetypal model of formalism is unwarranted. Mathematicians characteristically employ rhetorical as well as formal arguments in the course of determining what counts as knowledge. If there is a current fashion in

149

conceiving mathematical proofs, Davis and Hersh argue, it would be *away* from formalism:

At the turn of the century, one might have said that a proof is that which is verifiable in an absolutely mechanical fashion. Now that a much more thorough going mechanization is possible, there has been a reversal. . . . We recognize that mathematical argument is addressed to a human audience, which possesses a background knowledge enabling it to understand the intentions of the speaker or author. In stating that mathematical argument is not mechanical or formal, we have also stated implicitly what it is—namely, a human interchange based on shared meanings, not all of which are verbal or formulaic.[76]

The "continual and essential use" that mathematicians make "of rhetorical modes of argument and persuasion" constitute what Davis and Hersh call "mathematical rhetoric."[77]

Mathematization has produced a more unfortunate connection between rhetoric and mathematics. Davis and Hersh observe, with tongue in cheek, that there are now *three* "branches of mathematics—pure mathematics, applied mathematics, and rhetorical mathematics":

Rhetorical mathematics . . . is neither pure nor applied, obviously. Not pure, because nothing of mathematical interest is done, . . . and not applied, because . . . no practical consequences issue from rhetorical mathematics—except publications, reports, and grant proposals. . . . For example, you might develop a "mathematical model" for international conflict. The model might be just a list of axioms: an axiomatic model. Or it might be a collection of strategies with an associated payoff matrix: a game theoretic model. Or again, maybe a collection of "state variables" to specify the international military-political situation, together with a set of equations relating the values of state variables today to their values tomorrow. Program this into your computer, and you've got a simulation model.[78]

Rhetorical mathematics exists primarily in such "soft" sciences as biology, economics, and psychology. The characteristics Davis and Hersh find most offensive are (*a*) the fabrication of quantitative forms to "model" nonquantitative structures, and (*b*) the argument *ad ignorantum* used against opponents of mathematization. This last point is especially troublesome, since those who mathematize are inclined to claim unearned expertise in mathematics; "It is important to state publicly that among professional mathematicians the skepticism about behavioral-science mathematics and even about mathematical biology is much stronger than it is among non-mathematical behavioral scientists."[79]

One might think that a tendency to perceive every form as quantity

150

would be what Burke called "the occupational psychosis" of applied mathematics and its mutation, rhetorical mathematics.[80] My impression, however, is that the impulse to mathematize notions of form is a common motive among scholars who profess to deal with nonquantitative forms. They are forced into competition against mathematizers to establish their arguments as "knowledge," because of the insistence of scientistic philosophy on mathematization as a standard of logic, and because of the political significance of those sciences that are believed to be providing the intellectual capital for technology. Rhetorical mathematics is one symptom of this situation—the more you *sound* like a physicist, the more likely it is that your arguments will be heeded and your research funded. Even those who would avoid all numbers, if they were not addicted to paychecks and pagination, understand the very concept of form analogically, with "quantity" as the analogue. Writers conceive of "art form" and "mythic form," for example, with nary a number in mind; but the form, once conceived, is treated as if it were the number "2," a signifier emptied of specific content. So, for example, Lévi-Strauss's accounts of myth bear closer likeness to the symbolic logician's truth-table than to any story ever told—the mythic form is conceived as a way to collect certain privileged narratives for study, but what we know about mythic form in consequence of our researches must be expressed in terms foreign to the very idea of mythic form. "Form" is treated as an extraction from life, a residue left over when we strip from a thing any feature that marks it as bound in a particular time and space.

The attitude that form is an "essence" of some sort masks the fact that we *make* forms in the process of deciding what we want to count as knowledge. The kids in "Mr. Rogers' neighborhood" know that the structure of a table depends on the perspective of the naked eye or of the microscope, and on the intentions of the room designer who wants a smooth surface for aesthetic reasons, or the chemist who is interested in developing a new molecular bonding for paint. With discourse, the possibilities multiply, for nothing constrains a text as narrowly as nature constrains the character of matter. Of course, the temptation is to call one perception "real" and all others "appearance." Privileging one form over another as a matter of principle, however, denies that a designer knows anything, or that a treatise on smooth surfaces can have any sort of empirical relevance. Few would deny that room designers know something, so what is to be gained from pedantic formalisms that suggest otherwise? We need only remember that a designer's description of a smooth surface will not get a rocket to Saturn, and that a physicist's description of ever smaller subatomic structures will not get a room gracefully appointed.

"Formalizing" is thus more of a problem than "form." We need to account for cultural characteristics of the various communities who formalize knowledge in particular ways. In this essay, I have adapted a notion of communicative praxis from the work of Calvin Schrag for this task. Groups of physicists, or of room designers, agree upon an agenda of problems they aspire to solve, a vocabulary of special terms, and a library of texts to be used in two ways, (a) to frame the group's perspective, and (b) to disseminate what the group counts as its knowledge. My claim is that knowledge is determined in its mode of dissemination (in a journal article, for example, or in a classroom) and not in its mode of production (the scientific method, for example, applied through experiments or field surveys). If Davis and Hersh are right, this principle, including its hostile attitude toward transcendence and its explicit rejection of formalism, may be persuasive even among mathematicians:

The competent professional knows what are the crucial points of his argument—the points where his audience will focus their skepticism. Those are the points where he will take care to supply sufficient detail. The rest of the proof will be abbreviated. This is not a matter of the author's laziness. On the contrary, to make a proof too detailed would be more damaging to its readability than to make it too brief. Complete mathematical proof does not mean reduction to a computer program. Complete proof simply means proof in sufficient detail to convince the intended audience—a group of professionals with training and mode of thought comparable to that of the author. Consequently, our confidence in the correctness of our results is not absolute, nor is it fundamentally different in kind from our confidence in our judgments of the physical reality of ordinary daily life.[81]

We are accustomed to think of "experts" as producers of discourse, the expert witness in a trial, for example. Davis and Hersh want us to think of experts as "consumers," an audience certified to determine what counts as knowledge inside a particular field. The important practice of the expert is as an audience member and not as a speaker.

I do not believe that Davis and Hersh go quite far enough in their conception of praxis. Once we call attention to the cultural factors that determine knowledge, we cannot pretend that experts are a community unto themselves, nor can we say that they are the *only* members of the audience who determine knowledge. This is implicit in much of what Davis and Hersh argue. They designate practitioners of rhetorical mathematics as working in "so-called behavioral sciences," for example, thereby suggesting that experts disagree among themselves on grounds determined by membership in field-specific communities. Why, and under what conditions, must we privilege a mathematician's talk about mathematics over and against an economist's talk about mathematics? In another place, Davis and Hersh say disparagingly about applied mathematics that its "tasks are set and paid for by the military, and involve the preparation of the premature end of life on this planet."[82] This separates communities of experts in a research setting from those who use knowledge to do the business of the workaday world, in this case the business of preserving the national defense. Why, and under what conditions, should we privilege a mathematician's talk about mathematics over and against a business person's or a general's talk about mathematics? Such questions want new answers if we are to go beyond the notion that knowledge is a mirror of nature, perhaps toward an understanding of "science as solidarity," to use Rorty's language.[83] A comprehensive theory of communicative praxis, such as the one sketched in this essay, may prove useful.

Notes

1. Michael Polanyi, *Personal Knowledge* (Chicago: University of Chicago Press, 1958); Michael Polanyi, *The Tacit Dimension* (Garden City, N.Y.: Doubleday, 1966); Thomas S. Kuhn, *The Structure of Scientific Revolutions* (2nd. ed.; Chicago: University of Chicago Press, 1970).

2. One recent indication is the symposium involving representatives from fourteen disciplines in the human sciences at the University of Iowa. "The rhetoric of inquiry" was posed as an alternative to abstract empiricism. For an overview of the interest that conference organizers sought to tap, see John S. Nelson, Allan Megill, and Donald N. McCloskey, "Scholarship in Our Rhetorical World," paper presented at the University of Iowa Symposium on the Rhetoric of the Human Sciences, Iowa City, Iowa, March 28, 1984. Most of the symposiasts seemed to presuppose such indictments of scientism as Polanyi's and Kuhn's, though most were seeking true alternatives, positive solutions to particular problems in their fields. Other books of importance to symposiasts include (among many others): Chaim Perelman and L. Olbrechts-Tyteca, *The New Rhetoric: A Treatise on Argumentation*, trans. John Wilkinson and Purcell Weaver (1958; Eng. trans. Notre Dame, Ind.: University of Notre Dame Press, 1969); Stephen Toulmin, *Human Understanding*, vol. 1: *The Collective Use and Evolution of Concepts* (Princeton, N.J.: Princeton University Press, 1972); Paul Feyerabend, *Against Method* (London: Verso, 1975); Richard Rorty, *Philosophy and the Mirror of Nature* (Princeton N.J.: Princeton University Press, 1979); and Alasdair MacIntyre, *After Virtue* (Notre Dame, Ind.: University of Notre Dame Press, 1981).

3. Edwin G. Boring, *History, Psychology, and Science: Selected Papers* (New York: Wiley, 1963), p. 79.

4. See Calvin O. Schrag, *Radical Reflection and the Origin of the Human Sciences* (West Lafayette, Ind.: Purdue University Press, 1980).

5. See Richard J. Bernstein, *Beyond Objectivism and Relativism: Science, Hermeneutics, and Praxis* (Philadelphia: University of Pennsylvania Press, 1983).

6. Evan Fales, "Review of Richard Rorty's *Philosophy and the Mirror of Nature*," *Philosophy of the Social Sciences* 50 (1983):524–29.

7. Perelman and Olbrechts-Tyteca, *The New Rhetoric*, pp. 2–3.

8. See Kenneth Burke, *A Rhetoric of Motives* (Englewood, N.J.: Prentice-Hall, 1950), pp. 29–46; and cf. Bertrand Russell, *Unpopular Essays* (New York: Simon & Schuster, 1950), pp. 71–111.

9. MacIntyre, *After Virtue*, pp. 1–2.

10. See John S. Nelson, "Models, Statistics, and Other Tropes of Politics: Or, Whatever Happened to Argumentation in Political Science?" in David Zarefsky, Malcolm O. Sillars, and Jack Rhodes, eds., *Argument in Transition: Proceedings of the Third Summer Conference on Argumentation* (Annandale, Va.: Speech Communication Association, 1983), pp. 213–29.

11. See Toulmin, *Human Understanding*, esp. pp. 133–356; and Charles Arthur Willard, *Argumentation and the Social Grounds of Knowledge* (University: University of Alabama Press, 1983).

12. See Polanyi, *Personal Knowledge*, pp. 3–17, 132–202; and John Ziman, *Public Knowledge* (Cambridge, Eng.: Cambridge University Press, 1968), pp. 13–29, 77–101.

13. Fred R. Dallmayr and Thomas A. McCarthy, eds., *Understanding and Social Inquiry* (Notre Dame, Ind.: University of Notre Dame Press, 1977), p. 78.

14. Alvin W. Gouldner, *The Future of Intellectuals and the Rise of the New Class* (New York: Seabury Press, 1979), pp. 28–29.

15. The most forceful critique of this contradiction, and in many ways the most excessive, is Chomsky's recitation of the ways in which academics bend their interests and energies to serve power elites in business and government. The point can be made more simply by pointing to the gate-keeping function of professional journals and the degree to which academics adapt their thinking and research to a target audience of referees who decide both what is "publishable" and thus who is "tenurable." (See Noam Chomsky, *American Power and the New Mandarins* [New York: Pantheon Books, 1969].)

16. Gouldner (*Future of Intellectuals*, p. 35) suggests that the original and abiding interest of scientism has been revolutionary and "religious": "The new industrial and positivist society was to be rescued from scarcity, integrated and legitimated by the new science and technology, and the new scientists/technocrats were to become the 'priests' of this society." (See Rudolf Carnap, "The Old and the New Logic," trans. Isaac Levi, in A. J. Ayer, ed., *Logical Positivism* [New York: Free Press, 1959], pp. 133–45; and A. J. Ayer, "Verification and Experience," ibid., pp. 228–43.)

17. See Charles Bazerman, "Codifying the Social Scientific Style: The APA Publication Manual as a Behaviorist Rhetoric," paper presented at the Iowa Symposium on the Rhetoric of the Human Sciences, Iowa City, Iowa, March 30, 1984. See also Sharon Dunwoody and Michael Ryan, "Scientific Barriers to the Popularization of Science via Mass Media," *Journal of Communication* 35 (1985):26–42.

18. See Donald McCloskey, "The Literary Character of Economics," *Daedalus* (Summer 1984), pp. 97–119; and Donald McCloskey, *The Rhetoric of Economics* (Madison: University of Wisconsin Press, 1985).

19. Among the many versions of "narrativism," Fisher's stands out as the most forceful and ambitious since Barthes, perhaps excessively so in its procla-

mation that "narrative logic" is a revolutionary "new" paradigm. (See Walter R. Fisher, "Narration as a Rhetorical Paradigm: The Case of Public Moral Argument," *Communication Monographs* 51 [1984]:1–22. Cf. Hayden White, "The Question of Narrative in Contemporary Historical Theory," *History and Theory* 23 [1984]:1–33.)

20. See W. Lance Bennett, "Storytelling in Criminal Trials: A Model of Social Judgment," *Quarterly Journal of Speech* 64 (1978):1–22; and W. Lance Bennett, "Rhetorical Transformation of Evidence in Criminal Trials: Creating Grounds for Legal Judgment," *Quarterly Journal of Speech* 65 (1979):311–23.

21. See Michael Calvin McGee and John R. Lyne, "What Are Nice Folks Like You Doing in a Place Like This? Some Entailments of Treating Knowledge Claims Rhetorically," paper presented at the Iowa Symposium on the Rhetoric of the Human Sciences, Iowa City, Iowa, March 28, 1984.

22. Thomas B. Farrell and G. Thomas Goodnight, "Accidental Rhetoric: The Root Metaphors of Three Mile Island," *Communication Monographs* 48 (1981):271–300; and Jürgen Habermas, *Toward a Rational Society*, trans. Jeremy J. Shapiro (Boston: Beacon Press, 1971), pp. 81–122.

23. See Chantal Mouffe, "Hegemony and Ideology in Gramsci," in Chantal Mouffe, ed., *Gramsci and Marxist Theory* (London: Routledge & Kegan Paul, 1979), pp. 168–204; and Dick Hebdige, *Subculture: The Meaning of Style* (London: Methuen, 1979), pp. 5–19.

24. Calvin O. Schrag, "Philosophy and Rhetoric," manuscript of public lecture, University of Iowa, March 16, 1983, p. 4.

25. Hans-Georg Gadamer, *Reason in the Age of Science*, trans. Frederick G. Lawrence (Cambridge, Mass.: M.I.T. Press, 1983), p. 69.

26. Homer *Iliad* 2.84–458. See Gadamer, *Reason in Science*, pp. 88–138; *Truth and Method*, trans. and ed. Garrett Barden and John Cumming (New York: Crossroad, 1982), pp. 19–33, 278–89; and Lois S. Self, "Rhetoric and *Phronesis*: The Aristotelian Ideal," *Philosophy and Rhetoric* 12 (1979):130–45.

27. Calvin O. Schrag, "Hermeneutics, Communication, and Rhetoric," paper presented at the S. C. A. Regional Research Seminar on Directions in the Philosophy of Communication, Northwestern University, June 28–30, 1982.

28. The most lucid account of the logic of perspectivism I have seen is José Ortega y Gasset, *Meditations on Quixote*, trans. Evelyn Rugg and Diego Marin (1914; Eng. trans. New York: Norton, 1961), pp. 61–63.

29. Jacques Derrida, "Plato's Pharmacy," in *Dissemination*, trans. Barbara Johnson (1972; Eng. trans. Chicago: University of Chicago Press, 1981), pp. 65–171.

30. Fredric Jameson, *The Prison-House of Language: A Critical Account of Structuralism and Russian Formalism* (Princeton, N.J.: Princeton University Press, 1972).

31. Kenneth Burke, *The Philosophy of Literary Form* (3rd. ed.; Berkeley: University of California Press, 1973), pp. xv–xvi; and Kenneth Burke, *Language as Symbolic Action* (Berkeley: University of California Press, 1966), pp. 344–58.

32. See Lloyd F. Bitzer, "Rhetoric and Public Knowledge," in Don M. Burks, ed., *Rhetoric, Philosophy, and Literature* (Lafayette, Ind.: Purdue University Press, 1978), pp. 67–93; and Michael Calvin McGee and Martha Anna Martin, "Public Knowledge and Ideological Argumentation," *Communication Monographs* 50 (1983):47–65.

33. Rorty, *Mirror of Nature*, p. 157.

34. Karlyn Kohrs Campbell and Kathleen Hall Jamieson, eds., *Form and Genre: Shaping Rhetorical Action* (Falls Church, Va.: Speech Communication Association, 1978).

35. Kathleen M. Hall Jamieson, "Generic Constraints and the Rhetorical Situation," *Philosophy & Rhetoric* 6 (1973):162–70.

36. See, e.g., the influential reading of Greek and Roman classics, and the consequent formulation of rhetorical theory as topics of rhetorical criticism by Lester Thonssen and A. Craig Baird, *Speech Criticism: The Development of Standards for Rhetorical Appraisal* (New York: Ronald Press, 1948).

37. Edwin Black, *Rhetorical Criticism: A Study in Method* (New York: Macmillan, 1965).

38. Lloyd F. Bitzer, "The Rhetorical Situation," *Philosophy & Rhetoric* 1 (1968):1–14.

39. Jamieson, "Generic Constraints," pp. 162–63.

40. Campbell and Jamieson, *Form and Genre*, p. 3.

41. See Perelman and Olbrechts-Tyteca, *The New Rhetoric*, pp. 149–83.

42. Herbert W. Simons, " 'Genre-alizing' about Rhetoric: A Scientific Approach," in Campbell and Jamieson, eds., *Form and Genre*, pp. 33–34.

43. Bruce E. Gronbeck, "Celluloid Rhetoric: On Genres of Documentary," in Campbell and Jamieson, eds., *Form and Genre*, p. 140.

44. Edwin Black, "The Sentimental Style as Escapism, or the Devil with Dan'l Webster," in Campbell and Jamieson, eds., *Form and Genre*, pp. 75, 85.

45. Ernest G. Bormann, "Generalizing about Significant Form: Science and Humanism Compared and Contrasted," in Campbell and Jamieson, eds., *Form and Genre*, p. 67 n. 1.

46. Ernest G. Bormann, "Rhetorical Criticism and Significant Form: A Humanistic Approach," in Campbell and Jamieson, eds., *Form and Genre*, p. 185. Though Simons is excluded from Bormann's sermon, one should note that his idea of "scientific theory" is itself a transcendent, romantic set of procedures that result in confident proclamations about which arguments are and are not ideally theoretical: "Although there are few generic conceptualizations that deserve the name 'theory,' let alone 'useful theory,' there is one approach—in Bitzer, Hart, Jamieson and others—which bears great theoretical promise" ("Genre-alizing," p. 41). The question of what "authentic science" might be is still open, and entailed in that discussion is the issue of theoretical utility (see Gadamer, *Age of Science*, pp. 1–20).

47. See Robert Paul Wolff, Barrington Moore, Jr., and Herbert Marcuse, *A Critique of Pure Tolerance* (Boston: Beacon Press, 1965), pp. 81–117, for development of the concept "repressive tolerance," and pp. 53–79, for its application to the questions discussed here. I have discussed this issue in a different context in my essay "Another Philippic: Notes on the Ideological Turn in Criticism," *Central States Speech Journal* 35 (1984):43–50.

48. Michael Halloran, "Doing Public Business in Public," in Campbell and Jamieson, eds., *Form and Genre*, pp. 134–35.

49. Karlyn Kohrs Campbell and Kathleen Hall Jamieson, "Form and Genre in Rhetorical Criticism: An Introduction," *Form and Genre*, pp. 22–23.

50. Ibid., pp. 26–27.

51. If they constrain, recurrences invite the *Ideologiekritik* associated with

156

the Frankfurt School. (See Jürgen Habermas, "A Review of Gadamer's *Truth and Method*," in Dallmayr and McCarthy, eds., *Understanding and Social Inquiry*, pp. 335–63.)

52. If they "enable" or "liberate," recurrences invite the sort of "hermeneutic recovery" associated with philosophical hermeneutics. (See Gadamer, *Truth and Method*, pp. 235–74, 460–91.)

53. I refer to the considerable and growing literature on the question of connection between rhetoric and epistemology originally proposed in Robert L. Scott, "On Viewing Rhetoric as Epistemic," *Central States Speech Journal* 18 (1967):9–17. See also, Scott, "On Viewing Rhetoric as Epistemic: Ten Years Later," *Central States Speech Journal* 27 (1976):258–66.

54. See my note, "Social Movement as Meaning," *Central States Speech Journal* 34 (1983):74–77.

55. Lyndon Baines Johnson, *The Vantage Point* (New York: Holt, Rinehart & Winston, 1971), p. x.

56. See Richard Hofstadter, *Anti-Intellectualism in American Life* (1962; rpt. New York: Alfred A. Knopf, 1966).

57. See Ernst Nolte, *Three Faces of Fascism*, trans. Leila Vennewitz (1963; Eng. trans. New York: Holt, Rinehart & Winston, 1965), pp. 88–99. Fascist appeals to popular culture are a good illustration of the interpenetration of academic and political life, of discourse and action: as McGuire argues, idealizations of *volk* were originally philosophical positions. Today we see a spate of arguments (including some of my own, "Public Knowledge and Ideological Argumentation," e.g.) that tear hair over the increasing influence of intellectual elites. See Michael D. McGuire, "Rhetoric, Philosophy, and the *Volk*: Johann Gottlieb Fichte's *Address to the German Nation*," *Quarterly Journal of Speech* 62 (1976):135–44. See also, Murray Edelman, *Political Language: Words that Succeed and Policies that Fail* (New York: Academic Press, 1977); George Konrad and Ivan Szelenyi, *The Intellectuals on the Road to Class Power*, trans. Andrew Arato and Richard E. Allen (New York: Harcourt Brace Jovanovich, 1979); and Seymour M. Lipset and Asoke Basu, "The Roles of the Intellectual and Political Roles," in Aleksander Gella, ed., *The Intelligentsia and the Intellectuals* (Beverly Hills, Calif.: Sage Publications, 1976), pp. 111–50.

58. See Michael Altimore, "The Social Construction of a Scientific Controversy: Comments on Press Coverage of the Recombinant DNA Debate," *Science, Technology, and Human Values* 7 (1982):24–31. See also John R. Lyne, "Ways of Going Public: The Projection of Expertise in the Sociobiology Debate," in *Argument in Transition*, pp. 400–415.

59. See Anthony Giddens, *A Contemporary Critique of Historical Materialism* (Berkeley: University of California Press, 1981), pp. 15–20, 230–52.

60. George Steiner, interview, Time, March 29, 1982, p. 72.

61. George Steiner, *Portage to San Cristobal of A. H.* (New York: Simon & Schuster, 1981).

62. Jürgen Habermas, *Communication and Evolution*, trans. Thomas McCarthy (1976; Eng. trans. Boston: Beacon Press, 1979), pp. 1–68.

63. Stuart Hall, "The Rediscovery of 'Ideology': Return of the Repressed in Media Studies," in Michael Gurevitch, Tony Bennett, James Curran, and Janet Woollacott, eds., *Culture, Society, and the Media* (London: Methuen, 1982), pp. 56–90.

157

64. Hans-Georg Gadamer, *Hegel's Dialectic*, trans. P. Christopher Smith (New Haven, Conn.: Yale University Press, 1976), pp. 5–34, 100–116.

65. Sometimes amusing verbal gymnastics result when these writers resist the attempts of others to make "systems" (dare I say "sense"?) out of the discourse of deconstruction itself. See Jacques Derrida, *Positions*, trans. Alan Bass (1972; Eng. trans. Chicago: University of Chicago Press, 1981), pp. 38–91.

66. Walter Benjamin, *Illuminations*, ed. Hannah Arendt, trans. Harry Zohn (New York: Schocken Books, 1969), p. 255.

67. I agree with Burke that the figure "life is a drama" happens to be true. It differs from "life is a text" because it recognizes that life is not static, "written down" in a way that holds still for the sort of interpretation texts invite. The image of "drama" calls attention to what human beings *do* with the materials of life around them. As "actors," human beings may be constrained at times to follow scripts written for them by others and left lying about in history. But scripts cannot constrain perfectly, and no constraint can exist until it is manifested in the action of human beings—a story is just a story until people agree to enact it as part of their lives. There is distance in dramatism between a symbol and its actual embodiment, a distance analogous to the gap between a thing and its name. (See Kenneth Burke, *The Rhetoric of Religion: Studies in Logology* [Boston: Beacon Press, 1961], pp. 17–23.)

68. Habermas, *Communication and Evolution*, pp. 26ff.

69. See White, "Narrative in Comtemporary Historical Theory"; Hayden White, "The Value of Narrativity in the Representation of Reality," in W. J. T. Mitchell, ed., *On Narrative* (Chicago: University of Chicago Press, 1981), pp. 2–23; and MacIntyre, *After Virtue*, pp. 1–5, 11–48.

70. Adolf Hitler, *Mein Kampf*, trans. Alvin Johnson et al. (New York: Houghton Mifflin and Reynal & Hitchcock, 1939), pp. 456–57.

71. Ibid., p. 136.

72. Burke, *Rhetoric of Motives*, pp. 40–46.

73. José Ortega y Gasset, *Man and People*, trans. Willard R. Trask (New York: Norton, 1957), p. 247.

74. Philip J. Davis and Reuben Hersh, "Rhetoric and Mathematics," paper presented at the University of Iowa Symposium on the Rhetoric of the Human Sciences, Iowa City, Iowa, March 28, 1984.

75. Ibid., pp. 1–2.

76. Ibid., pp. 15, 18–19.

77. Ibid., p. 2.

78. Ibid., pp. 3–4.

79. Ibid., p. 6.

80. The phrase is actually Dewey's, corrected by Burke to show that an occupational psychosis is a *trained incapacity* to perceive the phenomena associated with one's occupation in what would now be called a "de-centered" light. (See Kenneth Burke, *Permanence and Change*, [2nd. ed. rev.; Indianapolis, Ind.: Bobbs-Merrill, 1965], pp. 44–49.)

81. Davis and Hersh, "Rhetoric and Mathematics," p. 19.

82. Ibid., p. 3.

83. Richard Rorty, "Science as Solidarity," paper presented at the University of Iowa Symposium on the Rhetoric of the Human Sciences, Iowa City, Iowa, March 28, 1984.

6

Michael J. Shapiro

LITERARY PRODUCTION AS
A POLITICIZING PRACTICE

THE PERSISTENCE OF THE KANTIAN QUESTION

And things, what is the correct attitude to adopt toward things?
Samuel Beckett, *The Unnamable*

Beckett's question evokes a substantial part of the history of philosophy, for in one form or another, the familiar philosophical systems since Plato give this question a privileged place. For present purposes we can begin with Kant, because his reorientation of the question still resounds in the depths of the philosophy of the social sciences. According to Martin Heidegger, who inherited but then recast Kant's question, Kant turned the question "What is a thing?" into the question "Who is man?"[1] Kant's new formulation was liberating inasmuch as it frees us from the tyranny of the object. Rather than looking for meaning in the world of things, Kant turned the gaze inward, positing the structure of human consciousness as the formal, a priori condition for our apprehension of things. But Kant's reorientation remained quarantined within the relentless grammatical metaphor of Enlightenment philosophy. Knowing remained for Kant a relationship between subjects and objects.

The Kantian revolution attacked one privilege, the privilege of the object, and substituted another, the privilege of the subject of consciousness. This privileging of the subject of consciousness is wholly compatible with the practice of science as it is understood within the still dominant grammatical trope of Enlightenment thinking. What Kant neglected, and what science as a practice brackets are the social practices or ways of being in the world that constitute man in any historical period. In focusing on the fact of objectification, the crafting of things as shaped by a subject's consciousness, Kant ignored the prior condition of the subject. As Heidegger put it, "He [Kant] does not inquire into and determine in its own essence that which encounters us prior to objectification into an object of experience."[2]

Heidegger viewed Kant's approach to the subject as a form of idolatry inasmuch as a fixed, conceptualizing subject fixes objects in a permanence that belies their predication on human practices. As soon as we reject Kant's subject and replace it with a historically, socially, and linguistically embedded one, we need an approach to understanding that rejects representation as the mode of relation between the subject and the world of objects. Science, to the extent that it rests on a neo-Kantian subject, rests on an idolatrous metaphysics, objectifying phenomena on the basis of a model of certainty of representation. Opposing this model of science, Heidegger said, "Science always encounters only what *its* kind of representation has admitted beforehand as an object possible for science."[3]

What science neglects, according to Heidegger, is what he called the "ground plan," that which is embedded in the practices of an age and which links and constitutes man, determining being in such a profound way that it gives rise to the questions of research. It is illusion, he believed, that things give themselves to thought.[4] In the modern age, science as calculation and research has rested on an epistemology of representation connected to a notion of man as a being with a viewpoint. According to this metaphysics of science, man is at the center of the problem of meaning, regarding his viewpoint as wholly conceptual or voluntary.[5] But this viewpoint, like the world that it beholds, harks back to something prior in the structure of human existence. Heidegger displaces the ego subject, the subject of consciousness, from the center of knowledge and puts in its place a historical, changing subject constituted as a set of skills and/or practices, including (and especially) linguistic practices, which "house" human existence.[6] The philosophy of modern science (and that of the social sciences) remains within the metaphysics of the subject of consciousness whose relationship to objects is one of representation and who thereby construes all experience as mediated by intentional content. This perspective includes the "perceptions" of empiricism and the "ideational acts of consciousness" of phenomenology. Heidegger pointed out that a science of any kind, even one that operates within such a cognitivist self-understanding, inevitably expresses the background practices from which it arises and which give it its predicates. As he put it, ". . . the sciences still speak about the Being of beings in the unavoidable suppositions of their regional categories. They just don't say so."[7]

Heidegger supplies a new set of questions in response to Beckett's request for direction on how to deal with "things." For Heidegger "things" are radically entangled with historically emerging practices.

160

These practices influence the identity of the "subject" or person for whom things have meaning. The kind of question that Heidegger evokes, then, relates to *how* the subject produces the "thing," given the practices within which the subject is embedded. Once we shift to "how" rather than "what" questions, part of our attention is directed toward the poetic or literary genre, which, in its modern realization, foregrounds its own practices to show both how such practices produce the person and the world and how alternative subjects and things can be produced.

THE PROBLEM OF GENRE AND POLITICAL UNDERSTANDING

. . . she applied for his reasons. Now though he had none, as we have seen, that he could offer, yet he had armed himself so well at this point, forewarned by the study that he had made of his cats-paw mind, that he was able to pelt her there and then with the best diligent enquiry could provide: Greek and Roman reasons, Sturm and Drang reasons, reasons metaphysical, aesthetic, erotic, anterotic and chemical, Empedocles of Agrigentum and John of the Cross reasons, in short all but the true reasons, which did not exist, at least not for purposes of conversation.
Samuel Beckett, *More Pricks Than Kicks*

Heidegger's attack on the primacy of the "viewpoint" and his alternative, which understands the world of persons and things as produced by prior practices embedded in language in general and speech practices in particular, provides an opening for the old "humanistic" genres that were, until recently, proscribed by those interested in the human sciences. If science, at one end of the continuum, has traditionally operated with a view of language as a transparent tool, an instrument devoid of ideational or otherwise practical content, literature, at the other end has seen language as opaque, and has accordingly seen its charge as one of penetrating the opacity in order to recover the commitments and practices contained in language. An increasing interest in the literary genre by social scientists has led to modes of social and political analysis, which both cast the social processes under investigation within aesthetically oriented imagery and foreground the language of inquiry itself. Describing this shift to aesthetic imagery in social theory, Clifford Geertz has noted that it involves, "the casting of social theory in terms more familiar to the gamester and aesthetician than to plumbers and engineers," and that it reflects an appreciation that language is necessarily opaque rather than clear, that its figures, its grammatical and rhetorical tropes (whether they are live and explicit or dead and therefore

161

naturalized) constitute persons and objects rather than simply adding extra means of expression.[8]

With this altered view of language and the complicity between the literary genre and social/political thought come the discursive objects that guide literary endeavors. Perhaps the most notable contribution that literary theory has lent to social and political understanding is the idea of the text. Not surprisingly, when the text metaphor is used in social and political theory such that, for example, human action, events, and situations become "readable," there develops an impetus to see that reading within a politicized language. Accordingly, modern thinkers have seen that reading as "polemical" (Ricoeur),[9] "rhetorical" (Gadamer),[10] "violent" (Foucault)[11] or, more directly, "political" (Jameson, who argues that the political perspective is, "the absolute horizon for all reading and all interpretation").[12] Moreover, the structure, form, or construction of the text itself becomes understood with political imagery, for example, Foucault's notion of the "discursive practice"—the combination of discursively engendered objects, concepts, enunciative modes, and themes—which creates privileged places for some subjects who are constituted as agents of knowledge while others are relegated to silence, and Jameson's notion of the "ideology of form," the sedimented, archaic practices sequestered in the style of the text, which coexist in both social and artistic practices and harbor structures of domination.

The more radical views of reading—for example, Foucault's and Jameson's—contrast with more traditional hermeneutic approaches in a way that addresses fundamental issues about how interpretation relates to social and political understanding. At the more traditional end of the continuum is Gadamer, who has recently tried to politicize his notion of hermeneutic understanding by conceiving of the process of understanding as involving embeddedness in a practical, politically oriented conversation. To the extent that he politicizes his approach, it is by problematizing the stance or perspective of the interpreter so that hermeneutics becomes a kind of practical activity that involves both the situatedness and the activity of the interpreter.[13] But Gadamer's approach maintains the privilege of genre in that he holds to the Aristotelian notion that there is a being intrinsic to that which is being interpreted. For example, in speaking of legal interpretation, he remarks that there is a nature or being to the legal text that plays a directing role in producing the principles of legal interpretation.[14] Given this respect for genre—the legal in this case—Gadamer's politics of interpretation is ultimately more collaborationist than partisan.

Foucault, by contrast, holds to a radical partisanship model of political interpretation and, accordingly, takes a firm stand against the hermeneutic tradition. Employing his violence imagery for reading the text of human events, Foucault has substituted genealogy for the traditional hermeneutics:

... if interpretation is the violent or surreptitious appropriation of a system of rules, which in itself has no essential meaning, in order to impose a direction, to bend it to a new will, to force its participation in a different game, and to subject it to secondary rules, then the development of humanity is a series of interpretations. The role of genealogy is to record its history: the history of the concept of liberty or of the ascetic life; as they stand for the emergence of different interpretations, they must be made to appear as events on the stage of historical process.[15]

A genre for Foucault is a historical production to be described rather than embraced. His lack of respect for the integrity of the genre of the text emerges in his historical investigations in which he consistently replaces the discourses of various professions and disciplines (e.g., the medical, penal, and psychiatric) or even the discourse of state power with a discourse that emphasizes control, subjugation, and domination. For example, he discusses "rights" (a discursive entity produced within the modern nation state) not within a legalistic discourse emphasizing the role of rights in establishing legal access to privileges, but in terms of the dimensions of power that have been generated by the development of this kind of human identity—persons with "rights." As he puts it, "Right should be viewed, I believe, not in terms of a legitimacy to be established, but in terms of the methods of subjugation that it instigates."[16]

This approach to knowledge, which essentially rewrites prevailing discursive formulation, is an increasingly familiar mode of poststructuralist analysis, and is sometimes referred to as "textualism." In its more radical formulations, textualism is clearly accompanied by a hyper-politicizing consciousness. Before elaborating the implications of modern textualism for purposes of understanding its politicizing tendencies, however, one needs a view of the political that articulates well with textualist philosophical conceits. This view of the political, immanent in his later studies, is characterized by Foucault as an "analytics of power."

THE DOMAIN OF THE POLITICAL

But what they were most determined for me to swallow was my fellow-creatures. In this they were without mercy. I remember little or nothing of these lectures. I cannot have understood a great deal. But I seem to have retained certain descriptions, in spite of myself.

Samuel Beckett, *The Unnamable*

There is an intimate connection between Foucault's antihermeneutic method and the political understanding toward which his investigations move. He argues that there is no meaning in the sense of an intent or cognized human goal beneath the surface of various sets of statements of a discipline or practice. Rather than looking for meanings in the texts of various social practices, he looks at what the statements *are* and why *they* rather than some other statements, conveying power for other kinds of subjects, are there. The "are" of the statements thus amounts to the statements' strategic significance, the resources they deliver to kinds of subjects.[17] Moving from his concern with the statement as a resource to the genealogical understanding of the modern age, Foucault focuses his analyses on how practices that are immanent in the discourses they form produce us as kinds of subject/objects—for example, with such individualized identities as the "onanistic child," the "hysterical woman," or collective identities such as the "population."[18] For example, speaking of the new discursive object, the "population," he notes:

One of the great innovations in the techniques of power in the eighteenth century was the emergence of "population" as an economic and political problem: population as wealth, population as manpower or labor capacity, population balanced between its own growth and the resources it commanded. Governments perceived that they were not dealing simply with subjects, or even with a "people," but with a "population."

Foucault is not asking what a population is in the sense of looking for the referent of the term. It is not the traditional problem of definition, but rather, the issue of how population as an idea grew out of the practices of an age and found its way into discourse as a technique of power. For Foucault, the prevailing discourses, those that harbor subjects and objects linked to the structure of domination, are productions of power rather than mere descriptions. Seeing power as immanent in what we *are* in any age, Foucault orients his analyses toward the processes by which humans are turned into subjects. For example, speaking about the proliferation of penalties in the history of penology, he notes that we must read power not as a mechanism to halt illegal actions but as a force that differentiates illegalities, creates multiple identities, and places a surcharge on them.[19] This politicizing approach of Foucault is not merely an interest in description or even the critique of ideology, for he contends that by capturing the way that power makes us what we are, the way that

164

it creates various discursive identities that are both collective in scope (the "population") or individualizing (the citizen with "rights"), we can resist power: "Maybe the target nowadays is not to discover what we are but to refuse what we are. We have to imagine and to build up what we could be to get rid of this kind of political "double bind," which is the simultaneous individualization and totalization of modern power structures."[20]

But first, we must be able to "read" power, and Foucault's pedagogy has been to teach us how to conduct this reading. When we begin to approach the understanding of the political domain within the context of reading (discovering power) and writing (the process by which power is inscribed and thus the mode of deconstructing power by the rendering of alternative discursivities), we legitimize, as political pedagogy, the range of thinking produced by modern textualists who have turned the reading/writing imagery into an anti-authority epistemology. The pedagogy that has come out of Foucault's reading and writing is not exhortation, for there are none of the conventional signs of the pedagogic discourse. The genre is more literary. Foucault politicizes through his writing, through the production of rhetorical and grammatical tropes that dislodge privileged subjects, objects, events, and modes of conduct. By writing in a figural language antagonistic to conventional discourse, Foucault shows how power resides in the production of discursive entities that become fetishized and parade around as literal descriptions. His violent imagery for creating subjects, using, for example, "the penetrating of bodies" for the traditional ideas of socialization, and training replaces pacifying figures that collaborate with existing power, with a figure that challenges it. Foucault's writing, in short, serves to disinherit the power that enjoy an abundance bequeathed in prevailing discursive practices.

TEXTUALISM

I would like to think that I occupy the center, but nothing is less certain.   Samuel Beckett, *The Unnamable*

Contemporary textualism has to be given credit for providing vehicles for moving interests ordinarily exclusively associated with literary studies into a central place in social and political theory. A consideration of the wide variety of orientations that fit within the general idea of textualism would interrupt the plot. For present purposes it suffices to highlight those positions that generate the most access from literary concerns to the domain of the political. The first and perhaps most significant contribution relates to Beckett's remark above about the location of the subject. While phenomenology as an interpretive strategy displaces the authority of the object and replaces it with the intentional consciousness of the subject, textualism denies epistemic privilege to both the object or referent of a statement and to the subject/author of the statement. What replaces the referent and the intentional consciousness of the subject is the text.

This displacement of the speaker/writer as a locus of possible meanings is indebted to Saussurean linguistics. Departing from traditions that locate meaning in a relationship between a name and its referent, Saussure developed the position that meaning emerges from the relational structure of signifiers. With this as background, the textualist sees language not as a set of symbols whose function is exhausted by the process of representation but as a set of signs that are part of a system for generating objects. Textualism, with its emphasis on the sign, promotes two views relevant to the argument here. The first is that there is a value system embedded in the process of signification. That system is responsible for producing the objects, acts, and events we entertain in our conscious awareness. In speaking of the emphasis on signs rather than symbols, Jameson has expressed this contribution of textualists well: "Its privileged object is . . . seen as the unconscious value system or system of representations which orders social life at any of its levels, and against which the individual, social acts and events take place and become comprehensible."[21]

The second contribution of textualism is that it privileges literature as the mode of discourse in which the process of signification that produces the world of subjects and objects can be experienced. Because the style of literary discourse is such as to foreground its own productive mechanisms (at least in the case of certain modernistic forms of writing), objects and subjects are seen as productions rather than as natural phenomena, lying outside of human productive activity. Roland Barthes was among the most prominent of those who promoted the literary genre as one that avoids the naturalizing of the sign and literary criticism as a denaturalizing analytic practice. This position emerged in his early work in which he construed mythologies as unself-reflective forms of writing that naturalize phenomena and thereby hide political content in signs. In his later writings he emphasized the way language naturalizes to the extent that it is treated as a transparent tool instead of a producer of a content.[22] Against such a naturalization of the sign, Barthes promoted a view of the text as a tissue of codes, separate fragments that invoke different

166

readings, subjects, and values but never provide a single, definitive reading for the text as a whole.[23] It is the tissue of codes, however, rather than the author that controls the text, for the text is run by "the order of the signifier"; no one discourse or code can claim privilege with respect to founding an appropriate interpretation.[24]

Jacques Derrida has also exalted the pluralistic nature of the text, and has produced vigorous critiques of attempts to locate an originating consciousness behind the production of a text or referent. The development of a text involves for Derrida a process of writing that he characterizes as a free play of signification, understandable more from the inner structure that it exercises than from the series of referents that it produces. Given this play of signification in the text, Derrida invariably tries to show how the texts of various thinkers harbor something that eludes the writers: elements of mythology or commitment hidden in the opacity of the text. The writer misses these because of treating the discourse as a neutral channel running from intention to objective.[25] For example, in his analysis of Benveniste's attempt to show how the language-thought distinction is invalid, Derrida shows that Benveniste makes use of something he is attempting to dismiss. The language that Benveniste uses to deal with the thought-language relationship already contains the acceptance of a rigid distinction between the two (e.g., the concept of "category," which depends for its meaning on a language-thought distinction).[26] There is no way, according to Derrida, to get outside of language to assess thoughts or consciousness. Accordingly, one cannot juxtapose language to something else that is thought to be less mediated or interpreted. Consciousness is manifested *in* writing; it is not an originating event to be expressed once it is generated.

In accord with this view Derrida develops a model of the Freudian subject *as* memory rather than a person with a consciousness who *has* a memory.[27] Memory is constructed by Derrida as a series of writings and erasures. Consciousness is thus a form of writing, and a given subject is constituted by the selections made from the systems and process of differences in the play of signification. Similar to Derrida's notion that the Freudian subject *is* memory, is Lacan's suggestion that it is inappropriate to say that an ego is frustrated. Rather, for Lacan, the ego is constituted *as* frustration.[28] But, and this is central to how his analysis privileges writing, Derrida sees the development of memory as constituted by fiction, by imaginative discourse (contrary to the classic Platonic distinction between reality and imagination). Lacan sees fiction as a clue to truth, a truth that lies outside the realities produced by fictionalizing.[29]

Because in thinking one is always writing—creating a text, according to Derrida—the approach to interpreting the written text, like the text itself, is shot through with nonpresent meaning, a meaning that eludes the writer. Self-consciousness, for the writer/interpreter, then, can consist only in a thoroughgoing suspicion of the language produced (and thus the thinking and reality produced) in the process of interpretation. Accordingly, after deconstructing the thought of Lévi-Strauss, Derrida produces a brief meditation on his own writing and acknowledges his figurative use of childrearing.[30] With this gesture, Derrida shows the pervasiveness of textuality, the inability to get outside the production of the world as a form of writing. This position, the political significance of which Derrida never seems to approach directly, relates importantly to the domain of the political nevertheless. By exposing the density of commitment in writing (or thinking *as* writing) that eludes the consciousness of the author/writer, Derrida shows how the conclusions in social and political thought are engendered in the writing process. The production of a text *and* its interpretation can thus be seen as ideologizing processes.

What Derrida does not provide is a purchase on the world, a way of thinking/writing that foregrounds the political dimension. Foucault's strategy has been to characterize the kind of subject/object that has been scripted by modernity and to denote the collective groupings (disciplines, agencies, etc.) that have disproportionately contributed to that scripting. As Said has put it, Foucault allows the text to "assume its affiliation with institutions, offices, agencies, classes, academies, corporations, groups, guilds, ideologically defined parties, and professions."[31] Foucault's historical and political problematics guide his readings while Derrida remains self-conscious about his own mythologizing but does not render that self as one that sides with those subjects he imagines as participating in a world resistant to subjugation and domination as does Foucault.

THE PROBLEM OF THE FETISH

The creation of the world did not take place once and for all time, but takes place every day. Habit then is the generic term for the countless treaties concluded between the countless subjects that constitute the individual and their countless correlative objects.

Samuel Beckett, *Proust*

As an approach to interpretation, textualism feeds off other radical epistemological strategies inasmuch as it is an attack on fetishes, on objects that enchant to the extent that they appear natural, universal, or in some way beyond human artifice or invention. A major dimension of

168

the establishment of fixed modes of authority among members of a society is the transformation of processes and possibilities into objects and *faits accomplis*. We are thereby left with totems or idols, which, when they are no longer recalled as arrests of the activities they represent, become objects of worship, things that one sees as external or outside of—to use Beckett's metaphor—treaty-making. From a political point of view, the fetish performs the ideological function of removing power and authority from the realm of direct contention. This recalls the Foucaultian model of political understanding sketched above. The fetish—kinds of scripted human subjects in Foucault's Nietzschean version of it—reflects or represents practices involving domination and subjugation. To point out or to dislodge the fetish is to show how it can be read politically as a product of power rather than a thing.

Various thinkers in different epistemological camps have attacked the fetish within different linguistic frames of reference but in ways that are strategically similar. All of these radical epistemologies—including the Marxian, Freudian, Nietzschean and poststructuralist—see the world of objects available to our immediate consciousness as a product of our discursive habits, a product that stands for (and hides) processes of production. The Marxian approach to the fetish, growing out of Marx's notion of the fetishism of commodities, is best elaborated by George Lukacs under the rubric of reification.[32] Lukacs, like Heidegger, opposed a radical distinction between subject and object, seeing it as the philosophical support for reification. His position, as Goldmann has noted, is that, "objects exist only as correlates to a subject in relation to this subject's praxis."[33] To attack reification is to show that we have become so habituated to things that emerge *from* our practices that we have lost the subjectivity that things carry as a result of their being produced *in* our practices and that we have thus lost our ability to analyze human relations and practices. The Marxist epistemological orientation is thus an attempt to recover the human relations lost in the reified discursive world of things.

Accordingly, the Marxist hermeneutic is a hermeneutic of suspicion that construes things (fetishes) as masks hiding processes. What is to be recovered in Marxist interpretation are the human relations that are hidden in such things as the commodity. Marx's reading of society was, in effect, an attempt to divulge a hidden text.

The Freudian hermeneutic can be similarly construed, even though it operates within a therapeutic rather than a political problematic. For Freud, the role of analysis is one of making a person's hidden text

169

transparent or available to that person. The world of fetishes—things that appear in fantasy life—are to be reduced to the underlying psychic processes that produce them. This understanding of the Freudian model of consciousness as the recovery of a lost text is encouraged by Freud's use of the mystic writing pad as an analogy for levels of consciousness. In order to show how a psychic text can be created without being available to immediate consciousness, Freud suggested that we conceive of the establishment of a psychic history as a form of writing. The medium of that writing is a mystic writing pad, a tablet with a plastic sheet over a wax surface. On such pads—still popular as children's toys—a pull on the plastic sheet to separate it from the wax surface makes the writing disappear from the sheet. To render this as a dynamic of consciousness, Freud argued that as the self engages in its own construction through a writing process, much that is written is lost to immediate consciousness (the plastic overlay). But the hidden text remains as an impression in the wax and remains there to be recovered.[34] The epistemological imagery is thus very similar for Marx and Freud, notwithstanding the vast difference in problematics directing their interpretive activities.

With Nietzsche we find yet another attack on the fetish. Like Marx and Freud, Nietzsche's interpretive approach seeks to show how the world that is experienced in ordinary imagery or the language of everyday affairs is mistakenly taken for an external reality of things that stand apart from human practices and contrivance. But, importantly, Nietzsche's approach is not interpretive in the traditional sense in that he saw no truth behind the mystifications in the world available to consciousness. As he put it, "What then is truth? A mobile army of metaphors, metonyms, and anthropomorphisms . . . to be truthful means using the customary metaphors.—in moral terms: the obligation to lie according to a fixed convention, to lie herd-like in a style obliging to all."[35] For Nietzsche the text to be recovered is the record of human contrivances wherein the world has been donated ("we put value into things and this value has an effect on us after we have forgotten that we were the donors.")[36] The problem of the fetish is in part the problem related to turning values into things. But more important than the "things" that hide human values are actions. The primary fetish for Nietzsche is the fetish of the subject, an invention that people add to actions and events.

The subject is a fiction that many similar states in us are the effect of one substratum; but it is we who first created the "similarity" of these states: our adjusting them and making them similar is the fact, not their similarity which had rather ought to be denied.[37]

170

Nietzsche's perspectivism—his view that subjects can never gain a comprehensive view of the world of things because that world is engendered from the practices or modes of being of humans, along with his view of the subject as a fetish—turned his attention to language. His particular interest in poetics, that form of language most self-conscious of its own style, stemmed from his view that it is in the tropics of language that we see the production of reality. Knowing is always caught within productive tropes and is thus an aggressive act to be understood not causally but aesthetically. To see how knowing produces the world is to pay attention to the textuality of human linguistic practices, the rhetorical and grammatical tropes that produce subjects and values. Nietzsche conveyed his notion that the style of language creates subjects, objects, and actions with careful attention to the style of his own writing. As Derrida has pointed out, for example, Nietzsche would produce purposeful contradictions in his own text in order to *show* that "truth" is plural.[38] In general, Nietzsche argued that the troped-up world can be understood only as a process, a process that must be recovered philologically. His analyses, therefore, sought to discover the linguistic formations that have given rise to what we "know." For Nietzsche, as was the case for Heidegger, understanding the world as a presence requires an understanding of the "how" of the construction of that world. Knowing within this context for Nietzsche is thus a kind of action or practice, not a unified form of consciousness. Nietzsche, more than any other philosopher, tied the trope intimately to the problem of knowing and understanding.

METAPHORS AND OTHER TROPES

Habit is the ballast that chains the dog to his vomit.

Samuel Beckett, *Proust*

In this brief fragment, Beckett challenges habituation not only through an implicit denunciation of it both as limit (the chain image) and as distasteful (the vomit) but also through his own transgression or habitbreaking. Because he uses a mixed metaphor, the statement has a jarring, dehabitualizing effect. It calls attention to itself because it does not work in the way expected of properly conceived metaphoric expressions. Dogs and chains "work" all right as a metaphor for limit, but chains and vomit do not; their linking up refuses the mind its accustomed rest.

Habituation to a reified world of **subjects** and "things," the failure to realize the structures of value, **legitimation** and power sequestered in the

171

way the world is discursively engendered are in part a failure to penetrate the tropes in prevailing discursive practices. The commitments and legitimations involved in the rhetorical and grammatical dimensions of discursive practices are ignored to a large extent because of a venerable metalinguistic position evident in the histories of philosophy and political thought. There is an epistemology of rhetoric whose tenacity has militated against an effective challenge to our habituation to language and the "things" it puts over on us. That disabling epistemology of rhetoric has been effectively identified recently in the writings of philosophers and literary theorists who, influenced by Nietzsche's notion of metaphors as productive, equalmaking enactments, have characterized tropes as aggressive and ideological, while traditional approaches, which see language as reproductive of thought, have conceived of metaphor as additional adornment to that process of reproduction.

For Aristotle, who began the tradition within a reproductive model of language, making a good metaphor was predicated on "seeing" a similarity. This he preferred within the context that knowledge is a function of "right talking."[39] John Locke promoted a primarily semantic view of language, regarding good or knowledge-related language as that which could serve as a conduit between thought and things. Within this view, he constructed his notion of figures of speech as elements that corrupt the relationship between an idea about things and the things themselves.[40] But, as Paul de Man has demonstrated, Locke's own discourse violates his view of language in general and figurative language in particular. He points out how Locke's view of the relationship between ideas and language, in which he consigns ideas to the extra-discursive realm of "simples" is confounded because one cannot separate thought and language. Within a semiological rather than a semantic approach to language it becomes evident that it is the structure of relationships among linguistic entities that produces our things, or "simples." And "idea" is not a thing that stands outside of language waiting to be expressed or spoken about. It comes from the Greek *eide*, which means "light." To understand "idea," then, is to appreciate the way that it is figuratively constructed. Metaphors cannot corrupt ideas, for "idea" *is* a metaphor.[41]

Given the pervasiveness of the figural, our traditional distinction between figural and literal language breaks down, and we are left with the recognition that some expressions are obviously or explicitly figural and some are not. In the case of the latter, the figurative is simply taken for the literal. Because aspects of our meanings, our enactments of reality, are embedded in our discursive practices, how we create our world is not easily available to conscious deliberation. It is un- or non-consciously

172

that we engender or celebrate our social and political world inasmuch as the given structure of legitimation, power, and domination is immanent in discourse producing both our self-understandings and the "things" we speak about.

If pruning away figures of speech in order to have a clear vision of the world is a misguided strategy for political understanding, our strategy has to be one of planting and nourishing a crop that will force out the older varieties or at least provide competition and challenge. This gardening metaphor for an epistemological shift translates into the promotion of the literary genre as a means for opposing the ideational commitments entrenched in linguistic practices, which, within the old epistemology of "clarity," go unnoticed. The creation of a new terrain of meaning requires the production of new figures opposing those of the old meaning system. Writers who have made this a practice, according to Derrida, include Ernst Renan, Nietzsche, Freud, and Henri Bergson, "all of whom, in their attentiveness to metaphorical activity in the theoretical or philosophical discourse, proposed or practiced the multiplication of antagonistic metaphor in order to better control or neutralize their effects."[42]

In a sense, then, theoretical discourses, when they are oriented toward literariness, that is, when they are constituted with a self-consciousness of their own figural practices, are politicized. They are politicized in that they oppose the authority and legitimacy sequestered in incumbent figures. To see such literariness as political requires, as recent poststructuralist thought has suggested, an adjustment in our metalinguistic conceits so that we see metaphor, for example, as ideational, value-creating, and aggressive instead of as a figure, which either succeeds or fails at creating clarity. As Derrida has pointed out the old view of metaphor in terms of clarity is owed to the predominant metaphor of metaphor, the "heliotrope" or trope based on the sun wherein metaphors are evaluated on the basis of the ability to shed light.[43]

When we see metaphor in particular and figural language in general from the point of view of their polemical effects, we become more sensitive to the politicizing implications of discursive selection. As I have suggested elsewhere, for example, there is a conservative bias in the increasing tendency to model political processes on language borrowed from information-processing activities (whence we come to view political participation as "providing input," thereby accepting an outsider status for all such "input" providers).[44] Or similarly, as Jean Baudrillard has suggested, there is a disguised political model promoted when we borrow from the domain of the "enjoyment of consumer goods" to speak about social stratification. Whereas one (like Baudrillard) might want to see inequality politicized, understood as control over economic and political decisions, the consumer discourse conjures away the issue of class antagonisms or conflicts of interest into a statistical dichotomy between two groups of consumers between whom the gap is narrowing. Such a choice of figuration, according to Baudrillard, creates an alibi for modern democracies.[45]

There is a political dimension of figuration. At times it is in the direction of mystification and legitimation, serving prevailing structures of power and authority, and at times it is in the direction of resistance. Figuration can politicize a domain that has been naturalized or obnubilated by a figuration that is too familiar, or too distantly associated with interest and power to evoke the idea that the issue of control is problematic. In this latter instance, politicization comes through the refiguration of the field. The metaphor involved in bringing together two previously remote linguistic domains creates what Ricoeur has called a "predicative impertinence," the creation of a productive clash between semantic fields.[46] Thus, for example, Foucault's placing of education, jurisprudence, and psychiatry, among other things, within the frame of "carceral functions" can be regarded as a literary gesture with political significance. The employment of a discourse borrowed from a punitive domain and lent to helping or ameliorative domains has the effect of rendering problematic what were, within their more familiar discursive frames, unproblematic, institutional descriptions.

THE EXPLICITLY LITERARY

He had a strong weakness for oxymoron.
                    Samuel Beckett, *More Pricks Than Kicks*

While all writing and all other discursive employments have a literary dimension, a style that contributes to the meanings of the statements, it is the explicitly literary or poetic that sees itself as governed not only by the referents it assembles but also (and often primarily, especially in the case of modernist writing) by a concern with how its language works. As an exercise of imagination, literature foregrounds the vehicle (linguistic effects) for imaginative production, while more realistic or denotative discourses bracket imaginative operations, ignoring the way that the discourse produces things and focusing on speaking about things. The brief examples from literary works that I shall now use are selected for the presence of linguistic self-consciousness, the extent to which they promote a form of interpretation through their style. In contrast to more

174

denotational discourses that are predicated on a social code with its reified subjects, objects, and relationships, the literature I shall consider is code-questioning, code-breaking, and code-producing.[47]

To highlight this consciousness of codes, literary discourse often makes use of metalinguistic emphases, focusing not on the relationship between language and objects but on the structure of the codes that produce objects and actions, that is, on the practices that are presupposed in utterances that do not reflect explicitly on their metalinguistic presuppositions. Thomas Mann implicitly offers several relevant metalinguistic meditations in his Joseph novels. For example, at the beginning of the third novel, the point at which Joseph is pulled from the pit and finds himself in the custody of wandering merchants, the dialogue begins thus:

"Where are you taking me?" Joseph asked Kedeema, one of the old man's sons as they were setting up the sleeping-huts, in the rolling, moonlit lowland at the foot of the mountains called Fruitlands.

Kedeema looked him up and down.

"Thou'rt a good one!" said he, and shook his head in token that he did not mean good at all but various other things such as pert or queer or simple. "Where are we taking thee? But are we taking thee anywhither? No, not at all. Thou art by chance with us, because our father hath purchased thee from harsh masters, and thou goest with us whither-ever we go. But taking thee that cannot be called."

"No? then not," responded Joseph. "I only meant: whither doth God lead me, in that I go with you?"

"Thou art and remainest a funny fellow," countered the Ma'onite, "and thou hast a way of putting thyself in the centre of things till one knoweth not whether to wonder or be put out. Thinkest thou, thou 'Come-hither,' that we are a-journeying in order that thou mayest arrive somewhither where thy God will have thee to come?"[48]

Whereas much literary discourse achieves its effects with the use of lexical tropes such as the metaphor discussed above, this passage, like many in realist prose, relies on the use of the grammatical trope. Mann here makes use of what Jacobson has referred to as 'the poetic resources concealed in the morphological and syntactic structure of language ... the poetry of grammar.'[49] Jacobson demonstrates grammatically oriented poetics in an analysis of the Mark Antony funeral oration from Shakespeare's *Julius Caesar*. Before considering the Mann passage here, Jacobson's analysis is worth reviewing because of the structural similarity in the two strategies. First of all, Jacobson notes that throughout the oration, Brutus's claims are rendered in abstract terms as belief states instead of reported facts:

The Noble Brutus hath told you Caesar was ambitious.

Shakespeare manipulates the grammar of the oration as Antony "lampoons Brutus's speech by changing the alleged reasons for Caesar's assassination into plain linguistic fictions."[50]

I speak not to disprove what Brutus spoke. But here I am to speak what I do know.

What Shakespeare/Antony manipulates through the play of the grammar of the passage is responsibility for action or the legitimation of models of agency. To show this, Jacobson cites the contrast between Brutus's claim, "He was ambitious," and Antony's query, "Did this in Caesar seem ambitious?" There is a clear transfer of agency from the agent to the action. So apart from the obvious irony (which produces a good deal of the oration's effects as well), the grammatical shifts have the effect of changing the locus of the indictment. With this shift Antony is again disclosing that "these reified attributes [e.g., ambition] are nothing but linguistic fictions."[51] There are then additional shifts, when "ambition" (as an abstract noun) becomes part of a "concrete passive construction":[52]

Ambition should be made of sterner stuff.

And then (as a predicate noun) "ambition" becomes part of an interrogative sentence:[53]

Was this ambition?

Mann's opening for *Joseph in Egypt* has a grammatical play with an effect parallel to that which Jacobson extracts from the funeral oration. What is shown is how linguistic constructions are not simply statements about facts or deeds but are also implicit vehicles for agency and responsibility. The modes of action and agency that distribute responsibility and thereby create what are regarded as deeds are inextricably linked with the grammar that delivers them.[54] Grammatical tropes thus have the effect of problematizing and thus politicizing modes of agency inasmuch as what becomes at issue is the locus of legitimacy. For example, the model of agency that Joseph begins with is one in which the Ma'onites are responsible for his destiny: "Where are you taking me?" This sentence nominates the Ma'onites as the actors and Joseph as an object being controlled. Kedeema responds by rejecting the grammar and the model of agency immanent in it. Noting that his father has purchased Joseph, that is, that Joseph is an object of the action called a purchase,

176

Kedeema states that, as for Joseph's destiny, "Thou goest . . . whither-ever we go." And he goes on to note that this grammatical construction cannot be translated to make them responsible for taking him some-where: "But taking thee that cannot be called."

Joseph's second grammatical attempt to hold on to a destiny model of his journeying (a model intimately tied to the mythological structure of the Old Testament) fails also: ". . . Whither doth God lead me, in that I go with you?" This is also not the grammar of agency that Kedeema can accept, and he again chides Joseph (through an opposing grammatical construction) for attempting to place himself at the center of the universe. Here the grammatical structure of the novel seems to be conveying the idea that we have a story about the new historical construction of a type of ego that we can derive from the biblical Joseph's story.

It is easy for a *reader* moving through Mann's Joseph novels to place Joseph at the center of the universe, for the story line revolves around him; and his journeys downward and upward, the swings of fortune he experiences, provide a major continuity and an emotional purchase for the reader. But at the level of grammatical style, Mann's novels fore-ground the problem of meaning, the difficulty of penetrating the text of a people's rules for legitimacy, authority, and responsibility. The diffi-culty that Joseph has in speaking to the Ma'onites at the beginning of his major journey downward mirrors the difficulty Mann experienced as he did his research in preparation for writing the novels. He saw himself explicitly attempting to penetrate the world of the Old Testament, which, for him, meant developing a style that would be an amalgam of the author and the subject matter, which, he felt, had its own style.[55] Joseph, like Mann, blends styles throughout the novels, for Mann regarded Joseph as a transparent figure in whom various traditions were mingled. This mingling is conveyed in the passage under analysis and throughout the novels as the resolution of grammatical variation, the movement toward a shared grammar and thus a shared model of agency and responsibility.[56]

Mann's political orientation in the Joseph novels clearly works in the direction of reconciliation and integration. He was, as he noted in reflecting on the enterprise of the novels, seeking that which unifies humanity, the typicality of that which is human residing in diverse cultural traditions.[57] But much literary production operates without this unificationist persuasion and works, instead, toward a destruction or sundering of the linguistic props that give us our legitimized subjects, objects, actions, and events. Instead of seeking to unify codes and bring people together within the same linguistic universe, much of the modernist writing seeks to question, problematize, or destabilize codes. One way that literary discourse produces this kind of effect is through what Russian formalists have called defamiliarization. Victor Shklovsky attributes this practice to Tolstoy who, he claims, "makes the familiar seem strange by not naming the familiar object. He describes an object as if he were seeing it for the first time, an event as if it were happening for the first time. In describing something he avoids the accepted names and instead names corresponding parts of other objects."[58]

Samuel Beckett's technique is also a form of defamiliarization, but unlike Tolstoy's, it is linguistically self-conscious in a radical way. He takes familiar figures of speech and dislocates them, using unfamiliar figures or antagonistic ones, to oppose stock forms of thinking and legitimation. Part of Beckett's effects are achieved through jarring the reader's sensibilities with mixed metaphors and oxymorons that do not allow the kind of comfortable purchase on reality that comes from treating language as a transparent medium. For example, in his opening story in *More Pricks Than Kicks* the issue or problem turns ultimately on an oxymoron that occurs in the second to last line. The story, "Dante and the Lobster," features Belacqua Shuah, a namesake (with the first name) of a character in Dante's *Purgatorio* who, if one simply follows the story line, has the task of bringing home a lobster for dinner. At least that is the story from Belacqua's point of view. From other points of view, including the lobster's, events beyond Belacqua's control conspire to achieve the result of getting the lobster to his aunt's table. Beckett, like Mann in the example above, uses grammatical structure to convey the different points of view; for example, the lobster's in such lines as, "Always assuming, of course, that the lobster was ready to be handed over." But when we heed the figures of speech, another kind of theme or story emerges, one that recalls the title of the story, a juxtaposition that, like the figures *in* the story, does not seem to work well together and therefore has a jarring effect (Dante and a lobster?)

After Belacqua gets the lobster home to his aunt's table he is horrified to learn that it is alive and is to be plunged into boiling water in this state.

She lifted the lobster clear of the table. It had about thirty seconds to live. "Well," thought Belacqua, "it's a quick death, God help us all."
It is not.[59]

The familiar way to read the passage, one that is not attuned to the lexical trope, is as a debate about whether this death is slow or fast and thus whether the lobster must endure much suffering. But the expression "quick death" is arresting and defies the easy interpretation because it is

178

an oxymoron. From the old English, old Teutonic, and Nordic languages comes the opposition between the "quick" and the "dead" (an opposition still "quick" in the Christian prayer). "Quick" still retains the meaning "characterized by the presence of life." Once we become aware of the oxymoronic quality of "quick death," our reading changes. We see Dante's and the Christian view of death as nondeath (a view connected to the notion of salvation) or living death. This is a view that clearly denies death, and that it comes from a Christian or God-related ideology becomes explicit. The "God help us all" coupled with the "quick death" no longer seems to be just an exclamation but, rather, a recognition that the idea of God is connected to the idea that death is not really death. The last line also changes. The "It is not" is not simply a captious reaction to the idea that the death of the lobster will involve minimal suffering; rather, it is a response to the contradictory notion that death is not death.

The issue thus leaves the narrow terrain of whether or not lobsters suffer when plunged alive into boiling water and enters the broader field of questions about the legitimate control over the concept of death. Why a lobster to represent such an issue? Beckett seems to think that it smacks of Christian symbolism, noting, for example, that when seen from above it is a "cruciform."[60] By presenting the issue with rhetorical play, Beckett is showing how the Christian idea of death as nondeath is more than a proclamatory position trumpeted from the pulpit. It has taken up residence more subtly within the rhetorical structure of common speech practices.

How should one describe, then, what it is that Beckett does with his mixed metaphors, oxymorons, and neologisms? If we equate literary discourse with the exercise of imagination, we get some help from Gaston Bachelard whose notion of the role of imagination resonates well with Beckett's style. "Imagination is always considered to be the faculty of *forming* images. But it is rather the faculty of *deforming* the images offered by perception."[61] Beckett, like Foucault, Derrida, and de Man, seems to view the rhetorical figures used to convey knowledge or thinking as particularly inapposite, because much of his deforming energy has gone into producing imagery antagonistic to the prevailing forms used to convey epistemological commitments. He likens the mind to a cat's-paw that grasps aggressively in the process of understanding, and at times the imagery becomes even more violent:

His plan therefore was not to refuse admission to the idea, but to keep it at bay until his mind was ready to receive it. Then let it in and pulverize it. Obliterate the bastard . . . . Flitter the fucker, tear it into pieces like a

179

priest. So far so good. But by what means? Belacqua ransacked his mind for a suitable engine of destruction.[62]

Beckett's wrenching of prevailing understandings by substituting conflicting imagery—thinking as flittering, pulverizing, etc.—is in accord with his notion that the subject is a victim of the dominant models of reason represented in prevailing speech practices. In his *The Unnamable* he anticipates Foucault's conception of power as a force that produces us, gives us an identity, and enforces a garrulousness that satisfies a growing surveillance aimed at rendering us predictable and fitting us into a set of legitimized identities that serve reason and order. The character in *The Unnamable* laments his pacification and resulting predictability, his absorption into prevailing models of one's destiny: "I have my faults, but changing my tune is not one of them. I have to go on as if there was something to be done, something begun, somewhere to go."[63]

Of course, part of the effect of this passage is achieved through the use of the ironic tone.[64] The suggestion really is that the fault lies elsewhere. Being predictable is a condition, not a fault. The fault lies in construing consciousness as an independent, causal force that, if it were, would render us *un*predictable. Beckett's view, ironically expressed here, of consciousness as epiphenomenal to something else—language practices—is further conveyed by the metaphor of the "tune," which contributes by suggesting that there is a conductor. The pedagogy of *The Unnamable* is similar to Foucault's approach to power. Power achieves its effect; grammatically speaking *it* is the actor, and rhetorically speaking *it* speaks through the mouth of the subject who subjugates himself with his own utterances: "I don't know why with their billions of quick and their trillions of dead that's not enough for them. I too must contribute my little convulsion, mewl, howl, gasp, rattle, loving my neighbor and blessed with reason."[65]

Beckett's writing, like Foucault's, is part of his resistance to power. His wildly shifting word play constitutes enactments that seek both to show how identities are epiphenomenal to speech practices and to resist them. Thinking and understanding are among his major targets. Like Foucault, Derrida, and de Man, he attacks the illusion that thinking is a relationship between a conscious subject and a world of objects. In a literary way, Beckett conveys the position that it is the background of practices, the sites and locations available to the subject, that produce the things that emerge in thought/language. Beckett's form of literary production, like Foucault's resemanticizations and refiguration, reveals domination and subjugation in discursive practices and shows how

180

subjects made by power are fetishized. His use of the figure of speech is a weapon against the deadening habituation to the world troped up in ordinary speech and then treated as if it were delivered in literal language. We can leave Beckett with a passage that achieves its effects with both the lexical and the grammatical figures:

I myself have been scandalously bungled, they must be beginning to realize it, I on whom all dangles, better still, about whom, much better, all turns, dizzily, yes yes, don't protest, all spins, it's a head, I'm in a head, what an illumination, sssst, pissed on out of hand.[66]

With his grammatical figure, the passive voice in the opening words, Beckett conveys the notion that the subject, the "I" is a product rather than an active, directing consciousness. In his substitutions of figures— "dangles," "turns"—he shows how the illusion of the "I" at the center of reality is merely a function of grasping at rhetorical devices. That the "I" is in the head, finally, is also an illusion. It is not in the head in the sense of being a directing, originating consciousness. Heaping scorn on this Cartesianism, Beckett places the "I" in a place where it *receives* the action. It is in a head, but the kind where it gets pissed on.

LITERARY READINGS OF THE NONLITERARY

I say what I'm told to say, that's all there is to it, and yet I wonder, I don't know, I don't feel a mouth on me, I don't feel the jostle of words in my mouth.
                                        Samuel Beckett, *The Unnamable*

Literary discourse, particularly in its modernist guise, is hyperpoliticizing. By producing alternative forms of thought *in* language, it makes a political point. By virtue of its departures from linguistic normality, it points to the way that institutions hold individuals within a linguistic web. But it goes beyond this demonstration. It deforms images to show how accepted models of the real are productions of grammatical and rhetorical constructions, and it forms antagonistic imagery that provides sites for resistance to domination. A failure to exercise a literary self-consciousness, then, amounts to the adoption of a depoliticizing posture, the acceptance of institutional imperatives. Following Beckett's musings, one might say that those who write in a primarily denotative genre cannot feel the words in their mouths. While the poetic or literary takes language as its object, nonliterary discourses, those that subordinate or bracket their literariness, aspire to making their language neutral (unchewy?).

But all writing, whatever its genre, is susceptible to a literary reading, to a concern with the relationship between its style or linguistic practices and argumentation about things that it presents. That literary analysis travels well across genres has been ably demonstrated by Hayden White in his literary analyses of historical writing. He argues that in addition to providing information and explanations or interpretations at an explicit level, historical, factually oriented accounts of events convey messages about the attitudes that the reader should adopt with respect to the "data" and interpretations.[67] Leaving aside the obvious epistemological problem involved in separating the "facts" and "interpretations" from the values and attitudes that the style of writing implicitly promotes—and White does this explicitly—his analyses show how historians build stories and develop tropes that produce attitudes toward historical events.

White fails to point out that "events," so called, become events only when shaped by the problematic and style of the discourse. This is demonstrated by Northrup Frye in his recent literary analysis of the Bible. Frye shows how the metaphoric and metonymic structures of biblical language constitute the biblical facts and events as well as the interpretive structure for developing an appreciation of the discursively engendered facts and events. For example, he shows how explanatory accounts in the Bible contain rhetorical structures that arrange words in the form of continuous prose so that a notion of causality for biblical events is almost inevitable.[68] All the Bible's tropic effects become coherent, Frye shows, in the context of the basic plot of the Bible. Frye's demonstration that the Bible is a story with "a specific social function . . . a program of action for a specific society,"[69] resembles White's demonstration that simple historical accounts of "fact" and "events" take place within an "emplotment"—a story designed to produce attitudes.

Within this program, the Bible then constitutes the facts and events discursively. For example, what man *is* is partly based on an identity produced, according to Frye, by "the legal metaphor that runs through the Bible, and sees man as under trial and subject to judgment."[70] Similarly, events described fit in with a purpose, the legitimation or rationalization of centralized authority. In the case of the Bible this is an authority based on the Covenant with God. As Frye points out, the account in Exodus bears only an oblique relationship to the historical condition of Egypt's control over the nation of Israel. "The evidence from history seems to suggest that Israel continued to be nominally subject to Egyptian power through most of the period covered by the Judges."[71] The Exodus story is thus not just an account of control, legitimate or illegitimate; however it might be construed to aid and abet future anti-imperialist movements. It is a deliverance story implicating God as an actor in such a way as to strengthen the legal bond between Him and the "children of Israel." That the story is oft repeated and that it is ritualized in period festivals designed to reenact the deliverance myth shows, according to Frye, how myths function. They are inseparable from notions of what is to be done. They justify actions that serve the authority the myth is designed to legitimate. The prose of the Bible, while seemingly innocent in places where it is primarily descriptive instead of proclamatory, legitimates modes of conduct and commitments of fidelity by dint of the way its style, the structure of the prose narrative, produces subjects, objects, events, and interpretive orientations. Frye sums up this case:

Accuracy of description in language is not possible beyond a certain point. The most faithfully descriptive account of anything will always turn away from what it describes into its own self-contained grammatical fictions of subject and predicate and object. The events the Bible describes are what some scholars call "language events," brought to us only through words; and it is the words themselves that have the authority, not the events they describe.[72]

Such a literary reading of prose styles can be used to politicize (in the sense of questioning the model of authority implicit in the style) even the more stylistically austere analyses that constitute the current corpus of public-policy and public-administration studies in the discipline of political science. When we examine such nonliterary discourses from a literary standpoint, as White and Frye have done with historical and biblical discourse respectively, we are seeking to pay attention to the "jostle of words" that speakers/writers hardly notice. And when this attention is paid from a political standpoint we are, as Foucault has done with various disciplinary practices, politicizing both by highlighting the discursive practices in the text and by offering alternatives.[73]

What we can learn by treating political commentary as though it were literary and attending to the "jostle of words" and its politicizing implications can be illustrated by examining James Q. Wilson's *The Investigators*. This book is a study of the Federal Bureau of Investigation and the Drug Enforcement Administration.[74] I choose to look at this particular study because from most perspectives it is an excellent study in the problem of "implementing" public policy. It is not very obviously marked by unconscious ideologizing. Like all of Wilson's studies, this one is well conducted. It is also well written in the sense that its claims are reasonable and even ingenious within the scope of the enterprise Wilson sets for himself. The interpretive frames that the work evokes involve the code of science and its criteria for truth and the code of responsibility that goes with a no-nonsense business mentality. To the extent that one stays within the boundaries of these codes, the study delivers useful truths. In short, in a number of ways, the work belongs to the genre of public-policy commentary.

If, however, we put *The Investigators* into a literary genre and apply to it the kinds of stylistic interpretations I have just discussed, we shall raise questions about structure and form. We shall ask what it is that Wilson does and how he does it, implicitly as well as ostensibly. We can begin with his self-understanding of what he was up to.

My motive for offering this analysis is not necessarily to make the work of the FBI or the DEA better or more rational, or to expose to public scrutiny additional problems in organizations that have, of late, been beset by controversy. Rather, it is my hope to explain how carrying out tasks within a governmental setting exposes managers and executives to constraints that render the devising of efficient and effective means to attain organizational objectives especially difficult or unlikely. In short, this is an account of the consequences of practicing public administration.[75]

This sounds innocuous enough, but we should not allow this brief statement of motives to throw us off the trail of Wilson's polemical program. Recall how Mark Antony pleaded a similar innocence with his modest claim about coming to bury Caesar instead of praising him. Then his discourse took over, and, as Jacobson showed us, the grammatical tropes did the job so that by the time he got through, the audience was indignant. Motives are not the place to look, at least not if motives are viewed as initiating, causal conditions. Wilson's approach to motives suggests that the value impetus that a discourse contains relates to the exogenous purposes of its immediate author, what that author thought he or she was up to in getting started.

More than forty years ago, C. Wright Mills pointed out that motives should not be seen as "the expression of prior elements within the individual."[76] Without rehearsing much of what has led up to this part of the analysis, I want to note, in agreement with Mills, that discourses contain a valuational impetus not so much by dint of what prompts them but by virtue of what they contain and how they act, how they create or perpetuate subjects (persons with identities), things, relationships, and contexts of agency. What is thought is *in* a discourse. It is not an initiating circumstance but part of what is said and how it is said. This is in fact the insight that Lacan offers on motives in his resurrection of speech as the privileged domain for psychoanalytic practice.[77]

What I suggest, therefore, with respect to *The Investigators*, is that we deauthorize it, carry it over into a genre that is not the one in which its "author" thought himself to be toiling. Within the genre of the reading I shall offer, *The Investigators* is an authority perpetuating mythology than can be explicated as myth from two perspectives. The first is that suggested by Frye. Myth, from Frye's perspective is not a concept meaning "not really true." In its fundamental (Greek) sense it simply means, "charged with a special seriousness and importance." The stories relating to aspects of a society that are told and retold as myths are those that legitimate the existing order and provide justifications for conduct conducive to order maintenance. Any discursive strategy that incorporates the prevailing language helps to legitimate the authority in existing institutions and thus has a mythical element.

But when the mythic function is in the background, there is an absence of exhortation, and the justifications for conduct are implicit in the grammatical and rhetorical tropes of a discourse whose surface appearance is primarily reportage and inference-making. It is clear, from the mythic elements in Wilson's study, even though those elements are not foregrounded, that the work of the FBI and the DEA ought to be done in the way it is being done, once some minor irrationalities caused by flaws at the level of organizational incentives are taken care of. Myth, as Frye points out, is inseparable from what ought to be done, and Wilson is telling us, indirectly, what ought to be done.[78]

Before dealing with any of the specific mythic elements in *The Investigators*, we should consider the second perspective from which the study can be read as mythological. This is Roland Barthes's perspective in which myth is viewed as a type of speech, speech that is "not defined by the object of its message but by the way in which is utters this message."[79] Without going into the details of how Barthes constructs his notion of the "way" of an utterance, it should suffice to note that a myth for Barthes is a second-order semiological system. The relationship between the original signifier and signified is a sign that contains another signifier-signified ralationship. For example, when Barthes saw on the front cover of the magazine *Paris Match* a black soldier saluting the Tricolor, he read the picture as a mythology. In this case, the mythic element is in the second-order relationship, which says "that France is a great Empire, that all her sons, without any colour discrimination, faithfully serve under her flag, and that there is no better answer to the detractors of an alleged colonialism than the zeal shown by this Negro in serving his so-called oppressors."[80] Barthes notes that the motive behind a myth is not the intentions of a person/author but a force intrinsic to the myth. It is the concept that motivates the form in which the myth develops. In the case of the saluting black soldier, the motivating concept is an apology for imperialism.

Wilson's mythological function is also one of apology, a genre of apology that is very much a part of modern mass culture. Barthes has described this genre succintly:

To instill in the Established Order the complacent portrayal of its drawbacks has nowadays become a paradoxical but incontrovertible means of exalting it. Here is the pattern of this new-style demonstration: take the established value you want to restore or develop, and first lavishly display its pettiness, the injustices which it produces, the vexations to which it gives rise, and plunge it into its natural imperfection; then, at the last moment, save it *in spite of* or rather *by* the heavy curse of its blemishes.[81]

Barthes's examples of how this genre works are from films and books dealing with organizational pettiness, intrigue, and venality in institutions like the army and the church, films and books that rescue and legitimize these institutions by contrasting the small blemishes and inefficiencies that occur when order is being maintained with the advantage of having that order (e.g., the film *From Here to Eternity*). The myth compresses, Barthes suggests, to the message, ". . . what is this trifling dross of order, compared to its advantages. . . . What does it matter, after all, if Order is a little brutal or a little blind when it allows us to live cheaply."[82]

This genre of apology is a very close fit with that of *The Investigators*. Throughout the study, the FBI and the DEA are shown to engage in actions that are not consonant with the alleged missions of their agencies. These shortcomings are then attributed to flaws in the agencies' incentive systems applied to the behavior of individual functionaries. The conduct encouraged in these functionaries results in a failure to "realize organizational goals" (primarily a failure to adopt the appropriate criteria for selecting "priority offenders"). Ultimately, the investigators in both agencies end up responding to political criteria for targeting various classes of "offenders." But in Wilson's telling, the worst shortcoming, the politicization of the conduct of the investigators (and of the agencies at all levels), turns out to be a strength. Here is the denouement of the mythic story of the investigators, worth quoting at length:

186

Excessive zeal in conforming to political demands has led the FBI to undertake some inquiries that had only partisan justification, and a preoccupation with maintaining public support has led it and the DEA to exaggerate their statistical accomplishments and to stimulate public concern over crime, subversion, and drug trafficking. But the same sensitivity to the political environment has also meant that, broadly speaking, these agencies have done what the public wanted done. When crime was on the increase, the FBI went after criminals; when public concern over threats to domestic security was at its peak, the FBI investigated subversives. . . .[83]

Wilson has told us, from his own reckoning, that excessive concern with its image has led the FBI and the DEA into various minor administrative shortcomings, primarily in the form of overly rigid demands for conformity within the organizations. This has produced conduct at the investigative level that leaves something to be desired. But, to repeat Barthes's insight into this kind of apology for power, "What is this trifling dross of order compared to its advantages?" Here we have from James Q. Wilson a mythology that is an analysis of the implementation of public policy at the first level and, at the second, the mythic level, a legitimation of part of the established order. It is hard to avoid this kind of conclusion once we are using the mythological framework, for it does not take a minute reading of the quotation above to see an "excessive zeal" for maintaining the story line of the myth. First we are told that the FBI and the DEA are so politicized that they exaggerate their accomplishments by the way they report statistics and that they "stimulate public concern over crime, subversion, and drug trafficking." But then these same agencies, which are characterized as producing the way the public deploys its concerns with respect to categories of wrongdoing, are described in the very next sentence as being responsive to public wants. Surely this is a contradiction. If you produce the wants and then respond to them, it is not convincing to make the case that those wants are responsible for initiating your activities. Only a dedicated mythologist, one committed to a story that gets the job done—which in this case is the job of selling our investigative agencies—could be willing to subordinate such contradictory details to the plot as a whole.

The literary reading reveals, then, a mythic story; it transforms an austerely written policy analysis into a legitimating pamphlet, a celebration of part of the existing order. Moreover, this part of the order is perhaps most difficult to celebrate from the point of view of values such as justice and fairness, and the like. This celebration is evident, not only when one takes the plot and the genre of the story as a whole. It is evident also when one does a closer, more detailed literary reading, paying attention to the lending discourses that govern the writing and produce kinds of subjects, objects, and modes of conduct. These details help the perpetuating myth. They help to get the job done.

The most important thing to notice is that, at the level of its language, *The Investigators* is largely ghostwritten. It incorporates the discursive patterns of the prevailing institutions and their legitimations. The FBI is described and analyzed within that agency's discourse, and likewise for the DEA. We are invited into a world of subject/objects called "investigators," "informants," "criminals," and "extremists" and their various actions or performances. These are all described within the code of business or administrative job performance. The investigators have "tasks" and function in the context of such things as "performance measures," while their adversaries (the criminals et al.) remain equally in character and engage in "violations," "subversion," "drug-trafficking," and so forth. Wilson worships all the fetishes or idols that the practice of federal-level law enforcement has erected, even though he is aware of processes immanent in them. For example, on the "criminal" he states that what gets criminalized is a function of political pressures felt by the agencies, but he then goes on to treat the "criminal" as a thing, a kind of object for the investigator. The temporal dimension of understanding, the processes wherein things become criminalized are bracketed: we are shown a frozen world of "things" that are the fixtures in the environment of the actors whose activities Wilson is promoting, the investigators.

Even at an explicit level of discourse about issues of justice and fairness, one might wonder about a practice like "instigation" in which an investigator and his informant encourage someone to commit a criminal act in order to get sufficient evidence for a successful prosecution. Such activities are spoken of as "proactive" as opposed to "reactive" methods of investigation. What some might call entrapment, bullying, infringement of rights, and the like become sequestered within a neutralizing Latinism.

What Wilson's language does becomes even more apparent in the context of what it fails to do, self-consciously politicizing the field he works. What is "drug-trafficking," for example, if we call off all legitimation bets for the moment and enter the issue with a historical as well as a politicized consciousness? In such a situation, we might wonder about the difference between "drug-trafficking" and "drug-marketing." Why are "the investigators" not hanging around the executives in the marketing divisions of large pharmaceutical companies? What is the process wherein some harmful substances have been encouraged and some discouraged by official agencies? In the case of the "dangerous drugs" produced by the pharmaceutical companies, controls consist of esoteric warnings (mostly in Greek and Latin) to the physicians whose medical training has promoted the substances in the first place. Those products that do not survive the loose screening of the Food and Drug Administration get marketed in places such as Latin America where citizens are not protected by regulatory agencies of the United States.

What historical sequence of events and what power-related process give rise to the differential identification of the marketing versus the trafficking person? In response to such a question what one would find is what Foucault has shown in his analysis of what he has called the proliferation of illegalities. The historical processes involved in this proliferation can be politically characterized; they relate to a growing structure of domination. The penalties on behalf of which the investigators operate are "facts" or "things" that harbor historical processes. Let us listen for a moment to someone not co-opted by the motives of power:

Penalty would thus appear to be a way of handling illegalities of laying down the limits of tolerance, of giving free reign to some, of putting pressure on others, of excluding a particular section, of making another useful, of neutralizing certain individuals and of profiting from others. In short, penalty does not simply "check" illegalities; it differentiates them, it provides them with a general "economy" and, if one can speak of justice, it is not only because the law itself in the way of applying it serves the interests of a class, it is also because the differential administration of illegalities through the mediation of penalty forms part of those mechanisms of domination.[84]

In contrast to this kind of politicizing statement, what we get from Wilson is a rhetoric of legitimation in the form of the traditional clichés of power and a grammar of absolution. To the extent that Wilson has a political program, it is not that of Foucault, that of showing how domination and subjugation, the allocation of punishment versus support is embedded within the discourse of the administration of penalities. Rather, it is one of supporting the existing enforcement system of those penal codes. One of his grammatical tropes that appears throughout the study is what Wilson calls the "task." This is a concept he nominates as an actor. In his preferred model for running investigative agencies, the tasks determine the investigators' behavior. Where is power in such a grammar? It has fled from the scene after it set up the "task" that Wilson promotes as the privileged actor. This control by the task is preferred by Wilson to what he calls the bogey of rational and effective law enforcement, the top-down perspective in administration, where the organization's executives control conduct through incentives and performance monitoring.[85]

Finally, when the major metaphor of *The Investigators*, the "task," is viewed as metaphor instead of as literal description, it undermines even the limited political motive that Wilson tacitly acknowledges, that of enhancing the already politically determined pursuits of the investigators. A "task" is not just a job or a piece of work outside the context of organizational exigencies. As a metaphor for some kind of activity, it borrows from the domain of fiscal management in hierarchical (top-down) structures. It is derived from *taxa, taxare*, a Latin verb denoting "a fixed payment to a king, lord, or feudal superior."[86] Even without benefit of the metaphoricity of "task," it should be evident that a task calls forth activity only in the sense that the person who is charged with the task has to defer to a superior, be that superior an individual person or an institutionalized collectivity whose power relations are implicit in each instance of an authorized task. Wilson's political program turns out to be vacuous. In addition to saying, qua his mythology, that we must celebrate the FBI and the DEA, he is saying that instead of running these agencies from the top-down, we should run them from the top-down.

How should we talk about the activities of the investigators? Above, quite inadvertently, I referred to their activities as "pursuits." For the sake both of continuity and of political conscientiousness I shall stick with this characterization. To pursue is "To follow with hostility or enmity; to seek to injure (a person), to persecute, to harass, worry, torment."[87]

Notes

1. Martin Heidegger, *What Is a Thing?* trans. W. B. Burton and Vera Deutsch (South Bend, Ind.: Regnery/Gateway, 1967), p. 224.

2. Ibid., p. 141.

3. Martin Heidegger, "The Thing," in *Poetry, Language, Thought*, trans. Albert Hofstadter (New York: Harper & Row, 1971), p. 170.

4. Martin Heidegger, "The Age of the World Picture," in *The Question Concerning Technology*, trans. William Lovett (New York: Harper & Row, 1977).

5. Ibid.

6. On these aspects of Heidegger's thinking, see Hubert L. Dreyfus, "Holism and Hermeneutics," *Review of Metaphysics* 34 (September 1980), and "The Dasein as a Whole," review of Martin Heidegger's *The Basic Problems of Phenomenology*, in *Times Literary Supplement*, Sept. 17, 1982, p. 1011.

7. Martin Heidegger, "The End of Philosophy and the Task of Thinking," in

On Time and Being, trans. Joan Stambaugh (New York: Harper & Row, 1972), p. 59.

8. Clifford Geertz, "Blurred Genres: The Refiguration of Social Thought," *American Scholar* 49 (Spring 1980):165–79.

9. Paul Ricoeur, "The Model of the Text: Meaningful Action Considered as a Text," in Paul Rabinow and William M. Sullivan, eds., *Interpretive Social Science: A Reader* (Berkeley: University of California Press, 1979), pp. 73–102.

10. Hans-Georg Gadamer, "On the Scope and Function of Hermeneutical Reflection," in *Philosophical Hermeneutics*, trans. David E. Linge (Berkeley: University of California Press, 1976), pp. 18–43.

11. Michel Foucault, "The Order of Discourse," trans. Ian McCleod, in Robert Young, ed., *Untying the Text* (Boston: Routledge & Kegan Paul of America, 1981), pp. 48–78.

12. Fredric Jameson, *The Political Unconscious* (Ithaca, N.Y.: Cornell University Press, 1981).

13. Hans-Georg Gadamer, *Reason in the Age of Science*, trans. Frederick G. Lawrence (Cambridge, Mass.: M.I.T. Press, 1982), p. 90.

14. Ibid., p. 136.

15. Michel Foucault, "Nietzsche, Genealogy, History," in Donald F. Bouchard, ed., *Language, Counter-Memory, Practice* (Ithaca, N.Y.: Cornell University Press, 1977), pp. 151–52.

16. Michel Foucault, "Two Lectures," in *Power/Knowledge*, trans. Colin Gordon (New York: Pantheon Books, 1980), p. 96.

17. Michel Foucault, *The Archeology of Knowledge*, trans. Alan Sheridan (New York: Pantheon Books, 1972), p. 120.

18. Michel Foucault, *The History of Sexuality*, trans. Robert Hurley (New York: Pantheon Books, 1978), p. 25.

19. Michel Foucault, *Discipline and Punish: The Birth of the Prison*, trans. Alan Sheridan (New York: Pantheon Books, 1977), p. 275.

20. Michel Foucault, "Afterward, the Subject and Power," in Hubert L. Dreyfus and Paul Rabinow, *Michel Foucault: Beyond Structuralism and Hermeneutics* (Chicago: University of Chicago Press, 1982), p. 216.

21. Fredric Jameson, *The Prison House of Language* (Princeton, N.J.: Princeton University Press, 1972), p. 10.

22. For the former, see Roland Barthes, *Mythologies*, trans. Anette Lavers (New York: Hill & Wang, 1972), and for the latter, Roland Barthes, "Literature Today," in *Critical Essays*, trans. Richard Howard (Evanston, Ill.: Northwestern University Press, 1972), pp. 151–62.

23. For an example of Barthes's later approach to texts as tissues of codes, see his "Textual Analysis of Poe's 'Valdemar,'" in Robert Young, ed., *Untying the Text*, pp. 133–61.

24. Roland Barthes, "From Work to Text," in Josue Harari, ed., *Textual Strategies* (Ithaca, N.Y.: Cornell University Press, 1979), pp. 73–81.

25. See Jacques Derrida's analysis of Rousseau, in *Of Grammatology*, trans. Gayatri Chakravorty Spivak (Baltimore, Md.: Johns Hopkins University Press, 1974), and his analysis of Plato, "Plato's Pharmacy," in *Dissemination*, trans. Barbara Johnson (Chicago: University of Chicago Press, 1981), pp. 61–172.

26. Jacques Derrida, "The Supplement of Copula: Philosophy before Linguistics," in Josue Harari, ed., *Textual Strategies*, pp. 82–120.

27. Jacques Derrida, "Freud and the Scene of Writing," in *Writing and Difference*, trans. Alan Bass (Chicago: University of Chicago Press, 1978), pp. 196–231.

28. Jacques Lacan, "The Function and Field of Speech and Language in Psychoanalysis," in *Ecrits*, trans. Alan Sheridan (New York: Norton, 1977), pp. 30–114.

29. See Spivak's "Translator's Preface," in Derrida, *Of Grammatology*, p. lxiv, for a comparative analysis of Lacan and Derrida.

30. Jacques Derrida, "Structure, Sign and Play in the Discourse of the Human Sciences," in *Writing and Difference*, pp. 278–94.

31. See Edward Said, "The Problem of Textuality: Two Exemplary Positions," *Critical Inquiry* 4, no. 4 (Summer 1978):673–714, and also Jonathan Culler, "Jacques Derrida," in John Sturrock, ed., *Structuralism and Since* (New York: Oxford University Press, 1979), pp. 154–80.

32. Georg Lukacs, "What Is Orthodox Marxism?" in *History and Class Consciousness*, trans. Rodney Livingstone (Cambridge, Mass.: M.I.T. Press, 1971), pp. 1–26. Jameson has restated Lukacs's position on reification as "The transformation of human relations into an appearance of relationships between things." (See his "Reflections in Conclusion," in Ernst Bloch, ed., *Aesthetics and Politics* (New York: Schocken Books, 1979), p. 212.)

33. Lucien Goldmann, *Lukacs and Heidegger*, trans. William Q. Boelhower, (Boston: Routledge & Kegan Paul of America, 1977), p. 70.

34. Sigmund Freud, "Note on the Mystic Writing Pad," quoted in Jacques Derrida, "Freud and the Scene of Writing," in *Writing and Difference*, pp. 222–23.

35. Friedrich Nietzsche, "On Truth and Lie in the Extra-Moral Sense," quoted in Eric Blondel, "Nietzsche: Life as Metaphor," in David Allison, ed., *The New Nietzsche* (New York: Delta, 1977), p. 167.

36. Quoted in Tracy Strong, "Texts and Pretexts: Reflections on Perspectivism in Nietzsche," paper delivered at the North American Nietzsche Association meeting, the American Philosophical Association, 1980.

37. Friedrich Nietzsche, *The Genealogy of Morals*, trans. Francis Golffing (Garden City, N.Y.: Doubleday, 1966).

38. Jacques Derrida, "The Question of Style," in Allison, *The New Nietzsche*, p. 187.

39. Aristotle's conception of science as "right talking" is developed in John H. Randall, *Aristotle* (New York: Columbia University Press, 1960).

40. Paul de Man, "The Epistemology of Metaphor," in Sheldon Sachs, ed., *On Metaphor* (Chicago: University of Chicago Press, 1978), pp. 11–28.

41. Ibid.

42. Jacques Derrida, "White Mythology: Metaphor in the Text of Philosophy," in *Margins of Philosophy*, trans. Alan Bass (Chicago: University of Chicago Press, 1982), pp. 207–72.

43. Ibid.

44. See my "Structuralist, Post Structuralism and Political Understanding," paper delivered at the International Political Science Association meeting, Rio de Janeiro, Brazil, August 1982.

45. Jean Baudrillard, "Sign Function and Class Logic," in *For a Critique of*

the Political Economy of the Sign, trans. Charles Levin (St. Louis, Mo.: Telos Press, 1981), pp. 29–62.

46. Paul Ricoeur, "The Function of Fiction in Shaping Reality," *Man and World* 12 (1979):132–33.

47. Julia Kristeva speaks of the literature-code relationship in this way in "From One Identity to Another," in *Desire in Language*, trans. Thomas Cora, Alice Jardine, and Leon Roudiez (New York: Columbia University Press, 1980), pp. 124–47.

48. Thomas Mann, *Joseph in Egypt*, trans. H. T. Lowe-Porter (New York: Alfred A. Knopf, 1938), p. 3.

49. Roman Jacobson, "Linguistics and Poetics," in Thomas A. Sebeok, ed., *Style in Language* (Cambridge, Mass.: M.I.T. Press, 1960), p. 375.

50. Ibid.

51. Ibid., p. 376.

52. Ibid.

53. Ibid.

54. This is analyzed at length by Kenneth Burke in his *A Grammar of Motives* (Berkeley: University of California Press, 1969).

55. Thomas Mann, *The Theme of the Joseph Novels* (Washington D.C.: Library of Congress, 1942), p. 9.

56. Mann explicitly states that he saw Joseph as a "transparent figure" (ibid., p. 15).

57. E.g., a poem sung to Joseph's father, Jacob, represents this by blending Hebrew cadences with the versification of German romantic poetry, according to Mann (ibid.).

58. Victor Shklovsky, "Art as Technique," in *Russian Formalist Criticism*, trans. Lee T. Lemon and Marion J. Reis (Lincoln: University of Nebraska Press, 1965), p. 13.

59. Samuel Beckett, *More Pricks Than Kicks* (London: Chatto and Windus, 1934), p. 22.

60. Ibid., p. 21.

61. Gaston Bachelard, *On Poetic Imagination and Reverie*, trans. Colette Gaudin (Indianapolis, Ind.: Bobbs-Merrill, 1971), p. 19.

62. Beckett, *More Pricks Than Kicks*, p. 53.

63. Samuel Beckett, *The Unnamable*, trans. Samuel Beckett (New York: Grove Press, 1958), p. 66.

64. See Kenneth Burke's discussion of the ironic trope in *A Grammar of Motives*, p. 503.

65. Beckett, *The Unnamable*, pp. 66–67.

66. Ibid., p. 119.

67. Hayden White, "Historicism, History and the Figurative Imagination," in *Tropics of Discourse* (Baltimore, Md.: Johns Hopkins University Press, 1978), p. 105.

68. Northrop Frye, *The Great Code: The Bible and Literature* (New York: Harcourt Brace Jovanovich, 1982), p. 81.

69. Ibid., p. 49.

70. Ibid.

71. Ibid.

72. Ibid., p. 60.

73. William Connolly has done this with a discourse in the philosophy of the social sciences. See his literary deconstruction of Richard Rorty in *Raritan*, forthcoming.

74. James Q. Wilson, *The Investigators* (New York: Basic Books, 1978).

75. Ibid., p. ix.

76. C. Wright Mills, "Situated Actions and Vocabularies of Motive," *American Sociological Review* 5 (December 1940):904.

77. Lacan, "The Function and Field of Speech and Language in Psychoanalysis."

78. Frye, *The Great Code*, p. 33.

79. Barthes, *Mythologies*, p. 109.

80. Ibid., p. 116.

81. Barthes, "Operation Margarine," in *Mythologies*, p. 41.

82. Ibid., p. 42.

83. Wilson, *The Investigators*, pp. 213–14.

84. Foucault, *Discipline and Punish*, p. 272.

85. See *The Investigators*, chap. 1, for this argument.

86. *The Shorter Oxford English Dictionary on Historical Principles* (Oxford: Clarendon Press, 1933).

87. Ibid.

PART II
THE PRESIDENTIAL INAUGURAL AS CASE STUDY

INTRODUCTION TO PART II

In Part I of this book we explored the concepts "form" and "genre" from several vantage points, using ideas suggested by rules theory, literary history and criticism, principles of taxonomy, theory of metaphor and imagery, concepts of praxis, and political criticism. Collectively the chapters make clear that problems of definition arise whenever concepts of "form" and "genre" enter into criticism of discourse. Nevertheless, it is also clear that there can scarcely be discussion of discourse without resort to comparisons and contrasts of patterns and presumed kinds. As Connors says in opening chapter 1, "The attempt to understand phenomena by referring them to other phenomena both similar and dissimilar is one of the basic human conceptual activities." On the other hand, as both Connors and Conley emphasize, classifying always invokes the dangers of solipsism and oversimplification and of becoming stultifyingly prescriptive. To illustrate both the possibilities and the problems of genre criticism applied to political rhetoric we offer the chapters comprising Part II in which generic conceptions are used in examining one of the least debatable "kinds" of political speaking.

The essays in Part II concentrate on a single rhetorical type—the presidential inaugural—and three of the essays focus on a single instance of that type. Several advantages accrue from this focus. First, because almost everyone agrees that American presidential inaugural addresses constitute a distinctive kind of political discourse, problems of defining the genre are thus minimized. Second, American presidential inaugurals comprise a manageable corpus of discourse, and their availability allows critics to make comparisons and contrasts that should show what is fundamental and what is discretionary or accidental in any instance of the presumed genre. Third, the opening essay, which assays all inaugurals, together with the three essays that focus upon Ronald Reagan's 1981 inaugural, present a range of critical possibilities. By comparing the essays with each other and with the theoretical advantages and disad-

197

vantages of generic analysis posited in Part I, we gain a practical check on the value of each approach and on the possibilities supposedly inhering in generic criticism. Reagan's 1981 inaugural address constitutes an especially useful "test case" for the methodological explorations we seek. Friends and foes alike concede that Ronald Reagan (with assistance from aides) is skillful in crafting and presenting political messages. By using his inaugural address as our "test case" we test the critical and explanatory power of genre theory against a "good" rather than a crude instance of the genre. Also, by using the 1981 inaugural address we have the advantages of studying a relatively recent instance of the genre but one for which after-the-fact data are available to round out the historical context of the speech. In Part II, then, we advance from theoretical considerations concerning the potentialities of generic criticism to practical tests of the method, using an expertly crafted instance of a genre that is minimally troublesome definitionally. Included in the appendix of this volume are the texts of Reagan's 1981 and 1985 inaugurals. One test of the chapters in Part II is whether or not they can help to illuminate Reagan's second inaugural address as well.

We conclude this introduction with observations concerning how the considering of Reagan's second inaugural address can highlight definitional and methodological issues suggested by the chapters in Part II.

We must remember at the outset that the setting for Reagan's second inaugural address was markedly different from the setting for his first such speech. On January 21, 1985, Reagan delivered his second inaugural address before a relatively small audience in the Capitol rotunda. It was the Monday after Inauguration Day, that day having been usurped by Super Bowl XIX. And it was cold—so cold that the inaugural ceremony had to be conducted indoors. Was this a bad augury for a President whose first inauguration had taken place in bright sunshine and was presented to the American people along with news that American hostages in Iran had finally been released? How the second inaugural was like and unlike the first is a matter that immediately confronts us with the definitional problems of genre theory, even for the relatively undisputed genre of American presidential inaugurals.

First, what are the recurring features of inaugurals? What are their variations? And how can we account for both their commonalities and their differences? Equally important, how can we be sure that we have accurately identified their distinguishing and variable characteristics? Operating from the assumption that recurring exigencies and situational constraints invite recurring rhetorical responses, Campbell and Jamieson deduce several key features of inaugurals, which follow from the inherent nature of the inaugural address as an epideictic address presented by an elected President in conjunction with a ceremonial event that marks the beginning of an administration.

To their credit, Campbell and Jamieson assay the entire corpus of inaugurals to test their claims about the genre's distinguishing features. For the most part, the characteristics they identify seem to be present in Reagan's second inaugural address as well. There are appeals to unity in the first third of the speech, in particular in the lengthy Adams-Jefferson parallel. The President's opening moment of prayer for Senator Stennis and Representative Long might well be interpreted as yet another unifying appeal, one that, in its reference to recent events, bespoke as well a sense of epideictic timelessness. From a comparison of the first and second inaugural addresses, one might conclude that the latter offers fewer unifying appeals, reconstituting appeals, and articulations of basic philosophy, but this, too, is predictable from Campbell and Jamieson's account.

Less certain is whether these and other alleged characteristics of the genre are as readily isolable as Campbell and Jamieson seem to suggest, a question ultimately of inter-observer reliability. Consider, for example, this passage from Reagan's second inaugural address.

We've come to a turning point, a moment of hard decisions. I have asked the Cabinet and my staff a question and now I put the same question to all of you. If not us, who? And if not now, when? It must be done by all of us going forward with a program aimed at reaching a balanced budget. We can then begin reducing the national debt.

Is this an invitation to contemplation, a call for action, a restatement of political principle, an appeal to unity, and perhaps more? We suggest that the amorphous nature of discourse continues to be a problem in genre studies, and may lead, on the one hand, to overemphasis on explicitly phrased generic markers, or to an unwarranted "reading in" of markers where discourse is more subtle or obscure.

Whereas Campbell and Jamieson view the inaugural as a type of epideictic discourse, and extract its characteristics from the practice of presidents, Bruce Gronbeck deduces its rules for competence from ancient rites of augury and investiture. Gronbeck argues that, as with other ceremonies of change, the inaugural serves symbolically to reorient and reassure the people at a moment of significant political transition. In a sense, the President's inaugural address (and accompanying ceremonies) is presented to audiences as a reading of the signs of the times (augury), and as an instrument for elevating the person to the Presidency (investiture). Again, an examination of the second Reagan inaugural address raises interesting theoretical and methodological questions. Gronbeck maintains that a major function of inaugurals, as of all ceremonies of transition, is celebration—signaled by references to peaceful transitions, favorable states of affairs, and promises of a bright future. If ever a speech should contain such references, one would think it would be the 1985 inaugural address, coming as it did after such a successful first term. There are, to be sure, numerous celebrative claims, but the speech is surprisingly spare in its references to the last four years. In four brief sentences interspersed through the speech, the President alludes to accomplishments but never elaborates. How, then, shall we judge this relative absence of self-congratulatory reference to the first Reagan term? Is it evidence of rhetorical ineptness—of a failure to seize upon invited opportunity? Or has he managed to fulfill the celebrative function without reference to his accomplishments?

In the second part of Jane Blankenship's provocative essay, she brings her model of rhetorical forms to bear upon a two-hour segment of ABC's television coverage of Reagan's inaugural address and the release of American hostages in Iran. In ABC's "twinning" of these events, Blankenship discerns the rhetorical energy of an emergent form, the oxymoron, as it reveals the intense, often confusing clash of inconsistencies to viewers: "the powerfulness of power (the inaugural) and the powerlessness of power (the hostage capture/release)."

Apart from insights into a theory of form, and the particular form of ABC's coverage, this essay points to a need for analysis of television coverage of important political genres associated almost entirely with that medium—the presidential press conference, candidacy announcements, campaign coverage, national party conventions, and so forth. Though an oxymoronic strain may be inherent to television, as Blankenship points out, might critics discern other emerging forms in the coverage of various types of political events? Are particular forms associated with particular genres? What effect might such forms have upon shaping future forms in televised political events? If there are influences, what is their potential political meaning and effect? The oxymoron in 1981 emerged as a result of an atypical confluence of events. Might coverage of more typical inaugurals be dominated by metaphors of restoration and continuity in a "text" beginning with preinaugural celebrations and extending through the oath-taking, the inaugural address, and postinaugural celebrations? Recall some of the images from the 1985 "text." The twinnings are not of the same

200

provocative, intense nature as in 1981, but they provide potential political readings by audiences.

Television presents the President and the First Lady as the very embodiments of stability as they move smoothly from event to event—steady, serene, confident. The President is twinned with Hollywood as he stands center stage at an inaugural gala telecast by ABC, with Frank Sinatra, Elizabeth Taylor, and Mr. T among those in the background. Is the President thereby twinned with his past, Hollywood, and the American Dream, or at least Hollywood's version of that dream? And if we are not sure of the values associated with that dream, Jimmy Stewart tells us when he describes Hollywood as "a place where concepts like patriotism and family were extolled." Viewers, of course, were not unmindful of Sinatra's Rat Pack and alleged connections with shady characters, Taylor's serial marriages, and Mr. T's ever imminent and explosive violence in the *A-Team*. (Perhaps the form here was irony.) We can be reasonably sure that coverage of religious ceremonies at the Washington National Cathedral provided another sort of twinning with the inaugural, reinforcing the "under God" theme pervasive in the President's text. On Sunday night, six hours after the official oath-taking, the President himself twinned inaugural events with Super Bowl XIX when he tossed a coin to determine the kick-off. Millions of Americans witnessed the Dolphins and 49ers gazing up at the electronic bust of the President on a giant TV screen in the stadium. Did this twinning lead audiences to view the President as honest broker in the political contests of America? Did it reinforce further their sense of Reagan as being as American as a gang tackle? There were surely other potentially important twinnings between commercials and inaugural events that could reinforce a dominant metaphor. A General Motors commercial during the postinaugural luncheon provided corporate legitimation of the ritual, albeit associated with crash-testing; a voiceover described the inaugural as "a proud ceremony of succession and renewal" and reminded Americans that once again "the torch has passed peacefully and with grace." When commercials for Sominex, Oil of Olay, and *My Wicked, Wicked Ways*, the story of Errol Flynn, a Hollywood cohort of the President, interrupted CBS's coverage of the luncheon, were viewers' habits so disciplined as to prevent a blend of ideas, images, values? If not, with what potential effect? We may ask, too, if bringing viewers' attention to the inaugural as ritual, as commentators did on CBS, influences viewers' participation in the ritual. After all, we are familiar with the chilling effect of the social dolt who, when the group is having fun, announces that the group is having fun. We are convinced that a conception of "text" as a lattice of twinnings, as Blankenship's essay seems to suggest, holds promise for more fruitful insights into televised political genres. But note, too, that our observations about the effects of the twinnings we have identified are merely speculative.

We come, finally, to Roderick Hart's essay, which in its use of computer-assisted content analysis provides the only instance in this book of a scientific study of rhetorical genres. At first glance, selecting 500 words from the middle portion of the first or the second Reagan inaugural address would seem to hold little promise. But we are convinced that Hart's "weak version of the scientific method" provides a valuable alternative to the humanistic approach and underscores the need for greater rigor in any approach to rhetorical genre. Hart wisely places his computer-assisted approach in the overall context of the critical enterprise; the computer may "sift" and "flag" but ultimately critical sensitivity is the final determinant of insights about rhetorical genres. The computer can give us a sense of the types of *words* used in the samples, but it remains for the critic to reflect upon nuances and strategies of sentences. For example, sampling might pick up references to God in this sentence from the first address: "Your dreams, your hopes, your goals, are going to be the dreams, the hopes, and the goals of this administration, so help me God." Or in this sentence from the second address: "My friends, together we can do this, and do this we must, so help me God." The critic might suggest that the strategy is to associate Reagan's commitment in the first instance, and a *collective* commitment in the second—with words from the oath of office.

Too, it would be the task of the critic to discern the effect of noncontiguous sentences. Consider the following phrases in the second inaugural address: "But there are many mountains yet to climb"; "And if we meet this challenge"; "Our nation is poised for greatness"; "The time has come for a new American emancipation"; "We've come to a turning point." The overall effect of optimism is cumulative, something which the computer alone would not pick up. It is the combination of a sound quantitative approach and a sensitive critic which invites, for example, Hart's trenchant observation about Reagan's first inaugural address: "His High Interest *and* Complexity scores earmark him as a kind of bastard son of Eleanor Roosevelt and Herbert Hoover."

7

Karlyn Kohrs Campbell and Kathleen Hall Jamieson

INAUGURATING THE PRESIDENCY

The presidential inaugural address is a discourse whose significance all recognize but few praise. Arthur Schlesinger, Jr., for example, acknowledges that, during inaugural addresses, "the nation listens for a moment as one people to the words of the man they have chosen for the highest office in the land,"[1] but he finds little merit in such speeches: "Even in the field of political oratory, the inaugural address is an inferior art form. It is rarely an occasion for original thought or stimulating reflection. The platitude quotient tends to be high, the rhetoric stately and self-serving, the ritual obsessive, and the surprises few."[2]

Conceivably, inaugurals mirror the alleged mediocrity of American presidents. In our view, presidential inaugurals are maligned because their symbolic function is misunderstood. Resolving this misunderstanding requires us to address several issues in the criticism of political rhetoric: Can inaugural addresses be treated as a group? Are they a distinct type, a rhetorical genre?[3] If so, what predetermines their characteristics?

Conventional wisdom and ordinary language treat inaugural addresses as a class. Critics have intuitively taken them to belong to a distinct rhetorical type, but generalizing about them has been difficult. Despite apparent dissimilarities among them, we hold that presidential inaugural addresses form a genre, and in this essay we attempt to identify the shared qualities that render them distinctive. In that process, we shall account for the recurrent and the variable in these speeches, explain the unique functions of the presidential inaugural, and illuminate the power of those inaugural addresses widely regarded as eloquent.

U.S. presidential inaugurals are a subspecies of the kind of discourse

An earlier version of this essay appeared in *Presidential Studies Quarterly* 15 (Spring, 1985):394–411; the revised version is published here with the permission of the Center for the Study of the Presidency, publisher of *Presidential Studies Quarterly*.

that Aristotle called epideictic, a form of rhetoric that praises or blames on ceremonial occasions,[4] addresses an audience that evaluates the rhetor's skill (*Rhetoric* 1354b.2–4), recalls the past and speculates about the future while focusing on the present (1358b.18–20), employs a noble, dignified, literary style (1414a.15), and amplifies or rehearses admitted facts (1368a.27).

In a recent work on rhetoric in the Catholic Church, John O'Malley noted that epideictic rhetoric presents speakers with a unique problem of invention—a problem in discovering and developing appropriate lines of argument. Unlike forensic (courtroom) or deliberative (legislative) speeches that deal "with more immediate and pressing issues" for which "classical theory proposed *topoi* or commonplaces, . . . [t]he occasional or ceremonial nature of epideictic often deprived it of obviously immediate issues."[5] As a result, *memoria*, or recollection of a shared past, becomes an exceptionally important resource for epideictic speeches. O'Malley also called attention to the distinctively contemplative character of this genre. He remarked: "Epideictic wants as far as possible to present us with works and deeds, . . . not for metaphysical analysis but quite literally for viewing . . . 'to look,' to 'view,' to 'gaze upon,' and to 'contemplate.' . . ."[6] Harry Caplan added that in epideictic discourse a speaker tries, by means of his art, "to impress his ideas upon [the audience], without action as a goal."[7]

Using these criteria one can see that presidential inaugurals are epideictic rhetoric because they are delivered on ceremonial occasions, fuse past and future in present contemplation, affirm or praise the shared principles that will guide the incoming administration, ask the audience to "gaze upon" traditional values, employ elegant, literary language, and rely on "heightening of effect" by amplification and reaffirmation of what is already known and believed.

The special character of presidential inaugural addresses is defined by these general epideictic features and by the nature of the inauguration ceremony. Inauguration is a rite of passage, a ritual of transition in which the newly elected President is invested with the office of the Presidency.[8] The fusion of epideictic features with the requirements of this rite of investiture creates the distinctive rhetorical type that is the U.S. presidential inaugural address.

Investiture necessitates participation in a formal ceremony in which a duly constituted authority, before appropriate witnesses, confers the right to play a certain role or to take a certain position. The ceremony usually involves a demonstration by the candidate for investiture of her

204

or his suitability for such elevation. In the inauguration ceremony, the President must swear an oath specified by the Constitution,[9] before "the people" as witnesses, and demonstrate by rhetorical enactment his worthiness, his capacity to be the President. More specifically, the President must show that he understands the principles of a democratic-republican form of government and the limits it imposes on executive power, and he must manifest rhetorically his ability to lead and to be the symbolic head of state who is President of all the people. All of these are culturally evolved expectations that specify the "appropriate" features of a presidential inaugural address.

The general qualities of epideictic rhetoric, modified by the nature of presidential investiture, generate a constellation of four interrelated elements that constitute the essential presidential inaugural address and differentiate it from other types of epideictic rhetoric.[10] The presidential inaugural (1) unifies the audience by reconstituting its members as "the people" who can witness and ratify the ceremony; (2) rehearses communal values drawn from the past; (3) sets forth the political principles that will govern the new administration; and (4) demonstrates that the President appreciates the requirements and limitations of the executive functions. Each of these ends must be achieved through means appropriate to epideictic address, i.e., while urging contemplation not action, focusing on the present while incorporating past and future, and praising the institution of the Presidency and the values and the form of the government of which it is a part.

The special "timelessness" of epideictic discourse is the key to fusing the elements of the dynamic that symbolically constitutes the presidential inaugural. The time of epideictic rhetoric, including inaugurals, is the eternal present, the mythic time that Mircea Eliade calls *illud tempus*, time out of time. Eliade writes: "Every ritual has the character of happening *now*, at this very moment. The time of the event that the ritual commemorates or re-enacts is made *present*, 're-presented' so to speak, however far back it may have been in ordinary reckoning."[11] This "time out of time" has two distinguishing features: (1) in it one experiences a universe of eternal relationships; in the case of inauguration, the relationship between the ruler and the ruled; and (2) it has the potential to be reenacted, made present once again, at any moment. This special sense of the present is central to the generic character of the inaugural because the address is about an institution and a form of government fashioned to transcend any given historical moment. The timelessness of an inaugural address affirms and ensures the continuity of the constitutional

205

system and the immortality of the Presidency as an institution, and timelessness is reflected in its contemplative tone and by the absence of calls to specific and immediate action.

In order to transcend the historical present, inaugurals need to reconstitute an existing community, rehearse the past, affirm traditional values, and articulate timely and timeless principles that will govern the administration of the incoming President. Inaugurals bespeak their locus in the eternal present in a "high" style that heightens experience, invites contemplation, and speaks to "the people" through time. The quality of epideictic timelessness to which inaugurals aspire was captured by Franklin Roosevelt in his 1941 address: "To us there has come a time, in the midst of swift happenings, to pause for a moment and take stock— to recall what our place in history has been, and to rediscover what we are and what we may be . . . ."[12]

RECONSTITUTING "THE PEOPLE"

Before an audience can witness and ratify an ascent to power, the audience must be unified and reconstituted as "the people." John Adams illustrated the reconstituting power of historical reenactment when he rehearsed the founding of the nation in 1797: "In this dangerous crisis [under the Articles of Confederation] the people of America were not abandoned by their usual good sense, presence of mind, resolution, or integrity. Measures were pursued to concern a plan to form a more perfect union . . ." (p. 10).* Jefferson sought to create a single people out of partisan division when he said: "We have called by different names brethren of the same principles. We are all republicans. We are all federalists" (p. 16).[13] More recently, after a close election and a divisive campaign, John F. Kennedy in 1961 began: "We observe today not a victory of party, but a celebration of freedom . . . (p. 269). As one would expect, explicit appeals for unity are most common in addresses that follow divisive campaigns or contested electoral outcomes.[14]

Partisan politicking is not the only source of division. Occasionally a major crisis or a war creates disharmony that must be set aside if a President is to govern all the people. Acknowledging the disunity created by the Civil War, McKinley in 1901 declared: "We are reunited. Sectionalism has disappeared. Division on public questions can no longer be traced by the war maps of 1861" (p. 180). In 1917, in the face of U.S. entry into World War I, Wilson affirmed the importance of unity: "[I]t is

*Page citations are to Lott. See n. 12.

imperative that we should stand together. We are being forged into a new unity amidst the fires that now blaze throughout the world" (p. 205).

Once the audience has been united as "the people," it can perform its role in the inaugural ceremony. Inaugural addresses themselves attest to the witnessing role of "the people." For example, in 1889, Benjamin Harrison said:

There is no constitutional or legal requirement that the president shall take the oath of office in the presence of the people, but there is so manifest an appropriateness in the public induction to office of the chief executive of the nation that from the beginning of the Government the people, to whose service the official oath consecrates the officer, have been called to witness the solemn ceremonial [p. 155].

Similar statements appear in many others. John Quincy Adams said: "I appear, my fellow citizens, in your presence and in that of heaven to bind myself . . ." (p. 51). "In the presence of this vast assemblage of my countrymen," said Cleveland, "I am about to supplement and seal by the oath which I have taken the manifestation of the will of a great and free people" (p. 151). "I, too, am a witness," noted Eisenhower, "today testifying in your name to the principles and purposes to which we, as a people, are pledged" (p. 263).[15]

Without the presence of "the people," the rite of presidential investiture cannot be completed. The people ratify the President's formal ascent to power by acknowledging his oath, witnessing his enactment of his role, and accepting the principles he lays down to guide his administration. Benjamin Harrison recognized the interdependence of the President and the people in this inaugural act:

The oath taken in the presence of the people becomes a mutual covenant. . . . My promise is spoken; yours unspoken, but not the less real and solemn. The people of every State have here their representatives. Surely I do not misinterpret the spirit of the occasion when I assume that the whole body of the people covenant with me and with each other today to support and defend the Constitution of the Union of the States, to yield willing obedience to all the laws and each to every other citizen his equal civil and political rights [p. 155].

That an inaugural address is an adjunct to or an extension of the oath of office is demonstrated dramatically in the shortest address, Washington's second. After describing himself as "called upon by the voice of my country" to "this distinguished honor," Washington said:

Previous to the execution of any official act of the President, the Constitution requires an oath of office. This oath I am now about to take, and in your presence: That if it shall be found during my administration of the Government I have in any instance violated willingly or knowingly the injunctions thereof, I may (besides incurring constitutional punishment) be subject to the upbraidings of all who are now witnesses of the present solemn ceremony [p. 7].

Although it consists entirely of a presidential reavowal of the constitutional oath, this inaugural also recognized the witnessing role of the audience in the rite of investiture.

That an inaugural address is an extension of the oath of office is certified by many of these speeches.[16] However, one of the more eloquent addresses derived its power in part from its construction as an extension of the oath of office and as an invitation to participate in a mutual covenant. In 1961 each assertion or promise articulated by Kennedy was phrased as a pledge jointly made by leader and people. His litany of mutual pledges culminated in the claim: "In your hands, my fellow citizens, more than mine, will rest the final success or failure of our course" (p. 271). Finally, he explicitly invited audience participation by asking: "Will you join in that historic effort?" (p. 271). By casting his speech as an extension of the oath of office and by inviting the audience to join him in these avowals, Kennedy underscored the ritualistic nature of the occasion.

The force of Lincoln's first inaugural also derived, in part, from his call for audience participation. Lincoln's speech made listeners peculiarly aware that contemplation is a precursor of action.[17] After offering his interpretation of constitutional principles, and defining his audience as those "who really love the Union," Lincoln said:

Before entering upon so grave a matter as the destruction of our national fabric, with all its benefits, its memories, and its hope, would it not be wise to ascertain precisely why we do it? Will you hazard so desperate a step while there is any possibility that any of the ills you fly from have no real existence? Will you, while the certain ills you fly to are greater than all the real ones you fly from, will you risk the commission of so fearful a mistake? [p. 120].

His conclusion drew participation from contemplation: "My countrymen, one and all, think calmly and *well* upon this whole subject" (p. 122), and, in the line paraphrased by Kennedy, he said: "In *your* hands, my dissatisfied fellow-countrymen, and not in *mine*, is the momentous issue of civil war" (p. 122). One reason that Lincoln's first inaugural is a great address is that the audience was asked to participate actively in contemplating the meaning of the constitutional principles Lincoln laid down and in judging whether these principles warranted secession.[18]

Each of the elements forming a presidential inaugural ought to facilitate the President's task of reconstituting his listeners as "the people." The traditional values rehearsed by the President need to be selected and framed in ways that unify the audience. Thus, for example, following a campaign replete with charges that he was an atheist, Jefferson's speech assured former adversaries that he recognized the power of the deity, "acknowledging and adoring an overruling Providence . . . , that Infinite Power which rules the destinies of the universe . . ." (pp. 16–17). Similarly, the founders were eulogized in early inaugurals but disappeared as the Civil War approached. Since Garrison and other abolitionists had widely publicized the founders' slaveholding, public veneration of them would ally a President with those who favored slavery and invite the enmity of its opponents. Van Buren's exceptional reference in 1837 to Washington and the other founders can be explained by his explicitly pro-slavery position.[19] The point to be noted is that when an appeal that was once a unifying recollection of past heroes interferes with the process of reconstituting the audience as a unified people, it is abandoned.

Just as recollection of the past and rehearsal of traditional values need to be non-controversial and unifying, so recommitment to constitutional principles unifies by assuring those who did not vote for this President that he will, nevertheless, scrupulously protect their rights. The same needs to unify the audience and to speak in the epideictic present also influence the language in which Presidents articulate the principles that will govern their administrations.

REHEARSING TRADITIONAL VALUES

To demonstrate his qualifications for the office, the President must venerate the past and show that the traditions of the institution continue unbroken in him. He must affirm that he will transmit the institution intact to his successors. Consequently, language of conservation, preservation, maintenance, and renewal pervades these speeches. What we conserve and renew is often sanctified as our "creed," our "faith," and our "sacred trust." Cleveland's statement in 1885 is illustrative: "On this auspicious occasion we may well renew the pledge of our devotion to the Constitution, which, launched by the founders of the republic and consecrated by their prayers and patriotic devotion, has for almost a century borne the hopes and aspirations of a great people through

209

prosperity and peace and through the shock of foreign conflicts and the perils of domestic strife and vicissitudes" (p. 151).

Presidential use of the principles, policies, and presidencies of the past suggests that, in the inaugural address, *memoria* or shared recollection is a key source of *inventio*, the development of lines of argument. Lincoln's final appeal in his first inaugural illustrates the rhetorical power and resources of the past: "The mystic chords of memory, stretching from every battlefield and patriot grave to every living heart and hearthstone all over this broad land, will yet swell the chorus of the Union, when again touched, as surely they will be, by the better angels of our nature" (p. 123). Coolidge put it more simply: "We cannot continue these brilliant successes in the future, unless we continue to learn from the past" (p. 215). Such use of the past is also consistent with the ritualistic process of representing beginnings, origins, and universal relationships.

The past is conserved by honoring past Presidents. Washington was praised by John and John Quincy Adams, Jefferson, Taylor, and Van Buren; Monroe and Jackson referred to their illustrious predecessors; Lincoln spoke of the distinguished citizens who had administered the executive branch. The past is also conserved by reaffirming the wisdom of past policies. Cleveland, for example, praised policies of Washington, Jefferson, and Monroe (p. 152); McKinley praised the policy of "keeping ourselves free from entanglement, either as allies or foes" (p. 17).

The past is also used analogically to affirm that just as we overcame difficulties in the past, so will we now; the venerated past assures us that the nation has a future. Thus, in 1932, in the face of severe economic problems, Franklin Roosevelt said: "Compared with the perils which our forefathers conquered because they believed and were not afraid, we have still much to be thankful for (p. 232), and in 1941 he reminded his audience of the difficult tasks that confronted Washington and Lincoln (p. 243).

In the world of inaugural addresses, we have inherited our character as a people; accordingly, veneration of the past not only unifies the audience but warrants present and future action, as recurring references to "no entangling alliances" have illustrated. A more recent example is found in the 1981 inaugural in which Reagan paraphrased a statement Jefferson made in 1801. Jefferson said: "Sometimes it is said that man cannot be trusted with the government of himself. Can he, then, be trusted with the government of others?" (p. 16). Reagan said: "But if no one among us is capable of governing himself, then who among us has the capacity to govern someone else?"[20]

As Reagan's use of Jefferson illustrated, a President must go beyond the rehearsal of traditional values and veneration of the past to enunciate a political philosophy that will inform the incoming administration. Because rhetorical scholars have focused on the specific political principles laid down in individual inaugurals, they have often failed to note that although these principles vary from inaugural to inaugural, all inaugurals not only lay down political principles but present and develop such principles in predictable ways.

ENUNCIATING POLITICAL PRINCIPLES

In many inaugurals, presidents indicate that they feel obliged to set forth the principles that will govern their tenure in office. Jefferson's explicit 1801 statement exemplified this: "About to enter, my fellow-citizens, on the exercise of duties which comprehend everything dear and valuable to you, it is proper you should understand what I deem the essential principles of our Government, and consequently those which ought to shape its Administration. . ." (p. 16). In keeping with the epideictic character of inaugurals, however, specific policies are proposed for contemplation, not action. Proposals are not an end in themselves but illustrations of the political philosophy of the speaker. This contemplative, expository function differentiates policy proposals embedded in inaugurals from those in State of the Union addresses, where there is a call to immediate action.[21]

So, for instance, in a relatively detailed statement of his political views, Polk discussed "our revenue laws and the levy of taxes," but this discussion was an *illustration* of the principle that "no more money shall be collected than the necessities of an economical administration shall require" (p. 93). Similarly, he aired his position on the national debt to *illustrate* the principle that "Melancholy is the condition of that people whose government can be sustained only by a system which periodically transfers large amounts from the labor of the many to the coffers of the few. Such a system is incompatible with the ends for which our Republican Government was instituted" (p. 93).

Because Taft conceived the inaugural address as a vehicle for articulating relatively specific policy, his speech provides a rigorous test of the claim that inaugurals deal with principles rather than practices. Taft said: "The office of an inaugural address is to give a summary outline of the main policies of the new administration, so far as they can be anticipated" (p. 189), but his tedious list of recommendations functions not as a call for specific, immediate action, but as evidence of continuity and of loyalty to the Constitution. He said, for example: "I have had the honor

211

to be one of the advisers of my distinguished predecessor, and as such, to hold up his hands in the reforms he has initiated. . . . To render such reforms lasting, however, . . . further legislative and executive action are needed" (p. 189). Such reforms ("the suppression of the lawlessness and abuses of power of the great combinations of capital invested in railroads and in industrial enterprises carrying on interstate commerce") were defined as means of maintaining the democratic character of the government. Again, they became illustrations of following broad principles.

The rite of investiture demands that the President do more than rehearse traditional values and enunciate a political philosophy. He must also enact his presidential role.

ENACTING THE PRESIDENCY

The audience, unifed as "the people," witnesses the investiture of the President. To complete and ratify the President's ascent to power, the inaugural address demonstrates rhetorically that this person can function as a leader within the constitutionally established limits of executive power and that he can perform the public, symbolic role as President of all the people.

The inaugural address is thus performative. It evinces presidential leadership by the very fact of its delivery. As President, the speaker appropriates the country's history and assumes the right to say what that history means; as President, the speaker asserts that some principles are more salient than others at this moment; as President, the speaker constitutes hearers as "the people"; and as President, the speaker asks "the people" to join in a mutual covenant to commit themselves to the political philosophy enunciated in the address.

Franklin Roosevelt's first inaugural dramatically underscored his role as a leader and the special importance of executive action. He spoke of "a leadership of frankness and vigor" and said: "I am convinced that you will again give the support to leadership in these critical days" (p. 231). "This Nation asks for action, and action now" (p. 232), and "With this pledge taken, I assume unhesitatingly the leadership of this great army of our people. . ." (p. 233). However, Roosevelt was aware that he was pressing the limits of executive power. He said:

It is to be hoped that the normal balance of executive and legislative authority may be wholly adequate to meet the unprecedented tasks before us. But it may be that an unprecedented demand and need for undelayed action may call for temporary departure from that normal balance of public procedure. I am prepared under my constitutional duty

212

to recommend the measures that a stricken nation . . . may require. . . . I shall ask Congress for the one remaining instrument to meet the crisis—broad Executive power to wage a war against the emergency, as great as the power that would be given to me if we were in fact invaded by a foreign foe [p. 234].

What is crucial here is that Roosevelt portrayed his leadership as constitutional. Special powers would be conferred by Congress, and those powers would be analogous to the extraordinary powers exercised by previous Presidents in similarly extreme circumstances.

An abiding fear of the misuse of executive power pervades our national history. Washington's opponents accused him of wanting to be king; Jackson was called King Andrew and Van Buren, King Martin; Teddy Roosevelt was attacked in cartoons captioned "Theodore Roosevelt for ever and ever"; Lincoln's abolition of habeas corpus and Franklin Roosevelt's use of executive power as well as his pursuit of a third and fourth term were damned as monarchical, or worse, as despotic.[22] The American Revolution was fought, the Declaration of Independence reminds us, in response to "repeated injuries and usurpations, all having in direct object the establishment of an absolute Tyranny over these States. . . ." To allay fears of incipient tyranny, the incoming President must assure the citizenry that he does not covet power for its own sake and that he recognizes and respects constitutional limits on his authority.

There is a paradox in the demand that a President demonstrate rhetorically a capacity for effective leadership while carefully acknowledging constitutional limitations. To the extent that the speaker promises strong leadership, there is a risk of being seen as an incipient tyrant. By contrast, should the President emphasize the limits on executive power, there is a risk of being seen as an inept or enfeebled leader. Eloquent Presidents have walked this tightrope with agility, as Lincoln did in his first inaugural when he responded to the fear that he would use executive power to abolish slavery: "I have no purpose, directly or indirectly, to interfere with the institution of slavery in the States where it exists" (pp. 117). He attested that this was a consistent position for him by citing statements from his campaign speeches and a plank from the Republican party platform. This material he characterized as "the most conclusive evidence of which the case is susceptible" (p. 117–18). Addressing abolitionist revulsion against the fugitive slave law, he quoted Article 4 of the Constitution and averred that the law was merely an extension of that article, a part of the Constitution he had just sworn to uphold. He added: "I take the official oath to-day with no mental reservations and with no purpose to construe the Constitution or laws by any hypercritical rules" (p. 118).

In recognizing the limits on presidential power, inaugurals not only affirm the balance of power and locate executive initiatives in the mandate of the people, they also offer evidence of humility. The new President humbly acknowledges deficiencies, humbly accepts the burdens of office, and humbly invokes God's blessings. The precedent for evincing humility was set in the first inaugural when Washington said: "[T]he magnitude and difficulty of the trust to which the voice of my country called me, being sufficient to awaken in the wisest and most experienced of her citizens a distrustful scrutiny into his qualifications, could not but overwhelm with despondence one who ought to be peculiarly conscious of his own deficiencies. . ." (p. 3). Washington's attitude was echoed in Carter's less felicitous comment in 1977: "Your strength can compensate for my weakness, and your wisdom can help to minimize my mistakes."[23]

Inaugurals typically place the President and the nation under God, and this, too, is part of the process of acknowledging limits. By calling upon God, the President subordinates himself to a higher power. References to God are not perfunctory. The God of the inaugurals is a personal God who is actively involved in affairs of state, an "Almighty Being whose power regulates the destiny of nations," in the words of Madison (p. 27), a God "who led our fathers," in the words of Jefferson (p. 22), a God who protects us, according to Monroe (p. 38), a God revealed in our history, according to Cleveland (p. 153), and a God who punishes us, according to Lincoln: "He gives to both North and South this terrible war as the woe due to those by whom the offense came. . ." (p. 126). The President enacts the presidential role by placing himself and the nation in God's hands. We should note, however, that it is only when the President is fully invested in office that he has claimed the authority to place the nation "under God." For this reason, perhaps, prayers or prayerlike statements have usually occurred near or at the end of inaugurals. This can explain why Eisenhower called the prayer he delivered prior to his first inaugural "a private prayer." Although he had taken the oath of office, he was not yet fully invested as the President and until he had performed further rhetorical acts of acceptance, he sensed that he lacked the authority to represent the nation before God.

The placement of prayers or prayerlike statements is a subtle indication that the inaugural address is an integral part of the rite of investiture. Some inaugurals have articulated the notion that the President becomes the President *through* delivering the inaugural address. For example, William Henry Harrison concluded his 1841 speech this way: "Fellow citizens, being fully invested with that high office to which the partiality of my countrymen has called me, I now take affectionate leave of you" (p. 86).[24]

If an inaugural address is to function performatively as part of the investiture, the President must speak in his public role as the President. An inaugural would not fulfill this function if the address pressed forward the personality or personal history of the incoming President.[25] When evidence is drawn from the President's personal past, it must reveal something about the presidency or about the people or the nation. Personal narrative is inappropriate in a rhetorical genre designed for the formal display of the President as the President. The functions of personal material in an inaugural are clearly different from the functions of like material in campaign oratory where a high level of self-disclosure and self-aggrandizement is not only appropriate but expected. The functions of self-references also distinguish the inaugural address from other presidential rhetoric.[26]

A dramatic example of inappropriate personal material appeared in the final paragraph of Grant's second inaugural. He concluded: "[T]hroughout the war, and from my candidacy for my present office in 1868 to the close of the last Presidential campaign, I have been the object of abuse and slander scarcely ever equalled in political history, which to-day I feel that I can afford to disregard in view of your verdict, which I gratefully accept as my vindication" (p. 135). The statements speak of Grant, the person, not of the presidency or of Grant, the President. In so doing, the statement called into question Grant's ability to fulfill the symbolic role of President of all the people.

By contrast, Franklin Roosevelt used his personal past effectively. In his fourth inaugural in 1945, he said: "I remember that my old schoolmaster, Dr. Peabody, said, in days that seemed to us then to be secure and untroubled: 'Things in life will not always run smoothly. Sometimes we will be rising toward the heights—then all will seem to reverse itself and start downward. The great fact to remember is that the trend of civilization itself is forever upward; that a line drawn through the peaks and valleys of the centuries always has an upward trend'" (p. 247). It was wartime; this statement brought hope out of tribulation and became the basis for Roosevelt's claim that although the Constitution is a firm foundation, it is still a document open to improvement. The lesson of his mentor allowed Roosevelt to say something he could not have asserted himself as effectively.

More recently, Carter's use of a statement by a former teacher illustrates a potential pitfall in using personal material. Immediately after thanking Gerald Ford for all he had done to heal the divisions in the nation, Carter said: "In this outward and physical ceremony, we attest once again to the inner and spiritual strength of our Nation. As my high school teacher, Miss Julia Coleman, used to say, 'We must adjust to changing times and still hold to unchanging principles.' "[27] As we have argued, the first duty of the President in an inaugural is to reconstitute his audience as "the people." Carter was attempting to forge an American community out of his listeners. However, only certain people have the standing to do that, and Miss Julia Coleman, however able she may have been as a high school teacher, was not one of them. Had Carter made her the voice of the people expressing a timeless truth, Coleman's aphorism might have been appropriate later in the inaugural. Despite Coleman's lack of authority, her adage might have served had it been an unusual, penetrating, immediately intelligible, vivid statement of the relationship between change and continuity. However, even such a claim is questionable. In Carter's statement we have the rhetorical equivalent of what would have occurred had Kennedy said, "To paraphrase my old headmaster, 'ask not what your country can do for you. . . .' "[28]

A presidential inaugural address is part of the process by which the President is invested in office. As a result, the audience expects the presidential role to be enacted: a demonstration of ability to lead, to recognize the limits of executive power, to speak and act in a presidential, rather than a personal, role. A President, as President, can unify the audience as "the people" and lay down the principles that will guide the coming administration. Finally, the President must demonstrate his understanding of the epideictic demands of a ritualistic event.

FULFILLING EPIDEICTIC REQUIREMENTS

The qualities Aristotle ascribes to epideictic discourse are qualities appropriate to ritualistic or ceremonial events. All U.S. presidential inaugurals are speeches of display inviting the audience to evaluate the rhetor's skill in enacting his role. Like other epideictic discourse, they praise or blame, affirm traditional values, heighten what is known and believed, use elegant language, and focus on the eternal present. Great inaugurals express the nuances of the relationship between the people and the President and respond to situational exigencies in a more subtle fashion than their more pedestrian peers. Inaugurals frequently praised include Washington's first, Jefferson's first, Lincoln's first and second, Franklin Roosevelt's first, and Kennedy's. Some add Theodore

Roosevelt's first, Wilson's first, and Franklin Roosevelt's second.[29] These especially admired inaugurals share certain characteristics: (1) they reinvigorate as well as rehearse traditional values; (2) they create memorable phrases that sum up who we are as a people and what the presidency is as an institution; (3) they involve us actively in redefining the nation as embodied in the principles guiding the incoming administration; and (4) they address timely questions timelessly, or, in the words of William Faulkner, their "griefs grieve on universal bones."[30]

Great inaugurals capture complex, situationally resonant ideas in memorable phrases. We still recall Jefferson's "peace, commerce, and honest friendship with all nations, entangling alliances with none" (p. 17) and Lincoln's "With malice toward none, with charity for all, with firmness in the right as God gives us to see the right, let us strive to finish the work we are in, to bind up the nation's wounds, to care for him who shall have borne the battle and for his widow and his orphan, to do all which may achieve and cherish a just and lasting peace among ourselves and with all nations" (p. 126). We remember Franklin Roosevelt's "So, first of all, let me assert my firm belief that the only thing we have to fear is fear itself" (p. 231) and Kennedy's "And so, my fellow Americans, ask not what your country can do for you: Ask what you can do for your country" (p. 271). Such phrases illustrate special rhetorical skill in reinvigorating traditional values; in them familiar ideas become fresh and take on new meaning.

Stylistically and structurally, great presidential inaugurals are suited to contemplation. Through the use of parallelism, for example, Kennedy revived our traditional commitment to the defense of freedom when he said: "[W]e shall pay any price, bear any burden, meet any hardship, support any friend, oppose any foe, in order to assure the survival and success of liberty" (p. 269). The memorable antithesis, 'Let us never negotiate out of fear. But let us never fear to negotiate" (p. 270), was a vivid restatement of our modern tradition of relationship to foreign nations. Kennedy's more famous antithesis asked citizens to contemplate a redefinition of who they were as a people, a redefinition based on sacrifice. Through the use of assonance, Kennedy underscored the nuclear peril when he spoke of "the steady spread of the deadly atom" (p. 270). By arresting attention, such literary devices invite listeners and readers to ponder these ideas, ideas less suited to contemplation when stated in more mundane language.

Inaugurals enable us to consider who and what we are as a people; great inaugurals invite us to see ourselves in new lights, to constitute ourselves as a people in new ways. In 1913, for example, Wilson said:

"We have been proud of our industrial achievement, but we have not hitherto stopped thoughtfully enough to count the human cost. . . . We have come now to the sober second thought" (p. 200). In 1865, Lincoln compelled listeners to consider God's view of the conflict between the North and the South when he said: "Both read the same Bible and pray to the same God, and each invokes His aid against the other. . . . The prayers of both could not be answered. That of neither has been answered fully. The Almighty has His own purposes" (pp. 125–26). In 1961, Kennedy spoke of "a call to bear the burden of a long twilight struggle, year in, and year out . . ." (p. 271), a call that suggested *Götterdämmerung* and denied easy victory or inevitable triumph.[31]

In a special and significant sense, the great inaugurals are timeless. They articulate a perspective that transcends the situation that parented them, and for this reason they retain their rhetorical force. For instance, although Lincoln's first inaugural encompassed the situation of a nation poised on the brink of civil war, Lincoln's message speaks to all situations in which the rights of constituent units are seen to clash with the powers of a central body. Similarly, the eloquent conclusion of Lincoln's second inaugural might be applied today to the wounds that remain in the nation from the conflict over the war in Vietnam. Although Franklin Roosevelt's first inaugural assured his hearers that they, as a people led by Roosevelt, could surmount that economic crisis, it also assures us that Americans can surmount all material problems. Kennedy's inaugural reflected the history of the cold war, but it also expressed the resoluteness required under any circumstances to sustain a struggle against a menacing ideology. Finally, George Washington's inaugural not only spoke to the immediate crisis but articulated what Arthur Schlesinger calls "a great strand that binds them [the inaugurals] together."[32] Washington said: "The preservation of the sacred fire of liberty and the destiny of the republican model of government are justly considered, perhaps, as *deeply*, as *finally* staked on the experiment intrusted to the hands of the American people" (pp. 4–5).

The great inaugurals not only re-present this fundamental idea, they reenact the process by which the President and the people "form a more perfect union." In recreating this mutual covenant, great inaugurals both reconstitute the audience as "the people," they constitute us as a people in some new way: as those entrusted with the success or failure of the democratic experiment (Washington I), as members of a perpetual Union (Lincoln I), as a people whose spiritual strength can overcome material difficulties (Franklin Roosevelt I), as a people willing to sacrifice for an ideal (Kennedy), as a people capable of counting the costs of industrial

218

development (Wilson I), as members of an international community (Wilson II), as limited by the purposes of the Almighty (Lincoln II), as a people able to transcend political differences (Washington I, Jefferson I). Notably, the great inaugurals dramatically illustrate the processes of change within a continuous tradition. In them, the resources of epideictic ritual are yoked to political renewal.

We have identified four major elements that constitute the American presidential inaugural as a genre. Our analysis suggests the processes by which a distinctive kind of epideictic rhetoric comes into being. Its broadest parameters are set by the general characteristics of epideictic discourse. A specific kind of ceremony and occasion refines the genre further. In this case, the presidential inaugural is part of a rite of passage, of investiture, a rite that establishes a special relationship between speaker and audience. The demands of investiture require a mutual covenant, a rehearsal of fundamental political values, an enunciation of political principles, and the enactment of the presidential persona.

The conventions of this rhetorical type also emerge because the Presidents we elect know the tradition and tend to study past inaugurals before formulating their own. So, for example, in 1809 in the sixth inaugural, Madison said: "Unwilling to depart from examples of the most revered authority, I avail myself of the occasion now presented to express the profound impression made on me by the call of my country" (p. 25).[33] Over time, earlier presidential inaugurals have frequently been quoted, especially those of Washington, Jefferson, Lincoln, and Franklin Roosevelt. This process of rhetorical introversion illuminates some remarkable coincidences. Harding and Carter, for example, quoted the same verse from Micah. Franklin Roosevelt and Carter quoted a former teacher; Franklin Roosevelt and Kennedy had a rendezvous with destiny, Reagan paraphrased Jefferson, Nixon paraphrased Kennedy, Kennedy echoed Lincoln, Polk rephrased Jackson, Reagan echoed Kennedy. In other words, Presidents recognize, capitalize on, and are constrained by the inaugurals of their predecessors which, taken together, form a tradition.

As we have said, presidential inaugurals are shaped by their epideictic character, by inauguration as a rite of investiture, and by the inaugural tradition. However, presidential inaugurals vary. What makes the U.S. presidential inaugural a genre is that the variation is of a certain sort. Circumstances vary as do the personalities of the presidents, but the variation among inaugurals is predictable.

Inaugural addresses vary substantively because presidents choose to rehearse aspects of our tradition that are consistent with the party or political philosophy they represent. Such selective emphasis is illustrated in Franklin Roosevelt's second inaugural address, in which he said:

Instinctively we recognize a deeper need—the need to find through government the instrument of our united purpose to solve for the individual the ever-rising problems of a complex civilization... In this we Americans were discovering no wholly new truth; we were writing a new chapter in our book of self-government.... The essential democracy of our Nation and the safety of our people depend not upon the absence of power, but upon lodging it with those whom the people can change or continue at stated intervals through an honest and free system of elections.... [W]e have made the exercise of all power more democratic; for we have begun to bring private autocratic powers into their proper subordination to the people's government... (pp. 237–38).

Later, he added: "Today we reconsecrate our country to long-cherished ideals in a suddenly changed civilization" (p. 240). Similarly, in 1981, Ronald Reagan chose to emphasize facets of the system in order to affirm values consistent with his conservative political philosophy. He said: "Our government has no power except that granted it by the people. It is time to check and reverse the growth of government which shows signs of having grown beyond the consent of the governed."[34]

A major variation occurs in inaugurals delivered by incumbent Presidents. Because a covenant already exists between a reelected President and "the people," the need to reconstitute the community is less urgent. Because the country is familiar with a sitting President's political philosophy, the requirement of stating one's philosophy is also muted. Reelected Presidents tend to recommit themselves to principles articulated in their prior inaugurals or to highlight only those principles relevant to the agenda for the coming term. In this respect, subsequent inaugurals by the same President tend to be extensions, not replications, of earlier inaugurals.

The inaugural addresses themselves articulate the reason for this generic variation. For instance, although he was a President in the midst of the most serious of crises, Lincoln said:

At this second appearing to take the oath of the Presidential office there is less occasion for an extended address than there was at the first. Then a statement somewhat in detail of the course to be pursued seemed fitting and proper. Now, at the expiration of four years, during which public declarations have been constantly called forth on every point and phase of the great contest which still absorbs the attention and engrosses the energies of the nation, little that is new could be presented (p. 125).[35]

220

Some Presidents have used a subsequent inaugural to review the trials and successes of their earlier terms. In so doing, they have rehearsed the immediate past, a move rarely made in first inaugurals. When subsequent inaugurals develop specific policies, these are usually described as continuations of policies initiated in the previous term, continuations presumably endorsed by the President's reelection.

Special conditions faced by some Presidents have caused some subsequent inaugurals to resemble first inaugurals. For example, in 1917 Wilson said: "This is not the time for retrospect. It is time rather to speak our thoughts and purposes concerning the present and the immediate future" (p. 203). In the face of the events of World War I: "We are provincials no longer. The tragic events of the thirty months of vital turmoil through which we have just passed have made us citizens of the world. There can be no turning back. Our own fortunes as a nation are involved whether we would have it so or not" (p. 204). The war prompted Wilson to constitute "the people" in a new way, as citizens of the world. Similarly, the events leading to World War II affected Franklin Roosevelt's choices in 1941. He said: "In this day the task of the people is to save the Nation and its institutions from disruptions from without" (p. 243). That statement of "the task" diverged sharply from the principles emphasized in 1933 and 1937.

CONCLUSION

Variability in inaugural addresses is evidence of an identifiable cluster of elements that fuse to form the *essential* inaugural act. Each apparent variation is an emphasis on or a development of one or more of the key elements we have described. Washington's second inaugural address underscored the role of the audience as witnesses and the address as an extension of the oath of office. Jefferson's first address was a call to unity through the enunciation of political principles; Lincoln's first inaugural was a dramatic appeal to the audience to join in the mutual covenant between the President and the people; his second was an exploration of what it means to say that this nation is "under God." Theodore Roosevelt explored the meaning of our "sacred trust" as it applies to a people with an international role; Franklin Roosevelt's first address explored the nature of executive leadership and the limits of executive power, whereas his second constituted the audience as a caring people; Wilson's first inaugural explored the meaning of U.S. industrial development. Finally, Kennedy's address exploited the possibilities of the noble, dignified, literary language characteristic of the epideictic to such an extent that his address is sometimes attacked for stylistic excess.[36]

221

The U.S. presidential inaugural as a genre, then, must reconstitute "the people" as an audience that can witness the rite of investiture. The inaugural must rehearse communal values from the past, set forth the political principles that will guide the new administration, and demonstrate that the President can enact the presidential persona appropriately. Still more generally, the presidential inaugural address is an epideictic ritual that is formal, unifying, abstract, and eloquent; at the core of this ritual lies epideictic timelessness—the fusion of the past and future of the nation in an eternal present in which we reaffirm what Franklin Roosevelt called "our covenant with ourselves" (p. 247): a covenant between the executive and the nation that is the essence of democratic government.

Notes

1. Arthur Schlesinger, Jr., Introduction to *The Chief Executive: Inaugural Addresses of the Presidents of the United States from George Washington to Lyndon B. Johnson* (New York: Crown Publishers, 1965), p. vi.

2. Ibid., p. vii. Generally, the literary quality of presidential discourse is not high. For example, in announcing that Thomas Jefferson's autobiographical writings and public papers would be included in the Library of America series, Daniel Aaron, president of the selection committee, commented that the works of only a few additional presidents—Lincoln, Grant, Wilson, and both Roosevelts—were likely to be included. The criteria for selection are literary, not political, and, in Aaron's words, "Some could write well, others were wooden." (Cited by Herbert Mitgang, "Jefferson's Prose Joins Library of America Series," *New York Times*, May 28 1984, p. 15Y.)

3. We are concerned here exclusively with addresses delivered every four years, following presidential elections. For an analysis of speeches by ascendant vice presidents, see Kathleen Hall Jamieson and Karlyn Kohrs Campbell, "Rhetorical Hybrids: Fusions of Generic Elements," *Quarterly Journal of Speech* 68 (May 1982):146–57.

4. Aristotle, *Rhetoric*, trans. W. Rhys Roberts, (New York: Modern Library, 1954), 1358b.12. Subsequent citations from the *Rhetoric* are identified in parenthesis in the text.

5. John W. O'Malley, *Praise and Blame in Renaissance Rome: Rhetoric, Doctrine, and Reform in the Sacred Orators of the Papal Court, c. 1450–1521* (Durham, N.C.: Duke University Press, 1979), p. 40.

6. Ibid., p. 63.

7. Harry Caplan, Introduction to *Rhetorica ad herennium* (Cambridge, Mass.: Harvard University Press, 1954), p. 173.

8. James L. Hoban, Jr., "Rhetorical Rituals of Rebirth," *Quarterly Journal of Speech* 66 (October 1980):282–83.

9. According to historian John McCollister in his book *So Help Me God* (Minneapolis, Minn.: Landmark Books, 1982), George Washington ad libbed the additional words "so help me God" in taking the oath of office, although these words are not part of the oath specified in the Constitution. His addition has

become part of the convention of the ceremony. (Cited by Francis X. Clines, "Presidents and Churchgoing, a Sensitive Subject," *New York Times*, March 23, 1982, p. 12Y.)

10. The idea of a rhetorical genre as a constellation of elements governed by a dynamic principle is developed in Karlyn Kohrs Campbell and Kathleen Hall Jamieson, "Form and Genre in Rhetorical Criticism: An Introduction," in Karlyn Kohrs Campbell and Kathleen Hall Jamieson, eds., *Form and Genre: Shaping Rhetorical Action*, (Falls Church, Va.: Speech Communication Association, 1978), pp. 9–32.

11. Mircea Eliade, *Patterns in Comparative Religion*, trans. Rosemary Sheed (Cleveland, Ohio: World Publishing Co., 1970), p. 392; cited in David Cole, *The Theatrical Event: A Mythos, A Vocabulary, A Perspective* (Middletown, Conn.: Wesleyan University Press, 1975), p. 8.

12. Davis Newton Lott, *The Presidents Speak: The Inaugural Addresses of the American Presidents from Washington to Nixon* (rev. ed.; New York: Holt, Rinehart & Winston, 1969), p. 243. Subsequent citations from inaugurals delivered through 1969 are from this source and are identified by page numbers in parentheses in the text and in subsequent notes.

13. Dumas Malone, *Jefferson and His Time*, vol. 4, *Jefferson the President: First Term, 1801–1805*, 4 vols. (Boston: Little, Brown, 1970), p. 20. Malone comments that Jefferson did not capitalize these key words and turn them into party names. (Cited in Gregg Phifer, "Two Inaugurals: A Second Look," *Southern Speech Communication Journal* 48 [Summer 1983] 385).

14. See, *e.g.*, Buchanan's 1857 address, which followed an election held during the conflict between pro- and anti-slavery forces in "bloody Kansas" (p. 111); Hayes's inaugural of 1877 (pp. 140–41); Cleveland's inaugural of 1885 (p. 151); Benjamin Harrison's address in 1889 (p. 162); Cleveland's speech in 1893 (p. 168); and Nixon's address in 1969 (p. 280), in addition to those cited in the text.

15. See, among others, Lincoln's first (p. 117) and McKinley's first (p. 171).

16. Van Buren spoke of "an avowal of the principles that will guide me . . ." (p. 65); Buchanan repeated the oath at the beginning of his address (p. 111); Cleveland referred to his speech as a supplement to the oath of office (p 151); Eisenhower said: "We are called as a people to give testimony in the sight of the world to our faith that the future shall belong to the free" (p. 257); Lyndon Johnson said: "[T]he oath I have taken before you and before God is not mine alone, but ours together" (p. 275).

For discussion of another rhetorical covenant pertinent to presidential discourse, see Roderick P. Hart, *The Political Pulpit* (West Lafayette, Ind. Purdue University Press, 1977), pp. 43–65.

17. For a discussion of this dimension of epideictic rhetoric, see Chaim Perelman and L. Olbrechts-Tyteca, *The New Rhetoric: A Treatise on Argumentation*, trans. John Wilkinson and Purcell Weaver (Notre Dame, Ind. University of Notre Dame Press, 1969), pp. 49–51.

18. Garfield made a moving plea that echoed Lincoln's first inaugural. In 1881 he said: "My countrymen, we do not now differ in our judgment concerning the controversies of past generations, and fifty years hence our children will not be divided in their opinions concerning our controversies. They will surely bless their fathers and their fathers' God that the Union was preserved,

that slavery was overthrown, and that both races were made equal before the law. We may hasten or we may retard, but we can not prevent, the final reconciliation. Is it not possible for us now to make a truce with time by anticipating and accepting its inevitable verdict?" (p. 146).

In a footnote to his analysis of Nixon's first inaugural, Robert L. Scott called attention to Nixon's excessive use of the pronoun "I." Such personal references, discussed below, not only violate the presidential persona that the speaker should assume but, as Scott noted, they also tend to preclude the joint action through which the President and the people covenant together. (See "Rhetoric That Postures: An Intrinsic Reading of Richard M. Nixon's Inaugural Address," *Western Speech* 34 [Winter 1970]. p. 47.)

19. The extent to which the founders, including George Washington, were identified with pro-slavery positions was illustrated by John C. Calhoun, speaking in the Senate on March 4, 1850. He said: "Nor can the Union be saved by invoking the name of the illustrious Southerner whose mortal remains repose on the western bank of the Potomac. He was one of us—a slaveholder and a planter. We have studied his history, and find nothing in it to justify submission to wrong." (Text as in A. Craig Baird, ed., *American Public Addresses, 1740–1952* [New York: McGraw-Hill, 1956], p. 83.)

20. Ronald Reagan, "Inaugural Address," *Vital Speeches of the Day* 47 (Feb. 15, 1981):258–59. Bert E. Bradley, "Jefferson and Reagan: The Rhetoric of Two Inaugurals," *Southern Speech Communication Journal* 48 (Winter 1983): 119–36, is an extended comparison of the inaugural addresses of 1801 and 1981.

21. Kathleen Hall Jamieson, *Critical Anthology of Public Speeches* (Chicago: Science Research Associates, 1978), pp. 28–30.

22. Marcus Cunliffe, *American Presidents and the Presidency* (New York: American Heritage Press, 1968), pp. 149, 152, 154–55, 158, 163, 172.

23. Carter's statement calls attention to the risks involved in confessing limitations. This remark could be taken as evidence of inability to lead forcefully.

24. In 1877 Rutherford B. Hayes expressed similar sentiments as he began his address: "We have assembled to repeat the public ceremonial, begun by Washington, observed by all my predecessors, and now a time-honored custom, which marks the commencement of a new term of the Presidential office" (p. 137).

25. See material from Scott cited in n. 18, above.

26. Roderick P. Hart's computerized analysis of 380 presidential speeches generated an 8.01 level of self-reference (all first-person pronouns were counted). By contrast, the nine inaugurals in this sample generate a 1.12 level of self-reference. (See *Verbal Style and the Presidency* [Orlando, Fla.: Academic Press, 1984], pp. 273, 279.) A further refinement of self-referencing has been made by Dan Hahn, who noted that in 1977 Carter used "we" forty-three times, "our" thirty-six times, but "I" only six times in his inaugural. (See "The Power of Rhetorical Form," a paper presented at the Fourth Annual Conference on Discourse Analysis, Temple University, March 1983, p. 6.)

27. Jimmy Carter, "Inaugural Address," *Public Papers of the Presidents of the United States*, Jimmy Carter, 1977, Book I (Washington, D.C.: U.S. Government Printing Office, 1977), p. 1.

28. The Rev. George St. John, headmaster of Choate, the preparatory school in Wallingford, Conn., attended by John F. Kennedy, used to say to his students,

"Ask not what your school can do for you; ask what you can do for your school" ("Walter Scott's Personality Parade," *Parade,* Dec. 15, 1968, p. 2).

29. Schlesinger, *The Chief Executive,* p. vii.

30. William Faulkner, "Nobel Prize Speech," in Stewart H. Benedict, ed., *Famous American Speeches* (New York: Dell, 1967), p. 223.

31. A number of other inaugurals include admonitions. See, e.g., the addresses of Eisenhower in 1957 (p. 264), Truman (p. 252), and Harding (p. 211).

32. Schlesinger, *The Chief Executive,* p. vii.

33. Eight years later, in 1817, Monroe said: "In commencing the duties of the chief executive office it has been the practice of the distinguished men who have gone before me to explain the principles which would govern them in their respective Administrations. In following their venerated example my attention is naturally drawn to the great causes which have contributed in a principal degree to produce the present happy condition of the United States" (p. 33).

34. Reagan, "Inaugural Address," p. 259.

35. In 1805 Jefferson reported that his conscience told him he had lived up to the principles he had espoused four years earlier (p. 19). In 1821 Monroe said: "If the person thus elected has served the preceding term, an opportunity is afforded him to review its principal occurrences and to give the explanation respecting them as in his judgment may be useful to his constituents" (p. 41).

36. E.g., Garry Wills wrote: "The famous antitheses and alliterations of John Kennedy's rhetoric sound tinny now" (*The Kennedy Imprisonment: A Meditation on Power* [New York: Pocket Books, 1982], p. 312).

More detailed treatments of the style of John Kennedy's inaugural address include Edward P. J. Corbett, "Analysis of the Style of John F. Kennedy's Inaugural Address," *Classical Rhetoric for the Modern Student* (2d ed.; New York: Oxford University Press, 1971), pp. 554–65; and Sam Meyer, "The John F. Kennedy Inauguration Speech: Function and Importance of Its 'Address System,' " *Rhetoric Society Quarterly* 12 (1982):239–50.

8

Bruce E. Gronbeck

RONALD REAGAN'S ENACTMENT OF THE PRESIDENCY IN HIS 1981 INAUGURAL ADDRESS

In moments of cultural transition, members of societies assemble to mark the transition ceremonially. The ceremonies performed at such moments link past with present and even future in symbolic acts of *remembrance, legitimation,* and *celebration:*

1. In ceremonies of transition, the past is selectively recited and ideologically interpreted so that its heroes may provide contemporary role models, so that its villains may be made consubstantial with contemporary enemies, and so that its myths may be employed to explain the collectivity's origins, present circumstances, and future glory.

2. The past also is an ally of legitimation processes, a vehicle for sanctifying institutional authority, authorizing acts of power, and articulating codes of collective as well as individual conduct. Because the past is thus an individual's and a culture's source of orientation, it is called up at times of sociopolitical transition so as to renew the collectivity's fundamental commitments to institutions, agencies of social control, and perceptions of what it means to be a "citizen" of the culture.

3. And the past is celebrated at times of transition. Celebratory actions can be motivated by diverse mutual needs, including a need to glorify past triumphs in hopes of future victories; a need to rehearse past orderly transitions so as to forestall disorderly transitions (coups, revolts) in the future; and, perhaps, a need to compare venerated heroes with a newly anointed leader in hopes that a Reign of Virtue will characterize the new leader's governance.

Ceremonies of cultural transition, then, are called for in moments of cultural fissure, in moments when mundane business-as-usual is interrupted. They require symbolic acts, both verbal and nonverbal, to smooth that transition and sometimes to heal a breach. More specifically, we can distinguish between *cyclical* and *unexpected* transitions. Often, the fissure is expected, even cyclical, as in presidential elections; at other times, the break is unexpected, leading to a sense of cultural rupture, as

226

when a President is assassinated. Unexpected cultural ruptures are inevitably accompanied by some degree of cultural anxiety, which adds deepened negative emotions to the ceremonies.[1] Cyclical and unexpected cultural fissures, then, can place varied demands upon rhetors; yet, because the break in civic business-as-usual is always minimally disturbing but may be strongly destructive, ceremonies of transition at base must provide collective reorientation for members of the culture. Themes of *time* and *space* pervade speeches delivered within these ceremonies precisely because our sense of temporal and spatial orders is our primary source of collective positioning. Liturgies—a concept coming from Greek etymological roots meaning, roughly, "folk-works"—are behavioral formulae that repeatedly define and position a collectivity temporally and spatially.

In American experience, we discover all manner of ceremonial discourses and other actions used to connect past and future. The speeches made are not confined to such persistent genres as the keynote speech, the commencement address, and the funeral oration for heads of state. They include, too, such archaic, quasi-religious forms as the thanksgiving sermon and the artillery election sermon.[2]

Each of these—and other—genres of political and quasi-religious speaking entails, in Berger and Luckmann's language, "reiterated performance of . . . [institutions'] prescribed roles by living actors."[3] The roles performed and performed again in ceremonial discourses sustain social institutions. That particular roles are performed rhetorically time after time does not mean the rhetoric of those performances is "empty." Ritualistic rhetoric often contains a discourse of power; observance of traditional forms gives formalisms the power to guide and constrain the consciousness of all those who participate in the rituals. Choices of terms, rhetorical amplification and diminution, themes emphasized and neglected, depiction and other imagistic devices of discourse—all these *define*, for the time being, the institutions that authorize the ritual or rhetorical ceremony.

The case studies in Part II focus on a single instance of one of the most traditional of rhetorical genres, the American inaugural address. We examine a single instance of that genre, the first presidential inaugural address by Ronald Reagan, delivered in 1981. The goal of this essay is to demonstrate the *institutional* implications of the presidential role as played out in that speech by President Reagan. In so doing, I hope to add credence to the much broader thesis that "empty" rhetoric of the type we normally associate with such ceremonial rhetorical performances as inaugural addresses is, in fact, not socioculturally or functionally empty

227

at all. It is discourse that defines institutions and restrains or opens their future development.

To accomplish my specific and more general goals, I shall venture outside the strictly American context of such discourse. "Inauguration," understood here as a series of symbolic acts undertaken since ancient ages by virtually all cultures in moments of change in leadership, transcends cultural boundaries. Taking the concept back to its primordial beginnings should help us better to understand the functions, forms, and *materia* of the American presidential inaugural, and, in particular, to assess the competency with which President-elect Ronald Reagan inaugurated his presidency in 1981.

INAUGURATION IN CIVIL CEREMONIES

As an act of cultural transition, inauguration is at once *an expression of hope* and *a rite of elevation*. That is, when changing leaders, cultures seek to articulate hope for future prosperity in new phases of their existence in much the same way they do during all forms of commencement ceremonies—graduation, ordination, Bar Mitzvahs, first Communions. The hope for future prosperity is founded upon both qualities of the leader being given office and traditional values being reasserted. More than that, the grounds for hope must be made explicit, given the vagaries and uncertainties that govern life. Like the augurs of old, modern societies still search for favorable signs of good luck. As a rite of elevation, inauguration must function to distance a leader from his or her people, for civil power must be exercised at a distance, not only physically in some "special place" but also psychologically by a "special person."

To secure a clearer picture of the grounds for hope and the dynamics of elevation, we should consider the arts of augury, which etymologically and connotatively ground our current rituals of inauguration, and the acts of investiture, which comprise enduring ceremonies of elevation. Augury and investiture, as facets of cultures' civil religions, inform or embed more modern notions of inauguration; therein we shall find clues to the forms and *materia* used to execute the functions of remembrance, legitimation, and celebration.

AUGURY

The divining *collegium*, tradition has it, was founded by Romulus for the purpose of consulting the *auspicii* ("auspices") in times of govern-

228

mental action or election. The *collegium*, later called the Augures, originally consisted of three patricians. By the period of the empire and well into the 4th century A.D., the number had been raised to sixteen, with each well-bred patrician and plebian augur serving for life. A reading of the auspices or "signs of the times"—an *augurium*—was taken any time a governmental institution or officer faced an important decision. *Comitia* and other centers for public business could not start without "inauguration"; generals would not cross rivers or enter battle without favorable signs; if a constitutional act were called into question, the college of augurs had the power to determine if there were a flaw (*vitium*) in it; and—important to our purposes—every officer took the auspices upon entering office.

The primary signs included the presence, flight patterns, and cries of eagles and vultures (*alites*) as well as of ravens, owls, and crows (*oscines*). All of these nighttime observations occurred from a tent, amid liturgical incantations.[4] Other signs included the eating habits of chickens, the movements of other animals, and thunder and lightning in the heavens. Even the falling or movements of natural objects were observed by augurs.

Now, of course, more than a millennium and a half have passed since the days of the augurs, yet our contemporary ceremonies of inauguration certainly are traceable to augury, and, indeed, I think modern inaugurations carry with them associations from ancient ages. In part, a contemporary inauguration involves a reading of the auspices and an assessment of future prosperity and good luck. Yet our sociopolitical structures differ significantly from those of the Roman empire. In the United States we have collapsed the priestly offices of the *colleqium* into the civic office of the Presidency. We expect a President both to project our future and to execute policies consistent with that vision. Regarding actual priestly offices, we possess only facsimiles of them. The Fourth Estate, the press, has taken upon itself the functions of divination. For us, the arts of augury are practiced by the chief political officer and by sets of social observers who see themselves as both the mirrors and the shapers of public consciousness.

Given the American civil religion and its reliance on mass-mediated voices, political augury—especially but not only at moments of cultural transition—occurs within the discourse of both inaugurees and the institutional commentators upon the ceremony. So, when we analyze Ronald Reagan's inaugural speech of 1981, we shall see him projecting his rationale for sociopolitical optimism. Like every other new President, he will read the "signs of the times" as he sees them. We shall need to

229

compare his readings with those of the many commentators who took notice of his "good luck" in being able to announce the release of the Iranian hostages shortly after his speech; of his selection of the west steps of the Capitol for his speech, thereby drawing attention visually to monuments to cultural achievement; and of the gala atmosphere of his inaugural balls. Both in Washington and around the country, a gala atmosphere was created as a vehicle for uplifting the national governors and for revitalizing the country's spirits after the gloomy last days of Jimmy Carter's administration.

In general, then, while America's sociopolitical institutions differ formally from those of Rome, as a culture we at least analogously have the auspices read when presidents, governors, and other executive officers are inaugurated.

INVESTITURE

If one of the primary metaphysical characteristics of inauguration is rooted in ceremonies of divination, another draws even more heavily from ancient rites of investiture. These, of course, vary from culture to culture, yet all investiture rites spring from a common foundation—practices that literally and symbolically allow an individual to "put on" an important religious or civic office. Even today, a church bishop dons robes, headgear, staff, and ring, each item of adornment signifying some aspect of power and authority. Just so, the ancient Roman *consul*, in being granted *imperium*, or power, by the Roman citizens assembled, whole, in the *comita centuriata*, took to himself the ivory necklace, the bundle of rods and two axes known as *fasces*, and the imperial *toga*. His corporeal body thus was literally fitted "inside" the institutional body of office.

The parallel between the first-century-B.C. *consul* and the contemporary American President can be extended. The *consul*, as a civic creature given power by the people and offered ratification by the Roman Senate, and a President, as a similar creature given power by the people in election and ratified by the Electoral College, both draw their powers, responsibilities, and limitations from remarkably similar fountainheads. And both Roman *consules* and American Presidents are expected to imprint those offices with their own marks or signatures. The Roman *consul*, as a civic-priestly ruler, was allowed (within limits) to pursue his own interpretations of the ancient Twelve Tables of Law. Roman history—its *res gestae* or record of "things done"—was largely a record of consular accomplishment; and indeed, until in later years it became

230

customary to identify the passing of political time by referring to emperors' appellations, Roman historical periods always were named after individual *consules*. Such was the power of "signature" or imprint upon urban, rural, and provincial business. In this country, we, too, expect individual Presidents to take on administrative and other executive duties, and also to guide the political state by offering legislative programs, proposing and pursuing foreign policies, setting the tone for public and personal morality. We even tend to identify political epochs by referring to presidential tenures-of-office, as in "Jeffersonian America" or "Jacksonian America."

Rites of investiture, then, are paradoxical ceremonies. On the one hand, a person puts on a *persona*—an officer puts on the Office. Someone who was merely a citizen-individual becomes an institutional personage. One who was merely a frail, temptation-prone, perhaps vain and limited human being is expected by the collectivity almost magically to be sagacious, temperate, wise, loyal, compassionate, and everything else we associate with benign governance. Yet, on the other hand, because "the Office" is only a symbolic abstraction—a role or civil fiction that takes "real" form only when *someone* plays that role or lives out that fiction—rites of investiture must give explicit, concrete expression to the Office. As members of the American culture, we can come to know, to understand, and to respond to the Office only insofar as we can see it exercised by somebody. The *Presidency* is in actuality but a succession-of-acts carried out by *Presidents*. In rites of investiture, therefore, citizen-witnesses participate in a bimodal ceremony, one that is simultaneously an *evocation* (a "calling up" of the Office) and an *embodiment* (a "physical expression" of the Office).[5]

If we think about inauguration in general, conscious of the ancient conceptions of augury and investiture, the following characterization of inaugural processes seems compelling and justified: in times of cultural transition—particularly of political transition—societies institute ceremonies of inauguration. The act of naming a new leader is a grave, serious act liable to produce either good or bad collective luck, so we look for the auspices, signs of good fortune. Further, the granting of *imperium* requires symbolic elevation of the leader-elect. Symbolic elevation is required in part because the Office itself is institutional and hence abstract. It is symbolically alive only in the collective consciousness that resides in written and unwritten constitutions: in an important sense, it thus exists "above" mundane reality. Yet the granting of *imperium* requires concrete descent to the level of living human beings, for actual

231

power is exercised or expressed only in the deeds and words of the persons evoking and embodying the Offices.

Thus we may define an inauguration ceremony as a ritual whereby an institutional role is called up or evoked symbolically and then expressed or embodied by the person filling it, amid positive auspices or fortuitous signs that point to future prosperity and fortune. In inaugural ceremonies, a social or mythic reality is articulated, and a leader-persona assumes and expresses power.

Given the analysis I have just presented, a competently performed inaugural ceremony should function to (1) legitimize both a leader and the culture (understood here as a web-of-collective-meanings); (2) celebrate the transition of leadership and followership; and (3) offer collective reassurance that the leader has the knowledge, wisdom, and vision to protect the culture from both internal and external devils, and to carry the society successfully into the future. Given what I have said about the need to link past with present and future so as to remember, to legitimate, and to celebrate, these ceremonial outcomes depend fundamentally upon discourse and other human acts that integrate the temporal and spatial orders so as to reorient the witnesses to the ceremony. I hope to show later that the functions that inauguration ceremonies must perform are most clearly visible in the ways in which inaugurees treat references to time and place as they seek to evoke and embody the office to which they have been elevated.

REAGAN'S 1981 INAUGURAL

Before we can assess Ronald Reagan's competence at performing the rites of augury and investiture associated with presidential ascension to office, we need to describe the features of his address that are germane to such judgments. I shall organize these features under two headings, formal or structuring characteristics of the speech, and attempts to fulfill the transitional functions of remembrance, legitimation, and celebration.[6]

More specifically, speakers select patterns of arrangement, connective words, and grammatical "voices" for *strategic* purposes. Organizational patterns provide conceptual maps demonstrating relationships between and among the ideas being articulated; connective words put those ideas in particular relationships with each other; and, voices—first, second, and third person—in discourse formally bind the speaker and audience into particular associations (as "we" unites them, "I" and "you" separate them, "we" and "they" gather a collectivity and divide it from another, etc.). Examining such "small" formal elements as connectives and voice, especially, is important, for they give us clues to the conceptual configurations into which ideas are being put and to the personal force the rhetor believes his or her voice has.[7] Once we have carried out this sort of close textual analysis, we can move easily from questions of form and material into an analysis of function. Our analysis of the functions of Reagan's first inaugural will be informed determinatively by what we shall have seen about Reagan's attempts to offer his constituents a temporal and spatial orientation to their place in history and the world today.

FORMAL AND MATERIAL CHARACTERISTICS OF THE SPEECH

The elements of form and material in which I am interested are arrayed in table 8.1. Let us locate these elements through a review of the speech section by section.

Introduction. The one-paragraph salutation, offered in the usual mode

Table 8.1 Formal Characteristics of Reagan's 1981 Inaugural Address

Paragraphs*	Segment of the Speech/Subject Matter	Mode-of-Address ("Person")
	Introduction	
1	Salutation	2nd, singular and plural
2–7	Announcement of transition	1st singular, 3rd plural
	Body	
8–28	Overview of domestic programs	1st singular (3rd plural in paragraph 22)
29–39	Valuative guides to conduct	1st singular, 1st plural
40–55	Expression of commitments	1st singular, 2nd plural, blending into 3rd plural
56–65	Overview of foreign policy	1st plural
	Conclusion	
66–75	Review of heroes (temporally and spatially)	1st singular, with referents in 3rd singular
76–81	Martin Treptow as Everyman	narrative 3rd singular, ending in 1st plural
82–83	Requirements for all	1st plural
84	Divine blessing	2nd-plural

* These paragraphs are set and numbered as in "Inaugural Address[,] Ronald Reagan," Wil A. Linkugel et al., eds., *Contemporary American Speeches; A Sourcebook of Speech Forms and Principles,* 5th ed.; (Dubuque, Iowa: Kendall/Hunt, 1982), pp. 374–80. They have drawn the text, in turn, from *Vital Speeches of the Day,* Feb. 15, 1981, pp. 258–60.

of direct address, is unexceptional (except, perhaps, for the fact that it does not identify the Chief Justice or the former President by name). More interesting, though not atypical, is the announcement of the transition-of-power treated in paragraphs 2–7. In using the first-person singular and plural in this section, Reagan is expressing both a personal and a collective commitment to the efficacy and efficiency of American political transition. His references to "the orderly transfer of authority" and "the continuity which is the bulwark of our republic" open the temporal themes that will dominate several sections of the discourse.

Body. After an almost perfunctory introduction, paragraph 8 starts the address proper, announcing the longest section of the speech—his treatment of domestic issues. This section breaks into three subsections.

Paragraphs 8–28 develop Reagan's overview of our domestic programs. By using the first-person plural predominantly, he makes America's problems—largely economic problems—shared phenomena. His only employment of a different mode of address comes in paragraph 22, when he refers to "special interest groups" without mentioning any specifically. Overall the audience is left with the impression that they share problems brought on by faceless, nameless interests (including government) existing outside themselves.

In paragraphs 29–39, the President offers a series of precepts and other guides-to-conduct for extricating America from its fiscal woes. Highlighting both personal and collective commitments with alternation of first-person singular and plural constructions, he first phrases the common commitments to "idealism," "fair play," "peace," "power . . . granted by the people," and the need "to curb the size and influence of the Federal establishment." He also expresses his personal intention *not* "to do away with government" (paragraph 34). The last five paragraphs in this section return to the first-person plural to express, using antitheses, what government is and is not. Interestingly, the precepts recited at the beginning of the section are drawn from campaign speeches; yet, forsaking his campaigning habits, Reagan works hard to emphasize their positive rather than negative force, through personal disavowal and the antithetical sharpening of valuative implications.

Having discussed problems and laid valuative foundations for solutions, Reagan moves into the third subsection (paragraphs 40–55). This subsection is reminiscent in tone of John Kennedy's exhortations. The performative thrust of the inaugural process is heightened brilliantly in these sixteen paragraphs. Echoing Kennedy, Reagan begins with a series of permissive "let us" constructions (paragraph 40). The next three paragraphs move into direct, second-person address, asking the audience to "look" and "see" heroes "every day going in and out of factory gates," "across a counter," and in other varieties of everyday circumstances. He then unites the "seeing" audience with the people they are "looking at" in paragraphs 44–45: "Now, I have used the words 'they' and 'their' in speaking of these heroes. I could say 'you' and 'your' because I'm addressing the heroes of whom I speak—you, the citizens of this blessed land." "I," "they," and "you" all become united within Reagan himself, as both observer and representative. Hence, in paragraphs 46–54 he can return to first-person singular and plural constructions, at times embodying the collectivity himself, at times sharing heroic status with his auditors. He and they, through individual and collective heroic efforts, can remove "the roadblocks," "reawaken the industrial giant," "lighten our punitive tax burden," and set "our first priorities" (paragraphs 50, 52–53).

I belabor these sixteen paragraphs of exhortation, which comprise almost a fifth of the speech, for several reasons. Materially, they force the speech to pivot on a depiction of everyday heroes who hold common commitments and aspirations. Modally or relationally, the section begins with "I," "you," and "they" separated, but ends with all three voices united, as leader and led are bonded together metaphysically or symbolically. Functionally, the past (See paragraphs 41, 54) is welded to the present so as to point the way to future reward. And formally, the introduction of exhortation in the middle of the speech allows Reagan to feature the sermonic thrust—and he assuredly is a preacher through the entire speech—but yet to return to his own version of heroic themes later.

The body of the speech ends with a brief discussion of foreign policy. The ten paragraphs, once again, are reminiscent of Kennedy, but with some important differences. Kennedy divided America's foreign constituencies into six groups as he sought to feature foreign policy, foreign aid, arms and arms control, and international scientific and cultural exchanges. Reagan puts all non-Americans into but two groups—"neighbors and allies" and "the enemies of freedom, those who are potential adversaries" (paragraphs 56, 59). He obviously has constructed a binary foreign vision, with others for or against us; his bipolar thinking is further reflected in the series of antitheses characterizing paragraphs 58–65.

Conclusion. With paragraph 66, Reagan is ready to galvanize the speech into one final, coherent vision, a vision needing nineteen paragraphs for development. The conclusion is framed in references to the guiding deity—with thanks for prayer meetings in paragraph 66 and an invocation of God's blessings in paragraph 84. Inside those religious

235

brackets is Reagan's second attempt to deal with heroes and heroic actions. Paragraphs 67–75 review the monuments to the war dead in Arlington National Cemetery and the accomplishments of George Washington, Thomas Jefferson, and Abraham Lincoln. Reagan's employment of the first-person singular obviously is forcing a direct identification of Reagan with these cultural forebears. Then he narrows his vision in paragraphs 76–81 to a "young man, Martin Treptow, who left his job in a small town barber shop in 1917 to go to France with the famed Rainbow Division." Treptow becomes Reagan's Everyman, the epitome of those everyday heroes referred to earlier, but with a difference. Treptow's sacrifice was ultimate.

With the mention of Treptow's death, Reagan can conclude the whole speech with a final, collective exhortation to what "we" can do, requiring "our best effort, and our willingness to believe in ourselves and to believe in our capacity to perform great deeds; to believe that together with God's help we can and will resolve the problems which now confront us" (paragraph 82). To seal that exhortation, he ponders, "And after all, why shouldn't we believe that? We are Americans" (paragraph 83). Uniting his personal optimism with that of the heirs to Treptow, he concludes.

By examining these rhetorical details of Reagan's inaugural, we can see Reagan's strategic interweaving of individual (his and the listeners') experiences, sociopolitical commitments, and mythic explanations of the American spirit. We likewise can see movement among the first-, second-, and third-person voices, sometimes expressing Reagan's personal opinions, sometimes exhorting listeners, and sometimes bonding the leader and the led together in common endeavor. These strategies are hardly exceptional, but yet, Reagan executed them in rhetorically and ceremonially significant ways. Couched in our analysis of formal and material elements are clues to Reagan's attempts to evoke and embody the Office and to portray that office's relationships to the people. Before drawing conclusions concerning these matters, however, let us move into the second analytical topic, Reagan's attempt to fulfill the sociocultural functions of inauguration.

CEREMONIAL FUNCTIONS OF THE SPEECH

Given what has been said about aspects of form and substance, it should come as no surprise that this speech contains almost no celebration, very little in the way of direct legitimation, and a good deal of remembrance.

Celebration. Apparently there was little to celebrate in 1981. Reagan half-smiled when thanking former President Carter for his help "in the transition process," when discussing the shopkeepers and other common heroes, and when concluding the speech. In other words, he appeared pleased with the pro-forma mechanical process of ascension, with the "little people" who acted as his social role models, and with the completion of his task of talking—but that was all. The bulk of the speech was expressed in unremittingly serious tones and language, tones and language bespeaking a crisis atmosphere. Celebration had almost no place because America had come dangerously close to death in its immediate past.

This is not to say, however, that Reagan saw no hope for the future; crisis or not, he played the hopeful augur. He told his audience that "this Administration's objective will be a healthy, vigorous, growing economy that provides equal opportunities for all Americans with no barriers born of bigotry or discrimination" (paragraph 25). That optimism seemed spawned by his commitments to precepts alluded to earlier (in paragraphs 29–39). The signs of the times *as they could be observed at the present* might be inauspicious. But, as we shall note soon, if one looks beyond the present and immediate past *to the more distant past*, Reagan augered, we would find nearly infallible signs justifying his sense of future prosperity.

Hence, while the 1981 inaugural address was anything but celebratory and while it posited a crisis atmosphere, it nonetheless held out hope for future prosperity. Ronald Reagan was grim but not despondent.[8]

Legitimation. There was little explicit legitimation in this discourse. Reagan noted only that he was elected in the quadrennial "ceremony" of presidential campaigns, that with Carter's help he was "maintaining continuity which is the bulwark of our republic," and that citizens' prayers could support him in his new job (paragraphs 4, 6, 66).

If direct references to legitimation occurred only thrice, however, there was no lack of *indirect* hints of Reagan's mandate to rule powerfully. The speech abounded with the valuative references and ideological truisms already noted. Reagan depicted himself as confirmed by the people and by God because he believed what they believe, valued what they value, knew what they know about everyday life, and professed virtues ordained by God. The resulting vision is biblical. As leader, Reagan positioned himself between divine, eternal verities and popular will. Legitimated from above and below, he committed himself to guiding propositions: "Government is not the solution to our problem; government is the problem"; "It is my intention to curb the size and influence of the Federal government and to demand recognition of the distinction

237

between the powers granted to the Federal Government and those reserved to the states or to the people"; "In the days ahead I will propose removing the roadblocks that have slowed our economy and reduced productivity"; "And as we renew ourselves here in our own land we will be seen as having greater strength throughout the world" (paragraphs 18, 32, 50, 56). Legitimated from above and below, he posited the style of presidential actions for his term of office. That style was derived from Reagan's version of the Great Chain of Being, with civic leaders dwelling in the symbolic space between God and humanity, a space doubly legitimated.

Remembrance. The biblical vision made remembrance *the* primary theme of the speech. Kennedy had pushed us boldly into the future with his themes of development, exploration, and a thousand days of lighting torches, but Ronald Reagan led us into the past. That past—depending on how near it was to us—was divided into two epochs.

The immediate past was negatively valued. Our immediate economic past, to Reagan, included "decades" of piling "deficit upon deficit, mortgaging our future and our children's future for the temporary convenience of the present" (paragraph 12). Further, "From time to time we've been tempted to believe that society has become too complex to be managed by self-rule, that government by an elite group is superior to government for, by, and of the people" (paragraph 19). That theme was continued in paragraph 38, where Reagan noted that "It is no coincidence that our present troubles parallel and are proportionate to the intervention and intrusion in our lives that result from unnecessary and excessive growth of Government." But, in contrast, the more distant past was positively valued in the roll call of great heroes: Dr. Joseph Warren, George Washington, Thomas Jefferson, Abraham Lincoln, the war dead, and, of course, Martin Treptow (paragraphs 49, 54, 70, 71, 72, 73, 76ff.).

Such a rhetorical manipulation of the past, of remembrance, is perhaps typical of inaugural addresses offered in times of perceived crisis; nevertheless, the manipulation provides our central clues to electee Reagan's visions for his society and for himself. His pattern of temporal reference gave the speech a markedly revivalistic thrust. The future was to be faced, not with Kennedy's "new" commitments, but with *renewal* and *rededication.* The verb "renew," together with such similar action words as "reawaken" and "lighten," recurred throughout the address. The present and the immediate past were characterized by ills, woes, burdens, even a sense of "inevitable decline" (paragraph 39). There was no solace in present and immediate past, no hope for survival and

238

progress. The future would belong to America only if it looked backward into the future. Most of American history since World War I must simply be excised from collective experience; that excision even removed his own party leaders—Nixon, Eisenhower, Hoover—from sociopolitical memory. Only the *distant* past could brighten the collective future. In the main, Ronald Reagan evoked ancient officers, and embodied the personages of long-dead Americans.

These references to evocation and enactment take us into large issues, and it is therefore appropriate to move from comparatively concrete to comparatively more abstract construct considerations.

REAGAN, INAUGURATION, AND ROLE COMPETENCY

I suggested earlier that standards for evaluating "a competently performed inauguration ceremony" may be derived in part from a broader genre of ceremonies of cultural transition, and also from consideration of ancient and modern rites of inauguration and investiture. There are two principal questions that should be asked about inaugural addresses, once they have been examined functionally and formally:

1. To what degree does the inaugural address function to bridge the cultural fissure created at times of change in leadership? That is, to what degree does the inaugural address reorient a citizenry via acts of remembrance, legitimation, and celebration?

2. To what extent is the inauguree able to evoke and embody the Office formally or ceremonially? Are the auspices well read and the investiture well executed—"read" well enough and "executed" surely enough to justify and sanctify *imperium*?

We have in Reagan's themes a fusion of past and future, a fusion that allows the past to guide the future, even to bypass the present. The remembrances offered are primarily valuative and ideological. The legitimation needed to rule powerfully comes partly from political or institutional structure, partly from popular mandate and, for Reagan, most emphatically from common commitments to cultural values and American ideological truisms. Celebration—though anything but featured in 1981—is possible because revival of past glories and dreams can be accomplished when the leader and the followers are one. The signs of the present times are not auspicious, perhaps, but a "new beginning" is possible through renewal of old commitments. All three of these inaugural functions were epitomized and personified in an ideal heroic type drawn from World War I—in a barber who went to war with a pledge.

239

Even more generally, we have noted that Reagan did little with the spatial order. There was no commentary on America's development from the wilderness, the frontier, or any other source of spatial *mythos* so often punctuating earlier inaugurals. Reagan had little to say spatially, except in the section on the West Front and the monuments. The temporal order, however, received the full force of his attention. The secular and sacred temporal orders were fused in American valuative premises, ideological tenets, and individual virtues—as well as in the person of the backward-looking/future-oriented leader himself. Insofar as he was able to convince us that *he* was Martin Treptow elevated to the Presidency, Reagan was able to overleap time, both to bridge the gap created by an unsavory present and to force the distant past and near future into an operative relationship.[9]

I would argue that Reagan most competently created a discourse capable of healing the transitional fissure produced by change in leadership and hence of reorienting the citizenry. After hearing this address, Americans ought to have understood that the work of government would be executed firmly and pointedly within a markedly traditional framework of commitments. After hearing this address, they ought to have known that they had elected a man able to reach for a future anchored solidly in the past.

Regarding evocation and embodiment, that is, investiture rites, some questions can be raised. For one thing, Reagan did not really invoke the Office. In paragraph 54, he mentioned "this Administration," but nowhere else did he refer to an abstracted Presidency. Whenever he talked about his power, it was discussed in personal and popular rather than in institutional terms. In other words, nowhere in this speech did Reagan "put on" the Office. As I have noted repeatedly, he instead identified himself directly with "the people," particularly with factory workers, shopkeepers, entrepeneurs, and, finally, a barber. Now, we may believe, following John Locke and the compact theory of government, that power springs from the people in trust of good leadership, yet we also know it is the mythically sanctified "Office" that enshrines presidential virtue and power. If he does not put on that office, Reagan is in danger of not working within its limitations and arenas of responsibility, in danger of depending for efficacy on his own charisma and poll ratings rather than on his role requirements. Those dangers, I would add parenthetically, have been borne out in his populist style of leadership in postinaugural days.[10] To neglect such evocation is to risk institutional powerlessness or, worse, noninstitutional power, that is, demagoguery.[11]

Reagan increased his institutional risks by identifying himself with a

240

virtuous barber. He even went so far as to say that few of us need make the kind of ultimate sacrifice Martin Treptow did. We need only work a little harder and keep our eyes on common cultural values, grounded in history and powerful enough to take us through present troubles into an optimistic future. Now, one need not disparage barbers, but they are hardly the stuff of which dreams and success are made. Treptow may well have personified Reagan's vision of volunteerism and dedication, but his mythic profile is faint. In a sense, Reagan-Treptow, in union, embody a Presidency at too mundane a level; the resulting vision was constrained, undramatic, and certainly not inspirational.[12]

What I am saying is that in embodying the Presidency in his inaugural, Ronald Reagan offered an equation of identity. In doing that, he collapsed the leader into the led; he destroyed the symbolic distance between the presidential institution and those who owe obedience to and trust in it. His own Great Chain of Political Being contained a missing link.[13]

We are justified in asking why. We cannot here trace through great mounds of public discourse to assess motive, but we can speculate a bit. Populism assuredly *was* a theme of Reagan's 1980 campaign, as Gary Woodward argues convincingly (see n. 10, above). In most forms of populism there is an inherent anti-institutionalism, even an antiformalism. Further, Reagan likewise had campaigned vigorously against the expanded Presidency he found in most of the twentieth century. On this point he cared little whether the occupant of the White House had been Republican (Nixon) or Democrat (Carter). He developed on his fabled campaign notecards little homilies that attacked the Imperial Presidency with harshness. One of his major campaign themes invoked a Reign of Virtue. In speech after speech, including his nomination acceptance speech, he postulated moral solutions to undoubtedly pragmatic problems. He seemed to assume that rededication to fundamentalist public morality and to principles of narrowed public stewardship would solve the problems of unemployment, stagflation, high tax levels, and individual rights.[14]

In sum, Reagan's 1980 campaign resembled Carter's 1976 campaign in several ways, principally in its anti-Washington themes. Yet there was an important difference between the two candidates. While Carter saw himself as *personally* untainted by the Washington of the post-Watergate era and yet *personally* capable of creating a "government as good as its people," Reagan saw the taint of government less in its officials than *in the offices themselves.* Carter's federal themes were phrased analogically: ". . . *as* good as its people." He sought to take the mantle of morality to

241

himself, and, thus clothed, to use the power of the Presidency for moral ends. But Reagan's themes emphasized that "government isn't the solution—it's the problem." Reagan saw that he had to do more than replace an incumbent, do more than be a "moral" president. He had to rework the very mechanisms of government. It is little wonder, therefore, that in his inaugural address he depicted his authority-to-rule in charismatic or popular terms, not in institutional terms. In 1981 he was evoking and embodying the Presidency, weak as that Presidency might be in the end, in ways he had talked about in 1980.

Overall, I am convinced that while Ronald Reagan fulfilled the ceremonial functions of inauguration and cultural transition in 1981, he failed to buoy up the Office and to set the country on a strong sociopolitical course. Perhaps he had worried too much about the size and power of the federal government for too long. He undoubtedly sold the Office short. He thereby may have crippled his own chances to make his programs a long-term success, for while he seized the office through electoral mandate, he manhandled its powers. In 1981 Ronald Reagan enacted a Presidency smaller than that which he had won. And even in 1984, when he won reelection, there was little doubt of Reagan's personal mandate to rule, yet many doubts about his abilities to sustain a program and carry his party through the 1988 elections.

A PARTING THOUGHT

In discussing legitimation and institutional roles, Peter L. Berger and Thomas Luckmann have written:

The institution, with its assemblage of "programmed" actions, is like the unwritten libretto of a drama. The realization of the drama depends upon the reiterated performance of its prescribed roles by living actors. The actors embody the roles and actualize the drama by representing it on the given stage. Neither drama nor institution exists empirically apart from this recurrent realization. To say, then, that roles represent institutions is to say that roles make it possible for institutions to exist, ever again, as a real presence in the experience of living individuals.[15]

This essay has given concrete illustration to these notions. More, I would hope, in articulating the functions, forms, and *materia* of inauguration both generally and specifically, it has added some little concreteness to Berger and Luckmann's constructionist theory of institutionalization and role competency.

Yet, of course, this essay is only a beginning. In approaching traditional subjects for rhetorical analysis—such subjects as rhetorical genres, strategies, forms, and judgments of competency—within a construction-

242

ist or sociocultural functionalist framework, the essay suggests a modest though I think important reorientation. It suggests that "empty" rhetoric of the type we normally associate with such ceremonial performances as inaugural addresses is, in fact, not empty at all. Rather, mere ritualistic rhetorical performances often contain the discourse of power, because institutional offices are evoked and embodied in them and because relationships between the leader and the led are articulated therein. Mere observance of formalisms provides those formalisms with the ability to guide and constrain consciousness by enacting their sources of legitimation. And, in such "little" words as modes-of-address or grammatical voice lie clues to the presumed governing relationships between and among institutions as well as between institutions and those owing allegiance to them.

Such are some of the theoretical propositions embedded in this essay. They are important propositions, I think, for they ask us to find "influence" and "persuasion" in discourse and symbolic acts which seem not to call overtly for conceptual, attitudinal, valuative, or behavioral change. Yet I also recognize that these propositions need considerably more development and exemplification before they can be incorporated in the corpus of rhetorical theory. I would hope, then, that others pick up the challenge of "empty rhetoric" and complete the job of filling it.

Notes

1. See the analysis of "marginal situations" in Peter L. Berger and Thomas Luckmann, *The Social Construction of Reality: A Treatise in the Sociology of Knowledge* (Garden City, N.Y.: Doubleday, 1967), passim. I extend their analysis somewhat in "The Rhetoric of Political Corruption: Sociolinguistic, Dialectical, and Ceremonial Processes," *Quarterly Journal of Speech* 64 (1978):155–72.

2. See, e.g., Harold Mixon, "Boston's Artillery Election Sermons and the American Revolution," *Speech Monographs* 34 (1967):43–50; Harry P. Kerr, "The Election Sermon: Primer for Revolutionaries," *Speech Monographs* 29 (1962):13–22; and Harry P. Kerr, "Politics and Religion in Colonial Fast and Thanksgiving Sermons, 1763–1783," *Quarterly Journal of Speech* 46 (1960):372–82. With some little more work, I think it could be demonstrated that election, artillery, and ordination sermons provided the rhetorical models for later genres of transitional discourse. Perhaps, indeed, the only major form of transitional discourse not given birth in those models was the commencement address, which developed more or less independently from its beginnings in seventeenth-century Harvard College.

3. Berger and Luckmann, *Social Construction*, p. 75.

4. I have drawn this and the following descriptions from *Oxford Dictionary of Classical Literature and Antiquities*, s.v. "Augur"; R. H. Barrow, *The Romans* (Harmondsworth, Eng.: Penguin Books, 1949), esp. p. 13; H. H. Scullard, *From The Gracchi to Nero: A History of Rome from 133 B.C. to 68 A.D.* (New York:

Frederick A. Praeger, 1959), esp. p. 241; F. R. Cowell, *Cicero and the Roman Republic* (1948; rpt. Harmondsworth, Eng.: Penguin Books, 1956), esp. chaps. 6–10; *The Encylopedia of the Classical World*, s.v. "Augur" and "Auspicia."

5. I discuss "embodiment" at greater length in my "Audience Engagement in Family," in Martin Medhurst and Thomas Benson, eds., *Rhetorical Dimensions in Mass Media: A Critical Casebook* (Dubuque, Iowa: Kendall/Hunt, 1984), pp. 4–32; cf. James E. Combs, *Dimensions of Political Drama* (Santa Monica, Calif.: Goodyear Publishing Co., 1980), esp. chap. 2, "Political Ceremonies: The Elite Dramatization of Symbols," pp. 18–48.

6. An earlier version of this paper—the one read at the Temple University Conference on Form and Genre in Political Communication (March 1983)—included a section treating Reagan's address as it compares with other presidential inaugurals. Following the lead of Donald L. Wolfarth, "John F. Kennedy in the Tradition of Inaugural Addresses," *Quarterly Journal of Speech* 47 (1961):124–32, I discussed the degree to which the 1981 speech was typical of inaugural addresses—in its salutation, its material topics, its syntactical features. Using Wolfarth's categories, one is led to conclude that the speech was totally unexceptional. Therefore I have not reprinted that analysis here.

7. In other words, I am interested in both the informational and the relational dimensions of messages, as discussed by Herbert W. Simons, *Persuasion: Understanding, Practice, and Analysis* (Reading, Mass.: Addison-Wesley, 1976), esp. p. 59; cf. Paul Watzlawick, J. H. Beavin, and D. D. Jackson, *Pragmatics of Human Communication* (New York: Norton, 1967).

8. We should note that Reagan's reference to a "new beginning" (paragraph 27) was picked up that day by the mass media's augurs. In general, they agreed that solutions to American's problems would not be easy to find; but, as noted earlier, in reading the signs of the times—the hostage release, the West Front setting, and the expressions of happiness seen at the inaugural balls—they, too, got caught up in the symbolism of a "new beginning." Reagan's style, openness, and optimism were contagious. The press's coverage of the hostage release, especially, intertwined as it was with the inauguration, demonstrated the union of the President's and the Fourth Estate's augurings. (See Ernest G. Bormann, "A Fantasy Theme Analysis of the Television Coverage of the Hostage Release and the Reagan Inaugural," *Quarterly Journal of Speech* 69 [1982]:133–45.) Only late in 1981 did the press generally begin to question his promises of prosperity. See some of the postinaugural rhetorical essays referred to in n. 10, below.

9. Worth pursuing, for students of Harold Adams Innis, is this address's strong emphasis on time and de-emphasis of space. If one accepts Innis's differentiation between time-bound and space-bound societies, then we are seeing in this address the true conservative—the oligarch or theocrat who possesses a monopoly of knowledge and secretive power. (See Harold Adams Innis, *Empire & Communications*, revised by Mary Q. Innis, and foreword by Marshall McLuhan [1950; rpt. Toronto: University of Toronto Press, 1972]).

10. See the first rhetorical analyses of Reagan's leadership style in such essays as Sara Russell Hankins, "Archetypal Alloy: Reagan's Rhetorical Image," *Central States Speech Journal* 34 (1983):33–43; Gary C. Woodward, "Reagan as Roosevelt: The Elasticity of Pseudo-Populist Appeals," *Central States Speech Journal* 34 (1983):44–58; Richard E. Crable and Steven L. Vibbert, "Argumentative Stance and Political Faith Healing: 'The Dream will Come True,' "

Quarterly Journal of Speech 69 (1983):290–301; Walter R. Fisher, "Romantic Democracy, Ronald Reagan, and Presidential Heroes," *Western Journal of Speech Communication* 46 (1982):299–310; Bert E. Bradley, "Jefferson and Reagan: The Rhetoric of Two Inaugurals," *Southern Speech Communication Journal* 48 (1983):119–36; Gregg Phifer, "Two Inaugurals: A Second Look," and Bert E. Bradley, "A Response to 'Two Inaugurals: A Second Look,'" *Southern Speech Communication Journal* 48 (1983):378–85; 386–90.

11. "Demagoguery" may seem too strong a term here, although I mean to use it with comparative neutrality to index an operative government where the leader and the led presumably are directly bonded, as in a fascist state. The fascist leader is the super-representative of the collectivity, with power simultaneously to rule *for* and *over* it. The fascist state has the authoritarian and absolutist characteristics of monarchy, although, in Weberian terms, its leader rules through principles of charisma rather than principles of heredity. The fascist leader is a demagogue, in a classic sense of that word. In a country as fully institutionalized as this one, I think demagogic relationships between leaders and the led are potentially dangerous, as they can circumvent the codified checks and balances written into our instruments of government. And I think that Presidents (and one can look at the years not only of Reagan in this century but also of Theodore Roosevelt and Jimmy Carter) who attempt to rule demagogically court political disaster.

12. In his fantasy theme analysis of this occasion, Bormann likewise notes Reagan's reliance upon Treptow, suggesting we can "share the fantasy about the persona of Martin Treptow, the common man hero in Reagan's peroration" ("A Fantasy Theme Analysis," p. 136). Yet, even though Bormann is attempting to wrestle with the mythic structure and the fantasies informing this discourse, he says no more about Treptow and this passage in the speech. Apparently Bormann is as unimpressed with its restorative power as I am.

13. For an alternative reading on Reagan and his heroic themes in this address, see Fisher, "Romantic Democracy," esp. p. 307. In interpreting the sections of the inaugural treating heroes, Fisher notes that "different from Carter, Reagan's stress was heroism rather than goodness. . . . It is noteworthy that whereas the image of 'goodness' appeals to conscience, to one's sense of ethical being, the image of 'hero' appeals to ego, to one's conviction that one can face hazard or hardship and prevail. The 'ethical person' is; the 'hero' does. . . . The 'hero' is led to feel good about him or herself no matter the adversity. In a time of distress and uncertainty, as now, the hero image is as rhetorically efficacious as any image one might conceive, . . ." I am not as convinced of the optimism in this address as Fisher is, nor am I as willing to collapse into a single vision the sections treating "everyday" heroes and the great men remembranced in the granite pantheons of Washington, D.C. We do both agree in the end, however, that, common or uncommon hero, the President's leadership was to be severely tested because of the partiality that seemed to characterize his programs and policies (Fisher, ibid., p. 310). While his personal ratings in the polls were sustained through most of his first term, he consistently had his programs evaluated harshly by the public, and his battles with Congress continued well into his second term.

14. See Crable and Vibbert, "Argumentative Stance."

15. Berger and Luckmann, *Social Construction*, p. 75.

9

Jane Blankenship

TOWARD A DEVELOPMENTAL MODEL OF FORM: ABC's Treatment of The Reagan Inaugural and the Iranian Hostage Release as Oxymoron

Observing that "*form* is always emergent," Carroll C. Arnold defined it as emerging shape that "transcends pattern" and describes form as "the outcome of selecting stimuli, noting and perhaps 'editing' their structures, and blending the information with experience to create a more or less holistic perception of 'what it's all about.' "[1] Kenneth Burke, somewhat similarly, suggested that a "work has form in so far as one part of it leads a reader to anticipate another part, to be gratified by the sequence" and he linked form to the actualizing of the "entelechial principle."[2] Noting that he used the term with some latitude, Burke viewed entelechy thus: "Since an action contains some ingredient of purpose, or end, Aristotle uses the term 'entelechy' ('having its end within itself') as synonym for 'actuality.' "[3] Later he observed: "We can look for the 'perfection' of the work in the principles of its construction, as embodied in its actual form."[4]

These are by no means the only conceptions of form with which one might begin this essay; indeed, the term "form" probably admits as much variation in usage as any in the lexicon of the rhetorical theorist/critic. Several central quarrels persist in the literature on form, and here, as elsewhere, I am clearly taking sides in a number of them.[5] This essay is much too brief to crystallize any of them very exhaustively and any crystallization is necessarily shaped by the purposes of the essay. Still, two key questions are useful to pose at the outset of our undertaking: (1) What is the essential relationship between form and content? and (2) Where do form and content "reside"?[6]

When we ask, "What is the relationship between form and content?" we call for definitions of both terms. Those who take the position that form and content are separable frequently schematize the relationship thus:

246

Content Designates	Form Designates
meaning	manner
thought	shape of thought
ideational content	means of presentation
the stuff of which something is made (matter)	arrangement and organization of material
material antecedent to the rhetor/artist	shape imposed by the rhetor/artist[7]

Such schemas treat form and content as if they were two separate entities or as two sides of the same coin. One view, for example, envisions form as something external, a "box" or "husk" into which content is somehow packed; form is a container and content is the contained. At the other extreme are those who hold to a kind of monism; they believe that there is no seam between two.[8] Others come close to believing that there is no such thing as content, claiming that "the form of [a] book . . . is the content."[9] I propose that the basic relationship between form and content is a reciprocal and developmental one. I shall take the view that form is not a containing principle but a shaping one. In this I follow Burke, who suggests that form is "a *way* of experiencing,"[10] and John Dewey, who calls it "a *way* of envisaging, of feeling, and of presenting experienced matter."[11]

The second key question is: Where does form-content "reside"? *In* texts? In a creative, recreative *dialogic* in which speaker/listener share? Those who answer, "In texts" tend to see rhetorical acts as objects, as artifacts to be charted.[12] Some even argue that a text is a stable, permanent form whose intrinsic configuration yields its signification.[13] I hold that form, like all other elements in a rhetorical context, is by nature dialogic.

What centrally unites Arnold's, Burke's, and the conception of form that I adopt is emphasis on development—on form as emergent, as dynamic not static, as *energetic*.[14]

Elsewhere, Barbara Sweeney and I have published an essay on "The 'Energy' of Form."[15] We briefly introduced in that essay a triumvirate of Aristotelian terms drawn largely from his *Physics*, *Ethics*, and *Rhetoric*. These terms help to illuminate the nature of form.[16] The terms and their rough equivalents in English are as follows:

1. *Dynamos*—the potential possibilities at the beginning of the creative act.

2. *Energeia*—the energy that sustains movement toward an end, the purposive aspect of shaping *toward*.

3. *Ergon*—the energy of perfected habit.

The set as a whole is "neat" in the sense of providing three terms that are clearly differentiable. Each term, on the other hand, is "messy" in the sense that it pulls together and gives coherence to a variety of materials. Nonetheless, I find the schema useful as a way of understanding rhetorical action.

A *rhetorical* action is a linguistic or symbolic action of a public, adaptive sort that is constrained by purpose and situation. Rhetorical action operates in the area of the contingent where choice is possible and where primarily (although not solely) pragmatic outcomes are obtainable. By virtue of exercising some choices (words, structures, etc.) rather than others, any rhetorical action "constructs" one interpretation of "reality" rather than another and, in that fundamental way, becomes "suasory."

In the essay immediately preceding this one, Gronbeck has illustrated how ceremonial discourse can maintain or sometimes reshape images of the institutions that authorize ceremonies. Using the same case, I propose to show how reportage of that event and other simultaneous events can develop an underlying form with "energy" to influence all who were exposed to the events as reported. The materials I shall analyze consist primarily of two hours of ABC coverage of Inauguration Day, 1981. The day was made especially significant because in addition to its being the occasion for a ritual celebration of Ronald Reagan's "new beginning," it was also the day on which the American hostages in Iran were released. In analyzing this body of communication, I shall make use of the concepts of dynamos, energeia, and ergon because they are helpful in making palpable the emergence of developmental forms. In the course of my analysis I hope to illustrate, also, how the various forms of form yield *reciprocities* of, for example, (1) "form" and "content"; (2) speaker(s) and listener(s), or, speaker-listener and speaker-listener in any rhetorical action; and (3) discourses over time (e.g., conversations, formal texts, constitutions, metaphysical systems).

I

A DEVELOPMENTAL MODEL OF FORM

In this part of the essay, I shall briefly sketch a developmental model of form: an organizational scheme centered on the three energies of form

248

outlined earlier—dynamos, energeia, ergon. In the treatment of each "energy" and its application to rhetorical actions, I set forth a series of assumptions about what each entails with specific focus on the case to be examined.

Although we sometimes talk about form and content as if they are different "entities" or as if form is a "box" into which content is "poured," I hope to show that to talk of form without "content" and content without "form" is very difficult and probably misleading. Form and content operate reciprocally, *together*—form to *shape* content and content to provide form with something *to* shape. It is this *inter*action that yields the "substance" of discourse.

In any communicative interaction, meaning is jointly arrived at by the participants in that interaction. This is most clearly seen in face-to-face informal conversation, but even in more formal one-to-many occasions most speakers know they do not merely "inject" information, arguments, or meanings into the minds of their audiences. Audiences participate at the very least in a "silent dialogue" with any speaker, agreeing, questioning, refuting, acknowledging, and the like. And, of course, they may "tell" the speaker what they think by applauding or booing. *Together*, audiences decide whether or not speech is meaningful to *them*.

To a very large extent, we all live in a Grand Conversation that began before we were born and that will continue long after each of us is dead. That conversation consists of all the informal and formal "talk" that precedes any one of our speech acts. "Talk," here, includes all those "texts" that have shaped our histories. In this sense, Constitution A may "talk to" Constitution B to help shape Constitution C; one theory of how the universe began may "talk to" another theory, and that dialogue or debate may inform another theory. The philosophical system of Aristotle may *interact* with the philosophical system of another person, to help illuminate both systems or to spark yet a third system. In significant and interrelated ways these reciprocities are at work in all utterance and in each utterance.

Dynamos, potential energy, *capacity* for, may represent the very beginning of a creative act, whether a brief sentence, a conversation, a formal speech, or a television production. In the abstract, dynamos may represent a nearly limitless set of possibilities constrained initially only by the nature of our perceptual and conceptual apparatus and by the most general rules of communication such as the necessity of reciprocity between speaker and listener. In the concrete, dynamos is shaped by constraints imposed both by the *nature of certain kinds of material* (e.g., bronze, language, film, video tape) and by the special capacities com-

249

monly associated with them for example, rhetorical action, wherein rhetors deal with *probabilities*, in the *contingent*, where choice is possible. (Recall Aristotle's definition of rhetoric as the faculty—the capacity—for finding in any given case the available means of persuasion.)[17] To illustrate, production of the inaugural/hostage-release television coverage was constrained by the "materials of TV," by what commercial TV can and cannot do (e.g., it typically does not run news stories uninterrupted by commercials), by what cameras could cover (the inaugural, but not the actual release of the hostages), what TV cameras can and cannot do (e.g., they can zoom in for close portraiture but cannot reproduce what is not lighted), by current electronic technology (e.g., dissolves, use of split screens, and the like). The inaugural/hostage-release story was constrained further by the "materials" the viewers brought to the ABC production. People have, for example, the capacity to "receive, sort, and stack" information.[18] They also have a certain television literacy that tips them off to what certain kinds of television shots mean.

It is useful here to keep in mind two underlying principles of dynamos as it functions in rhetorical action: (1) A "capacity," Burke reminds us, is not something static; it does not lie dormant until used. A capacity is "a command to act in a certain way," and a capacity for rhetorical action requires that we act in some ways, rather than others.[19] (2) An absolutely essential aspect of rhetorical action, is the *participatory* dimension, which we may refer to as an "insidedness." Let us explore these two briefly.

The urge to rhetorical action, to "participation" or "sociality," is everywhere at hand, and even casual observers understand this principle. The "participatory" is a fact of life from birth, and it continues at every turn thereafter. As Richard Gregg, drawing from Kenneth Burke, observes:

. . . at each level form involves action, from those fundamental principles of symbolic forming that are covert, primal acts of mind through the acting of principles and ideas in repetitive, progressive movement, to the summing up act of perceiving the forming structures which encompasses all. At each level, the action includes an inducement to participate; to participate is to act in terms of the building expectancies and to be gratified by the fulfillment provided.[20]

Moreover, rhetors and audiences share a happy understanding of this quite palpable "insidedness." At the end of the 1936 film *Fire over England*, after a momentary triumph over her transitory enemies, the middle-aging Queen Elizabeth/Flora Robson happens to glance at herself in a mirror, saying: "That *mirror* is old and tarnished. I will have no more mirrors in my rooms." We know, and the poet knows we know that still *lively* convention. And we, together, know that our celluloid Elizabeth knows it. Just as we "know" formal conventions, so we "know" typical scenarios for playing out situations. In the 1981 inaugural story, for instance, TV viewers brought with them certain expectations based on viewing past inaugurals; they had some intuitive repertoire of scenarios through which this drama could be played out. In both the formal convention of the mirror and the playing out of inaugural scenarios, participants knew or thought they knew where they were going.

Thus we are brought to the second of the "energies," energeia—energy directed toward an end. Forming, here, includes "the *for what* aimed at."[21] ABC, for example could have covered the inaugural and the hostage-release stories as twin examples of "new beginnings" and proceeded through metaphors such as "rebirth" or "restoration." But they did not. Instead, ABC covered the simultaneously emerging events as separate stories revealing two sharply different faces to United States power: the powerfulness of power (the inaugural) and the powerlessness of power (the hostages' capture/release). Reporters, directors, and producers created form and energy wittingly and unwittingly. Through the many details of their verbal and visual coverage, an oxymoron emerged. My argument is not that ABC consciously decided at the outset to cover the stories that way: rather, I contend that the direction of particular decisions about what to show and say moved toward "construction" by oxymoron rather than "construction" by metaphor. As John Dewey put it, "the act itself is exactly what it is because of *how* it is done."[22] Thus, form entails a relationship between means and ends—of means as ends *in process*.

Energeia entails purpose (including the decision to speak or not), intentionality, direction, and expectancy (as in I. A. Richards's notion of "feedforward").[23] It also entails notions that one is *in process*, that one is going somewhere, that one has a repertoire of "expectancies," and of "places" to go, including "categorical expectancies"; for example, reaffirmation, defense of one's behavior as in apologia, and so forth. And one has a repertoire of detailed ways of working out such "progressions"; for example, qualitative progression as in detailing urgency via tone and language intensity.

Energeia entails choice, which may be exercised with all aspects of verbal and visual language—in the sound, grammatical, syntactical, and lexical aspects. Certainly during the inaugural proceedings, controlled choice in selecting among phenomena was abundantly evident. ABC had the drive to the capitol by President Carter and President-elect Reagan mapped out, with cameras and reporters posted in particular places. When things were slow before and after the ceremony, reporters had "set pieces" at their command (e.g., Frank Reynolds, George Will, and others swapped stories of past inaugurals); the inaugural speech was in their possession before the TV audience saw it.

Choice lies within both communicator and perceivers. Viewers had, at the very least, elementary notions of "configuration" about how "new beginnings" sound and look, and they had underlying notions of what transition in the American Presidency is *expected* to sound and look like. Reciprocally, ABC *chose*, but viewers *chose* from among alternative perspectives open to them—perspectives allowing them to decide what they thought ABC was "up to."

For centuries the most penetrating writers on rhetoric have insisted that wherever communication takes place, maker and perceiver must have engaged in *reciprocal* relationships. The Aristotelian conception of enthymeme, in which listeners supply part of the "proof" for what is said, reflected understanding of the inevitably reciprocal relationship of speaker and listener.[24] Those who speak or write a given language, or who hear or read, tacitly understand their joint participation in interpreting that code. In persuasion, the wise persuader understands, as Patrick Henry must have, that people do not take up arms or otherwise act because the persuader "persuades"; auditors respond because they persuade *themselves* that the "persuasion" offered makes sense.

Those engaged in the dialogue called "rhetorical action" may be aware that as they enter any given speech act, they enter a world of discourse "governed by rules that antedate the speaker's [speakers'] appearance and postdate his [their] disappearance"; that is, they participate in "the long dialogue of history."[25] For example, television viewers on January 20, 1981, entered into the hostage portion of the story well aware that the story had begun over 400 days before and would continue after they turned off their sets. They were also aware that they shared some responses to that longer story. Still, they were also, at least intuitively, aware of the uniqueness of each speech act and that, as Stanley Fish posits, "propositionality is radically personal."[26] They were at least intuitively aware, too, of the uniqueness of each news bulletin and comment on what was going on in Teheran.

Still further, rhetors are aware, for example, that some forms (induction) differ from some others (deduction) and that some types of speeches tend to function in one way and some in another. That is, there are eulogies, apologias, inaugurals, even though most will not label them "matrix forms" or "constellations/genres"[27] as rhetorical scholars are inclined to do.

People who create rhetoric have many tacit understandings, whether they can articulate them or not. They understand some of the constraining limitations; they are aware of audience psychology and that certain patterns recur. Moreover, even relatively unsophisticated rhetors may come to understand that forms "are grounded, not merely upon technical plot devices, rhyme scheme, and textbook pedagogy, but upon culturally imposed criteria for thinking."[28] They know, too, that form moves thought and feeling toward various perceptions: toward actualizing (exemplifying) an underlying principle; toward a resolution; toward "logical" conclusions—as in syllogisms; toward *habits* of perceiving relationships, interpreting, defining, formulating, arguing; toward completion, wholeness, configuration rather than single detail or discrete details; toward typical ways of making conceptual leaps, when warrants are supplied for conclusions or when figures of thought imply general "rules"; toward the types of effects that come about in consequence of particular forms: oxymorons, metaphors, synecdoches, denouements, and the like.

This potentiality to "move toward" is the most significant feature of form, rhetorically. Form gives energeia to symbolization in at least these ways: moving from expectedness to unexpectedness; any call for movement from acknowledgment to understanding; any call for movement from sight to *in*sight; questions that require answers: the movement from the interrogative to the declarative; alchemic movement as in metaphor and oxymoron. This is what "energeia" entails.

"Ergon" is a concept that designates the influence that *habit* has on *choice* in rhetorical formulation. No rhetor's choices are invariably original; every sophisticated or unsophisticated rhetor creates her or his communications according to presumed "rules" of the language used, the styles presumed to be appropriate in various situations, the accepted conventions of responding to the circumstances confronted.

The concept of "dynamos" points to the creative possibilities through which a rhetor may work, but the concept of "ergon" reminds us of the degree to which this rhetor's choice will be constrained, even fossilized, by habit. The latter phenomenon was pointed to by Aristotle when in his *Ethics* he observed that even in attaining virtue we are and must be guided by "perfected habit"; that is, we shall learn virtue only by performing virtue until habituated to virtue. In much the same way, we learn to express ourselves well or ill, in part through received conventions or forms and through practice.[29] The problem is that habit and convention in communication may confine as easily as free a communicator. In any case, when we examine a person's rhetoric we must examine the degrees of tension between the opportunities of free choice and the constrictions of habit and of received form.

II

In this section I shall use my earlier treatment of a developmental model of form to examine a two-hour segment of ABC's coverage on January 20, 1981, of Ronald Reagan's inauguration and of the release of the fifty-two Americans held hostage in Iran for 443 days.[30] Some supporting materials come from coverage of the stories in other electronic and print sources and from discussions with viewers of a videotape of the ABC coverage.

ABC's attempt to construct the simultaneously evolving stories develops a pervasive underlying form—oxymoron, that always jarring and frequently dizzying compressed juxtaposition of contradictory terms. The oxymoron that emerges from ABC's telecast resides in the sometimes simultaneously functioning dual faces of "power"—the powerfulness of power and the powerlessness of power. The discussion that follows allows us to glimpse the development of that oxymoron in both its verbal and its visual aspects.

I have already discussed what I believe are the reciprocal relations involved in any rhetorical action and the energizing and constraining forces of form. Since I propose to illustrate the usefulness of these concepts by examining an instance of broadcast journalism, it is useful to add that I believe, with Peter Dahligren, that news is a "form of social knowledge, a way of defining and making sense of the world."[31] And, as I have implied throughout the first section of this essay, I assume that this "sense of the world" is "formed by the way [data] . . . are processed"[32] for and in presentation. In examining a unit of broadcast news, we must also understand that viewers place what they receive from the medium within a larger dialogue in which they continuously participate. This larger dialogue includes conversations with friends, experience of past inaugural speeches, statements about the hostage situation, and the entire array of "texts" or "documents" known. Additionally, the total dialogue of experience will include notions about how things "ought to go" and all other elements that shape the conceptual structures comprising the "universe of discourse" in which the viewers have been and are participants.

254

If we ask ourselves what the dynamos dimension of rhetorical action draws attention to, the possibilities for communicative action seem at first almost limitless. Those possibilities, however, become at once limited as soon as we consider the many constraints that also shape particular rhetorical actions. Possibilities and constraints operate no less energetically in commercial television than elsewhere.

Complex, live-action news coverage is, for example, constrained by the requirement of presenting several fundamentally different kinds of "reality" in serial proximity to one another. The effect is inherently oxymoronic, as we can see if we consider how all televised news coverage functions.

We must note that at least on commercial television "real dramas" (items of news) and "manufactured dramas" (commercials) are presented next to one another, often interrupting each other and, in any case, vying for our attention and our participation first in one "reality" and then in another.[33] One may say that both "real dramas" and "manufactured dramas" are *constructions* of reality, but not even a die-hard constructivist would maintain that the "real" and the "manufactured" are identical kinds or orders of constructions. Our special case illustrates this point. On January 20, 1981, viewers who experienced the hostage-release/inaugural stories through ABC experienced those stories interspersed with stories of other life crises—coping with severe headaches, purchasing a car, keeping the kitchen drain from clogging, and selecting wholesome and attractive pet food.

Not only did the viewer have many dozens of "mini-dramas" played out along with the lengthier stories on ABC, but the two kinds of dramas "represented" fundamentally different views of life. Even in presentations of news "realities," the audience was required to move quickly back and forth between discussions of different kinds of solutions and sometimes different judgments over the possibility of solution(s). The hostage-release story had lasted nearly fifteen months; the inaugural story had lasted at least from the start of a two-year primary campaign (and some would say from 1968). Both were long, continuing, messy dramas, and both were likely still to continue. News reports presented two long stories of false starts, reversals, not infrequent ineptness, and the like, and these were continually juxtaposed with short, neat, complete, carefully controlled, commercial "mini-dramas." The scripts of the mini-dramas were clear: disaster threatens, a wise friend or confidant suggests a solution, a turning point occurs, a happy conclusion ensues—pain-free heads, unclogged drains, the right car, a wholesome pet. Commercial-land was a land of assured outcomes in which we, along with the woman in the

H & R Block commercial, could exclaim: "They guarantee it. It's great!" The complex, long-continuing political process and problems were continually juxtaposed with quickly and simply solved purchase and consumption processes, problems, and solutions. Neither vanquished (Jimmy Carter) nor victor (Ronald Reagan) controlled the release of the hostages or the timing of that release. Neither the Associated Press, nor United Press International, nor Reuters, nor ABC could initially, at least, accurately announce their release. Even the Reverend Moomaw, the Reagans' own minister, in his preinaugural prayer incorrectly assumed that the hostages *had* been released. The powerlessness of power, personified.

All commercially televised news is marked and constrained by the necessity of presenting both "real" and "manufactured" accounts of life. All television is further constrained by what cameras can and cannot see, and by what presenters of news can and cannot see. Neither the audience nor ABC personnel could see the plane with the fifty-two Americans take off from Mehrabad airport. ABC cited the wire services and on at least one occasion cited a wire service citing "a policeman at the airport." The viewer could not see a sign at Frankfurt airport saying, "Welcome Home." Peter Jennings told about it. The viewer could not clearly make out a second plane on the runway at Andrews Air Force Base, nor see former Secretary of State Cyrus Vance board it; viewers were told what that fuzzy shape in the background was. On the other hand, TV cameras could capture the carefully controlled pace of the motorcade to the Capitol for the inaugural ceremony, and later, now former President Jimmy Carter's review (to the cadence of a 21-gun salute) of the honor guard at Andrews Air Force Base. The television cameras could zoom in to let viewers catch close portraiture of the new President as he recounted the "pledge" of "a young man, Martin Treptow," who left his job in a small-town barbershop in 1917 to go to France "with the famed Rainbow Division." Treptow, President Reagan told his audiences, wrote in his diary:

America must win this war. Therefore I will work, I will save, I will sacrifice, I will endure, I will fight cheerfully and do my utmost, as if the issue of the whole struggle depended on me alone.

The camera could dissolve from the American flag at Andrews Air Force Base, to the cannons firing a farewell salute, then to the Carters and Mondales, then to the flag. "Cuts" would have separated these entities as merely continuous elements; "dissolves" allowed them, literally, to merge. Television could also allow viewers to be in two or more places at

256

the same time. They watched the new President chat and drink champagne in the Capitol building while Peter Jennings, in Frankfurt, told them the latest details about the hostages. By means of a chroma-key, television could allow viewers to watch Jimmy Carter preparing for departure at Andrews Air Force Base while they also watched Ronald Reagan signing his first Executive Order at the Capitol.

Television is limited, but so is the "material" viewers can handle. We can receive, sort, and stack information, but we are most efficient in doing that when we view one story at a time. The task of receiving, sorting, and stacking information about two stories, sometimes with picture coming from one country and voice from another, tended to intensify the oxymoronic character of experience. As Ernest Bormann observed:

All this pushing, popping, stacking created a montage which aroused emotions such as suspense, despair, hope and weariness. Over the months the hope and despair over the hostages had created a symbolic climate conducive to getting the hostage problem out of the consciousness of the viewers and letting them turn to something else, to start anew with a different drama, one less frustrating and more hopeful.[34]

Even if viewers were not suffering from a kind of emotional and intellectual vertigo because of the ongoing juxtapositions in the harried world of live-action TV, they were consistently juggling the trivial with the consequential. For example, the inaugural story consisted not merely of the oath of office and the firm words of the inaugural speech, but the story as covered included speculation about whether Reagan's younger son would or would not shake hands with President Carter (he had vowed not to), whether Nancy Reagan had suggested that Barbara Bush dye her white hair, and whether Senator Barry Goldwater, who had worn a cowboy hat to the inaugural platform, would put it on when the cameras were aimed in his direction.

There were other kinds of "juggling acts" to be performed as well. Both before and after the formal ceremony, ABC news reporters vied with each other for major roles with the other players in the drama, and they were frequently asked to switch quickly from role to role. They became:

—persons who talk directly to the President and his people (e.g., *Sam Donaldson*: "Mr. President, are the hostages out yet?") and then,
—persons who talk *about* their talking directly (e.g., *Susan King*: "I yelled at [Deaver] but he walked away quickly. . . ."), and then,
—persons who give both trivial and significant information (e.g., "the

257

plane has taken off we believe"; identifications of Senators Byrd, Hatfield, and lesser lights; knowers of intimate details such as "Jody Powell snores, you know"), then,

—persons who interpret (". . . maybe that's what robbed Jimmy Carter of the election"), then,

—persons as persons (e.g., Frank Reynolds reminded viewers that not only had Carter and his staff been up for many nights but so had ABC correspondent Sam Donaldson; or, as Donaldson confided, ". . . my eyesight's not as good as it used to be").

Thus the large cast of news reporters did not merely tell the inauguration story, they participated in it.

We can perhaps assume that today's television viewers possess at least an implicit knowledge of the grammar and syntax of television and a basic capacity to understand reporters' juggling their roles, but we still have ample reason to believe that viewers of Inauguration Day, 1981, experienced what one observer called "a turbulent swirl of competing events."[35] I present below a description of the verbal/visual stimuli provided by ABC in one small segment of the total coverage.* The segment was immediately preceded by a medium shot of the American flag, dissolved to a long shot of the band, followed by a zoom in, and then a dissolve to the Carters and Walter Mondale at attention. The image of President and Vice President dissolved, to be followed by a long shot of cannons and then a plane, dissolving back to the Carters and Mondales, dissolved to an image of the flag, followed by a medium close-up of the Carters. All of this took place while the "Star-Spangled Banner" was being played and a 21-gun salute was being fired in the background.

Immediately following the above, the sequence of communications described below occurred.†

Visual	Verbal
#1 MCU of Carters and Mondale.	*Jarriel*: . . . 21 gun salute for the former chief executive. You see Rosalynn standing facing the honor guard here at Andrews Air Force Base. *Frank Reynolds*:

* Excerpts from ABC News Courtesy ABC News, Copyright 1981 American Broadcasting Companies, Inc.
† CU, close up
  LS, long shot
  MCU, medium close up
  MLS, medium long shot
  MS, medium shot

And Tom, I'm seeing on another monitor his successor in a room in the Capitol preparing

#2 Cut. MS of Reagan surrounded by dignitaries. Zooms in on Reagan, tilts down to hands, then up. Zooms in on hands signing and zooms back.

to sign the first official document. Here is President Reagan.

Reagan: I'm happy to be taking this action in this historic room—a sign of what I hope will be full cooperation between Congress and the Executive branch. This is a memorandum ah for the heads of executive departments and agencies that of course will be implemented by the Office of Management and Budget.

#3 Cuts to LS airplane on runway.

Reynolds: He's signing the ah nominations for his cabinet officers and its just worth—noteworthy to point as you watch him affix his signature he's signing at a table I believe that was first used by Abraham Lincoln.

Now I think we have we have seen him sign his first official document as President let's go on back out to Andrews Air Force Base where former President Carter is preparing to get aboard Airforce One not for the merely traditional flight home home But ah for the long journey that ah apparently will take him to Germany and back. Yes Tom.

#4 Dissolves to MLS of Carter reviewing Honor Guard, tracking shot.

Go ahead Tom. *Jarriel*: Frank, President Carter is now reviewing the troops, the Honor

259

#5 Cut to MLS of same action, camera at back of Carter reviewing Honor Guard.

Guard assembled here but also and some distance away which you can't see too clearly on camera is the aircraft with ah former Secretary of State Cy Vance and the team of approximately 30 medical specialists who are about to leave ah to go to

Frankfurt Germany for the debriefing of the American hostages. Mr. Carter, here, receiving a a formal send off—

a 21-gun salute, first, for the former chief executive and now he is reviewing the troops.

#6 Cut to LS.

His Cabinet, his senior staff, they're all here and as they arrived here we could tell that *they* knew what we learned

#7 Cut to MS of Carter and military officer walking toward camera (music heard throughout).

moments later, that the hostages had indeed been freed. There was no sadness on their faces as they passed us here just a few moments ago.

#8 Chroma-key zooms in upper right within yellow border.

They were smiling because they had finally received the word

#9 CU of Reagan, then slight zoom-in.

that it was indeed a fact.

This juggling of images and talk was not random, of course. ABC's purposes in covering the swirl of events on that January morning dictated choices throughout much of the coverage. One purpose was to compete with CBS and NBC in covering the inaugural in all of its pomp and circumstance. That required covering not only the inaugural address but the fuller setting as well: the President-elect's arrival at the White House to meet the outgoing President; their motorcade to, and disembarking at, the Capitol building; entry to the "holding rooms" where the President-elect and wife wait (where viewers were given a glimpse of Reagan looking at a TV set); the announcements and arrivals of Mondale, Bush, Carter, and Reagan; and the formal protocols leading up to Reagan's speech.

Television viewers, as other participants in dialogue, had notions of the end(s) toward which they were moving; they had some implicit notions of entelechy, of an underlying principle, a resolution, of wholeness or configuration. They neither expected nor constructed random "stacks" of details. In the inaugural story they were given evidence of a smooth transition from Carter to Reagan and the continuing tradition of the peaceful transfer of American political power. No hitches appeared during the carefully practiced ceremonials. Despite the double momentousness of the day and uncertainties about the hostage release, preinaugural amenities were observed and shown to television viewers. Susan King reported, ". . . the President and the President-elect stood together and waved to photographers. . . ." Barbara Walters sought to know whether Reagan and Carter had talked about the hostages but was told they just engaged in "small talk." She commented: "Just pastry and coffee, huh?" At the Capitol well-established protocol was followed, determining who emerged when, who was present on the platform, and the seating arrangement. On television, differences in clothing were duly noted; for example, Walters observed that Mrs. Bush's coat was "a Bill Blass blue coat we understand and . . . Mrs. Carter said she just bought hers off the rack."

Timing was given attention by commentators. As the dignitaries left for the Capitol building, Susan King, who was stationed at the White House, pointed to the precision of the schedule: "They seem to be spacing the time as they each walk out. It is all very organized here as you might expect. Protocol is called in time. . . ." The new President took the oath of office on time. Thus, "categorical expectancies" were fulfilled in fact and in mediated presentation. Notions of how things ought to go were reaffirmed.

Much of this part of the inaugural drama was under artistic control. The central actors, including reporters, had a precise schedule of events. Reporters had copies of the inaugural address. Cameras were placed, set pieces were available as "fillers." Both the President-elect/President and the network were in control: the White House protocols and the formalities on the platform were largely familiar: the Marine Band, the familiar hymns, and the orders of movement and of actions. In ABC's

261

presentation, however, viewers were reminded that all was not under total control:

Visual	Verbal
#1 Camera (MS) on R. Carter, in white coat, greeting others. Joan Mondale at her side.	*Reynolds*: . . . yes, I guess this is a great day for the fashion designers if there's going to be a Nancy look and a Nancy hairdo
#2 MS of Nancy Reagan and others surrounding her, Barbara Bush in blue coat to the left of the Nancy Reagan whose red coat was thus balanced.	and all that other jazz that is usually associated with our our celebration of celebrities. Mrs. ah Bush in, well, I guess I'd call it—is that just a vivid blue, huh? *Walters*: Ah! you told me you weren't going to give any fashion notes
#3 MCU, R. Carter in white, framed.	and you're stealing my thunder! *Reynolds*: (from about "you're"): Well I'd better not. Maybe it's purple. *Walters*: It's a Bill Blass blue coat we understand, and as we said, Mrs. Carter just said she bought
#4 CU of R. Carter, side view, pans right to J. Mondale, zooms out to MLS, R. Carter still in frame, then continues zoom to LS of platform then extreme LS.	hers off the rack. *Reynolds*: We have a report Barbara, excuse me, I am just told that the Associated Press reports that the hostages are leaving the airport. Now we can't go any further than that on that report but it comes to us from Associated Press. I don't know whether it's filed—it must be filed from Teheran, and they say that the hostages are leaving the airport. Imagine that! We are within half an hour
#5 MS of N. Reagan and son.	of the transition of power, Barbara. *Walters*: You know,

262

Frank when you were talking a
moment or two ago about
Jimmy Carter, as we look at the
Reagan family, he's only

#6 Aerial, high angle behind
platform, extreme LS of scene
looking on to mall.

Walters: 56 years old and still
has a long life ahead of him one
hopes. . . .

At times, the televised presentation made matters seem even more out of
control. For example, in the midst of Walter's remarks about the
memoirs of past presidents:

Visual	*Verbal*
#1 LS of group at Andrews Air Force Base (10 sec.).	*Reynolds:* Here is Andrews Air Force Base now, and the people you see there are waiting, I believe, to board a plane that will fly to Rheinmein Air Force Base in West Germany.
# 2 Shot of N. Reagan. Very brief (1–2 sec.), treated as a switching error and cut to LS of inaugural platform.	*Reynolds:* We're back at the Capitol now.

During the inaugural coverage many cameras were used, a plethora of
different camera shots was offered with different angles on the scene. For
example, cameras tracked (MS) congressional leaders walking inside the
Capitol, zoomed out toward the physically present audience, showed an
aerial view, looking from the inaugural platform toward the mall. In
short order, viewers saw the inaugural from inside, outside, and from on
high. Meanwhile they were quickly "confronted" with the unseen story:

Visual	*Verbal*
#1 From an aerial view, Cut, MS of Sen. Mark Hatfield and several others talking. Reagan looks at TV monitor. Jiggly camera work.	*Donaldson:* Frank, we're all anticipating now the moment when the President of the United States and the President-elect will come through this doorway on the West front—walk down the red carpet to the special platform and the transfer of power will be made. . . . ["Hail

to the Chief" played in background]

#2 MS of Secret Service men with Carter, coming out, and of Capitol and down steps to platform.

We'll see if he's heard about the hostages. Here he comes.

#3 MS of Carter, side view; Sam Donaldson in frame; camera follows Carter and moves in closer.

Mr. President are the hostages out? *Carter*: Can't say yet. *Reynolds*: Not yet Sam, not yet. *Donaldson*: Is that what he said Frank? I couldn't hear it. *Reynolds*: He said "Not yet Not yet." *Donaldson*: Not yet! Not yet! They've cheated him! They're cheated him right down to the end.

The inaugural speech itself was the epitome of careful, even perfect, execution of preplanned choices. The President and his staff seemed to produce and direct most of this part of the show. There was no doubt that this was Ronald Reagan's moment. In the two hours of coverage we are examining, about twenty-nine minutes were taken up by presentation of formal, scripted, and rehearsed speech. During the speech itself all but two and a half minutes were devoted to shots focused directly and solely on Ronald Reagan, close up or waist high.

Other essays in this book focus on details of the inaugural speech itself. I shall therefore offer only a few observations about it. The President was verbally in control, "Let there be no more misunderstanding—we are going to act beginning today."

Of government, he said he would "make it work—work with us, not over us; . . . stand by our side, not ride on our back . . . provide opportunity, not smother it; foster productivity, not stifle it."

Of national renewal, he said: "It is time for us to realize that we are too great a nation to limit ourselves to small dreams. . . . So, with all the creative energy at our command let us begin an era of national renewal. . . . We have every right to dream heroic dreams."

Of international interests, he said: "When action is required to preserve our national security, we will act. We will maintain sufficient strength to prevail if need be. . . ."

Not only did the President call the shots verbally, he frequently appeared to summon up the cameras' *visual* shots as well:

[Extra long shot] Standing here, one faces a magnificent vista, opening [zoom into long shot and tilt up to monument] up on this city's special beauty and history.

At the end of this open [dissolve to long shot of monument from another angle] mall are those shrines to the giants on whose shoulders we stand.

Directly in front of me, the monument to a monumental man, George Washington, father of our country. A man of humility who came to greatness reluctantly. He led America out of revolutionary victory into infant nationhood. [Pan right, still a long shot, Vista, Jefferson monument included.] Off to one side, [dissolve back to close up of Reagan] the stately memorial to Thomas Jefferson. The Declaration of Independence flames with his eloquence.

And then beyond the Reflecting Pool, the dignified columns of the Lincoln Memorial. Whoever would understand in his heart the meaning of America will find it in the life of Abraham Lincoln.

Beyond those moments, monuments to heroism, is the Potomac River, and on the far shore the sloping hills of Arlington National Cemetery [dissolve to direction of cemetery] with its row upon row of simple white markers bearing crosses or Stars of David. [Close up of Reagan.] They add up to only a tiny fraction of the price that has been paid for our freedom.

Each one of those markers [camera draws back to waist high, medium long shot of Reagan] is a monument to the kind of hero I spoke of earlier.

Their lives ended in places called Belleau Wood, the Argonne, Omaha Beach, Salerno and halfway around the world on Guadalcanal, Tarawa, Pork Chop Hill, the Chosin Reservoir, and in a hundred rice paddies and jungles of a place called Vietnam.

Under such a marker lies [close up of Reagan] a young man, Martin Treptow, who left his job in a small town barber shop in 1917 to go to France with the famed Rainbow Division. [Close up continues to end of speech.]

How appropriate a match for a President who frequently proceeds from the anecdotal and a medium, television, with its special capacity for portraiture, anecdote, and intimacy. ABC coverage and CBS coverage as reported on by Bormann seemed to take direction from the commander-in-chief. Says Bormann:

The script editors in the control room could hardly have done a better job of portraying the speech itself if the Reagan people had written the video directions. They did not interrupt the speech once to go to "our man in Wiesbaden" or any place else. They did not even distract the viewer by superimposing a running tape to the effects, "There are reports that the hostages are leaving Iran. No official confirmation as yet."[36]

Still, the portrayal of the inaugural address was surrounded by vivid pictures of even persons most typically seen as "knowledgeable"— Presidents, the State Department, anchor persons, and other highly visible scriptwriters—seeming harried, frustrated, ill-equipped and from time to time less than articulate. Amid all the carefully designed orderliness, commentary not infrequently drew viewers' minds away from orderliness and displayed for them the confusion that existed in commentators' minds and doubtless within the bureaucracy.

Three examples, two of talk before and the other of talk after the inaugural speech, serve to illustrate this point.

1. *Reynolds*: "Let's go back now to Barbara. Oh? We're going to go to Betina Gregory who has a good view of the motorcade. *Gregory*: They're just beginning to pass by here at 15th and Pennsylvania . . .

2. *Walters*: And you know you know Frank that when we talk about the hostages and it may very well be this situation that robbed Jimmy Carter of his election [*Reynolds*: Yes] hoping weeks and weeks ago that what is happening today might have happened perhaps in October—the significance of it, the symbolism of it, the irony of it,— so many different things that we can say.

   Reynolds: Yes, well, here they are. *King* [yelling at Carter]: Mr. President is there any word about the hostages? Have they taken off? *Reynolds*: Susan. *King*: Any word from the hostages? *Reynolds*: Why what we have, Susan, is a report, and it's a wire service report I believe. We're not able to confirm it as yet independently that one of the planes—the Algerian Airline planes has taken off. . . .

3. (*Reynolds* turns over to Koppel.) *Koppel*: I'm in a position that I literally don't know what I'm leading into except that I know that Peter Jennings has it. . . .

As if we viewers already did not know something of the confusion, the confused talked *about* the confused:

Koppel: We're in one of these curious ah, well, we're in a transitional period even though the official transition of power has taken place, something less than the official or orderly transition has taken place at the State Department and at the White House and there's still a little bit of confusion at both those centers of power.

266

Ceremonial "good order" had been clearly displayed, but constrasting irregularities if not disorder were present also. Ronald Reagan looked at a television set to see what was going on. It was Barbara Walters, not the State Department, who told Louisa Kennedy, wife of a hostage and chief spokesperson for the Family Liaison Action Group (F.L.A.G.), that the hostages had been released:

Walters: Well, Frank, ah, somewhat different thoughts. Just a moment or two ago I telephoned Louisa Kennedy who is the wife of now, ex-hostage Moorehead Kennedy . . . and I said "Louisa, Hallelujah, Congratulations!" and she said "For what? Has it happened yet?" and I said "Yes it has" and we told, we told *her* the news. Evidently they weren't watching television and the State Department had not told them. . . .

Newspersons, along with many viewers, worried that we might have been tricked again and that even though in the air, the hostages would not be safe until out of Iranian air space:

Britt Hume: And what was your understanding about how long it would take them to get out of the air space, Sir? *Tip O'Neill*: About an hour— 600 miles they figure they were inside Iran property. . . . it'll take them about an hour to get out. . . . *Koppel*: . . . as you heard Speaker O'Neill say a few moments ago, it's about 600 miles, from 50–60 minutes to get them out of Iranian air space. . . .

Uncertainty rather than certainty surfaced again: Could we, even yet, be subject to another trick of the Ayatollah?

In discussing a developmental model of form I suggested that ergon (habit) facilitates the development of expectancies and of patterns within which to view large amounts of information. There was much in ABC's presentation that habit could grasp. The new President certainly was no newcomer to the American political stage. He had not come "out of nowhere" as had Jimmy Carter. Long accustomed to his voice and face, viewers were at least generally aware of many of his long-held *topoi*. It was no surprise to hear him proclaim them again in his inaugural speech; the speech had, as the *Orlando Sentinel Star* put it, "much of the same anti-government, pro-individual political philosophy that he formulated on the speaking circuit in the 1950's":[37]

. . . government is not the solution to our problem; government is the problem.

We are a nation that has a government—not the other way around.

. . . the Federal Government did not create the states; the states created the Federal Government.

267

It is time to reawaken this industrial giant, to get government back within its means and to lighten our punitive tax burden.

These were familiar themes that fulfilled expectancies, as did Reagan's summons to a brighter tomorrow:

. . . we are too great a nation to limit ourselves to small dreams.

The familiar *topoi*, a touch of restraint in statement, and what the *Indianapolis News* termed "a taste of the honey of hope"[38] resonated in the American language and tradition. Reagan, at least, appeared to be what viewers had learned to expect.

Just as many viewers could have their expectations fulfilled by the predictable Reagan *topoi*, so too were they familiar with certain of his linguistic habits and with their nonverbal correlates, including characteristic tilts of the head and emotional overtones in vocal timbre. Certainly, all the visual and nonverbal vocal signs of genuineness, geniality, optimism, and firmness were there when Reagan ended with: ". . . after all, why shouldn't we believe that [in our 'capacity to perform great deeds . . .']? We are Americans." How appropriate (if predictable) when his voice cracked perceptibly on "Americans"! And how appropriate (if predictable) it was when he "choked visibly when he read that passage from the diary of a World War I soldier, giving it special poignancy to the quoted words."[39]

Viewers in 1981 could "read" Ronald Reagan and find what he said consonant with what they expected him to say. Moreover, from thousands of hours of television viewing they had gained the capacity to make the maneuvers required by shifts in the foci of television cameras and directors' choices of scenes and talk. They knew enough about the sorts of Reagan's stories to predict their outcomes and enough about the "genres" of televised productions to foresee the outcomes of many of them. They knew Reagan's anecdotes would tend to be "upbeat" and that television directors would try to supply "action" rather than "talking heads," "stills," and "file film." My point is that experienced viewers of "the inauguration" knew in at least a rough way what to expect of the speaker and of the televised presentation of the event. The start of a story or the initial type of camera shot would forecast for viewers the form of what would probably follow. Watching the inauguration *as produced*, viewers had the visual literacy to anticipate whence "energy" would flow when camera zooms focused on the hands of Reagan signing his first Executive Order, panned from the Bushes and the Reagans posing for the still photographers, or the images dissolved from cannon salutes to a band and then to the faces of the Carters and the Mondales in process of relinquishing their offices.

Viewers knew intuitively the conventional themes of the occasion. They came to ABC's coverage of the inaugural event with energies of perfected habits in their heads, with scenarios for the drama to be played out:

The old order giveth way to the new.

Even in time of trial, the United States can have a smooth transition of power.

It is sad (or it is poetic justice) that Carter is punished by the Iranians to the very end.

This is a day of twin deliverance, from the "lowered expectations" of the Carter administration to the "heroic dreams" promised in the Reagan campaign, and from an "America" held hostage to "America" delivered.

No doubt some viewers brought to the telecast darker scenarios, or if they did not, the broadcasters encouraged them to call up pessimistic prospects, such as:

The hostages' plane may not take off.

The plane may take off, but it may not contain all of the hostages.

The plane could be turned back or be shot down while still in Iranian air space.

Like any other, this plane could crash before reaching Algeria, or Frankfurt, or the United States.

Audiences sitting in their living rooms knew how to play out any of several scenarios hinted at by ABC commentators. There would be those ready to say with Sam Donaldson, "I don't know *how* I knew it but" it seemed the hostages would not be released until *after* President Carter's "watch" was over. Many could, with Betina Gregory, associate the grayness of the day with anxiety for the hostages and be quite unsurprised by Carter's reply to Donaldson's query: "Not yet," Others would associate their thoughts with Frank Reynolds's suggestion that the sun's breaking through was a "sign," portending joy. In these and many other ways viewers were prepared by experience, by the energy of ergon to exercise a kind of "artistic control" over reported and portrayed events that sometimes seemed almost intolerably out of control. Those who were regular ABC viewers could co-author even more smoothly, possessing as they did at least an implicit knowledge of ABC's reporters' inclinations, the network's "philosophy of news," typical techniques, and the verbal and nonverbal habits of the reporters.

The habits of viewers also included implicit knowlege of the genres into which stories would fall: there would be inaugural-address stories, stories about the hostages' release, and "breaking-news" stories. From the first, viewers on January 20, 1981, knew much of what to expect to see and hear: the outgoing and incoming Presidents would meet at the White House and ride to the Capitol building, the vanquished and the victor would be seen together; they would go to separate places to await their summons to the inaugural platform; they would be surrounded by whomever protocol dictated. Dignitaries would assemble on the platform wearing clothing worth a commentator's notice. There would be special political topics to be touched on by commentators: if "Happy" Rockefeller were there, it would be to "represent Nelson's views," or if General of the Army Omar Bradley were present, it would be to summon up past triumphs. The Marine Band would play, and performers would sing such long-known songs as "America the Beautiful." Oaths of office would be taken, and the new President would give an address. The outgoing President and his family would leave Washington, the seat of government. Viewer after viewer was fully prepared to predict, well in advance of Inauguration Day, that all of these events and observations would occur on January 20, 1981. Such is the energy and force of what I have called ergon, the energy derived from perfected habit, an inescapable dimension of all rhetorical action.

If fulfillment of perfected habit were all there were to experiencing rhetorical actions, the experiencing would be far simpler and far more predictable than it is in fact. Despite the fulfillments of the habitual expectations I have just sketched, viewers' "literacy" was taxed on Inauguration Day, 1981. Consider this example of philosophical antinomy, of oxymoron, in the verbal-visual mixes ABC's viewers experienced on Inaugural Day:

Visual	*Verbal*
MLS of Bushes and Reagans posing for still pictures (4 people facing camera, centered).	*Koppel*: Ah, I understand now that Peter Jennings is standing by again in Frankfurt. Peter, what is the latest word you have? *Jennings*: Well, Ted, just to tell you that we, too, have just recently been

270

Some camera pans over to still photographers, zooms in on a single still photograph (photographed from side), pans back to the two couples, then zooms in on CU of Nancy Reagan.

talking to Teheran within the last couple of minutes; they are quoting PARS [Iranian News Service] and saying that the hostages took off a few minutes ago which brings me back to the thought that you offered some many minutes ago that perhaps there *was* a decision made to wait, *if* these reports are correct. . . .

The "visual dialectic" is heightened (becomes even more powerful) by

Reagan's moving right,

Camera moving left,

to mix with the visual-verbal dialectic. Note also that viewers saw but didn't hear the inaugural scene. When they "heard" the inaugural scene it was from Frank Reynolds speaking from another scene to listeners who were in yet a third: "Ronald Reagan as you can see in your picture . . . ."

Viewers knew there were multiple ways of "handling" the simultaneously developing inaugural and hostage-release stories. One scenario would have been to center on the person of Ronald Reagan. Some news writers pointed their audiences that way. Consider three editorials. The *Rocky Mountain News* (Denver) editorial started: "A few minutes after Reagan took the oath office, Iran released the 52 hostages."[40] A second way of interpreting events was to look for "auguries" and "omens." One such report said that Ronald Reagan was lucky and that other nations "are quick to move close to a newcomer who can come up with a national seven on the first roll" (*Globe and Mail*, Toronto).[41] A fuller treatment of this scenario appeared in the *Washington Post*:

The differences between nature and art all but dissolved as Ronald Reagan became the nation's 40th president. It was a scene as theatrical as any in which Mr. Reagan's played in Hollywood—the only thing missing was a sudden shaft of sunlight [the sun *did* come out] but for all of its larger-than-life qualities it was incontrovertibly real. When Mr. Reagan arrived at the Capitol, America was still being "held hostage"—a sense of Iran's unspeakable deceitfulness and the United States' painfully cloying vulnerability suffused the air. Virtually as Mr. Reagan took his oath, however, the final knots binding the hostages were coming untied, and, by the time he left the Capitol, America seemed to be a different place. It seemed, uncannily, precisely the place Mr. Reagan has been saying it is through 16 years of public life, and again in his inaugural address.[42]

271

In this or in other ways, an ongoing scenario could have focused on the broad theme of Ronald Reagan, what he "stands for," is the vessel of, and on "new beginnings."

A third possible scenario could have centered on the whole story using the metaphors of "renewal and restoration." Thus events could have been given overarching meaning though separated by the distance between Washington and Teheran.

In ABC's treatment there were moments illustrative of such possibilities, but they did not dominate. For example, there was a faintly sketched theme of deliverance:

Koppel: . . . if it is possible for this diverse nation of two hundred twenty-six million to have unanimity on anything perhaps the time is now to give an unanimous "Hallelujah" . . . .

Reynolds: The major news the important thing here is that they're free— they're gone. Thank God!

In ABC's treatment there were, in fact, few metaphors as single terms and few attempts at metaphors embedded in phrases. The closest metaphorical treatment can be illustrated by these tentative and brief tries:

Gregory: It's a fairly gray day here. One that, of course, is overshadowed by the news that overshadows this whole event and that is the unresolved nature—everybody on the street is asking what about the hostages. They are worried and concerned. The motorcade passing by now . . . .

Reynolds: Well, the sun has appropriately enough ah come out now and begun to shine once again on this beautiful Capital City. I guess that's ah an indication of how the country feels too, not merely about the inauguration of the new president, but about the glorious news that the American hostages on their 444th day of imprisonment, of kidnapping, have ah finally been released. . . .

There are some hints about *why* no overarching metaphor(s) appeared. There were in ABC's coverage hints that the inaugural was seen as an end-to-the-campaign event, rather than as a new beginning. Walters cast the hostage-taking as an event that may have "robbed" Carter of the election. Reynolds twice referred to Bush's ups and downs on the campaign trail, recalling his declaration about "Big Mo" after winning the Iowa caucus: "He's got the momentum now, hasn't he Sam?" Reynolds referred, too, to the debate in Nashua, New Hampshire, when Ronald Reagan declared: "I paid for this microphone." Said Reynolds, "Maybe he [Bush] wanted to go up to get the microphone and maybe somebody said, 'That's not your microphone, Mr. Bush!' " Sander Vanocur observed that the inaugural address "sounded like" a campaign speech and that Carter's departure seemed something like a "campaign stop." Reynolds gave another clue that, although the two major stories occurred on the same day, they were not "equivalent" images. He attempted to tell why this inaugural was "so different, so different":

Not only is Jimmy Carter in the unique position of being voted out of office after only one term, but here is Ronald Reagan who came to fame as an actor and then established his legitimacy as an executive and administrator by becoming governor of California. And, *over all* this was the tremendous drama of the release of the hostages in Iran.

My contention is that what ABC viewers were given was oxymoron— a miscellany of contrasting information, interpretations, and modes of presentation. "Real life" and "manufactured" mini-dramas were juxtaposed. A "real-life" ceremonial event, supremely under control, was juxtaposed to an equally "real-life" drama that was not only suspenseful but that seemed capable of careening out of control and that was unquestionably sometimes out of the control of reporters and of the United States government. One story was predominantly *seen*; the other was almost entirely *talked about*, with the two processes frequently occurring at the same time. Sentences of reportage were repeatedly at odds with next sentences, as when a statement about "a Bill Blass coat" was followed by "The Associated Press reports that the hostages are leaving the airport." Contrasting sights and sounds were presented, and contrasting visual images appeared simultaneously on the screen, as when Carter was shown receiving a last salute while Reagan was being shown signing his first Executive Order. Sometimes movements in different directions were shown simultaneously by means of chroma-key. Finally, there was ABC's attempt to cover two stories simultaneously rather than treating them as one story, as might have been possible by formulating some transcendent metaphor applicable to both of the major dramas.

My claim is not that ABC set out to cover the inauguration and the release of the hostages as oxymoron; rather, it is that ABC's presentation, in parts and in the whole, constantly confronted viewers with experience of dialectical tensions—with energies emerging in the form of oxymoron. There seems little doubt that this was the result of responses to the pressures of flowing events and information rather than the product of design. But ABC's viewers, with a considerable repertoire of tropes or terministic screens by means of which to give structure to their experi-

273

ence, were sorely "tested" by this presentation. My suggestion is that January 20, 1981, would seem to them a day of heightened, compressed *contrasts*, if they lived it through ABC television.

Notes

1. Carroll C. Arnold, *Criticism of Oral Rhetoric* (Columbus, Ohio: Charles E. Merrill Publishing Company, 1974), pp. 137, 131, 133. Aristotle, *Physics*, trans. Richard Hope (Lincoln: University of Nebraska Press, 1961), 194b. 27–29. In that same treatise, Aristotle also calls form "the subject in process" (191b. 20–22). In Aristotle, form enters his discussion both as an explanatory principle (formal cause) and as the essence of a definition of substance (final cause).

2. Kenneth Burke, *Counter-Statement* (Berkeley: University of California Press, 1968), p. 124 (first published in 1931).

3. Kenneth Burke, *Grammar of Motives* (Berkeley: University of California Press, 1967), pp. 261–62 (originally published 1945). See also Kenneth Burke, *Dramatism and Development* (Barre, Mass.: Clark University Press, 1972), pp. 39–43, and William E. Ritter, "Why Aristotle Invested the Word Entelecheia" *Quarterly Review of Biology* 7 (1932):377–403, and 9 (1934): 1–35.

4. Kenneth Burke, *Grammar*, p. 262.

5. Jane Blankenship, "The Influence of Mode, Sub-mode, and Speaker Predilection on Style," *Speech Monographs* 41 (1974): 85–118, and Jane Blankenship and Barbara Sweeney, "The 'Energy' of Form," *Central States Speech Journal* 31 (1980):172–83.

6. The next paragraphs draw heavily from Blankenship and Sweeney, "The 'Energy' of Form."

7. Blankenship and Sweeney, "The 'Energy' of Form," p. 172.

8. Benedetto Croce, *Aesthetic*, trans. D. Ainslie (rev. ed.; New York: Noonday Press, 1983; originally published in 1909). See also Ramon Queneau, *Exercises de Style* (Paris: Gallimard, 1947).

9. Dorothy Van Ghent, *The English Novel: Form and Function* (New York: Rinehart & Co., 1953), p. 113.

10. Kenneth Burke, *Counter-Statement*, p. 143.

11. John Dewey, *Art as Experience* (New York: G. P. Putnam's, 1958), p. 109.

12. See a brief treatment of two alternative approaches in Blankenship and Sweeney, "The 'Energy' of Form," p. 175.

13. See, e.g., Michel Foucault, *The Archeology of Knowledge*, trans. A. M. Sheridan-Smith (New York: Pantheon Books, 1972), p. 122.

14. E.g., from the outset I assume "dynamos" (potential energy) includes sentience, specialized sentiences, propensity toward gestalts and nexus, a "logic of consciousness," and the function of the "symbolic." See, e.g., Susanne K. Langer, *Problems of Art* (New York: Charles Scribner's Sons, 1957), pp. 26, 48; Susanne K. Langer, *Feeling and Form* (New York: Charles Scribner's Son 1953), pp. 39–53; Michel Foucault, *Archeology of Knowledge*, p. 72; and Susanne K. Langer *Philosophical Sketches* (Baltimore, Md.: Johns Hopkins Press, 1962), particularly "On a New Definition of 'Symbol,' " pp. 54–65.

15. Blankenship and Sweeney, "The 'Energy' of Form," pp. 172–83.

16. Clearly these terms are more complex and resonant than I have been able to indicate here; e.g., none of the three is tied solely to "form." Useful related reading may be found in Aristotle's *Metaphysics, Poetics,* and *On Generation and Corruption (On Coming to Be and Passing Away).* The preface of Richard Hope's translation of the *Physics* (Lincoln: University of Nebraska Press, 1961) is particularly suggestive.

17. William M. A. Grimaldi, S. J., *Aristotle, Rhetoric I: A Commentary* (New York: Fordham University Press, 1980), p. 5. "Rhetoric as a δύναμις in a person is the possession of the rules and principles which constitute the τέχνη, and which consequently endow the person with the capacity to see all the elements in a subject which can lead to the desired goal of the speaker (or writer)."

18. I am using these terms, drawn from cognitive psychology, as they are also used in Ernest G. Bormann, "A Fantasy Theme Analysis of the Television Coverage of the Hostage Release and the Reagan Inaugural," *Quarterly Journal of Speech* 68 (1982):133–45.

19. Kenneth Burke, *Counter-Statement,* p. 142.

20. Richard B. Gregg, "Kenneth Burke's Prolegomena to the Study of the Rhetoric of Form," Communication Quarterly 26 (1978):10.

21. Aristotle *Physics* 194b. 27–29.

22. John Dewey, *Art as Experience,* p. 109.

23. I. A. Richards, "The Secret of 'Feedforward,' " *Saturday Review* (Feb. 3, 1968), pp. 14–17.

24. Lloyd F. Bitzer, "The Rhetorical Situation," *Philosophy and Rhetoric* 1 (1968):13. See, e.g., his "Aristotle's Enthymeme Revisited," *Quarterly Journal of Speech* 45 (1959):408. In "The Rhetorical Situation," Bitzer observes that comparable situations prompt comparable responses; "hence rhetorical forms are born and a special vocabulary, grammar and style are established . . . because we experience situations and the rhetorical response to them, a form of discourse is not only established but comes to have a power of its own—the tradition itself tends to function as a constraint upon any new response in the form." Burke, in *Rhetoric of Motives* (Berkeley: University of California Press, 1969), p. 58, observes: ". . . many purely formal patterns can readily awaken an attitude of collaborative expectancy in us. . . . Once you grasp the trend of the form, it invites participation regardless of the subject matter. Formally, you will find yourself swinging along . . . even though you may not agree with the proposition that is being presented in this form."

25. Richard Ohmann, "Speech Acts and the Definition of Literature," *Philosophy and Rhetoric* 4 (1971):1–19. Ohmann says elsewhere: "A written literary work preserves in its words a record of purported speech acts. They are frozen in the text, to be brought alive whenever a reader re-enacts them as a participant" ("Literature as Act," in Seymour Chatman, ed., *Approaches to Poetics* [New York: Columbia University Press, 1973], p. 101). Burke observes on a similar point: ". . . the reader in participating in the poem breathes into the atomic structure a new physiological vitality that resembles, though with a difference, the act of its maker, the resemblance being in the overlap between writer's and reader's situation, the difference being in the fact that the two situations are far from identical" (*Philosophy of Literary Form* [New York: Vintage Books, 1957, rev. and abridged by Burke], p. 76). He also reminds us: "Few statements are made simply in 'themselves.' They are *answers* to other

statements. And this function is part of their intrinsic form" (*Grammar of Motives*, pp. 270–71n12).

26. Stanley Fish, "Facts and Fictions: A Reply to Ralph Rader," *Critical Inquiry* 1 (1975):883–91. Here Fish argues that propositionality appears "less a formal attribute of the text than a posture of the reader." Later: ". . . my unit of analysis is interpretive or perceptual, and rather than proceeding directly from formal units of language, it determines what those units are . . .; [it] is formed (or forms itself) at the moment when the reader hazards interpretive closure, when he enters into a relationship . . . with a proposition" (ibid., pp. 888–89. Of this point, William Ray goes so far as to say, ". . . Fish posits a model in which memory is relocated within the act of defining the signifier; and *the signified, as conceptual construct, vanishes from the picture entirely*" (italics added; "Supersession and the Subject: A Reconsideration of Stanley Fish's 'Affective Stylistics,' " *Diacritics* 8 [1978]:7).

27. W. Ross Winterowd, *Rhetoric: A Synthesis* (New York: Holt, Rinehart & Winston, 1968), p. 191; Karlyn Kohrs Campbell and Kathleen Hall Jamieson, eds., *Form and Genre: Shaping Rhetorical Action* (Falls Church, Va.: Speech Communication Association, 1978), pp. 24–25.

28. Bruce E. Gronbeck, "Celluloid Rhetoric: On Genres of Documentary," in Campbell and Jamieson, eds., *Form and Genre*, p. 141.

29. Aristotle *Ethics*, trans. Ernest Barker, 1103b.20–25: "Thus, in one word, states of character arise out of like activities. This is why the activities we exhibit must be of a certain kind; it is because the states of character correspond to the differences between these. It makes no small difference, then, whether we form habits of one kind or another from our very youth; it makes a very great difference, or rather *all* the difference."

30. The tapes were loaned by the Vanderbilt University Television News Archives. These and related tapes were provided as part of University of Massachusetts Faculty Research Grant 2033–23. The author wishes to thank Carolyn Anderson for reviewing certain sections of the tapes with her and Debra Madigan for her help in the preparation of this manuscript.

31. Peter Dahligren, "TV News and the Suppression of Reflexivity," in Elihu Katz and Tames Szecska, eds., *Mass Media and Social Change* (Beverly Hills, Calif.: Sage Publications, 1981), p. 101.

32. Gaye Tuchman, "The Exception Proves the Rule: A Study of Routine News Practices," in Paul Hirsh, Peter Miller, and F. Gerald Kline, eds., *Strategies for Communication Research* (Beverly Hills, Calif.: Sage Publications, 1977), p. 44.

33. Martin Esslin, "Aristotle and the Advertisers: The Television Commercial Considered as a Form of Drama," in Horace Newcomb, ed., *Television: The Critical View* (3rd ed.; New York: Oxford University Press, 1982), pp. 260–75.

34. Bormann, "A Fantasy Theme Analysis of the Television Coverage of the Hostage Release and the Reagan Inaugural," p. 137.

35. Don Morrison in the *Minneapolis Tribune*, Jan. 28, 1981, p. 12A, as cited in Bormann, "A Fantasy Theme," pp. 133–34. Morrison concluded: "Yesterday presented a turbulent swirl of simultaneous events, each competing for what should have been our undivided attention and, together, turning everyone's fever chart of emotions into a jagged up-and-down-blur . . . ."

36. Bormann, "A Fantasy Theme," p. 137.

276

37. Editorial, *Orlando Sentinel Star*, Jan. 21, 1981, in *Editorials on File* (New York: Facts on File, Jan. 16–31, 1981), p. 78. Hereafter, *EOF*.

38. Editorial, *Indianapolis News*, Jan. 20, 1981, *EOF*, Jan. 16–31, p. 76.

39. Editorial, *Daily Oklahoman*, Jan. 23, 1981, *EOF*, Jan. 16–31, p. 80.

40. Editorial, *Rocky Mountain News*, Jan. 21, 1981, *EOF*, Jan. 16–31, p. 77.

41. Editorial, *The (Toronto) Globe and Mail*, January 1981, *EOF*, January 16–31, p. 85.

42. Editorial, *Washington Post*, Jan. 21, 1981, *EOF*, Jan. 16–31, p. 85.

10

Roderick P. Hart

OF GENRE, COMPUTERS, AND THE REAGAN INAUGURAL

Generic scholarship in rhetorical studies has moved apace during the 1970s.[1] The decade has been awash in generic investigations of cultural ceremonies,[2] social movements,[3] political events,[4] and religious sermonizing.[5] In their best moments, such studies have been pattern-seeking; in their worst, pattern-imposing. But even the most modest of them has been a welcome change of pace from the case-specific studies dominating research on public address heretofore.

This is not to say that generic research is all of a piece. In fact, in recent research one can identify two theoretical approaches: the humanistic and the scientific. The humanistic approach has been best articulated by Kathleen Jamieson and Karlyn Campbell in their individual investigations[6] and in their contributions to *Form and Genre: Shaping Rhetorical Action*.[7] In the introduction to *Form and Genre*, they neatly defined the distinctive features of the humanistic thrust in critical investigations:

The critic who classifies a rhetorical artifact as generically akin to a class of similar artifacts has identified an undercurrent of history rather than comprehended an act isolated in time. Recurrence of a combination of forms into a generically identifiable form over time suggests that certain constants in human action are manifest rhetorically. One may argue that recurrence arises out of comparable rhetorical situations, out of the influence of conventions on the responses of rhetors, out of universal and cultural archetypes ingrained in human consciousness, out of fundamental human needs, or out of a finite number of rhetorical options or commonplaces. Whatever the explanation, the existence of the recurrent provides insight into the human condition.[8]

The "humanistic" approach, then, tends to isolate features of discourse, which, in turn, point up people's basic ways of knowing and feeling. From such a vantage point, generic research serves the larger goal of commenting upon (perhaps eventually improving upon) the human condition.

278

Of Genre, Computers, and the Reagan Inaugural

Herbert Simons and I have pursued the "scientific" option in generic
studies. In a 1976 essay, for example, I argued that generic research is
important because it opens up, virtually demands, theory-centered
considerations. I urged scholars to attend "to rhetorical systems which
perseverate, for in such perseverations lie the glimmerings of rhetorical
genres, and in such rhetorical genres lie the building blocks of theory
necessary to explain the over-arching forms which rhetoric-in-general
takes in everyday public life."[9] In other words, from a scientific point of
view, study of genres is useful because of its breadth of scope and because
of its tendency to isolate rhetorical phenomena suggestive of larger
communicative principles. Whereas those using a humanistic approach
focus on rhetorical patterns in order to shed light on particular historical
trends or basic human experiences, those using a scientific perspective are
more interested in what can be documented about communication
generally.

The scientific approach is thus field-intensive while the humanistic
approach treats rhetorical data as implicit markers of humanness, and
the rhetorical scholar as but another worker in the humanistic vineyard.
Those approaching the concept of genre from a scientific vantage point
would find little need to *evaluate* the discourses examined and would
probably be less interested than the humanist in the *historical* antecedents
(or consequences) of those messages. Rather, the scientific student of
genre would be concerned to (1) obtain a wide and diversified sample of
genre-prone messages, (2) develop and use reliable and valid methods for
inspecting characteristics of those messages, and (3) discover what the
resulting rhetorical patterns say about human, communicative behavior.

One should not push this humanistic/scientific distinction too far. In
practice, the differences are subtle, and neither approach—as an approach—has emerged as superior. Students of genres of public rhetoric
are more alike than they are different, with one exception: method.
Herbert Simons's essay in *Form and Genre* is particularly instructive in
this regard, for he argues that generic researchers must adhere as best
they can to the principles of classification, control, sampling,
operationalization, and unitization that constitute the scientific
method.[10] Simons acknowledges that such principles must be adapted to
the sort of "soft" data with which students of rhetoric deal, but he also
claims that scholars who follow such principles are most likely to
discover communicative patterns worthy of the name "pattern."

Most generic research in rhetorical studies, in recent years, has been of
the humanistic sort. One of the first of the few "scientific" studies of
genres was my doctoral dissertation in which I posited the existence of

five broad classes of discourse—situations ranging from "true belief" to open hostility.[11] Some years later Thomas Clark attempted a major replication of this study and published a series of reports outlining areas of convergence and divergence with my work.[12] More recently I developed a set of analytical tools capable of making interesting discriminations among pieces of discourse, and I have applied those methods to American presidential speechmaking. In *Verbal Style and the Presidency: A Computer-Based Analysis*,[13] I report certain generic features of presidential discourse, features seen in sharpest relief when compared to corporate, religious, movement, and campaign discourse. I shall not recast those findings here, but I shall indicate how such methods can be used, why they are especially helpful to the generic researcher, and how Ronald Reagan's 1981 inaugural address (or any other inaugural address) can be freshly appreciated when examined with these techniques.

GENERIC RESEARCH AND QUANTITATIVE METHODS

Humanistic study of genres has so far aimed at discovering "likenesses" among instances of discourse, but the scientific approach to study of genres has sought to determine *how much* likeness there is among them compared to a *universe* of discourses. To the scientifically minded, generic study of rhetoric virtually requires the use of quantitative assumptions and techniques, since it focuses on what might be called deviations from normality. For methodological purposes, the scientist posits that the world is entropic, that phenomena are, by their very nature, unpatterned and discontinuous. It thus becomes the scientist's job to pierce this fabric of apparent randomness and to find regularities of movement or structure that the untrained eye cannot observe. With regard to rhetorical genres, the scientific analyst presumes that there are *no* meaningful clusters of discourse in the natural world, that a given communicative situation is unrelated to all previous communicative situations, that speakers, audiences, and messages are unique *until proved otherwise*. Such "negative" thinking places the burden of proof on data that, in the case of genre research, would be descriptions of verbalizations/situations recurring with sufficient regularity and having sufficient structural integrity to "stand apart" from the larger population of messages and message-situations.

The foregoing, of course, is the "strong" version of the scientific method. The "weak" version is probably more useful and realistic. After all, even hard scientists are optimists in the sense that they guess that there *are* regularities in nature, that these regularities have been somehow

280

"hidden" from them by nature, and that their job is to uncover such mysteries. Naturally, the scientist understands that the burden of proof is on him or her to determine that such regularities are, in fact, regularities. And so the scientist examines the data that nature presents, carefully noting the temporal, spatial, and morphological forces operating when an event recurs or when two events co-occur.

Operating from this "weak" version of the scientific method, the rhetorical analyst interested in genres presumes: (1) that communication is *not* randomly structured, since people do not receive stimuli randomly, nor do they respond to those stimuli in random ways; (2) that some communicative rules are persistent and some rarely in force (e.g., God is always mentioned in an inaugural address, but war is mentioned only on occasion); (3) that patterns of communicative behavior differ in their recognizability as patterns (e.g., it is easier to tell when one is being greeted than when one is being praised); (4) that there are powerful and less powerful generic markers; that is, some communicative patterns point toward systemic regularities, toward the theoretical essentials of a rhetorical situation, while others do not (e.g., both Christian and Jew must say "I do" to be wedded but only one of them crushes a glass underfoot); (5) that there are useful and nonuseful generic delimiters; some categorizations of discourse (e.g., "the diatribe")[14] are more theoretically provocative than others (e.g., "Fourth of July oratory") because they account for more of the subtlety and complexity of the communicative situation and hence point beyond themselves; (6) that a rhetorical situation cannot be interpreted meaningfully unless one understands the communicative norms operating or being violated in that situation (in this sense, *all* rhetorical critics are, knowingly or unknowingly, generic commentators); (7) that an *explicit* understanding of communicative norms will allow rhetorical messages and genres to be described more precisely than will an implicit understanding of them; (8) that a *quantitative* description of a given message's communicative features and a *quantitative* description of its attendant norms will best help to establish the existence or nonexistence of a rhetorical genre.

Clearly, each of these assumptions can be sharply questioned. Indeed, most already have been.[15] But they are the assumptions that guide the research I shall report here, and from a scientific standpoint they are fairly orthodox assumptions. I do not wish to say that all generic research should proceed on these assumptions, nor do I mean to say that following these assumptions will inevitably produce generic insight. I do mean that such assumptions ensure that other scholars are afforded a clear and explicit delineation of how one has gathered one's data and, therefore, that others are given an opportunity to examine in detail the *understructure* of any claims made on the basis of that method.

Practically speaking, the assumptions I have itemized force the generic analyst (1) to develop a systematic method of data collection and (2) to assemble a normative data base sufficiently large and varied so that comparisons between sample and total population can be made. Neither of these matters is of small moment. The data-collection methods to be described here took some six years to develop. Moreover, the considerable labors involved in finding, selecting, and analyzing messages for comparison were themselves sufficient to tempt one to find another line of work. But these efforts have helped me to see features of persuasion I could not have seen otherwise and, therefore, the efforts seem justified.

It should also be pointed out, however, that *after* data have been gathered—by "scientific," "critical," or even "impressionistic" means— all scholars operate in much the same fashion. They sift through the assembled data looking for especially important findings; they interpret those findings by recourse to their unique assumptions and biases; and they weave those interpretations into a theoretical tapestry richly brocaded with the researcher's own limitations as a researcher. In this sense, of course, all researchers are humanists in that they move *from* their data bases to higher levels of abstraction via human intuitions. The scientific student of rhetorical genres is no different in these ways. The comments made about Reagan's 1981 inaugural address in this essay are factually based, but they become important only if the researcher is sufficiently sensitive to discourse generally to isolate the most significant findings and then relate them to some overriding set of rhetorical phenomena. Science investigates. It does not prove. Only human logic can do that.

THE DICTION PROGRAM[16]

The particular techniques I developed for exploring generic features of rhetoric have been described in detail elsewhere.[17] Therefore I shall outline here very briefly the procedures used and the rationales for those procedures. The method of study adopted was computerized language analysis, a procedure by which the text of a message (a poem, a letter, an editorial, a presidential speech) is converted into machine-readable characters (often by key-punching), and a computer is then asked to "pass over it" and to "look" for certain features of language. The computer can perform such operations because it is guided by a software program, in this case a program named DICTION, expressly developed for generic research. Using similar computerized techniques, scholars have

studied the imagery in Shakespeare's plays,[18] determined the authorship
of the disputed *Federalist Papers* (by comparing the long-standing verbal
habits of the rival authorial candidates to those in the unattributed
papers),[19] produced concordances to the Bible,[20] judged the psychological patterns of suicide notes[21] and, with a surprisingly high rate of
success, distinguished the remarks of liars from those of nonliars in
controlled laboratory sessions.[22] One value of such a computerized
program is that it can perform its analyses with incredible speed. The
hundreds of messages examined here were each analyzed from thirty
different vantage points and yet the process required only a few minutes
of computer time. Moreover, with the aid of the computer, a researcher
can examine *combinations* of words that he or she could hardly conceive
of, never mind calculate, without machine assistance.

In computerized language analysis, lists of words (or "dictionaries")
are built into the program and used to search a given passage. These
dictionaries must be carefully constructed so that they accurately measure what they are designed to measure. A dictionary called "Household
Pets," for example, might contain such words as dog, cat, goldfish, and
parakeet. Employing this dictionary as a sorting tool, we would expect to
find greater usage of such words in a child's letter to a friend than, say,
in a speech by Governor Mario Cuomo of New York. Herein lies both
the greatest danger and the greatest advantage of computerized language
study: computer-based investigation is no better than the dictionaries
employed. If the dictionaries are silly, the study itself will be foolish.
Reporting that Cuomo rarely mentions household pets in his public
remarks will surely say more about the reporter than about the intellectual habits of the Governor.

After numerous false starts, I developed four major dictionaries and
seven minor dictionaries. In each case, certain words were seen as
"contributing" to and others as "detracting" from the concept measured.
The four master dictionaries were labeled "Activity," "Optimism,"
"Certainty," and "Realism." A given speech could range from a low of
0 to a high of 300 on each of these dimensions. The four variables turned
out to be statistically quite independent of one another. This indicates,
for example, that knowing a president's "Realism" score for a particular
speech does *not* enable one to guess at his "Activity" score for that same
address. The dictionaries used in this study were the following:

Major Dictionaries

ACTIVITY: Statements referring to motion, change, or
the implementation of ideas. Subcategories

contributing to Activity include aggressiveness (fight, attack), accomplishment (march, push, start), etc. Passive words (quiet, hesitate) and words referring to mental functions (decide, believe) were seen as detracting from Activity.

OPTIMISM: Statements endorsing someone or something, offering positive descriptions, or predicting favorable occurrences. Words indicating praise (good, loyal, sweet), enjoyment (exciting, cheerful), or inspiration (courage, trust) were treated as though they contributed to Optimism, while negations (won't, cannot) and terms of adversity (conflict, despair) were treated as detracting from the Optimism scores.

CERTAINTY: Statements indicating resoluteness, inflexibility, and completeness. Leveling terms (all, everyone), collective nouns (bureau, department), and rigid verbs (will, shall) make for assured statements, while qualifying terms (almost, might), specificity (e.g., numerical citations), and first-person pronouns signaled an individual's refusal to speak ex cathedra.[23]

REALISM: Expressions referring to tangible, immediate, and practical issues. Factors contributing to Realism included concreteness (building, family), present-tense verbs, spatial and temporal references (now, day, city, south), and person-centered remarks (child, us). Realism scores decreased as past-tense verbs and complicated linguistic constructions (e.g., polysyllabic words) increased.

Minor Dictionaries

EMBELLISHMENT: Expressed through a selective ratio of adjectives-to-verbs based on the idea that heavy use of adjectival constructions makes for a "literary" style that "slows down" a verbal passage.

SELF-REFERENCE: Signals a willingness to invest oneself in one's message directly and immediately. This dictionary included all first-person pronouns.

VARIETY: Also known as the type-token ratio. Variety was calculated by dividing the number of

284

different words by the total number of words. A high score indicates a speaker's unwillingness to be repetitive, a decision that produces a "wordy" style.

FAMILIARITY: Consists of C. K. Ogden's "operation" and "direction" words, which he calculated to be among the 750 terms most frequently encountered in everyday speech.[24] A high score thus becomes a measure of colloquialness.

HUMAN INTEREST: An adaptation of Rudolph Flesch's notion that multiple references to human beings give discourse a lively, down-home quality.[25] Includes such words as you, me, father, themselves, etc.

COMPLEXITY: A simple measure of the average number of characters per word in a given passage. Borrows Flesch's notion that big words confuse more than they clarify.

SYMBOLISM: A list of the nation's "sacred" terms that have long been a part of public discourse in the United States. This category contains both "designative" terms (America, national, people) and "ideological" terms (democracy, freedom, law).

In essence, the computer was asked to count how often and where a given speaker used the types of words just described. Such a procedure is obviously not without its problems. For example, the computer cannot analyze the context within which a given word is used but can only report its frequency. In addition, these computerized counts do not take into consideration such important, albeit subtle, features of language as syntax, imagery, rhythm, and arrangement. Many of these limitations become less troublesome when we remember the computer's greatest strength: it deals capably with tremendous *amounts* of verbal information. It can help us track a given speaker across a great many speaking situations during several years in the public eye. It can therefore aid us in assessing his or her overall rhetorical style, his or her universe of discourse—the very sorts of things that may affect the average listener.

Perhaps the main value of the DICTION program is that it searches a speech for words that most speakers treat as unimportant. Even when exercising conscious control over one's words, for example, it is all but impossible to monitor the complex of verbs and adverbs that connotes resoluteness, or to match the enthusiasm of today's speech to that of last

285

week's. Because DICTION operates at the microstylistic level of language use, its discriminatory powers are considerable. Naturally, most speakers scrutinize (and often sanitize) their main ideas when preparing their remarks. The DICTION program, however, is interested only in *how* those remarks are eventually presented. Such a method of analysis holds out the intriguing possibility of discovering individual worldviews and cultural assumptions that are encoded without the knowledge of the encoder.

Space does not permit a more complete presentation of the theoretical assumptions built into DICTION or its methods of operation. Readers interested in DICTION's specific capabilities and a more complete defense of computerized language analysis are referred elsewhere.[26]

Clearly, the user of any sort of automated analysis of human language is confronted with numerous methodological and theoretical problems. But these problems are no different in magnitude from those confronted by an impressionistic critic (though the problems are different in kind). The acid test of any tool of research is whether or not it sheds important light on aspects of human intellectual activity and behavior. If a computer can note things that humans are not capable of noting or if a computer can force a researcher to be more precise and comprehensive in his or her thinking, then surely that computer has served the cause of scholarship. In the eyes of its creator, at least, DICTION does these things and more.

METHODS OF COMPARISON

A particularly helpful feature of DICTION is that it compares any passage being analyzed to a large data bank of other texts. Previously, researchers who did not have such comparison measures at their disposal had to rely on such indefinite claims as "Almost 30 percent of the sentences contain *allness* terms. One cannot avoid allness terms; they are part of the fabric of our everyday conversation, but to use them in three sentences out of ten in a Senate campaign seems excessive."[27] If this researcher had had access, say, to a sufficiently diverse sample of Senate campaign speeches and if, say, norms for "allness" terms were printed out adjacent to the counts for the passage in question, his claims could have been decidedly more precise and meaningful. DICTION prints out precisely such information for the user; thereby, it allows him or her to determine the rough generic shape of the passage in question. As DICTION continues to be used in research, the program will increment these norms each time a passage is examined, thereby ensuring an increasingly meaningful mapping of texts being processed.

286

Of Genre, Computers, and the Reagan Inaugural

So far, DICTION has been used to analyze roughly 900 passages of contemporary American public discourse. For a variety of reasons (many of which have to do with matters of comparability), only the middle 500 words of a given speech are subjected to computerized analysis.[28] Naturally, this very necessary solution to one problem produces problems of its own: DICTION is more helpful in analyzing a set of discourses (e.g., modern inaugural speeches) than a given subset of them (e.g., Ronald Reagan's 1981 inaugural). Similarly, DICTION is better able to account for a speaker's overall encoding habits than for the peculiar rhetorical devices used in a particular speech. Thus I have found its analysis of a given passage to be meaningful only if comparison data for the author of that passage (and/or of the context in which it was presented) were also available.

Commenting in detail here about the Reagan inaugural, I am doing so *for purposes of illustration only*, since, as has been suggested before, the single-instance or case-study approach is really more a "humanistic" (than a scientific) research procedure because it is often unconcerned with generalizability. The scientific concern for generalizability is problematic for the traditional critic interested in particular instances of discourse. Much of our best modern rhetorical criticism, after all, has involved individual analyses of individual speeches: Marie Hochmuth on Lincoln's inaugural address;[29] Hermann Stelzner on Roosevelt's war message;[30] Edwin Black on John Jay Chapman's Coatsville Address.[31] Yet, genre critics, myself included, are simply uninterested in commenting in detail on single instances of discourse. Perhaps because we wish to contribute to the theoretical rather than the historical record, some of us choose to discuss individual messages only insofar as they exemplify larger rhetorical phenomena or serve as negative instances of those phenomena. We are especially interested in suasory fashion, cultural continuities, and speakers' styles. My purpose in the remainder of this essay is to offer neither the first nor the last word on Reagan's 1981 inaugural address. Only to the extent that that address sheds light on Ronald Reagan's habitual way of speaking or on inaugurating activities in general does that message have interest for me.

A number of different speech samples have been analyzed by DICTION. One such sample consisted of thirty-eight speeches each for Presidents Truman through Ford. For each President, nineteen addresses were chosen from the first half of the administration and nineteen from the second half. In all cases, domestic audiences were being addressed. Also, roughly half of the speeches were delivered to national audiences via the electronic media; the remainder were presented to local listeners only.

Finally, a wide range of speaking situations was included: ceremonies, conferences, political gatherings, briefings, and so forth.

The Carter sample was a bit more ambitious so that I could gain a developmental glimpse of presidential language across a single administration. Thirty-eight speeches from each of Jimmy Carter's four years were selected for analysis. The Reagan sample, in contrast, was less comprehensive, consisting of twenty-four speeches delivered during his first year in the Presidency.

In preparing these samples, care was taken to achieve equivalence among three speech topics, since what is said can obviously affect how it is said. The topics included (1) *pragmatics*—speeches focusing on such tangible problems as the economy, energy, labor, and party politics; (2) *values*—speeches detailing the overriding principles and goals of the American people such as freedom, civil rights, justice, and national destiny; (3) *strife*—speeches describing domestic and international conflicts such as Vietnam, the Middle East, and nuclear disarmament.

Clearly, then, DICTION has been asked to search a great many verbal passages, thereby doing what computers do best: count, and remember what has been counted. But is such counting meaningful? Can computers enrich our understanding of rhetoric? Of genres of rhetoric? Can the computer add to a sensitive critic's tool kit? Indeed, can the computer even improve upon a twelve-year-old's powers of discrimination? I believe that the answer to all these questions is Yes. The proof lies partly in the pudding served up by Ronald Wilson Reagan on January 20, 1981.

THE REAGAN INAUGURAL, 1981

As the Reagan Presidency reached the end of its second year, it impressed most people, certainly most journalists, as a communication-centered Presidency. Newspaper and magazine headlines alone were revealing:

Wall Street Journal: "Reagan Misstatements Accumulate But So Far Do Little Harm."

New York Times: "Marketing The President."

Newsweek: "Reagan's Articulation Gap."

U.S. News and World Report: "Silver Tongue Pays Off For Reagan."[32]

Reagan's rhetorical dexterity was the product of an adulthood spent in front of motion picture and television cameras. Having begun his career as an actor, Reagan naturally regarded a public speech as "a theatrical event," according to his biographer Lou Cannon.[33] Cannon also recounts how Reagan's work for the General Electric Corporation between 1954 and 1962 (he served as a touring spokesperson after his film career had ended) marked his transition from the poetic to the rhetorical. During this time, says Cannon, "Reagan made the most of a unique opportunity to develop and polish a basic speech before captive audiences,"[34] thereby learning the difference between encouraging audiences to suspend disbelief and prompting them to believe him implicitly.

It is also significant that Reagan's introduction to the national political scene came as the result of his suasory abilities. His pretaped campaign speech for Barry Goldwater, presented on October 27, 1964, was the only bright light in that year's Republican blackness. But from that devastation rose a rhetorical giant, one who has been described as "the most effective American political orator since Franklin Delano Roosevelt,"[35] who has been linked to Winston Churchill as a "combination orator-rhetorician-leader and *performer*,"[36] whose listeners are said to "sense a whiff of the Kennedy magic and glamour."[37]

Ronald Reagan is very much a twenty-first-century chief executive. He knows, and what's more important he *feels*, what it takes to lead a people housed in bungalows connected to the White House by endless loops of thin black cable. It was thus a twenty-first-century compliment paid to Reagan by his aides when one of them said: "The staff doesn't presume to tell him, if it's a question of how you persuade people. No one challenges him because he's far better than anyone on the staff."[38]

Certainly Reagan's first speech in office evidences his rhetorical talent. The data I have gathered indicate that *Reagan's inaugural address was a generic hybrid—part inaugural, part campaign speech.* Because he has a natural ability to deal with people, he also has a natural ability to adapt to people. And his inaugural address is indeed adapted—to a nation tired of having its citizens jailed in Iran, tired of being unable to afford housing, tired of Jimmy Carter being tired of his job. Reagan's inaugural implicitly acknowledged these realities while simultaneously honoring traditional ceremonial demands. To phrase it more technically, his speech bore the imprint of an ancestral genre (its archetype) as well as its maker's personal and philosophical mark (its "signature").[39] The result was a piece of discourse that was Reaganesque to its core.

TRADITIONAL ASPECTS

Table 10.1 presents DICTION-derived facts concerning the Reagan inaugural, the nine immediately preceding inaugurals, twenty-four of

289

Table 10.1 Comparative Data concerning the Reagan Inaugural
Address (1981) (As analyzed by program DICTION)

Variable	Presidential Speech Generally (N = 380)	Other Presidents' Inaugurals (N = 9)	Overall Reagan (N = 24)	Reagan Inaugural
Activity	200.6	212.9	198.3	210.4
Realism	192.3	193.9	188.4	184.1
Certainty	185.5	215.7	181.1	230.1
Optimism	218.7	221.6	221.3	187.1
Complexity	5.11	4.88	5.89	7.60
Variety	.489	.475	.490	.480
Self-Reference	8.01	1.00	9.04	2.00
Familiarity	102.1	102.1	102.1	110.0
Human Interest	27.5	36.6	28.0	39.0
Embellishment	.067	.059	.072	.038
Symbolism	4.99	8.66	6.15	20.0

Reagan's first-year speeches, and a large sampling of other presidential discourse delivered between 1945 and 1980. This assemblage of data permits us to make a number of interesting cross-comparisons and to ask questions of an institutional, personal, and generic nature. The small sample sizes for inaugural speeches do not allow tests of statistical difference to be made, but the mean comparisons are suggestive nonetheless.

For example, table 10.1 indicates that Reagan's predecessors used the inaugural situation to produce what might be called visionary bluster, a distinctively American art form. When inaugurating their administrations, they used unusually high amounts of Activity and Certainty to indicate that important changes were in the offing and that their presidential eyes were trained on unassailable truths. Richard Nixon, for example, said, "For all of our people, we will set as our goal the decent order that makes progress possible and our lives secure . . . . In pursuing our goals of full employment, better housing, excellence in education, in rebuilding our cities and improving our rural areas, in protecting our environment and enhancing our quality of life, in all these and more, we will and must press forward urgently."[40] Strong inaugural words like these are comforting. Even if listeners do not accept their literal truth, listeners are heartened to discover that the new President has learned the lyrics of American indomitability so quickly. On Inauguration Day, at least, Americans are willing to luxuriate a bit and imagine that the new President will one day learn the legislative tune needed to go with these fine words. Americans are, to the dismay of many others on this planet, an assured, can-do people. The inaugural address echoes that fact.

Because they are *Americans*, Presidents are also required to used folksy platitudes on Inauguration Day. Later, when farm subsidies, nuclear-waste disposal sites, arms negotiations, and inflationary spirals occupy their attention, Presidents will be permitted to speak more technocratically. But on their first day in office, Presidents use less Complexity and Variety and more Human Interest and Symbolism than they will habitually use later on. Freshly minted Presidents thus use a combination of simple and emotional words for defining simple and emotional truths. In describing the American faith, for instance, Dwight Eisenhower opined, "This faith rules our whole way of life. It decrees that we, the people, elect leaders not to rule but to serve. It asserts that we have the right to choice of our own work and to the reward of our own toil . . . . And it warns that any man who seeks to deny equality among all his brothers betrays the spirit of the free and invites the mockery of the tyrant."[41] As many Americans remember, Eisenhower was not always able to speak this elegantly, but the inaugural situation brought out felicity of phrasing from both him and his writers.

Predictably, the Presidents decreased their Self-References during the inauguration, an adaptation signaling (1) the formality of their circumstances and (2) the self-abnegation expected of kings newly robed. To behave otherwise would be a faux pas—even for a plainspoken American speaking to plainspeaking Americans. None of the most recent Presidents used more than three Self-References in the 500-word passages analyzed; two, Kennedy and Johnson, never referred to themselves. On this dimension, apparently, the inaugural address must be all archetype, no signature.

Although he did not decrease his Complexity, Ronald Reagan followed the inaugural trail blazed by his predecessors as regards Activity, Certainty, Variety, Human Interest, Symbolism, and Self-References. Indeed, Reagan had always appreciated ceremonial speaking, perhaps because he had played the parts of a good number of trailblazers in his days on the silver screen, perhaps because he had a natural talent for hagiography, perhaps because ceremonies insulated him from the perplexities of reporters' questions. Ceremonial speeches permit the safe overstatement and invocation of national symbols. Speeches of this sort allowed Ronald Reagan to return to the simple themes of his General Electric days. "Because he believed in these pieties," says Lou Cannon, "he could get away with saying what other politicians were unable to say."[42] Ceremonial settings, of course, also permit use of a *script*, a script that an experienced speaker like Ronald Reagan had long since committed to memory. As Wayne Valis said, "Reagan can make an adequate script good; good material he makes excellent."[43]

The Reagan inaugural of 1981 was a veritable litany of the Tory virtues its author so admires. It was pellucid, personably unyielding, exceptionally colloquial, and, once again, pellucid: "With the idealism and fair play which are at the core of our system and our strength, we can have a strong and prosperous America, at peace with itself and the world. So, as we begin, let us take inventory. We are a nation that has a government—not the other way around. And this makes us special among the nations of the Earth. Our government has no power except that granted it by the people."[44] Although he was a new President, these were hardly new words for Reagan. He had said them at Eureka College; he had said them on *Death Valley Days*; he had said them standing at Barry Goldwater's side; he had said them to the radicals at Berkeley; he had said them during each of his presidential campaigns. Ronald Reagan did not mind in the least that much of his inaugural address was traditional, for he respected the formulas. Indeed, he was the formulas.

NONTRADITIONAL ASPECTS

There is also something of the radical in Ronald Reagan. He is not one to be dictated to by conventions unless those conventions serve him well. During the 1980 campaign, for example, he did not mind mixing it up with hecklers, upstaging his Republican rivals during a debate that George Bush "had bought and paid for," implicitly belittling Jimmy Carter with his "There you go again, Mr. President."[45] It would not be appropriate to call Ronald Reagan a rhetorical tactician (as one might call Richard Nixon), but he has a devastatingly fine sense of communication—an ability to determine how much weight a public platform will bear, and a gutsiness to load it up just short of that weight. As a consequence, there was a distinctive tone to his 1981 inaugural address, a warning that Reagan already knew his way around the presidential block.

Table 10.1 reveals that he used slightly less Realism (i.e., a greater number of abstractions) than did his predecessors in their inaugurals; and he used *much* more Certainty and Symbolism. Reagan's score of 230 on Certainty places him in the 90th percentile for that variable among the more than 400 presidential messages analyzed by DICTION. The *combination* of generous amounts of Certainty and Symbolism with little Realism pushes Reagan's 1981 inaugural beyond the philosophical to the

292

ideological, beyond the chauvinistic to the jingoistic. There was a kind of genetic assurance to his remarks, a hortatory quality found more often in the Washington Cathedral than in the White House. Reagan pounded home his themes of less government and more responsibility with a kind of epigrammatic logic: "government is not the solution to our problems; government is the problem"; ". . . the price for this freedom is high. But we have never been unwilling to pay the price"; and "[our economic ills] will not go away in days, weeks, or months, but they will go away."[46]

Wrapped in Inauguration Day bunting as he was, there was probably little danger that Reagan would be upbraided for such partisan overenthusiasm. American listeners tend to give their newly sworn-in Presidents rhetorical license; in his first inaugural address, Reagan used all that was given him. Commenting on Reagan's speech, Hedrick Smith implies that the new President's style was virtually dictated by the American people: "The time imperative presses him [Reagan] to produce an immediate sense of forward motion, to produce the feeling that he has taken charge and begun to halt the drift and uncertainty that caused such an explosive burst of voter frustration against the Democrats. And he has signaled that he intends his first day in office to convey a sense of urgency."[47] Thus, even if Reagan did not have an undisputed political mandate as a newly elected President, his inaugural speech, at least, had a fairly clear rhetorical mandate.

Reagan's address was more than just ideological. It was also somewhat apocalyptic. His Optimism score of 187 was lower than Harry Truman's in his saber-rattling speech on the war against Japan (Aug. 9, 1945), lower than Richard Nixon's resignation speech, and almost as low as Gerald Ford's second State of the Union speech (in which he declared that the state of the union "is not good"). Reagan's inaugural was almost forty points lower on Optimism than either his normal rate or the average rates of the other Presidents. The speech was peppered with unsettling phrases like "economic ills," "bear the burden," "terror of runaway living costs," "fate that will befall us," and "doomed to an inevitable decline."[48] Undoubtedly, we see here something of the incumbent-gouging that had characterized Reagan's just completed campaign speaking. This suggests that Reagan may still have been nursing a rhetorical hangover. Extending the metaphor a bit, we might think of Ronald Reagan's 1981 inaugural celebration as having turned into something of an Irish wake.

Turning to other aspects of his style, we might note that no published commentator has had the temerity to suggest that Ronald Reagan is a stylist. Certainly nothing in his 1981 inaugural address suggested otherwise. There was precious little grace or panache there, no interesting phraseology or startling imagery. An interesting finding is that Reagan's Complexity rating for the inaugural was dramatically higher than his predecessors' scores and considerably higher than those in his later speeches. A passage that averages better than seven and one-half characters per word sounded more like a technical report to stockholders than a conversation with the folks.

Two factors—one semantic and the other syntactic—may account for Reagan's use of dense language. Apparently, his public-speaking vocabulary contains a large number of polysyllabic terms, many of which are born of Republican loins: "inventory," "productivity," "entrepreneurs," "equitable," "establishment," "administration."[49] This is language of the board room, a language embracing the hypostatizations that, according to the New Republicans, can make government more responsible to its employers—the American people. It was reflective of Reagan's rhetorical genius that he could use such terms in the very same passage in which he referred to the "men and women who raised our food, patrol our streets, man our mines and factories, teach our children, keep our homes, and heal us when we're sick."[50] Reagan's first inaugural, like Reagan's politics itself, was a fascinating blend of Republican assumptions and Democratic language. His high Human Interest *and* Complexity scores earmark him as a kind of bastard son of Eleanor Roosevelt and Herbert Hoover.

Reagan's Complexity scores also result from his dependence on complex sentences, the passive voice, and imbedded clauses. Adlai Stevenson used big words, too, but he also had a marvelous ability to fold them into simple, active constructions such that pace and harmony emerged. Apparently, Reagan's speechwriters were not gifted in these ways. Reagan's cumbersome use of language during his press conferences suggests that he himself is not thus gifted either. The difficulty with using grammatically complex constructions, of course, is that once one enters a sentence, one's words expand inexorably while searching for an exit. Those few American schoolchildren who are still able to diagram English sentences would have their work cut out for them with Reagan's speech: "It is my intention to curb the size and influence of the Federal establishment and to demand recognition of the distinction between the powers granted to the Federal Government and those reserved to the States or to the people,"[51] or "It is no coincidence that our present troubles parallel and are proportionate to the intervention and intrusion in our lives that result from unnecessary excessive growth of government."[52]

294

A final element distinguishing the Reagan inaugural address was his avoidance of Embellishment. Reagan's later speeches were normally twice as embellished as his first set of remarks. The result was a spare inaugural address. Indeed, compared to Jimmy Carter's fleshy first speech, Reagan's was gaunt. In the Carter address, commitments were "resurgent commitments"; glories were "remembered glories"; nations were "proudly idealistic" nations; and worlds were not only "just and peaceful" but "truly humane" as well.[53] In the Reagan passage analyzed here, only one triple modifier and five double modifiers appeared. The remaining 150 nouns took a single modifier or, more typically, received no modification at all. Trading on basic American affirmations apparently makes modifiers superfluous. Thus, when lionizing the nation's citizens, Reagan used no adjectival flattery at all. He simply called the roll: "professionals, industrialists, shopkeepers, clerks, cabbies, and truckdrivers."[54]

Although I have discussed various devices of language in isolation here, rhetoric becomes rhetoric only by their combination. How has Reagan combined them? What is an assured, symbolic, negative, familiar, and unadorned speech? It was a classic piece of stump oratory, a let's-drive-the ingrates-out-of-Washington speech and yet it also retained ceremonial markings. His speech was thus the product of equal parts of tradition and innovation, a rhetorical amalgamation suited both to the new President's radical agenda and to his curious political personality as well. The Reagan inaugural was an ideational—and stylistic—signal that there was a new fellow in town who had a new broom and who could at least *talk* about using it. His postinaugural days would temper his rhetoric, as days in Washington, D.C., inevitably do, but the Reagan inaugural speech nevertheless served the classic functions of an inaugural address—to introduce, to remind, to warn, and to promise. In key-noting his administration, however, Reagan did it in a Reaganesque way.

CONCLUSION

An analytical tool like DICTION cannot so much lay bare a political message as it can offer a *perspective* on that message. The perspective it offers is uniquely rhetorical because the computer can report on language usage vis-à-vis a community of language users. When examining Reagan's speech in such comparative lights, I found he did some incipiently revolutionary things with words. That determination was made by comparing his remarks to those of his predecessors. Because they were computer-based, these comparisons were orderly, systematic, equivalent, quantitative, and generic. None of these features, of course, gives such comparisons privileged status. As an analytical program, DICTION is primarily useful for flagging the critic's attention, for directing him or her to features of rhetoric that may, additively, have great impact on listeners but that may be so subtle as to escape the attention of even the most careful listener or reader. DICTION does little more than record, remember, and report. A critic must then perform the operations that critics have always performed—sift among the data for useful data, interpret those facts worth interpreting, share those interpretations that should be shared. These are the time-honored procedures of humanistic research. The fact that a computer was used to advance these procedures does not necessarily improve the research—nor, I would add, does it necessarily make it less humanistic.

Notes

1. For a sample of the state of discussion in the mid-1970s, see Karlyn Kohrs Campbell and Kathleen Hall Jamieson, eds., *Form and Genre: Shaping Rhetorical Action* (Falls Church, Va.: Speech Cummunication Association, 1978).

2. Carol Jablonski, "Richard Nixon's Irish Wake: A Case Study of Generic Transference," *Central States Speech Journal* 30 (1979):156–63.

3. Richard Fulkerson, "The Public Letter as a Rhetorical Form: Structure, Logic, and Style in King's 'Letter from Birmingham Jail,' " *Quarterly Journal of Speech* 65 (1979):121–36.

4. Bruce E. Gronbeck, "The Rhetoric of Political Corruption: Sociolinguistic, Dialectical, and Ceremonial Processes," *Quarterly Journal of Speech* 64 (1978):155–72.

5. Thomas Clark, "An Exploration of Generic Aspects of Contemporary American Christian Sermons," *Quarterly Journal of Speech* 63 (1977):384–94.

6. See, especially, Kathleen H. Jamieson, "Antecedent Genre as Rhetorical Constraint," *Quarterly Journal of Speech* 61 (1975):406–15, and Karlyn K. Campbell, "The Rhetoric of Women's Liberation: An Oxymoron," *Quarterly Journal of Speech* 59 (1973):74–86.

7. Campbell and Jamieson, eds., *Form and Genre.*

8. Ibid., pp. 26–27.

9. Roderick P. Hart, "Theory-Building and Rhetorical Criticism: An Informal Statement of Opinion," *Central States Speech Journal* 27 (1976):75.

10. Herbert Simons, " 'Genre-alizing' about Rhetoric: A Scientific Approach," in Campbell and Jamieson, eds., *Form and Genre*, pp. 33–50.

11. Hart, "Philosophical Commonality and Speech Types," unpublished Ph.D. diss., Pennsylvania State University, 1970.

12. See Clark, "An Exploration of Generic Aspects"; also his "An Analysis of Recurrent Features of Contemporary American Radical, Liberal, and Conservative Political Discourse," *Southern Speech Communication Journal* 44 (1979):399–422, and "An Exploration of Generic Aspects of Contemporary American Campaign Orations," *Central States Speech Journal* 30 (1979):122–33.

13. Hart, *Verbal Style and the Presidency: A Computer-Based Analysis* (New York: Academic Press, 1984).

14. Theodore Windt, "The Diatribe: Last Resort for Protest," *Quarterly Journal of Speech* 58 (1972):1–14.

15. See, e.g., Ernest G. Bormann, "Generalizing about Significant Form: Science and Humanism Compared and Contrasted," in Campbell and Jamieson, eds., *Form and Genre*, pp. 51–69.

16. Portions of this section have been culled from Hart, *Verbal Style and the Presidency*.

17. Ibid.

18. Dolores M. Burton, *Shakespeare's Grammatical Style: A Computer-Assisted Analysis of "Richard II" and "Anthony and Cleopatra"* (Austin: University of Texas Press, 1973).

19. Fredrick Mosteller and David L. Wallace, *Inference and Disputed Authorship: "The Federalist"* (Reading, Mass.: Addison-Wesley, 1964).

20. For a general commentary on the uses of the computer in "literary" matters, see George Gerbner et al., eds., *The Analysis of Communication Content: Developments in Scientific Theories and Computer Techniques* (New York: Wiley, 1969).

21. Philip Stone and Earl Hunt, "A Computer Approach to Content Analysis: Studies Using the General Inquirer System," *Proceedings of the Spring Joint Computer Conference* (Washington, D.C.: Spartan Books, 1963).

22. Mark Knapp, Roderick Hart, and Harry Dennis, "Deception as a Communication Construct," *Human Communication Research* 1 (1974):15–29.

23. This variable has been used, in slightly modified form, in my "Absolutism and Situation: Prolegomena to a Rhetorical Biography of Richard M. Nixon," *Communication Monographs* 43 (1976):204–28.

24. C. K. Ogden, *Basic English: International Second Language* (New York: Harcourt Brace Jovanovich, 1968).

25. Rudolph Flesch, *The Art of Plain Talk* (New York: Collier, 1951).

26. See my "Systematic Analysis of Political Discourse: The Development of DICTION," in Keith Sanders, Dan Nimmo, and Lynda Kaid, eds., *Political Communication Yearbook: 1984* (Carbondale, Ill.: Southern Illinois University Press, 1985).

27. Herbert E. Knepprath, "Computer-Assisted Criticism: The 1968 Campaign Speaking of Max Rafferty," in G. P. Mohrmann, Charles Stewart, and Donovan Ochs, eds., *Exploration in Rhetorical Criticism* (University Park: Pennsylvania State University Press, 1973), pp. 138–57.

28. The main reason for eliminating the beginning and ending portions of the speeches was that such segments typically contain localized and personalized cues unique to the speaking occasion, thus making cross-comparisons meaningless. Typically, the middle 500 words of a public speech are not as heavily affected by contextual factors.

29. Wayland Parrish and Marie Hochmuth, *American Speeches* (New York: Longmans, Green, 1954), pp. 21–71.

30. Stelzner, " 'War Message,' December 8, 1941: An Approach to Language," *Speech Monographs* 33 (1966):419–37.

31. Black, *Rhetorical Criticism: A Study in Method* (New York: Macmillan, 1965).

32. Rich Jaroslovsky, *Wall Street Journal*, June 15, 1982, p. 33; Sidney Blumenthal, *New York Times Magazine*, Sept. 13, 1981, pp. 43ff.; Melinda Beck and Eleanor Clift, *Newsweek*, June 29, 1981, p. 20; Alvin P. Senoff, *U.S. News and World Report*, March 2, 1982, p. 29.

33. Lou Cannon, *Reagan* (New York: G. P. Putnam, 1982), p. 36.

34. Ibid., p. 72.

35. Robert Lindsey, "Creating the Role," in Hedrick Smith et al., eds., *Reagan the Man and the President* (New York: Macmillan, 1980), p. 24.

36. Wayne Valis, "Ronald Reagan: The Man, the President," in W. Valis, ed., *The Future under President Reagan* (Westport, Conn.: Arlington House, 1981), p. 34.

37. Hedrick Smith, "Mr. Reagan Goes to Washington," in Smith et al., *Reagan*, p. 150.

38. Quoted in Blumenthal, *New York Times Magazine*, p. 110.

39. The language is that used by Anthony Hillbruner in "Archetype and Signature: Nixon and the 1973 Inaugural," *Central States Speech Journal* 25 (1974):169–81.

40. Nixon, "World Freedom and Peace" [second inaugural address], *Vital Speeches of the Day* 19, no. 8 (1953):253.

41. Eisenhower, "First Inaugural Address," *Inaugural Addresses of the Presidents of the United States* (Washington, DC: U.S. Government Printing Office, 1961), p. 259.

42. Cannon, *Reagan*, p. 371.

43. Valis, "Ronald Reagan," p. 35.

44. Reagan, "Inaugural Address," *Weekly Compilations of Presidential Documents* 17, no. 4 (1981):2.

45. The last reference, of course, is to Reagan's remarks during his debate with then President Jimmy Carter; see "Presidential Debate," *Weekly Compilations of Presidential Documents* 12, no. 41 (1976):1445–59.

46. Reagan, "Inaugural Address," pp. 2, 3.

47. Hedrick Smith, "Reformer Would Reverse New Deal's Legacy," *New York Times*, Jan. 21, 1981, p. B2.

48. Reagan, "Inaugural Address," pp. 2, 3.

49. Ibid.

50. Ibid., p. 2.

51. Ibid.

52. Ibid., p. 3.

53. Carter, "Inaugural Address," *Weekly Compilations of Presidential Documents* 13, no. 4 (1977):88, 89.

54. Reagan, "Inaugural Address," p. 2.

PART III
COMMENTARY

Richard A. Joslyn

KEEPING POLITICS IN THE STUDY OF POLITICAL DISCOURSE

INTRODUCTION

When the editors of this volume asked me to serve as a roving critic at the Fourth Annual Conference on Discourse Analysis, I accepted with some reluctance. On the one hand, the topic of the conference—political discourse—was one that was of special interest to me and had become the subject of most of my writing. On the other hand, I knew almost nothing of the speech-communication literature and even less, if that is possible, about that body of research known as "form and genre." I therefore approached the task of criticizing the research efforts of the community of scholars gathered in Philadelphia in March 1983 with considerable trepidation.

The conference turned out to be a delight. In contrast to my own discipline's general disdain for political rhetoric, here was a group of thoughtful, energetic, productive scholars who clearly considered political "talk" to be important. It was a rejuvenating experience and reinforced my opinion that political science's neglect of political rhetoric was a serious shortcoming.

In the pages that follow, I have attempted to fulfill my original critical role in writing. Given my lack of familiarity with the more theoretical and historical issues with which this community of scholars has grappled, I have decided to focus primarily on the "research" chapters in this volume, especially those chapters in the second section that analyze the Reagan inaugural. For it is in the analysis of the 1981 inaugural that the approaches to political discourse utilized here take on their most concrete and immediate application.

Throughout this chapter I have tried to keep one overriding question central: In what ways and to what extent do these analyses help us better understand political processes in general and political discourse in particular? In the following pages I take a number of cracks at this question by raising, but probably not answering to anyone's satisfaction, a number of subsidiary questions about the research included in this volume.

IDENTIFYING A GENRE OF POLITICAL DISCOURSE

An appropriate place to begin is with the concept of a rhetorical genre itself. Since a few of the chapters included in this volume are written by those who believe that it is useful to think in terms of genres of political discourse, we might well ask whether that presumption is well justified by the authors represented here. What sorts of arguments are made and evidence presented in support of the notion of a genre of political discourse? In particular, how compelling is the claim that the case of political discourse studied most extensively here—the presidential inaugural—represents a distinctive rhetorical genre?

One striking feature of the justification for genres of political discourse presented in this volume is that the need for justification is not taken terribly seriously. Those supporting the claim that presidential inaugurals constitute a genre of discourse, for example, generally do so through assertion or, at best, selective illustration. Seldom is the need for a careful, systematic, empirical accounting of the genre manifested; rather, the existence of the genre is generally assumed. As a result, those who question the whole feasibility of classifying political discourse into genres are unlikely to be persuaded by the justifications offered herein. Or, to put it another way, the generic claims made in this volume are not advanced explicitly or extensively enough even to engage many of Conley's fears concerning the "Linnaean Blues."

Campbell and Jamieson make the boldest generic claims in their analysis of the inaugural as a genre of political discourse. Their assertion rests largely on their observation that "conventional wisdom and ordinary language treat presidential inaugurals as a class," and that "critics have intuitively taken them to belong to a distinct rhetorical type." In addition, they assert that inaugurals are a subspecies of epideictic discourse of a "distinctive kind," consisting of "four interrelated elements."

The claim that presidential inaugurals constitute a rhetorical genre, then, rests on the empirical claim that they contain the "four interrelated elements." Campbell and Jamieson attempt to demonstrate this claim by illustrating each of the four elements in a variety of inaugurals. This process of illustration raises two questions germane to the generic claim.

First, do all inaugurals contain all four of the specified elements? Second, does any other class of speech also contain the four elements? Campbell and Jamieson are, unfortunately, silent on the first question, although in places there is some hint that not all inaugurals are equally satisfying of the generic classification. Is an inaugural any less a member of the genre if it is absent one or two of the four elements?

Similarly, it is unclear whether or not there are other cases of political discourse that also contain the four elements specified by Campbell and Jamieson. State of the Union addresses, late October campaign speeches by a runaway front-runner, and even contemporary nomination acceptance speeches delivered by incumbent Presidents would seem likely also to contain the elements of discourse identified as typical of inaugurals. If so, then what Campbell and Jamieson may have discovered is not just a genre of presidential inauguration but a much broader genre of political legitimation and consensus-building. In fact, the first two of Campbell and Jamieson's four elements—reconstituting the audience and rehearsing communal values drawn from the past—may be the elements that define legitimizing or celebration rhetoric, while the other two elements simply define the presidential variation of this rhetorical type. Any number of occasions of discourse—the preambles of significant statutes, the speeches delivered on a nation's political holidays, and the speeches given at other celebrations such as the Olympics or the Bicentennial of the writing of the U.S. Constitution—reconstitute the audience and rehearse communal values. It is perhaps only in the presidential inaugural, however, that the connection is made with presidential actions and the Presidency.

This line of reasoning—from the identification of the general elements of legitimizing or celebratory discourse to the analysis of presidential inauguration—is, in fact, the path toward a generic claim taken by Gronbeck. He argues that the discourse that takes place upon the occasion of ceremonies to mark periods of cultural transition includes elements of "remembrance, legitimation, and celebration." By this broader understanding Gronbeck asserts that any number of rhetorical cases—keynotes, commencement addresses, funeral orations for heads of state, thanksgiving sermons, artillery election sermons—along with presidential inaugurals, form a recurring pattern of political rhetoric. In other words, Gronbeck does raise the second question asked above—Does any other class of speech share significant attributes with presidential inaugurals?—and he answers it in the affirmative.

Gronbeck is also more forthcoming on the first question raised above:

303

Have all inaugurals included the rhetorical characteristics of the genre of which they are presumably representative? Gronbeck does this by specifying his three key elements of ceremonial speech—remembrance, legitimation, and celebration—and then leaving open the question of whether any particular address satisfies these criteria. It is a pity that he, having specified a general set of criteria by which to judge inaugural addresses, then turns his analytical gaze upon only one case: Ronald Reagan's 1981 inaugural. However, posing the question in this way forces Gronbeck to keep open the question of generic fit in a particular case and allows him to conclude, as he does in the Reagan case, that a particular inaugural address may be bereft of the elements of ceremonial speech.

Roderick Hart pursues the discovery of the regularities or patterns in a genre of discourse in a significantly different manner. He *presumes* that there are "powerful and less powerful generic markers; that is, some "communicative patterns" that "point toward systemic regularities." Unlike Campbell and Jamieson, and Gronbeck, Hart begins with no a priori expectations of the rhetorical content of presidential inaugurals. There is nothing in his analysis even vaguely resembling Campbell and Jamieson's "four elements" or Gronbeck's three aspects of inauguration. Instead, Hart proceeds in a purely, one might say radically, inductive fashion. The content of presidential inaugurals across eleven language dictionaries (unjustified *here* at least in their content or inclusion) is measured and contrasted with presidential speech in general. The outcome of this procedure is taken to be the measurement of what is distinctive about inaugural addresses, in contrast to the form of presidential discourse generally.

The main virtue of Hart's approach is that it specifies a procedure that could be used, efficiently, to address the first question raised above: Do all instances of presidential inaugurals contain some common set of rhetorical elements? (A question that Hart, like Gronbeck, answers only for the Reagan case here.) However, the key to how illuminating such a procedure will be for the identification of genres is the extent to which the language dimensions used are important for understanding the content of the genre. In Hart's essay, the case is never made (or even attempted) for this particular selection of the language dictionaries.

Are all eleven dimensions important for this genre? Are all eleven dimensions *equally* important? Is it the frequency on each dimension separately that is important, or some combination of language use? Hart provides us with little guidance on this matter. Instead, each "dictionary" is dealt with separately, and we are never told how each enhances generic classification.

Ironically, Hart does provide a truncated description of the rhetorical elements of another form of political discourse: the campaign speech. It, Hart says, is "an assured, symbolic, negative, familiar, and unadorned speech," a statement that tells us what to expect when campaign speeches are analyzed with his eleven dictionaries. Unfortunately, no such clear statement exists for presidential inaugurals, hence preventing the reader from developing a general expectation for his analysis of inaugurals.

It is with regard to the comparative question—Do other cases of political discourse share the generic characteristics of presidential inaugurals?—that Hart's procedure has the most potential. The computerized analysis of political discourse facilitates comparisons across cases and types of political rhetoric. Unfortunately, the comparison made here— with presidential speech generally—is problematic, for as far as I know no one has ever suggested that all presidential speech constitutes a genre of its own. Hence, all we know is that inaugurals are different from an amalgam of presidential speech. But of what genre, then, are inaugurals a part? Are they a subspecies of ceremonial speech in general, as Gronbeck suggests, and hence similar to keynote and commencement addresses? Or are they a subspecies of political legitimation speech and consequently similar to the preambles to statutes, the founding documents of civil societies, and calls to arms? Or are they a subspecies of celebratory discourse and, thereby, similar to speeches given on patriotic holidays and celebrations of the achievements of Olympic athletes? Hart's procedure will permit an answer to these questions, provided the rhetorical elements of the genres are well defined and captured by his "dictionaries."

In short, there is a general failure in this volume to substantiate adequately or to test the claim that there are such things as genres of political discourse, and that presidential inaugurals in particular constitute one such genre. The comparative question—Do all instances of a type of discourse exhibit consistently, equally, some concrete set of characteristics?—is only halfheartedly addressed by Campbell and Jamieson (though the potential exists in Hart's approach). The inclusiveness question—Are there other types of discourse that share the features of inauguration?—is addressed only by Gronbeck. Perhaps there is no need to establish such a claim; perhaps those toiling in this area have settled this question to their satisfaction long ago. To an outside observer, however, as well as to Conley and McGee, such assertions are clearly in need of more careful and extensive justification.

305

Part III: Commentary

WHAT CAUSES GENRES OF POLITICAL DISCOURSE?

If one accepts that there are, indeed, patterns of political rhetoric, which might be called rhetorical genres, the next question that arises concerns the origins of these patterns. Why is it that different instances of political discourse share common elements? Is it because of the situation or setting faced by the rhetor? Is it because of the expectations of the audience? Is it due to the constraints imposed by the medium through which the discourse is transmitted? Is it the result of genetic influences? Or is it, more simply, a case of imitation and habit among a community of speech writers?

Five of the chapters in this volume attempt to explain why there should be patterns of political rhetoric. Campbell and Jamieson, and Gronbeck clearly believe that the ceremonial occasion is crucial for understanding the generic patterns of presidential inaugurals. In fact, in the view of Campbell and Jamieson the ceremony itself *necessitates* the content of the inaugural. For example, they argue that the investiture ceremony dictates that a President *"must* show that he understands the principles of a democratic-republican form of government and the limits it imposes on executive power, and he *must* manifest rhetorically his ability to lead and to be the symbolic head of state who is President of all the people" (emphasis added). Later, this notion of necessity appears again: "Before the audience can witness and ratify the ascent to power, it *must* be unified and reconstituted as 'the people,' " . . . "the President *must* venerate the past and show that the traditions of the institution continue unbroken in him. He *must* affirm that he will transmit the institution intact to his successors"; (emphasis added), and "a president *must* go beyond the rehearsal of traditional values. . . ." Campbell and Jamieson speak of "the demand that a President demonstrate rhetorically a capacity for effective leadership" and, finally, "the President *must* demonstrate his understanding of the epideictic *demands* of a ritualistic event" (*emphasis added*).

What is it, exactly, that creates this necessity so central to Campbell and Jamieson's analysis of inaugurals? They never say. Besides a vague reference to the importance of the ceremonial setting in which inaugurals occur ("the demands of investiture *require*"), the only other explanation provided is that "the audience expects the presidential role to be enacted" (emphasis added). But if that is what creates the necessity, how are these expectations communicated to Presidents? Have Presidents tested the boundaries of these expectations so that their successors have known what *not* to do?

306

Campbell and Jamieson also entertain parenthetically another possible explanation for the patterns of presidential inaugurals. They admit that much of the similarity across inaugurals may simply be because one President's speech writers study past inaugurals and imitate them when writing their own. In general, however, Campbell and Jamieson are relatively unconcerned with explaining how it is that the generic necessity, so central to their understanding of presidential inaugurals, is created.

Hart's approach to explaining the patterns in political discourse is also distressingly truncated and vague. He mentions communicative rules and norms, but never illustrates what they are, where they come from, or how they operate on a rhetor. Like Campbell and Jamieson, he also apparently believes that the ceremonial setting creates traditional demands: "Presidents are . . . required to use folksy platitudes on Inauguration Day." Unlike Campbell and Jamieson, however, he apparently thinks that the life-experience of each rhetor and the mood of the citizenry make significant contributions to each inaugural address. So, he concludes, Reagan's speech "bore the imprint of an ancestral genre (its archetype) as well as its maker's personal and philosophical mark (its 'signature')." In one place Hart combines the audience expectation and individual rhetor explanations by asserting that in 1981 Reagan used all of the "rhetorical license" granted him by his audience. The result was a speech that was "equal parts tradition and innovation."

Perhaps it is unfair to criticize the explanations for presidential rhetoric in two pieces that do not have explanation as their major goal. However, the language used by Hart and by Campbell and Jamieson leaves an impression, and it is primarily an impression, of rhetorical constraint, necessity, or determination that is almost mystical in nature. The language comes close to equating the patterns in inaugurals with the patterns that *must* be in inaugurals without explaining why that is the case. Other than brief indications that ceremonial settings, audience expectations, and rhetorical experience shape political discourse, little is said about *how* communicative norms, rules, traditions, conventions, similarities, or patterns are established.

Gronbeck, Blankenship, and Simons and Aghazarian are much more helpful in explaining the similarities in political discourse delivered by different rhetors. For Gronbeck, it is the political setting in which a speech is given that is crucial for understanding the patterns in presidential inaugurals. The conditions of the polity at this moment of cultural-political transition, he argues, create the expectations of the audience and the needs of the rhetor. This is a useful observation, for it points us in the direction of a phenomenon that exhibits meaningful variation and that could be helpful in explaining the variation in the content of inaugurals and other ceremonial addresses. In some political systems, transfers of power are episodic, and take place generally at a time of civic uncertainty and political change. In other political systems, such as our own, transfers of power are more cyclical and may or may not take place during times of unrest, strife, anxiety, or turmoil. From this we would expect that the content of inaugurals will not be identical over time or varied only in terms of personal stylistic eloquence, but rather, will reflect meaningful variations in the political conditions extant at the time of the address. If one assumes, for example, that legitimation is required more in times of cultural stress, then we would expect it to vary as a component of inaugurals with the amount of recent civil strife at inauguration times.

Blankenship also attempts to provide a more extensive explanation for the origin of an act of political communication. Her view of the development of form combines elements of both constraint and choice. The rhetor is delimited by purpose, situation, *materia*, and the perceptual and conceptual apparatus of one's audience, but also exercises considerable choice in the selection of rhetorical content.

On the one hand, rhetors are constrained in what they may sensibly do when "engaged in the dialogue called rhetorical action." The mode of communication, the purpose for the discourse, and the abilities and expectations of the audience delimit what may reasonably be accomplished by a rhetor. Quoting Richard Ohmann, Blankenship maintains that any speech act is "governed by rules that antedate the speaker's [speakers'] appearance and postdate his [their] disappearance."

On the other hand, within the parameters circumscribed by these limits, rhetors make rhetorical choices. They make choices about "all aspects of verbal and visual language—in the sound, grammatical, syntactical, and lexical levels." Some of these choices may be serendipitous or accidental, but they are choices nonetheless. And, as Blankenship observes, "By virtue of exercising some choices (words, structures, etc.) rather than others, any rhetorical action 'constructs' one interpretation of 'reality' rather than another and, in that fundamental way, becomes 'suasory.' "

This view of the development of form in political discourse is probably one with which Campbell and Jamieson would agree. However, by recognizing the range of choices made by rhetors, Blankenship provides a valuable corrective to the mechanistic, deterministic necessity implied by them. In fact, Blankenship goes on to observe in her discussion of

308

ergon that rhetorical choices may become habitual—an important observation for the explanation of similarities in presidential inaugurals. However, even in her discussion of habit, Blankenship reminds us that there are "opportunities of free choice."

Simons and Aghazarian make the most extensive and self-conscious attempt to develop an approach for explaining the patterns in discourse that may be observed across different rhetors ("We . . . urge genericists to utilize their talents for discovering order and coherence amid diversity and flux . . ."). By advancing what is really a fairly simple explanatory scheme they challenge researchers to reveal what it is about a rhetorical occasion that delimits but does not completely determine the rhetor's response, and the process by which similar responses to rhetorical situations by different rhetors occur.

As is the case for several other authors in this volume, the starting point for Simons and Aghazarian is the *situation* in which rhetoric occurs. It is the situation, after all, that influences the expectations of the audience and the "concomitant obligation on the speaker" to perform in a particular way. While there is a disagreement of sorts between Simons/Aghazarian and Campbell/Jamieson about just how constraining situational factors are, there is essential agreement that the situation makes "demands" upon a rhetor, which must be responded to in some way.

The way in which rhetors respond to situation demands, according to Simons and Aghazarian, may be understood in terms of the *role* adopted by the rhetor. The concept of a role suggests both constraint and choice, for there is usually more than one available role that may be chosen by a rhetor from a more extensive "menu." This recognition of the range of rhetorical choice which most situations permit is where Simons/Aghazarian and Campbell/Jamieson part company. In contrast to the sense of *necessity* implied by the latter pair of authors, Simons and Aghazarian clearly believe that rhetors are less constrained by the rhetorical situations to which they respond: "We are not convinced . . . that the strategies persuaders select are always required by situation. We suspect, rather, that there is usually more than one way of coping with situational demands and more than one way of construing those demands and of interpreting them to others."

Having recognized the importance of rhetorical choice, however, and the variation in rhetorical responses to similar situations, Simons and Aghazarian are quick to reaffirm that rhetorical choices are not random or idiosyncratic. Instead, they are patterned, recurrent, and "sometimes become conventionalized" as rhetors learn and apply *rules* when responding to rhetorical situations. These rules indicate "what behavior is obligated, preferred, or prohibited in certain contexts" and it is rules that make genres of discourse recognizable and predictable.

This approach to explaining the patterns in rhetoric across rhetors is extremely helpful. It makes explicit how it is that situations create a kind of necessity for or demand upon rhetors while still allowing rhetorical choice and rule violation. Yet, if one were to adopt the Simons and Aghazarian approach, at least three questions would need to be explored more deeply.

First, researchers will want to investigate what attributes of a rhetorical situation are important for understanding a rhetor's response. To observe that the situation is important in delimiting rhetorical choices is helpful and sensible (and perhaps even noncontroversial), but it does not really take us very far down the road to explaining rhetorical patterns. For example, suppose we wanted to explain the patterns in rhetorical appeals made by political candidates in their televised spot advertisements. What attributes of this situation might be useful? A number of possibilities come readily to mind, including the office being contested; the party of the candidate; the geographical location of the race; the type of election (primary or general, nonpartisan versus party); the candidate's status as challenger, incumbent, or contestant for an open seat; the economic condition and experience of the media consultant (prosperous versus bankrupt, political versus commercial background); the financial resources of the candidate; the nature of political discourse and the issue agenda at the time of the election; the appeals made by and the extant perceptions about the opponent; and so on. A truly helpful theory of rhetorical choice would not only reaffirm the importance of the situation but also help us to decide what attributes of the situation are worth exploring and which ones may be ignored safely.

Second, attention should be given to the Campbell/Jamieson and Simons/Aghazarian debate over the mix of constraint on the latitude available to rhetors. Simons and Aghazarian argue that Campbell and Jamieson have overestimated the degree of constraint on rhetors and that rhetors have much more freedom to be creative, inventive, and unconventional than they have implied. Further, they assert that "a rules-oriented generic perspective helps us to distinguish between situational requirements and strategic options." But how are we to tell in a particular set of responses to a rhetorical situation whether rhetors are complying with "situational requirements" or inventing "strategic option"? How are we to accumulate and evaluate evidence about the observed mix of constraint and choice so that we can then understand the variation in that mix across different rhetorical situations? When, or in what situations, would we expect rhetors to be more inventive? Simons and Aghazarian advance one tantalizing hypothesis, that rhetors are less inventive in political than in literary and dramatic settings. Yet it is unclear how we would ever empirically evaluate that claim or how we would go about navigating our way through the waters of the constraint/choice debate. In short, the Simons and Aghazarian observation concerning the overestimation of rhetorical demands or necessity is a useful corrective to deterministic thinking. It is not clear, however, how to proceed past their observation that "situational requirements may be satisfied by a variety of rhetorical strategies."

Third, more thought needs to be given to the nature of the "rules" relied upon by Simons and Aghazarian to capture rhetorical recurrences, and in particular to what sort of evidence will be appropriate for advancing a claim about the rules of a particular rhetorical situation. One problem is that since rules can be violated it will be difficult to tell when a rule is followed often enough to be a prescription for rhetorical behavior. Another problem is that rules may be apparently both empirical and prescriptive. This obviously presents a difficulty when rhetors consistently make rhetorical choices that are unpersuasive. If a group of rhetors respond similarly, yet unsuccessfully, to a rhetorical situation, are they abiding by or violating the rules? Implicit in the rule approach may be an assumption that rhetors, over time and with experience, adapt successfully to rhetorical situations. Even a casual glance at the history of political discourse suggests that such an assumption would be a dubious one.[1]

In general, to the extent that the authors in this volume are attempting to *explain* similarities in the rhetoric of political figures, there is a consensus of sorts about what will be the rough shape of those explanations. Such rhetorical "genre-alizing" will (1) have a consideration of the rhetorical situation as the analytical starting point; (2) involve a comparison of the rhetoric of different rhetors to a similar situation rather than the case study of a single rhetor; (3) allow for rhetorical choice and creativity as well as rhetorical imitation and similarity; and (4) lead to the explicit advancement of a set of rules to guide both rhetors and critics alike. This consensus is encouraging and indicates that the starting point for this endeavor is probably a sensible one. That such essentials would need to be pondered and justified, however, also reveals what a new endeavor this is for this community of scholars and how much more work needs to be done before anything approaching an empirically verified explanation for rhetorical patterns can be advanced.

WHAT IS GAINED BY A FORM-AND-GENRE APPROACH TO POLITICAL DISCOURSE?

Apparently, one of the claims that is made by form-and-genre researchers is that their approaches to political discourse will yield fresh analytical dividends. These dividends seem to be of two general types. First, there is the possibility that their approaches will uncover "otherwise-likely-to-be-missed" meaning in the discourse. Second, there is the possibility that their approaches will provide a more certain standard for assessing the eloquence of political speech. Let us turn our attention now to the contribution that the works in this volume make to each of these attractive goals.

UNCOVERING OTHERWISE-LIKELY-TO-BE-MISSED MEANING

To what extent does the research contained in this volume contribute to an enhanced understanding of the content of political discourse? Do the approaches represented here help us "see" aspects of the discourse that are both politically meaningful and likely to be missed?

It is difficult to divine the political significance of political discourse as analyzed by Blankenship and Hart. While Blankenship's essay is provocative when it comes to the origins of form in general and of oxymoron in particular, it is unclear what the political significance of her developmental approach to form is in this particular case. Her assertion that ABC brought contradictory terms ("the powerfulness of power and the powerlessness of power") "sharply together in a kind of controlled dizzying" is persuasively argued. However, one is hard pressed to deduce from this conclusion what the political significance of this way of presenting the inaugural might be. What others would take to be the more explicitly political meaning of the inaugural—by which I mean what Reagan had to say about his beliefs regarding government, his assessment of our international interests, his plans for domestic policy proposals, and his attempt to portray an appropriate public persona—are given only cursory attention by Blankenship, as if to say such utterances are little more than window dressing in the oxymoron that drives ABC's coverage. We are left, then, wondering what Blankenship concludes are the political implications of the form she has so insightfully discovered. Apart from completely confusing the audience, did this form advance or retard the interests of the newly inaugurated President? Did it serve to threaten or reassure the audience? Did it prevent an "educative" experience for the audience or interfere with the new President's attempt to present the political principles that would guide his administration? It is almost as if the discovery of the form in this case has relegated the political meaning of the inaugural as re-presented by ABC to the proverbial back burner.

Despite this general inattention to the politics of inaugural discourse, Blankenship makes a tantalizing observation, the political significance of which is potent. Blankenship notes that television viewers see two very different kinds of stories: the "short, neat, complete, carefully controlled, commercial 'mini-dramas' and the "long, continuing, messy dramas" of real news programs. One wonders what effect this has on television audiences. Do we become more impatient with political authorities when they can't provide us with "fast relief"? Does continual exposure to advertisements prepare us for the thematic, dramatic form of television news stories and render comprehension of the inverted-pyramid stories of the print media more difficult? Do the simplified portrayals of heroes and villains in product ads encourage us to understand political conflicts and controversies in the same way (e.g., the making of the federal budget becomes personalized as a mini-drama between David Stockman and Thomas "Tip" O'Neill à la the Crest protectors and "cavity creeps" in a toothpaste commercial rather than as an episode of ideology and interest advancement, evaluation of public policy alternatives, and authoritative allocation of political values)? In Blankenship's provocative observation about the forms of television stories there is the hint of attention to political meaning; one wishes she would have been more attentive to the *political* significance of form.

In short, while Blankenship's analysis of form is praiseworthy on many grounds—it presents a persuasive theory of the origin of form and analyzes rhetoric as represented by news-gatherers—it nevertheless strips this case of political discourse of its political significance. Or at least the political meaning of the form is left unexplored here.

The political meaning of the Reagan inaugural is also difficult to discern in Hart's analysis of Reagan's discourse. For Hart the content of a political speech may be understood through the use of eleven word "dictionaries." These dictionaries appear to be designed more to capture the style of a piece of rhetoric than its political meaning. Of the eleven dictionaries, only one—Symbolism—takes an aspect of political discourse that has some immediate political meaning. A couple of the other dictionaries—Activity and Realism, for example—might be indirectly

313

relevant for an appreciation of the political meaning of an inaugural, but the rest measure aspects of a rhetor's style that would be of little help in understanding that rhetor's political belief system or behavioral intentions. Consequently, Hart is able to dispense with the political content of the Reagan inaugural in only a couple of phrases ("beyond the philosophical to the ideological, beyond the chauvinistic to the jingoistic" and "themes of less government and more responsibility").

I do not doubt that this type of stylistic analysis is informative for those interested in the structure of language and rhetorical choice. Hart's analysis, after all, leads him to the interesting conclusion that the Reagan inaugural was more of a campaign stump speech delivered by a nonincumbent than a typical inaugural by a President comfortable with assuming the office. However, a mode of analysis that cannot distinguish the rhetoric of liberals from conservatives, of moralists from pragmatists, of ideologues from nonideologues, or of isolationists from internationalists seems to a political scientist to be a peculiar approach to political discourse. It does not help an observer understand the rhetor's worldview, philosophy of government, the political interests the rhetor is likely to be responsive to, or his or her programmatic intentions. Like the Blankenship piece, then, the Hart chapter strips the object of study of its political meaning and significance.

What, then, is the political meaning of a piece of political discourse? To a political scientist political discourse is to be taken seriously for what it reveals about political belief or behavioral intentions, or what one political scientist has defined as the core concern of political science: "the authoritative allocation of value."[2] This suggests that political discourse is important for what it reveals about one or more of the following aspects of political life:

1. The rhetor's worldview. What does the discourse reveal about the belief system of the rhetor? Does the rhetor have a tightly constrained belief system? What are the core values that anchor the belief system, that provide coherence and stability? How may we characterize the belief system of the rhetor—populist, progressive, liberal, libertarian, conservative, anarchist, internationalist, and so forth?

2. The rhetor's behavioral intentions. What does the discourse reveal about the predispositions of the rhetor? If the rhetor is in a policymaking position, what are his or her programmatic preferences? Should we expect policy change or continuity? Incremental or nonincremental change? Innovation or repetition?

3. The locus and intensity of political conflict. What does the discourse reveal about the intensity of political conflict? About the interests

dominating the political agenda? About how those interests are being aggregated? About the interests that are contributing to political conflict? About the willingness and ability of public officials to accommodate the interests making claims upon government?

4. The locus and legitimacy of political power. What does the discourse reveal about the holding and exercise of power in a political system? Is power a personal or an institutional phenomenon? How does institutional power-holding change over time? What are the origins of political power? Is the distribution of power legitimate or illegitimate? Is there consensus about the fundamental characteristics of a political regime, and the norms and values that shape public policymaking?

5. The role of the public. What expectations or norms about popular participation are revealed and encouraged in political discourse? Is the public's role a circumscribed one of observation, obedience, quiescence, and occasional indications of consent? Or is the public encouraged to take a more active role in public affairs? Is the public encouraged to be skeptical or reassured? Is the public encouraged to be participant or quiescent? Is the public encouraged to be allegiant or resistant? Are the public's belief systems challenged, rearranged, expanded, extended, or reinforced? Does discourse politicize or narcotize the public?

If one accepts this is as a rough and admittedly incomplete guide to the political meaning of political rhetoric, then it is the analyses of Gronbeck, Campbell and Jamieson, Shapiro, and Osborn that keep our attention focused squarely on the *political* content of discourse. For Campbell and Jamieson the content of inaugural addresses is important because of what they reveal about the fundamental political values, particular political principles, and enactment of a presidential persona. While Campbell and Jamieson do not ignore stylistic questions entirely—they discuss the use of time, the dignity of the address, and whether an inaugural contains "memorable phrases," for example—most of their analysis focuses on the twin problems of reinforcing and benefiting from cultural consensus and establishing the political belief system that will guide that administration's programmatic efforts. The political meaning of inaugural addresses becomes clear as a result of this analysis. Inaugurals attempt to persuade citizens of the fundamental legitimacy of the political regime, of the "fit between a particular political office/role and the new occupant of that office, and of the President's mandate to achieve his programmatic objectives." Inaugurals, then, reveal much about the legitimacy of political power and the worldviews of Presidents. Their political intention is to enhance what political scientists call "diffuse support" (the noncontingent reservoir of support for and loyalty to a political regime),

315

to keep the population quiescent and to inform both other power-holders in the political system and the public at large of what to expect programmatically over the next four years. Although inaugurals do not typically contain detailed, specific, policy proposals, nor represent calls for immediate citizen action, they do give some insight into the belief system that will guide the actions of the incoming administration. Inaugurals, however, contain mainly what one might call *riskless* rhetoric. That is, they contain little that anyone could disagree with, little that reveals valuative or programmatic choice, and little that is challenging or thought-provoking.

Gronbeck agrees that the political significance of presidential inaugurals lies more in their attempts at legitimation and personification than in their expression of programmatic choice. For him inaugurals are "a vehicle for sanctifying institutional authority, authorizing acts of power, and articulating codes of collective as well as individual conduct." They also provide "collective reassurance that the leader has the knowledge, wisdom, and vision to protect the culture from both internal and external devils, and to carry the society successfully into the future," and articulate "common commitments to 'idealism,' 'fair play,' 'peace,' power . . . granted by the people."

This is the language of consensus-building, legitimation, and quiescence. It reveals that inaugurals are intended to avoid controversy, to ignore policy choice, and to buy time and goodwill for political authorities. They are meant to comfort rather than challenge, legitimate rather than politicize, quiet rather than energize. In Murray Edelman's words, inaugurals, just as most campaign discourse, seem well designed to "dull the critical faculties of men."

For Gronbeck, then, inaugurals reveal more about a collectivity's values than about the values of the particular President. The Reagan inaugural, while it does reveal something about the worldview of Reagan himself (Reagan's "binary foreign vision, with others for or against us," the juxtaposition "of the immediate past" with "the more distant past," and the "markedly revivalistic thrust" of the Reagan inaugural) is more informative for what it reveals about the public's role expectations, belief in mythical explanations of social phenomena, and appetite for institutional legitimation. In other words, in a "well-performed" presidential inaugural we encounter not just a particular rhetor, but ourselves as well.

Campbell and Jamieson, and Gronbeck, then, keep our focus squarely on the political meaning of presidential rhetoric. Inaugurals, in particular, reveal much about the processes by which political power is legitimized; the public is confined to a narrowly circumscribed, "observational" role;

316

popular belief systems are reinforced; and political role expectations are satisfied. They also tell us a little about presidential worldviews but hardly anything about programmatic intentions or choices.

Shapiro and Osborn, in their analyses of nonpresidential discourse, also reveal much that is interesting politically about this discourse. For Osborn, rhetoric is thoroughly imbued with political significance. Through "depiction" there are many ways in which the rhetoric he has studied affects, politically, individuals, societies, and cultures. In particular, "depiction may provide a benign moment of sharing, as rhetors overcome abstraction to disclose the world as it is revealed to them," for "it can be a cynical hoax. . . that poses as disclosure for the sake of exploitation." In short, depiction "can insinuate itself into our consciousness, where it becomes difficult to dislodge."

At the individual level, depiction can affect all aspects of an individual's belief system. If we consider the standard dimensions of belief systems—cognitive, affective, and conative[3]—it is easy to see the myriad ways in which depiction engages and shapes all three.

The cognitive dimension of belief systems involves beliefs about and beliefs in the world and perceptions of how that world works and what one's place is in it. Depiction, for example, involves the use of "repetitive presentations" to "show us what we already know and accept, but in a manner that attempts to reinforce our acceptance. The cumulative effect of repetitive presentation is to imprint certain symbolic configurations upon our minds, to charge such formulations with an especially intense cultural energy." These presentations result, among other things, in the promotion of stereotypes, beliefs which Osborn points out, and years of public opinion research have shown, are most often "accepted without question and without awareness of their service as anchors of the social order."

The affective dimension refers to preference statements or feelings, including what one values, what one prefers, and what one likes and dislikes. The rhetoric of intensification, according to Osborn, relies on depictions "to color what we see and make our reactions smolder," and the rhetoric of group identification promotes feelings that become "sanctified as patriotic and worthy of further intensification." Consequently, certain presentations "facilitate daily commerce in communication" and "become authorized as legitimate group perspectives."

Finally, the conative dimension is the action component of a belief system, containing and revealing judgments about the efficacy and appropriateness of different forms of action. The rhetoric of implementation, according to Osborn, is "depiction's time of action." Implementation "has to do with designs for the future" and offers guidance about "some potential course of action." Furthermore, implementation "must sustain action to its conclusion" by using "the depictive powers of communicators to show what is at stake, to renew hope, and to remind audiences of the dedication required of them." The failure of rhetoric, then, will result in the absence of political action, social movements, and social change.

Clearly, then, Osborn believes that depiction has a continuing and pervasive impact on the belief systems of the populace. Political beliefs, perceptions, myths and stereotypes; political values, preferences and attitudes; and the forms and extent of political participation are all likely to be engaged and affected by rhetorical imagery of the type present in the literary, political, and cinematic works analyzed by Osborn.

It is not only individuals who are likely to be affected by depiction, however. Depiction is also an essential part of social and cultural processes, affecting the level of social consensus and tension, system legitimacy and identification, and balance between stability and change. For example, one of the consequences of depiction is that such symbols "imply shared evaluative outlooks, which are a necessary condition to mass cooperative action." There is much at stake here for a civil society, for, according to Osborn, "In our time great masses of people, often having much political power and therefore increased recalcitrance, must be joined in mega-communities" and "sustained by simple but mythic pictures that embody common values and goals." In the absence of such agreement on fundamentals, social mistrust and civil strife would presumably increase.

Depiction also affects the development of societies and cultures through the rhetoric of renewal. Here the challenge of rhetoric is to "maintain the structures of society against the ravages of time, the erosion of memory, and the decay of commitment." The difficulty is to encourage flexibility short of chaos, stability shy of rigidity, and continuity without fossilization. In Osborn's view, nothing less is at stake for human collectivities than the process of contemplating "the great moral truths that continue to offer meaning and direction to our lives" and strengthening "the grounding of those enthymemes vital to social judgment and deliberation."

At both the individual and the societal levels, then, Osborn reveals clearly what is important about the rhetorical process and what the many dimensions of political meaning in the cases of discourse he has analyzed are. When political discourse is hypothesized to affect not only individual belief systems but social consensus, stability, integration, flexibility, and

advancement, there can be little doubt about either the general significance or the political importance of the rhetoric under consideration.

Shapiro also keeps our attention focused squarely on the political
significance of the discourse he studies. *The Investigators*, he discovers, is
not simply a dispassionate analysis of the conduct of two national
law-enforcement agencies but is also mythology in disguise. Through the
use of particular terms (such as "task"), the language of agency personnel, and the adoption of a particular genre of discourse (a modern variant
in the apology), Wilson constructs a "mythic story" that "transforms an
austerely written policy analysis into a legitimating pamphlet, a celebration of part of the existing order." Such a story, as Shapiro poignantly
acknowledges, can serve well the interests of the existing law-enforcement system in the United States.

In contrast with Blankenship and Hart, then, the contributions of
Campbell and Jamieson, Gronbeck, Osborn, and Shapiro are much more
forthcoming about the political significance of political discourse. Processes by which citizen belief systems are shaped, system legitimacy
altered or maintained, social consensus influenced, and political participation delimited or encouraged are at the core of any study of politics. To
the extent that the latter selections enhance our understanding of these
processes, our appreciation of political processes is enriched as well.

ASSESSING THE ELOQUENCE OF POLITICAL DISCOURSE

A second reason for performing a generic analysis of political discourse is so that the eloquence of a particular instance of discourse may
be judged. As I understand it, once the "significant form" of a genre has
been established, it may be used as an ideal against which to compare a
particular speech. A speech that conforms to the form of its genre will be
judged to be eloquent; one that does not will be found wanting.

This volume contains two attempts at this style of criticism. Gronbeck,
once he has defined the significant elements of presidential inaugurals,
turns his attention to Ronald Reagan's 1981 performance and evaluates
that performance in terms of the ceremonial demands of the occasion.
Campbell and Jamieson also use a set of essential elements of inaugurals
and then proceed to discuss the comparative eloquence of a number of
them.

Gronbeck proceeds more clearly from general principle to particular
conclusion. He argues that a "competently performed inaugural ceremony" should "(1) legitimize both a leader and the culture . . . ; (2)
celebrate the transition of leadership and followership; and (3) offer

319

collective reassurance that the leader has the knowledge, wisdom, and vision to protect the culture from both internal and external devils, and to carry the society successfully into the future."

If the three functions of inauguration of which Gronbeck speaks are a suitable guide to the eloquence of an inaugural address, then one could critique Reagan's eloquence by analyzing the extent to which he satisfies the requirements of legitimation, celebration, and remembrance. In fact, this is just what Gronbeck does, and he concludes that the Reagan 1981 inaugural contained "almost no celebration, very little in the way of direct legitimation, and a good deal of remembrance."

Was the Reagan inaugural eloquent, then? Gronbeck's answer would seem to be a qualified No, since he finds the speech "anything but celebratory," and filled almost exclusively with only "*indirect* hints" of legitimation. Only in the area of remembrance does the speech fulfill extensively the inaugural "necessities."

This seems straightforward enough. But then Gronbeck does something puzzling. He goes on to argue, first, that the Reagan inaugural is far more consistent with the "three requisites" than originally indicated. In fact, Gronbeck argues that "Reagan most competently creates a discourse capable of healing the transitional fissure produced by change in leadership and hence of reorienting the citizenry." This is surprising, for if Reagan's inaugural lacked one of the three rhetorical requisites of inaugurals, and only indirectly accomplished a second, isn't it then peculiar that the rhetoric should be judged "most competent"? Or, put another way, if the Reagan address performs the inaugural functions admirably and yet lacks at least one of the three requisites of such discourse, then what is the status of the three requisites? It would seem that something other than simply the presence or absence of the three elements is guiding the rhetorical criticism of this anlayst. To Gronbeck eloquence is something more complicated that simply whether a speech contains elements of celebration, legitimation, and remembrance.

There is something, though, that bothers Gronbeck about the Reagan performance. It is not the lack of celebration, however, or the indirect quality of the legitimation contained in the address. Rather, what bothers Gronbeck is that Reagan's inaugural shows he is "in danger of not working within its [the office's] limitations and arenas of responsibility, in danger of depending for efficacy on his own charisma and poll ratings rather than on his role requirements." Further, Gronbeck criticizes Reagan for presenting a vision of the Presidency that is "constrained, undramatic, and certainly not inspirational" and for destroying "the symbolic distance between the presidential institution and those who owe obedience to and trust in it." In the final analysis, Gronbeck concludes, Reagan's inaugural reveals him to be, horror of horrors, a populist.

I fail to see why this is a rhetorical mistake or how this is evidence that the inaugural lacks eloquence. In fact, I would argue just the opposite: that presidential oratory which presents a competing image to that of the "imperial" Presidency, which reduces the distance between leader and led, which demonstrates that a public official possesses empathy with and appreciation for the belief systems of the body politic, and which argues that moral virtue will guide public policy is apt to be very eloquent speech indeed. It may offend those who find the speech unduly symbolic or vague, and it may not please those who believe political leaders should be revered rather than trusted, but in our political culture such rhetoric is neither surprising nor worrisome. Certainly, it is at least arguable whether Ronald Reagan's inaugural "crippled his own chances to make his programs a long-term success." Until the balance of power in Washington shifted a bit as a result of the 1982 congressional elections, Ronald Reagan seemed to be enacting his Presidency in a way that showed little reluctance to use the office's powers and no exceptional tendency to stoop to demagoguery. In short, Gronbeck's conclusion regarding Reagan's rhetorical failures is not supported by the analysis that precedes it.

Campbell and Jamieson, in their overview of presidential inaugurals, also address the issue of presidential eloquence. However, they assess eloquence in a way quite different from Gronbeck. Recall that Campbell and Jamieson assert that there are "four interrelated elements . . . which differentiate it [the presidential inaugural] from other types of epideictic rhetoric." However, when it comes to judging eloquence, the standard is different. "Great" inaugurals "reinvigorate as well as rehearse traditional values; . . . create memorable phrases that sum up who we are as a people and what the presidency is as an institution; . . . involve us actively in redefining the nation as embodied in the principles guiding the incoming administration; and . . . address timely questions timelessly, or, in the words of William Faulkner, their 'griefs grieve on universal bones.' "

This set of characteristics is perfectly fine as a rhetorical guide to eloquence: it is an explicit, fairly specific, and reasonable set of criteria. What is peculiar, however, is the process by which the criteria were arrived at. It seems that eloquence was determined, first, in a reputational manner ("Inaugurals frequently praised. . . . Some add . . .") and then this subset of speeches was found to contain at least some of the attributes mentioned above. Not only are we left wondering whether all the great inaugurals possess *all* of the attributes of eloquence enumerated,

321

but one also wonders what would happen if the criteria of eloquence were applied fairly to the whole set of inaugurals, without a prejudgment of how they are regarded and, ideally, without the critic's knowing who gave which speech (extremely difficult to accomplish, I realize). Would the assessment of eloquence via a set of abstract principles agree with the reputation for eloquence that the speeches have? Perhaps a speech obtains a reputation for eloquence because of factors other than those presumed by Campbell and Jamieson to characterize great inaugurals—such as by being exceptionally reassuring in a time of unusual cultural or political anxiety and uncertainty.

In short, it is difficult to see in this volume how the generic approach enhances the critique of eloquence. Campbell and Jamieson's attempt suffers from a troubling danger of tautology, and Gronbeck's conclusion is a questionable application of what appear to be reasonable criteria. Perhaps the generic claims themselves are not yet well enough established to further rhetorical criticism; in any event, the efforts here are either silent or unpersuasive on the issue of rhetorical eloquence.

ASSESSING THE SIGNIFICANCE OF POLITICAL DISCOURSE

If we assume for the sake of argument that the form-and-genre approach to political discourse is a worthwhile endeavor, that it helps reveal the political meaning of political rhetoric and provides an aid to rhetorical criticism, then one would hope that it would tell us something of significance about the place and importance of political discourse in the life of a polity. This, in turn, raises at least two related questions. First, how does one decide which cases of political speech, out of all those instances available, one studies? Second, what do these analyses tell us about the likely effects of political discourse on attentive audiences?

SELECTING CASES OF POLITICAL DISCOURSE FOR STUDY

There is a multitude of instances of political discourse that one might wish to understand. Given the limited resources of researchers, however, choices must be made of the political discourse to be studied. In this volume the major case of political discourse selected for analysis is the presidential inaugural. While this type of speech may have been selected mainly for illustrative purposes, or because it yields a manageable number of rhetorical cases with which to deal, one still wonders whether this choice is a sensible one. Is the presidential inaugural a significant

322

rhetorical event in the life of the Amerian polity? Are Campbell and Jamieson justified in their claim that the "presidential inaugural is a discourse whose significance all recognize but few praise"? What selection criteria are appropriate for researchers who wish to enhance our understanding of political discourse?

First, one might select for analysis examples of political discourse based on the number of people exposed to or participating in the discourse. The reason for such a selection criterion would be simply that the more people exposed to or participating the more likely it is that that discourse will play a meaningful role in and have a significant influence on the body politic. Conversely, those instances of political discourse in which only a handful participate might be judged less crucial to understand simply because the number of belief systems or behaviors affected will be miniscule.

Second, an instance of political discourse might be selected for analysis because the discourse involves some particularly crucial political decision or event in the life of a polity. So, for example, justifications for calls to arms or discourse involving the founding of a body politic itself might be judged to be significant because they involve decision points of unusual magnitude and consequence. So, too, the political discourse accompanying a partisan realignment or period of civil strife might be judged important for what it reveals about the locus and intensity of political conflict and political values, goals, and interests achieving political ascendancy during a particular segment of time.

Third, instances of political discourse might be selected for study because they are viewed as credible and/or binding by those who attend to them. Since credibility is thought to be a key predictor of persuasive effect, instances of discourse perceived to be credible might be selected on the presumption that they are more likely to have had some behavioral effect. Similarly, when political discourse is taken to be binding by important political actors—as is the case with Supreme Court decisions and presidential Executive Orders—it may be presumed that it is more likely (though not, of course, certain) that the discourse has some behavioral consequence.

Fourth, the discourse of those who are more important by virtue of their political influence may be analyzed for what it reveals about those who achieve positions of political power in a political system. This criterion, it must be admitted, is almost the antithesis of the first one, since in most modern polities it is the few rather than the many who have political power. By this criterion the discourse of United States Presidents, Supreme Court Justices, committee chairmen in Congress, top

323

federal and state bureaucrats, military chiefs, "Fortune 500" corporate executives, foundation and banking heads, and leaders of interest groups would probably be of interest to the political analyst.

Fifth, discourse might be selected for study based on its unusual, abnormal, or provocative nature. If the reaction to discourse is taken to be an indication of the boundaries of what is politically acceptable behavior for rhetors, then perhaps that discourse that is the *least* comforting, reassuring, familiar, and persuasive ought to be studied for insights into the shape of a polity's rhetorical boundaries. In the same way that judging behavioral acts as deviant allows a community to reassess and reestablish boundaries of normal, acceptable behavior, so, too, the *rejection* of political discourse may reveal much about a polity's belief systems and political values.

The criteria above are nothing more than an attempt to judge the political significance of an instance or genre of political discourse in the life of a polity. If we were to apply these criteria in the selection of discourse for study, what types of discourse might survive our selection process?

Advertisements. The political discourse contained in many advertisements, both commercial and otherwise, would certainly meet many of these selection criteria. As Blankenship points out, advertisements may be looked at as "manufactured dramas" in which outcomes are assured and the stories are neat, short, and complete. Advertising contains political meaning—including dramatic presentations of what is of value, what is acceptable behavior, what are suitable roles—and reaches a vast and geographically dispersed audience. Furthermore, advertising represents the discourse of those with economic and political power, speaking to those who are relatively powerless. Candidates' advertisements are clearly important cases of political discourse: they reveal much about ascendant political values, enduring beliefs and preferences, our role expectations of various political offices, and the locus and content of competing political ideologies. Furthermore, they now consume the bulk of resources of those vying for significant elective office. However, it is not only candidates' advertisements that contain political messages. Product advertisements convey myths, ideologies, and value statements, and the so-called advocacy ads are hardly subtle in their use of political discourse. It would seem, then, that a group of discourse analysts as insightful as those represented in this volume, might profitably turn their attention to the discourse of advertisements.

News. Most members of the body politic are dependent upon others to relate to them the meaning of government and public affairs. The population is simply too remote from an increasingly distant, bureaucratized government to observe directly much of that government.

Consequently, those who "tell stories" about government or public affairs to a large, minimally attentive, and trusting population certainly engage in a meaningful form of political discourse. In contemporary American society, journalists are certainly among the most significant of "storytellers," exercising discretion about the political phenomena to be "covered," the themes to be presented, the dramas to be highlighted, the threats to be publicized, and the political actors to be elevated to celebrity status.

Drama. Theater and drama have been important instances of political discourse for centuries. Today, various dramatic forms remain the locus of political rhetoric, which is widely attended, engagingly presented, and focused on the important events and enduring questions of a body politic. Furthermore, it is often in drama that the boundaries of acceptable discourse are tested and fought over.

Social scientists have tended not to take the political meaning of drama very seriously. This is certainly true of political scientists, who have almost completely ignored the role of drama in the political life of the body politic.[4] Yet it is clear that dramatists are storytellers, too, just as journalists are, and that they portray politics, politicians, social conflicts, and ethical dilemmas to appreciative and attentive audiences. They, too, exert political influence, as Gerbner would say, through their shaping of our symbolic environment.

While live theater has undergone a secular decline in this century, other types of drama continue to be or have become politically important. Television entertainment fare, Hollywood films, and works of fiction continue the tradition of dealing with politics and government in a literary fashion. Add to these the political humor of cartoons and the lyrics of popular music, and the sheer amount of dramatic treatments with political meaning is enormous.

JUDICIAL, BUREAUCRATIC, AND LEGISLATIVE DECISIONS

While judicial, bureaucratic, and legislative decisions are seldom *spoken*, they clearly represent important instances of the use of language in ways that are politically significant. Though these communicative acts are seldom attended by large numbers of people, they achieve their significance from their binding, authoritative nature and the select audience that takes them seriously.

Here the point need hardly be belabored that the writing of a governmental decision represents an important use of language. Statutes, administrative decisions, and judicial opinions are the life-blood of our official political behavior and are of concern to those called upon to obey, interpret, and implement them.

This, of course, is the discourse most frequently studied by political scientists. For example, Murray Edelman has attempted to demonstrate the different types of political language used by different rhetors in different settings, and how that language can constrain and influence political behavior.[5] Theodore Lowi has studied the language of federal statutes in his attempt to reveal Congress's abrogation of significant law-making responsibilities and the concomitant political ascendancy of bureaucracies and interest groups.[6] Benjamin Ginsberg has used both party platforms and federal statutes as an indication of the locus and intensity of political conflict throughout American history,[7] and a host of judicial scholars has studied judicial opinions as both a reflection of the political values of individual justices and as an indication of the meaning of emerging judicial doctrines.[8]

These forms of political discourse have clearly not been received with the same indifference as, say, political drama has, but I am curious what a generic approach might reveal about such discourse. Are there genres of statutes, for example, as Lowi claims? Do these genres take on particular, enduring forms? Are some statutes/opinions more "eloquent" (less confusing) than others because they adhere to a conventional form? In short, could generic analysts improve those forms of political discourse that are actually binding on members of the body politic?

Scholarly Research. We seldom subject our own "story-telling" to the critical stance we take toward others. Yet it is clear that, just as journalists attempt to "cover" public affairs and construct mediated versions of political reality for their audiences, academic writers and speakers do the same. Political scientists, in particular, engage in political talk and writing that "reconstructs" our understanding of politics for our audiences.

It could be argued that the importance of our discourse satisfies a number of our selection criteria. Our audiences are large, they are minimally attentive (probably more attentive than the broadcast news audience; less attentive than the audience of dramas), and our talk is somewhat binding on students (that is, they are expected to "learn it" and will be "tested" on it).

The instances of political discourse selected for study in this volume correspond to these selection criteria and recommended rhetorical types unevenly. The only author who analyzes the discourse of journalists is

326

Blankenship, in her treatment of developmental form. To her, a presidential inaugural is not just a speech, but a *news story*, mediated, amplified, and presented by a news organization, and experienced by the audience as a visual and auditory drama, not just as a spoken text. This approach tells us less about the rhetor, and more about the storytellers who are mediating this rhetoric for the body politic, for whom the inaugural becomes something more than just a speech.

Even Blankenship's approach, however, stops short of giving journalists their due as political storytellers. Most people probably did not experience Reagan's 1981 inauguration even in the mediated version artfully analyzed by her, but, rather, through a much shorter version of the story on the 6:30 news, on the next morning's front page, or in *Time* magazine's cover story. One wonders what the storytellers did with the inaugural after they had had some time to reorganize the material and tell the story their way. In fact, perhaps ABC *did* tell the story of the inaugural as a two-dimensional story of "a new beginning" that night, once the uncertainty of the outcome was eliminated, rather than as the oxymoron of the live telecast. (This is just what Gronbeck suggests happened.) If this were the case, which version of the story would be the more important one?

In general, I wish the generic scholars would turn their attention more to the political discourse of journalists. It is through their eyes and ears that most of the body politic's understandings are gained; I would be interested in what forms and genres are present in the storytelling that they do.

Two of the other researchers represented in this volume have selected for analysis discourse of the type recommended above. Osborn presents a refreshing exception to our tendency to ignore dramatized political discourse. His insightful analysis of both cinematic and literary sources is a sensible approach to discourse analysis.

Similarly, Shapiro turns his critical gaze toward one of the types of discourse—academic research—mentioned above as fulfilling our selection criteria. Political scientists are not used to thinking of themselves as rhetors, but Shapiro shows clearly that we are.

But most of the discourse analyzed in this volume is, of course, the discourse of Presidents on Inauguration Day. Indeed, a major scholarly commitment has been made here to the inaugural as a type of speech that generic researchers can handle well.

I make this observation for one straightforward reason. It is simply not evident to me that presidential inaugurals are terribly significant instances of political discourse in the life of our body politic. They *do*

327

represent the discourse of a politically important figure (and his speech writers), and they do accompany a significant ceremonial occasion for our polity. But to say of the inauguration of a President and the orderly transfer of power that that act has been important throughout our history is not to say that the inaugural speech itself is also significant. The act of inauguration, and the fact that we have accomplished this act without civil strife or political turmoil clearly sets our polity apart from most contemporary regimes. The fact that this act is accompanied by ritual that has certain features of more ancient celebrations and ceremonies also tells us much about how human populations mark such transferrals of political power. However, to hold also that the speech given upon this occasion is an important form of political discourse is in need of some further discussion. It may be, for example, that inaugural addresses *are*, as Schlesinger opined, "inferior art forms," and that the American people find such speeches singularly unremarkable, unengaging, and uninformative.

In other words, perhaps there are other forms of political discourse that could also be the subject of generic analysis but that are more significant for understanding the life of the American polity. I have attempted to suggest above what some of these instances might be. It would be a shame for such an insightful and skillful group of analysts to spend their time understanding a manageable corpus of uninfluential discourse.

THE LIKELY EDUCATIVE EFFECT OF POLITICAL DISCOURSE

The second question I would like to raise about the political significance of the analysis conducted in this volume concerns the likely effect of this discourse. In particular, I would like to discuss what these authors indicate are likely to be the educative impacts of this discourse on attentive audiences. Although the studies represented here are not "effects" studies of the social-scientific variety, they are suggestive of what those effects are likely to be, and of how to approach the question of political learning. In particular, political scientists are interested in whether political rhetoric advances or retards the civic education of the populace and the possibilities for self-government.

Most contemporary varieties of democratic theory include the notion that for a citizenry to participate in a meaningful way in the making of political decisions that citizenry must have attained some minimal level of political understanding. Robert Dahl refers to this property as the "enlightened understanding" of the citizenry,[9] and James David Barber tersely opines that it is a necessary ingredient of effective political participation: "Normatively speaking, consent from ignorance can never be genuine, no more so than conversion by the sword."[10] May the examples of political discourse analyzed within these pages be said to enhance the enlightened understanding of the citizenry? Or, put another way, what is an attentive citizenry apt to learn from presentations of the type analyzed here?

The authors in this volume present a number of answers to this question. Campbell and Jamieson, for example, argue that the discourse of newly inaugurated Presidents informs the audience of the political principles that "will govern their tenure in office." Gronbeck also believes that inaugurals have an educative effect. He believes that, after hearing the Reagan (1981) inaugural, "Americans ought to have understood that the work of government would be executed firmly and pointedly within a markedly traditional framework of commitments. After hearing this address, they ought to have known that they had elected a man able to reach for a future anchored solidly in the past." And similar assertions of effect are made by the other authors.

Blankenship is alone in suggesting that what is learned might not be so directly derived from the text of the speech itself. She argues that it is difficult to say in advance what an audience will learn from a case of political discourse because they are active co-authors in the construction of the meaning of political addresses. Audiences possess "a vast storehouse of dramas 'likely' to be played out" and exert "energia" as they participate in the formation of political meaning. Presumably, then, the members of the audience for the Reagan inaugural were significant co-authors in the meaning of the inaugural event and used a variety of "topical systems" to understand the day's events.

If fact, Blankenship is the only author to ponder seriously the possibility that the mediated re-presentation of a political speech may actually confuse the audience, hence inhibiting political learning of any type. The oxymoron of ABC's coverage of the Reagan inaugural and the Iranian hostage release, she says, created an event in which viewers were confronted "with experience of dialectical tensions" and "were sorely 'tested' " by the presentation.

In other words, each of the authors in this volume has something different to say about the educative impact of the discourse they have chosen to study. Yet there *is* a common theme running through all of these efforts. It is that one way of evaluating the educative effect of political rhetoric is in terms of whether it is likely to have a "conserving" or a "radicalizing" effect on the audience. This may be viewed, for the

329

moment, as an educative dimension on which one end-point would be conserving rhetoric, by which I mean political talk that is apt to preserve the status quo by bolstering, reminding, or reinforcing values, beliefs, and attitudes already held or preferred. Gronbeck recognizes this potential when he observes that one of the purposes of ceremonial rhetoric is to serve as "a vehicle for sanctifying institutional authority, authorizing acts of power, and articulating codes of collective as well as individual conduct," and as a means of renewing "the collectivity's fundamental commitments to institutions, agencies of social control, and perceptions of what it means to be a 'citizen' of the culture." Shapiro also raises this possibility when he refers to how the "political dimension of configuration" can at times serve the purpose of "mystification and legitimation, serving prevailing structures of power and authority" and by Osborn, who observes that what he calls the "rhetoric of reaffirmation" normally performs its duty of guarding "the sacred fire around which a nation or a subculture gathers periodically to warm itself in recognition of its being."

The other end-point of the dimension, here called radicalizing rhetoric, would be represented by rhetoric whose likely effect was to produce large-scale change in belief or preference. This possibility is also recognized by a number of authors, most notably by Osborn, who observes that "metaphor has the power to explode the failed presentation in a new perspective-by-incongruity that cleanses and reorients the public mind with its verbal shock treatment." Osborn also argues that "novelists are often regarded as outriders who are not blinded by the fog of self-serving rhetoric that social structures may generate to protect themselves from doubt and change." Shapiro recognizes that rhetoric can at times work "toward a destruction or sundering of the linguistic props that give us our legitimized subjects, objects, actions, and events."

This dimension, defined by the end-points of conserving and radicalizing rhetoric, does not have ideology, as in liberal-conservative disagreements, as its underlying attribute, since conserving rhetoric may serve to reinforce all manner of political belief systems: liberal, conservative, fascist, socialist, populist, or whatever. Similarly, radicalizing rhetoric seeks change in prevailing attitudes and beliefs, no matter the belief attacked or the direction of change required. Determining where political rhetoric is located along this dimension, however, does require a knowledge of the political belief systems extant in the rhetor's audience.

What if we use this dimension to summarize what these authors have to say about the likely effect of political rhetoric? It is clear that different authors have reached different conclusions about the nature of the rhetoric chosen for analysis.

At the conserving end of the scale is Osborn's analysis of Frank Capra's *War Comes to America* and Shapiro's treatment of James Q. Wilson's book about the Federal Bureau of Investigation and the Drug Enforcement Administration. Osborn finds that Capra's film is an example of the rhetoric of renewal, which "attempts to maintain the structures of society against the ravages of time, the erosion of memory, and the decay of commitment." This rhetoric "seeks to regenerate vital culturetypes and appropriated archetypes through stylistic innovation," and is "novelty engaged in the cause of continuity." Capra reaffirms "a vision of America the Beautiful, built upon the central moral principle of 'We the People.' "

Shapiro, in turn, finds that Wilson's book is "a celebration of part of the established order . . . . what we get from Wilson is a rhetoric of legitimation in the form of the traditional clichés of power and a grammar of absolution. To the extent that Wilson has a political program, it is . . . one of supporting the existing enforcement system of those penal codes." This is accomplished, according to Shapiro, by adopting the mode of discourse of those being critiqued, worshiping "all the fetishes or idols that the practice of federal law enforcement has erected," utilizing the metaphor of the "task," apologizing for and minimizing the misconduct by these authorities, and, thereby, perpetuating the myth of depoliticized law enforcement.

To say that rhetoric is conserving is not to say that it is necessarily completely familiar, uncreative, lacking in innovation, or permitting of no attitudinal or belief change. In fact, Capra's films do attempt to create attitudinal change by portraying German and Japanese soldiers as "subhuman" and "loathesome," and the Russian and Chinese people as honorable. However, this attitudinal change is subservient to the overall, pervasive intent to bolster nation-state identity, political-system legitimacy, and belief in the higher good of the war effort.

Representative of the radicalizing end of this dimension is much of the literary and cinematic rhetoric studied by Osborn. He finds that John Steinbeck's *The Grapes of Wrath*, Harriet Beecher Stowe's *Uncle Tom's Cabin*, CBS's *The Guns of Autumn*, the *Triumph of the Will*, and Martin Luther King's Memphis speech all serve the goal of radically altering extant beliefs and attitudes. Steinbeck records the "progressive disintegration" of a capitalist system that cannot see beyond a 'what's in it for me preoccupation' "; Stowe uses "radical innovation in presentation" to challenge the established view of black people as something less or other than human"; CBS challenges the myth of the American hunter; *Will* attempts "to develop and impose a vocabulary of . . . the new social values," which depict "Hitler's new order and articulate the nature of the rebirth he promised Germany"; and Martin Luther King depicted the Memphis sanitation workers strike "as just one more instance of contradiction between the national reality and the national dream, between the lives people led and the religious and social ideals they professed."

Even radicalizing rhetoric of this type cannot proceed without some element of conservation within it as well. Radicalizing rhetoric does not usually begin with nothing or attempt to create a belief system where there was a complete absence of belief before. Instead, even radicalizing rhetoric attempts to use values and beliefs already in place but to apply them or draw associations with them in novel ways. So CBS's "radical" portrayal of hunters depends on our cultural affinity for deer and bears, paired with the application of the "Thou Shalt Not Kill" dictum to a group of people—hunters—generally perceived to be exempt from its application. Similarly, Stowe relied on the belief in Christ's crucifixion to power her depiction of slavery as an "impossible moral contradiction"; *Will* depicts Hitler as "the fulfillment of the German national legend, the superman who redefines good and evil"; and King depended on a variety of Christian and historical beliefs in his depiction of the sanitation workers' strike as part of an ongoing God-ordained quest for freedom.

If these instances of political rhetoric represent the end-points of this dimension of educative effect, where does the main case studied in this volume—presidential inaugurals—fall? And where, in particular, does the Reagan 1981 inaugural reside?

In general, presidential inaugurals are found to be near if not at the conserving end of the spectrum, designed largely to promote the status quo by reinforcing prevailing myths, belief systems, and values, and reminding the audience that these are shared by many. So, for example, Campbell and Jamieson claim that presidential inaugurals "affirm or praise" shared principles, accomplish the "amplification and reaffirmation of what is already known and believed," rehearse "communal values drawn from the past," "affirm traditional values," and "heighten what is known or believed."

In fact, there are a number of ways in which we can say that inaugurals are conserving. One is by simply repeating the clichés, platitudes, and cultural values that are familiar to all in attendance. Hence, Campbell and Jamieson find that inaugural discourse is "noncontroversial and unifying," and Hart opines that "Presidents are

... required to use folksy platitudes on Inauguration Day." This discourse is probably intended largely to reassure the "political losers" in the previous election, who may have some reservations about the future course of governmental action emanating from public officials whom they opposed. By repeating consensually held values, the rhetoric of presidential inaugurals may reassure losers that they need not become alienated or rebellious. As Campbell and Jamieson note, "explicit appeals for unity are most common in inaugural addresses that follow a divisive campaign or a contested electoral outcome." This is also accomplished by "assuring those who did not vote for this President that he will, nevertheless, scrupulously protect their rights." Clearly, this is evidence that newly inaugurated Presidents are speaking to their opponents.

A second way in which inaugural discourse is conserving is by focusing the attention of the populace on their identification with the political community and the legitimacy of the political regime. This is frequently done in inaugurals by reaffirming our support for the electoral process and the primacy of our identity as Americans. One of the more remarkable aspects of ABC's coverage of the 1981 Reagan inaugural, revealed in Blankenship's essay, is the extent to which ABC amplified the legitimizing themes of Reagan's discourse by displaying the icons of our political culture.

Campbell and Jamieson refer to this activity as reconstituting "an existing community," and they find that it is accomplished in presidential inaugurals by eulogizing the founders, other past heroes, and past Presidents; by "reaffirming the wisdom of past policies" through constructing a re-presentation of the "venerated past," by exhibiting presidential humility and the appreciation of and reverence for constitutional limits; by promoting the belief that the American political system is blessed by Providence; and by forming a "mutual convenant" between the President and the people. Hart agrees that the "invocation of national symbols" is an integral part of ceremonial speeches in general, and inaugurals in particular.

Blankenship extends this analysis to include more than just the text of the inaugural itself. Hence the television presentation of the inaugural also included visual aspects of "the continuing tradition of the peaceful transfer of American political power." Power is transferred smoothly, protocols observed, and expectations met in a "carefully practiced ceremonial" of live television coverage.

This is clearly the language of conserving rhetoric. It is rhetoric designed to bolster rather than challenge, reassure rather than disturb, placate rather than arouse. It is the language of social control, of the engineering of consent.

Despite this general picture of inaugurals as conserving, they are not completely devoid of innovation and risk. For instance, Campbell and Jamieson claim that eloquent inaugurals "reinvigorate as well as rehearse traditional values" and that "familiar ideas become fresh and take on new meaning." Furthermore, "great inaugurals invite us to see ourselves in a new light, to constitute ourselves as a people in a new way."

What of the Reagan inaugural in 1981? Was it a thoroughly conserving speech or a mixture of conserving and radicalizing rhetoric?

On balance, the first Reagan inaugural was a conserving one. Reagan attempted to legitimate his own taking of office by expressing "common commitments to cultural values and American ideological truisms," by urging us to "keep our eyes on common cultural values," and by reaffirming "American valuative premises, ideological tenets, and individual virtues." This was accomplished in terms of "sociopolitical commitments" through an acknowledgment of "the efficacy and efficiency of [the] American political transition," the celebration of the accomplishments of the founders, and expression of a desire for "a healthy, vigorous, growing economy that provides equal opportunities for all Americans with no barriers born of bigotry or discrimination." Reagan also conserved by exhorting the audience to see each other as heroic, to "believe in ourselves and . . . our capacity to perform great deeds," and to believe in divine intervention into the American political experience. This is surely conserving rhetoric, pointing us toward a "new beginning" through the "renewal of old commitments." As Gronbeck concludes: "After hearing this address, Americans ought to have understood that the work of government would be executed firmly and pointedly within a markedly traditional framework of commitments."

On the other hand, the Reagan inaugural was not entirely conserving. Reagan branched out in some moderately challenging, novel directions. He expressed a personal value system that was not simply the reaffirmation or the representation of cultural beliefs and values. Thus Reagan talked about the need "to curb the size and influence of the Federal establishment" and to "demand recognition of the distinction between the powers granted to the Federal Government and those reserved to the states or to the people." In the foreign sphere Reagan informed his audience of his personal worldview. According to Gronbeck, he "puts all non-Americans into but two groups—'neighbors and allies' and 'the enemies of freedom,' those who are potential adversaries." Reagan "obviously has constructed a binary foreign vision, with others for or against us."

Blankenship and Hart agree that Reagan's inaugural address was not completely without risk and that portions of it were apt to challenge, disturb, and create resistance from a nontrivial portion of the audience. Reagan took the opportunity presented by the inaugural to articulate his own political belief system. Although Blankenship argues that the audience should not have been surprised to hear him articulate, as the *Orlando Sentinel* put it, "much of the same antigovernment, pro-individual political philosophy that he formulated on the speaking circuit in the 1950s," it was, after all, a personal rather than a cultural belief system that was presented.

Hart agrees. To him, the 1981 inaugural was replete with the "Tory virtues" so admired by Ronald Reagan. In fact, Hart finds that Reagan's inaugural goes "beyond the philosophical to the ideological," and "beyond the chauvinistic to the jingoistic." This is rhetoric about which there is likely to be some disagreement and which may stimulate more challenge than comfort, worry than reassurance. Reagan's articulation of a public philosophy of "less government and more responsibility," while clearly not unique in American history, could be expected to be met with some resistance and disagreement by many unlike-minded citizens. Consequently, Reagan did take a (slight) risk in 1981, a risk of "educating" the citizenry rather than simply celebrating the occasion or legitimizing his assumption of the presidential office.

In summary, it is notable that most of the examples of political discourse analyzed in this volume are of the conserving type—the only major exceptions are the literary and cinematic works included in Osborn's essay. Wherever these analysts turn—to presidential talk, the live storytelling of journalists, the books written by academics—they encounter the language of legitimation, quiescence, and compliance.

This is a profound observation but one that the critics here do not seem to take seriously. It suggests, at a minimum, that the rhetoric emanating from various power centers in the United States (the state, the academy, and the press) and amplified and transmitted to our geographically dispersed citizenry via various mass distribution and communication techniques, is apt to contribute to civic education in a most delimited, conservative fashion. It also suggests that the capability for social control contained within political talk is a potent force within the life of modern, developed nation-states and is both impressive and worrisome. Finally, it would seem to cast doubt on the various claims made within this volume that epideictic rhetoric in general and presiden-

335

tial inaugurals in particular are unconcerned with "action as a goal." If one understands obedience, compliance, and quiescence as political action, then clearly most of the rhetoric studied here, no matter how "contemplative," has action as a pervasive, enduring, and consequential goal.

CONCLUSION

In the preceding pages I have attempted to raise some questions about the research reported in this volume. Although I have found it encouraging that this group of scholars takes political discourse seriously and studies it so insightfully, there remain a number of reservations about the political significance of these analyses. Let me summarize them here.

First, it is unclear how the claim that a set of political discourses constitutes a genre of discourse is supported. In particular, the "genre" of most immediate concern here—presidential inaugurals—is generally assumed or asserted to exist rather than demonstrated to share some set of attributes that differentiate it from other discourse. The authors most insistent on making this generic claim—Campbell and Jamieson—are fairly casual about supporting their claim that the interrelationships among four rhetorical elements uniquely define this class of political rhetoric.

Second, there is a large measure of disagreement, ambiguity, and fuzzy thinking about the origins of the similarities in the political discourse of different rhetors. The possible explanations are numerous—the setting, the expectations and abilities of the audience, the motives and purposes of the rhetor, imitation, habit, rules, the material with which the discourse is crafted—and include uncertain quantities of both constraint *on* the rhetor and choice *by* the rhetor. Only Blankenship, and Simons and Aghazarian really take the need for an explanation of rhetorical patterns seriously, and even their chapters do more hypothesis-advancing than hypothesis-testing. As a result, this volume offers precious little contribution to the question of *why* rhetorical similarities and contrasts appear. In the case of the inaugural, the types of explanatory concepts that would be used by a political scientist—the amount of extant civil strife, the intensity of opposition to a newly elected president, the balance of power with other governmental institutions, the extent of perceived external threat to the political community, and the margin of the electoral victory of the newly inaugurated President—are hardly mentioned as offering clues to the content of inaugural addresses.

Third, some of the analyses of political discourse in this volume strip the rhetoric of its political meaning. Political beliefs, worldviews, ideologies, and intentions are occasionally mentioned, but only in passing, in favor of attention to the more stylistic aspects of the discourse. While this is not uniformly true of all or even most of the chapters in this volume, and while this approach may be a sensible one for nonpolitical scientists, it is troubling when political discourse is depoliticized so thoroughly.

Fourth, it is unclear how one assesses the eloquence of a case of political discourse, particularly in the absence of any observation of the audience's response. The possibility that audiences ignore, are confused by, misperceive, rationalize, or personally interpret political discourse seems hardly to have entered into these analyses—nor to have been considered germane to the assessment of eloquence. Instead, eloquence here is largely reputational or personal.

Fifth, I remain unconvinced that the cases of political discourse studied the most intensely in this volume—the presidential inaugural—are meaningful ones in the life of our body politic. They seem to be generally ignored or discounted by the citizenry, and to contribute little of significance to the life of our polity. I suspect there are far more potent cases of rhetoric that celebrate and legitimize the political regime and community than inaugurals—election night news coverage and athletic pageantry, for example.

Sixth, although many of the authors draw attention to the legitimizing/conserving and radicalizing/challenging dimensions of political rhetoric, few reflect on the consequences of this flow of information for the body politic. Has there been a secular shift of late in industrialized nations in favor of conserving/legitimizing rhetoric? What avenues are available for rhetoric that challenges rather than reassures, and for the rhetoric of participation instead of the rhetoric of acquiescence? And what are the consequences of this type of rhetoric for the civic education of the public?

Finally, let me conclude abruptly—for I have surely overstayed my welcome by now—by simply asserting that in spite of the reservations advanced above, the research reported in this volume, taken alone, advances our understanding of political discourse more than the entire last ten years of political-science research. I hope that this community of scholars persists in their analyses, and attempts to answer some of the questions raised here.

Notes

1. The authors' discussion of the rules approach is also misleading in at least one way. In their attempt to distinguish the behavioral and generic approaches to generalizations, they have overstated the differences. For example, they claim that

behavioralists do experiments while "the genericist studies messages naturalistically." This is no longer, if it ever was, an accurate contrast. Behavioral researchers have for years been studying political rhetoric "naturalistically." A few examples include Thomas E. Patterson and Robert D. McClure, *The Unseeing Eye* (New York: G. P. Putnam's Sons, 1976); Thomas E. Patterson, *The Mass Media Election* (New York: Praeger, 1980); Arthur H. Miller and Michael Mackuen, "Learning about the Candidates: The 1976 Presidential Debates," *Public Opinion Quarterly* 43 (1979):326–46; Doris Graber, *Processing the News* (New York: Longman, 1984); Alan I. Abramowitz, "The Impact of a Presidential Debate on Voter Rationality," *American Journal of Political Science* 22 (1978):680–90; George F. Bishop, Robert G. Meadow, and Marilyn Jackson-Beeck, eds., *The Presidential Debates* (New York: Praeger, 1980); Robert S. Erikson, "The Influence of Newspaper Endorsements in Presidential Elections: The Case of 1964," *American Journal of Political Science* 20 (1976):207–33; Benjamin I. Page, *Choices and Echoes in Presidential Elections* (Chicago: University of Chicago Press, 1978); Donald L. Shaw and Maxwell E. McCombs, *The Emergence of American Political Issues: The Agenda-Setting Function of the Press* (St. Paul, Minn.: West Publishing Co., 1977).

2. David Easton, *A Framework for Political Analysis* (Englewood Cliffs, N.J.: Prentice-Hall, 1965), p. 50.

3. See Jarol B. Manheim, *The Politics Within* (Englewood Cliffs, N.J.: Prentice-Hall, 1975), and Chester A. Insko and John Schopler, "Triadic Consistency: A Statement of Affective-Cognitive-Conative Consistency," *Psychological Review* 74 (1967):361–76.

4. Exceptions include Dan Nimmo and James E. Combs, *Mediated Political Realities* (New York: Longman, 1983), and George Gerbner, Larry Gross, Nancy Signorielli, M. Morgan, and Marilyn Jackson-Beeck, "The Demonstration of Power: Violence Profile No. 10," *Journal of Communication* 29, no. 3 (1979):177–96.

5. Murray Edelman, *The Symbolic Uses of Politics* (Urbana: University of Illinois Press, 1964).

6. Theodore Lowi, *The End of Liberalism* (New York: Norton, 1979).

7. Benjamin Ginsberg, *The Consequences of Consent: Elections, Citizen Control and Popular Acquiescence* (Reading, Mass.: Addison-Wesley, 1982).

8. E.g., David J. Danelski, "Values as Variables in Judicial Decision-Making: Notes toward a Theory," *Vanderbilt Law Review* 19 (1966);721–40.

9. Robert Dahl, "On Removing Certain Impediments to Democracy in the United States," *Political Science Quarterly* 92 no. 1 (1977):1–20. See also his *Dilemmas of Pluralist Democracy: Autonomy vs. Control* (New Haven, Conn.: Yale University Press, 1982).

10. James David Barber, "Characters in the Campaign," in James David Barber, ed., *Race for the Presidency: The Media and the Nominating Process* (Englewood Cliffs, N.J.: Prentice-Hall, 1978).

PART IV
APPENDIXES

A. INAUGURAL ADDRESS OF RONALD REAGAN, JANUARY 20, 1981

1 Thank you. Senator Hatfield, Mr. Chief Justice, Mr. President, Vice President Bush, Vice President Mondale, Senator Baker, Speaker O'Neill, Reverend Moomaw, and my fellow citizens:

2 To a few of us here today this is a solemn and most momentous occasion. And, yet, in the history of our nation it is a commonplace occurrence.

3 The orderly transfer of authority as called for in the Constitution routinely takes place as it has for almost two centuries and few of us stop to think how unique we really are:

4 In the eyes of many in the world, this every-four-year ceremony we accept as normal is nothing less than a miracle.

5 Mr. President, I want our fellow citizens to know how much you did to carry on this tradition.

6 By your gracious cooperation in the transition process you have shown a watching world that we are a united people pledged to maintaining a political system which guarantees individual liberty to a greater degree than any other. And I thank you and your people for all your help in maintaining the continuity which is the bulwark of our republic.

7 The business of our nation goes forward.

8 These United States are confronted with an economic affliction of great proportions.

9 We suffer from the longest and one of the worst sustained inflations in our national history. It distorts our economic decisions, penalizes thrift and crushes the struggling young and the fixed-income elderly alike. It threatens to shatter the lives of millions of our people.

This speech is reprinted from *Contemporary American Speeches*, (5th edition), pp. 375–80, edited by Wil A. Linkugel, R. R. Allen, and Richard L. Johannesen. Dubuque, IA: Kendall/Hunt, 1982.

10 Idle industries have cast workers into unemployment, human misery and personal indignity.

11 Those who do work are denied a fair return for their labor by a tax system which penalizes successful achievement and keeps us from maintaining full productivity.

12 But great as our tax burden is, it has not kept pace with public spending. For decades we have piled deficit upon deficit, mortgaging our future and our children's future for the temporary convenience of the present.

13 To continue this long trend is to guarantee tremendous social, cultural, political and economic upheaval.

14 You and I, as individuals, can, by borrowing, live beyond our means but for only a limited period of time. Why then should we think that collectively, as a nation, we are not bound by that same limitation?

15 We must act today in order to preserve tomorrow. And let there be no misunderstanding—we're going to begin to act beginning today.

16 The economic ills we suffer have come upon us over several decades.

17 They will not go away in days, weeks or months, but they will go away. They will go away because we as Americans have the capacity now, as we have had in the past, to do whatever needs to be done to preserve this last and greatest bastion of freedom.

18 In this present crisis, government is not the solution to our problem; government is the problem.

19 From time to time we've been tempted to believe that society has become too complex to be managed by self-rule, that government by an elite group is superior to government for, by and of the people.

20 But if no one among us is capable of governing himself, then who among us has the capacity to govern someone else?

21 All of us together—in and out of government—must bear the burden. The solutions we seek must be equitable with no one group singled out to pay a higher price.

22 We hear much of special interest groups. Well our concern must be for a special interest group that has been too long neglected.

23 It knows no sectional boundaries, or ethnic and racial divisions and it crosses political party lines. It is made up of men and women who raise our food, patrol our streets, man our mines and factories, teach our children, keep our homes and heal us when we're sick.

24 Professionals, industrialists, shopkeepers, clerks, cabbies and truck drivers. They are, in short, "We the people." This breed called Americans.

25   Well, this Administration's objective will be a healthy, vigorous, growing economy that provides equal opportunities for all Americans with no barriers born of bigotry or discrimination.

26   Putting America back to work means putting all Americans back to work. Ending inflation means freeing all Americans from the terror of runaway living costs.

27   All must share in the productive work of this "new beginning," and all must share in the bounty of a revived economy.

28   With the idealism and fair play which are the core of our system and our strength, we can have a strong, prosperous America at peace with itself and the world.

29   So as we begin, let us take inventory.

30   We are a nation that has a government—not the other way around. And this makes us special among the nations of the earth.

31   Our Government has no power except that granted it by the people. It is time to check and reverse the growth of government which shows signs of having grown beyond the consent of the governed.

32   It is my intention to curb the size and influence of the Federal establishment and to demand recognition of the distinction between the powers granted to the Federal Government and those reserved to the states or to the people.

33   All of us—all of us need to be reminded that the Federal Government did not create the states; the states created the Federal Government.

34   Now, so there will be no misunderstanding, it's not my intention to do away with government.

35   It is rather to make it work—work with us, not over us; to stand by our side, not ride on our back. Government can and must provide opportunity, not smother it; foster productivity, not stifle it.

36   If we look to the answer as to why for so many years we achieved so much, prospered as no other people on earth, it was because here in this land we unleashed the energy and individual genius of man to a greater extent than has ever been done before.

37   Freedom and the dignity of the individual have been more available and assured here than in any other place on earth. The price for this freedom at times has been high, but we have never been unwilling to pay that price.

38   It is no coincidence that our present troubles parallel and are proportionate to the intervention and intrusion in our lives that result from unnecessary and excessive growth of Government.

39   It is time for us to realize that we are too great a nation to limit

ourselves to small dreams. We're not, as some would have us believe, doomed to an inevitable decline. I do not believe in a fate that will fall on us no matter what we do. I do believe in a fate that will fall on us if we do nothing.

40   So, with all the creative energy at our command let us begin an era of national renewal. Let us renew our determination, our courage and our strength. And let us renew our faith and our hope. We have every right to dream heroic dreams.

41   Those who say that we're in a time when there are no heroes—they just don't know where to look. You can see heroes every day going in and out of factory gates. Others, a handful in number, produce enough food to feed all of us and then the world beyond.

42   You meet heroes across a counter—and they're on both sides of that counter. There are entrepreneurs with faith in themselves and faith in an idea who create new jobs, new wealth and opportunity.

43   There are individuals and families whose taxes support the Government and whose voluntary gifts support church, charity, culture, art and education. Their patriotism is quiet but deep. Their values sustain our national life.

44   Now, I have used the words "they" and "their" in speaking of these heroes. I could say "you" and "your" because I'm addressing the heroes of whom I speak—you, the citizens of this blessed land.

45   Your dreams, your hopes, your goals are going to be the dreams, the hopes and the goals of this Administration, so help me God.

46   We shall reflect the compassion that is so much a part of your makeup.

47   How can we love our country and not love our countrymen? And loving them reach out a hand when they fall, heal them when they're sick and provide opportunity to make them self-sufficient so they will be equal in fact and not just in theory?

48   Can we solve the problems confronting us? Well the answer is a unequivocal and emphatic yes.

49   To paraphrase Winston Churchill, I did not take the oath I've just taken with the intention of presiding over the dissolution of the world's strongest economy.

50   In the days ahead I will propose removing the roadblocks that have slowed our economy and reduced productivity.

51   Steps will be taken aimed at restoring the balance between the various levels of government. Progress may be slow—measured in inches and feet, not miles—but we will progress.

52 It is time to reawaken this industrial giant, to get government back within its means and to lighten our punitive tax burden.

53 And these will be our first priorities, and on these principles there will be no compromise.

54 On the eve of our struggle for independence a man who might've been one of the greatest among the Founding Fathers, Dr. Joseph Warren, president of Massachusetts Congress, said to his fellow Americans, "Our country is in danger, but not to be despaired of. On you depend the fortunes of America. You are to decide the important question upon which rest the happiness and the liberty of millions yet unborn. Act worthy of yourselves."

55 Well I believe we the Americans of today are ready to act worthy of ourselves, ready to do what must be done to insure happiness and liberty for ourselves, our children and our children's children.

56 And as we renew ourselves here in our own land we will be seen as having greater strength throughout the world. We will again be the exemplar of freedom and a beacon of hope for those who do not now have freedom.

57 To those neighbors and allies who share our freedom, we will strengthen our historic ties and assure them of our support and firm commitment.

58 We will match loyalty with loyalty. We will strive for mutually beneficial relations. We will not use our friendship to impose on their sovereignty, for our own sovereignty is not for sale.

59 As for the enemies of freedom, those who are potential adversaries, they will be reminded that peace is the highest aspiration of the American people. We will negotiate for it, sacrifice for it; we will not surrender for it—now or ever.

60 Our forbearance should never be misunderstood. Our reluctance for conflict should not be misjudged as a failure of will.

61 When action is required to preserve our national security, we will act. We will maintain sufficient strength to prevail if need be, knowing that if we do we have the best chance of never having to use that strength.

62 Above all we must realize that no arsenal or no weapon in the arsenals of the world is so formidable as the will and moral courage of free men and women.

63 It is a weapon our adversaries in today's world do not have.

64 It is a weapon that we as Americans do have.

65 Let that be understood by those who practice terrorism and prey upon their neighbors.

66 I am told that tens of thousands of prayer meetings are being held

on this day; for that I am deeply grateful. We are a nation under God, and I believe God intended for us to be free. It would be fitting and good, I think, if on each inaugural day in future years it should be declared a day of prayer.

67 This is the first time in our history that this ceremony has been held, as you've been told, on this West Front of the Capitol.

68 Standing here, one faces a magnificent vista, opening up on this city's special beauty and history.

69 At the end of this open mall are those shrines to the giants on whose shoulders we stand.

70 Directly in front of me, the monument to a monumental man. George Washington, father of our country. A man of humility who came to greatness reluctantly. He led America out of revolutionary victory into infant nationhood.

71 Off to one side, the stately memorial to Thomas Jefferson. The Declaration of Independence flames with his eloquence.

72 And then beyond the Reflecting Pool, the dignified columns of the Lincoln Memorial. Whoever would understand in his heart the meaning of America will find it in the life of Abraham Lincoln.

73 Beyond those moments, monuments to heroism is the Potomac River, and on the far shore the sloping hills of Arlington National Cemetery with its row upon row of simple white markers bearing crosses or Stars of David. They add up to only a tiny fraction of the price that has been paid for our freedom.

74 Each one of those markers is a monument to the kind of hero I spoke of earlier.

75 Their lives ended in places called Belleau Wood, the Argonne, Omaha Beach, Salerno and halfway around the world on Guadalcanal, Tarawa, Pork Chop Hill, the Chosin Reservoir, and in a hundred rice paddies and jungles of a place called Vietnam.

76 Under such a marker lies a young man, Martin Treptow, who left his job in a small town barber shop in 1917 to go to France with the famed Rainbow Division.

77 There, on the Western front, he was killed trying to carry a message between battalions under heavy artillery fire.

78 We are told that on his body was found a diary.

79 On the flyleaf under the heading, "My Pledge," he had written these words:

80 "America must win this war. Therefore I will work, I will save, I will sacrifice, I will endure, I will fight cheerfully and do my utmost, as if the issue of the whole struggle depended on me alone."

346

81   The crisis we are facing today does not require of us the kind of sacrifice that Martin Treptow and so many thousands of others were called upon to make.

82   It does require, however, our best effort, and our willingness to believe in ourselves and to believe in our capacity to perform great deeds; to believe that together with God's help we can and will resolve the problems which now confront us.

83   And after all, why shouldn't we believe that? We are Americans.

84   Gold bless you and thank you. Thank you very much.

B. INAUGURAL ADDRESS OF RONALD REAGAN, JANUARY 21, 1985

1 Senator Mathias, Chief Justice Burger, Vice President Bush, Speaker O'Neill, Senator Dole, Reverend Clergy and members of my family and friends, and my fellow citizens: This day has been made brighter with the presence here of one who for a time has been absent. Senator John Stennis, God bless you and welcome back.

2 There is, however, one who is not with us today. Representative Gillis Long of Louisiana left us last night. And I wonder if we could all join in a moment of silent prayer.

3 Amen.

4 There are no words to—adequate to express my thanks for the great honor that you've bestowed on me. I will do my utmost to be deserving of your trust.

5 This is, as Senator Mathias told us, the 50th time that we, the people, have celebrated this historic occasion. When the first President, George Washington, placed his hand upon the Bible, he stood less than a single day's journey by horseback from raw, untamed wilderness. There were four million Americans in a Union of 13 states.

6 Today we are 60 times as many in a Union of 50 states. We've lighted the world with our inventions, gone to the aid of mankind wherever in the world there was a cry for help, journeyed to the moon and safely returned.

7 So much has changed. And yet we stand together as we did two centuries ago.

8 When I took this oath four years ago, I did so in a time of economic stress. Voices were raised saying that we had to look to our past greatness and glory. But we, the present-day Americans, are not given to looking backward. In this blessed land, there is always a better tomorrow.

This speech is reprinted from *Vital Speeches of the Day*, February 1, 1985, pp. 226–28.

348

9   Four years ago I spoke to you of a new beginning, and we have accomplished that. But in another sense, our new beginning is a continuation of that beginning created two centuries ago when, for the first time in history, government, the people said, was not our master. It is our servant; its only power that which we, the people, allow it to have.

10   That system has never failed us. But for a time we failed the system.

11   We asked things of government that government was not equipped to give. We yielded authority to the national government that properly belonged to states or to local governments or to the people themselves. We allowed taxes and inflation to rob us of our earnings and savings and watched the great industrial machine that had made us the most productive people on earth slow down and the number of unemployed increase.

12   By 1980 we knew it was time to renew our faith, to strive with all our strength toward the ultimate in individual freedom consistent with an orderly society.

13   We believed then and now there are no limits to growth and human progress when men and women are free to follow their dreams. And we were right. And we were right to believe that. Tax rates have been reduced, inflation cut dramatically and more people are employed than ever before in our history.

14   We are creating a nation once again vibrant, robust and alive. But there are many mountains yet to climb. We will not rest until every American enjoys the fullness of freedom, dignity and opportunity as our birthright. It is our birthright as citizens of this great republic.

15   And if we meet this challenge, these will be years when Americans have restored their confidence and tradition of progress; when our values of faith, family, work and neighborhood were restated for a modern age; when our economy was finally freed from government's grip; when we made sincere efforts at meaningful arms reductions by rebuilding our defenses, our economy, and developing new technologies helped preserve peace in a troubled world; when America courageously supported the struggle for individual liberty, self-government and free enterprise throughout the world and turned the tide of history away from totalitarian darkness and into the warm sunlight of human freedom.

16   My fellow citizens, our nation is poised for greatness.

17   We must do what we know is right and do it with all our might.

18   Let history say of us, these were golden years—when the American Revolution was reborn, when freedom gained new life and America reached for her best.

19 Our two-party system has solved us—served us, I should say, well over the years, but never better than in those times of great challenge, when we came together not as Democrats or Republicans but as Americans united in the common cause.

20 Two of our Founding Fathers, a Boston lawyer named Adams and a Virginia planter named Jefferson, members of that remarkable group who met in Independence Hall and dared to think they could start the world over again, left us an important lesson. They had become, in the years spent in government bitter political rivals. In the Presidential election of 1800, then years later, when both were retired and age had softened their anger, they began to speak to each other again through letters.

21 A bond was re-established between those two who had helped create this government of ours.

22 In 1826, the 50th anniversary of the Declaration of Independence, they both died. They died on the same day, within a few hours of each other. And that day was the Fourth of July.

23 In one of those letters exchanged in the sunset of their lives, Jefferson wrote, "It carries me back to the times when, beset with difficulties and dangers, we were fellow laborers in the same cause, struggling for what is most valuable to man, his right of self-government. Laboring always at the same oar, with some wave ever ahead threatening to overwhelm us, and yet passing harmless we rode through the storm with heart and hand."

24 Well, with heart and hand, let us stand as one today; one people under God determined that our future shall be worthy of our past.

25 As we do, we must not repeat the well-intentioned errors of our past.

26 We must never again abuse the trust of working men and women by sending their earnings on a futile chase after the spiraling demands of a bloated Federal establishment.

27 You elected us in 1980 to end this prescription for disaster. And I don't believe you re-elected us in 1984 to reverse course.

28 The heart of our efforts is one idea vindicated by 25 straight months of economic growth; freedom and incentives unleash the drive and enterpreneurial genius that are the core of human progress.

29 We have begun to increase the rewards for work, savings and investment; reduce the increase in the cost and size of government and its interference in people's lives.

30 We must simplify our tax system, make it more fair and bring the rates down for all who work and earn.

31   We must think anew and move with a new boldness so every American who seeks work can find work; so the least among us shall have an equal chance to achieve the greatest things—to be heroes who heal our sick, feed the hungry, protect peace among nations and leave this world a better place.

32   The time has come for a new American emancipation, a great national drive to tear down economic barriers and liberate the spirit of enterprise in the most distressed areas of our country.

33   My friends, together we can do this, and do it we must, so help me God.

34   From new freedom will spring new opportunities for growth, a more productive, fulfilled and united people and a stronger America, an America that will lead the technological revolution and also open its mind and heart and soul to the treasuries of literature, music and poetry, and the values of faith, courage and love.

35   A dynamic economy, with more citizens working and paying taxes, will be our strongest tool to bring down budget deficits. But an almost unbroken 50 years of deficit spending has finally brought us to a time of reckoning.

36   We've come to a turning point, a moment for hard decisions.

37   I have asked the Cabinet and my staff a question and now I put the same question to all of you. If not us, who? And if not now, when?

38   It must be done by all of us going forward with a program aimed at reaching a balanced budget. We can then begin reducing the national debt.

39   I will shortly submit a budget to the Congress aimed at freezing government program spending for the next year. Beyond this, we must take further steps to permanently control government's power to tax and spend.

40   We must act now to protect future generations from government's desire to spend its citizens' money and tax them into servitude when the bills come due.

41   Let us make it unconstitutional for the Federal Government to spend more than the Federal Government takes in.

42   We have already started returning to the people and to state and local governments responsibilities better handled by them.

43   Now, there is a place for the Federal Government in matters of social compassion. But our fundamental goals must be to reduce dependency and upgrade the dignity of those who are infirm or disadvantaged.

44   And here a growing economy and support from family and

community offer our best chance for a society where compassion is a way of life, where the old and infirm are cared for, the young and, yes, the unborn, protected, and the unfortunate looked after and made self-sufficient.

45   Now there is another area where the Federal Government can play a part.

46   As an older American, I remember a time when people of different race, creed or ethnic origin in our land found hatred and prejudice installed in social custom and, yes, in law.

47   There's no story more heartening in our history than the progress that we've made toward the brotherhood of man that God intended for us.

48   Let us resolve: There will be no turning back or hesitation on the road to an America rich in dignity and abundant with opportunity for all our citizens.

49   Let us resolve that we, the people, will build an American opportunity society in which all of us—white and black, rich and poor, young and old—will go forward together, arm in arm.

50   Again, let us remember that, though our heritage is one of blood lines from every corner of the earth, we are all Americans pledged to carry on this last best hope of man on earth.

51   And I have spoken of our domestic goals, and the limitations we should put on our national government.

52   Now let us turn to a task that is the primary responsibility of national government—the safety and security of our people.

53   Today we utter no prayer more fervently than the ancient prayer for peace on earth.

54   Yet history has shown that peace does not come, nor will our freedom be preserved, by good will alone.

55   There are those in the world who scorn our vision of human dignity and freedom.

56   One nation, the Soviet Union, has conducted the greatest military buildup in the history of man, building arsenals of awesome offensive weapons.

57   We've made progress in restoring our defense capability. But much remains to be done. There must be no wavering by us, nor any doubts by others, that America will meet her responsibilities to remain free, secure, and at peace.

58   There is only one way safely and legitimately to reduce the cost of national security, and that is to try to reduce the need for it.

59   And this we're trying to do in negotiations with the Soviet Union.

352

60   We're not just discussing limits on a further increase of nuclear weapons. We seek, instead, to reduce their number. We seek the total elimination, one day, of nuclear weapons from the face of the earth.

61   Now for decades we and the Soviets have lived under the threat of mutual assured destruction; if either resorted to the use of nuclear weapons, the other could retaliate and destroy the one who had started it.

62   Is there either logic or morality in believing that if one side threatens to kill tens of millions of our people, our only recourse is to threaten killing tens of millions of theirs?

63   I have approved a research program to find, if we can, a security shield that will destroy nuclear missiles before they reach their target.

64   It wouldn't kill people, it would destroy weapons. It wouldn't militarize space, it would help demilitarize the arsenals of earth. It would render nuclear weapons obsolete.

65   We will meet with the Soviets hoping that we can agree on a way to rid the world of the threat of nuclear destruction.

66   We strive for peace and security, heartened by the changes all around us.

67   Since the turn of the century, the number of democracies in the world has grown fourfold.

68   Human freedom is on the march, and nowhere more so than in our own hemisphere.

69   Freedom is one of the deepest and noblest aspirations of the human spirit.

70   People worldwide hunger for the right of self-determination, for those inalienable rights that make for human dignity and progress.

71   America must remain freedom's staunchest friend, for freedom is our best ally, and it is the world's only hope to conquer poverty and preserve peace.

72   Every blow we inflict against poverty will be a blow against its dark allies of oppression and war. Every victory for human freedom will be a victory for world peace.

73   So we go forward today a nation still mighty in its youth and powerful in its purpose.

74   With our alliances strengthened, with our economy leading the world to a new age of economic expansion, we look to a future rich in possibilities.

75   And all of this is because we worked and acted together, not as members of political parties, but as Americans.

76   My friends, we, we live in a world that's lit by lightning.

77   So much is changing and will change, but so much endures and transcends time.

78   History is a ribbon, always unfurling; history is a journey.

79   And as we continue on our journey, we think of those who traveled before us.

80   We stand again at the steps of this symbol of our democracy, or we would've been standing at the steps if it hadn't gotten so cold.

81   Now, we're standing inside this symbol of our democracy, and we see and hear again the echoes of our past.

82   A general falls to his knees in the hard snow of Valley Forge; a lonely President paces the darkened halls and towers, ponders his struggle to preserve the Union; the men of the Alamo call out encouragement to each other; a settler pushes west and sings a song, and the song echoes out forever and fills the unknowing air.

83   It is the American sound: It is hopeful, big-hearted, idealistic—daring, decent and fair. That's our heritage, that's our song. We sing it still.

84   For all our problems, our differences, we are together as of old.

85   We raise our voices to the God who is the author of this most tender music. And may He continue to hold us close as we fill the world with our sand, sound—in unity, affection and love.

86   One people under God, dedicated to the dream of freedom that He has placed in the human heart, called upon now to pass that dream on to a waiting and a hopeful world.

87   God bless you and may God bless America.

SELECTED BIBLIOGRAPHY

The literature on form and genre is so vast that we have decided to focus, in the first two sections of this bibliography, and particularly in the "Form and Genre Studies" section, on works in speech-communication. The third section provides substantive as well as bibliographic introductions to more specialized literature in political rhetoric.

THEORETICAL WORKS ON FORM AND GENRE

Aristotle. *Rhetoric*. W. Rhys Roberts, trans. In *The Basic Works of Aristotle*, Richard McKeon, ed. New York: Random House, 1941.

Arnold, Carroll C. *Criticism of Oral Rhetoric*. Columbus, Ohio: Charles E. Merrill, 1974.

Baker, Virgil L. "The Development of Forms of Discourse in American Rhetorical Theory." *Southern Speech Communication Journal* 18 (1953):207–15.

Bass, Jeff D. "The Rhetorical Opposition to Controversial Wars: Rhetorical Timing as a Generic Consideration." *Western Journal of Speech Communication* 43 (1979):180–91.

Baxter, Gerald D., and Bart F. Kennedy. "Whitehead's Concept of Concrescence and the Rhetorical Situation." *Philosophy and Rhetoric* 8 (1975):159–64.

Bennett, W. Lance. "Political Scenarios and the Nature of Politics." *Philosophy and Rhetoric* 8 (1975):23–42.

Benoit, William Lyon. "In Defense of Generic Rhetorical Criticism: John Patton's 'Generic Criticism: Typology at an Inflated Price.' " *Rhetoric Society Quarterly* 10 (Summer 1980):128–34.

Bitzer, Lloyd F. "Functional Communication: A Situational Perspective." In *Rhetoric in Transition*, Eugene E. White, ed. University Park: Pennsylvania State University Press, 1980; pp. 21–38.

———. "Political Rhetoric." In *Handbook of Political Communication*, Dan D. Nimmo and Keith R. Sanders, eds. Beverly Hills, Calif.: Sage Publications, 1981; pp. 225–48.

———. "The Rhetorical Situation." *Philosophy and Rhetoric* 1 (January 1968):1–14.

Black, Edwin. *Rhetorical Criticism: A Study in Method.* New York: Macmillan, 1965.

Booth, Wayne C. *A Rhetoric of Irony.* Chicago: University of Chicago Press, 1974.

Bormann, Ernest G. "Fantasy and Rhetorical Vision: The Rhetorical Criticism of Social Reality." *Quarterly Journal of Speech* 58 (1972):394–407.

———. "Generalizing about Significant Form: Science and Humanism Compared and Contrasted." In *Form and Genre: Shaping Rhetorical Action*, Karlyn Kohrs Campbell and Kathleen Hall Jamieson, eds. Falls Church, Va.: Speech Communication Association, 1978; pp. 51–69.

———. "Rhetorical Criticism and Significant Form: A Humanistic Approach." In *Form and Genre: Shaping Rhetorical Action*, Karlyn Kohrs Campbell and Kathleen Hall Jamieson, eds. Falls Church, Va.: Speech Communication Association, 1978; pp. 165–87.

Branham, Robert J., and W. Barnett Pearce. "Between Text and Context: Toward a Rhetoric of Contextual Reconstruction." *Quarterly Journal of Speech* 71 (1985):19–36.

Brinton, Alan. "Situation in the Theory of Rhetoric." *Philosophy and Rhetoric* 14 (Fall 1981):234–48.

Brock, Bernard, and Robert L. Scott. *Methods of Rhetorical Criticism: A Twentieth-Century Perspective.* 2nd ed. Detroit, Mich.: Wayne State University Press, 1980.

Brown, Robert L., Jr., and Martin Steinmann, Jr., eds. *Rhetoric 78: Proceedings of Minnesota Center for Advanced Studies in Language, Style, and Literary Theory*, 1979.

Burke, Kenneth. *Attitudes toward History.* Boston: Beacon Press, 1961.

———. *Counter-Statement.* Berkeley: University of California Press, 1953.

———. *A Grammar of Motives.* Englewood Cliffs, N.J.: Prentice-Hall, 1945.

———. *The Philosophy of Literary Form.* Baton Rouge: Louisiana State University Press, 1941.

———. *A Rhetoric of Motives.* Berkeley: University of California Press, 1969.

Campbell, Karlyn Kohrs. "Contemporary Rhetorical Criticism: Genres, Analogs, and Susan B. Anthony." In *The Jensen Lectures: Contemporary Communication Studies*, John I. Sisco, ed. Tampa, Fla.: University of South Florida, 1983; pp. 117–32.

———. "Criticism: Ephemeral and Enduring." *Communication Education* 23 (1974):9–14.

Campbell, Karlyn Kohrs, and Kathleen Hall Jamieson. "Form and Genre in Rhetorical Criticism: An Introduction." In *Form and Genre: Shaping Rhetorical Action*, Karlyn Kohrs Campbell and Kathleen Hall Jamieson, eds. Falls Church, Va.: Speech Communication Association, 1978; pp. 9–32.

Campbell, Karlyn Kohrs, and Kathleen Hall Jamieson, eds. *Form and Genre: Shaping Rhetorical Action.* Falls Church, Va.: Speech Communication Association, 1978.

Cathcart, Robert S. "Defining Social Movements by Their Rhetorical Form." *Central States Speech Journal* 31 (1980):267–73.
———. "Movements: Confrontation as Rhetorical Form." *Southern Speech Communication Journal* 43 (1978):233–47.
———. "New Approaches to the Study of Movements: Defining Movements Rhetorically." *Western Journal of Speech Communication* 36 (1972):82–88.
Cawelti, John. *Adventure, Mystery, and Romance.* Chicago: University of Chicago Press, 1976.
Chase, J. Richard. "The Classical Conception of Epideictic." *Quarterly Journal of Speech* 48 (1961):293–300.
Chesebro, James W. "Political Communication." *Quarterly Journal of Speech* 62 (1976):289–300.
Chesebro, James W., and Caroline D. Hamsher. "Contemporary Rhetorical Theory and Criticism: Dimensions of the New Rhetoric." *Communication Monographs* 42 (1975):311–34.
Colie, Rosalie L. *The Resources of Kind: Genre Theory in the Renaissance.* Berkeley: University of California Press, 1973.
Conley, Thomas. "Ancient Rhetoric and Modern Genre Criticism." *Communication Quarterly* 27 (1979):47–53.
Consigny, Scott. "Rhetoric and Its Situations." *Philosophy and Rhetoric* 7 (1974):175–86.
Conville, Richard. "Northrop Frye and Speech Criticism: An Introduction." *Quarterly Journal of Speech* 51 (1970):417–25.
Cox, J. Robert. "Argument and the 'Definition of the Situation.' " *Central States Speech Journal* 32 (1981):197–205.
Culler, Jonathan. *Structuralist Poetics.* Ithaca, N.Y.: Cornell University Press, 1975.
Derrida, Jacques. "The Law of Genre." Avital Ronell, trans. *Critical Inquiry* 7 (1980):55–82.
Dubrow, Heather. *Genre.* London: Methuen, 1982.
Edelman, Murray. *The Symbolic Uses of Politics.* Urbana: University of Illinois Press, 1964.
Fearing, Franklin. "The Problem of Metaphor." *Southern Speech Communication Journal* 29 (1963):47–55.
Fisher, Walter R. "Genre: Concepts and Applications in Rhetorical Criticism." *Western Journal of Speech Communication* 44 (1980):288–99.
———. "A Motive View of Communication." *Quarterly Journal of Speech* 56 (1970):131–39.
Frye, Northrop. *Anatomy of Criticism: Four Essays.* Princeton, N.J.: Princeton University Press, 1957.
Genette, Gerard. "Genres, 'Types,' Modes." *Poetique* 32 (1977):389–421.
Gregg, Richard B. "Kenneth Burke's Prolegomena to the Study of the Rhetoric of Form." *Communication Quarterly* 26, no. 4 (1978):3–13.

————. *Symbolic Inducement and Knowing.* Columbia: University of South Carolina Press, 1984.

Griffin, Leland M. "A Dramatistic Theory of the Rhetoric of Movements." In *Critical Responses to Kenneth Burke*, William H. Rueckert, ed.

————. "The Edifice Metaphor in Rhetorical Theory." *Communication Quarterly* 27 (1960):279–92.

————. "On Studying Movements." *Central States Speech Journal* 31 (1980):225–32.

Gronbeck, Bruce E. "Rhetorical History and Rhetorical Criticism: A Distinction." *Communication Education* 24 (1975):309–20.

————. "Rhetorical Timing in Public Communication." *Central States Speech Journal* 25 (1974):84–93.

Gustainis, J. Justin. "The Generic Criticism of Social Movement Rhetoric." *Rhetoric Society Quarterly* 4 (1982):259–60.

Harrell, Jackson, and Wil A. Linkugel. "On Rhetorical Genre: An Organizing Perspective." *Philosophy and Rhetoric* 11 (1978):262–81.

Hart, Roderick. "Absolutism and Situation: Prolegomena to a Rhetorical Biography of Richard M. Nixon." *Communication Quarterly* 43 (1976):204–28.

————. "Theory-Building and Rhetorical Criticism: An Informal Statement of Opinion." *Central States Speech Journal* 27 (1976):70–77.

Hastings, Arthur. "Metaphor in Rhetoric." *Western Journal of Speech Communication* 34 (1970):181–94.

Heath, Robert L. "Kenneth Burke on Form." *Quarterly Journal of Speech* 65 (1979):392–404.

Hernadi, Paul. *Beyond Genre: New Directions in Literary Classification.* Ithaca, N.Y.: Cornell University Press, 1972.

Hunsaker, David M., and Craig R. Smith. "The Nature of Issues: A Constructive Approach to Situational Rhetoric." *Western Journal of Speech Communication* 40 (1976):144–56.

Jameson, Fredric. *The Political Unconscious: Narrative as a Socially Symbolic Act.* Ithaca, N.Y.: Cornell University Press, 1981.

Jamieson, Kathleen Hall. "Antecedent Genre as Rhetorical Constraint." *Quarterly Journal of Speech* 61 (1975):406–15.

————. "Generic Constraints and the Rhetorical Situation." *Philosophy and Rhetoric* 6(1976):162–70.

————. "The Standardization and Modification of Rhetorical Genre: A Perspective." *Genre* 8 (1975):183–93.

Jamieson, Kathleen Hall, and Karlyn Kohrs Campbell. "Rhetorical Hybrids: Fusions of Generic Elements." *Quarterly Journal of Speech* 68 (1982):146–57.

Jauss, Hans Robert. *Toward an Aesthetic of Reception.* Timothy Bahti, trans. *Theory and History of Literature.* Vol. 2. Minneapolis: University of Minnesota Press, 1982.

358

Johnson, Mark, ed. *Philosophical Perspectives on Metaphor*. Minneapolis: University of Minnesota Press, 1981.

Jordan, Mark D. "A Preface to the Study of Philosophical Genres." *Philosophy and Rhetoric* 14 (1981):199–211.

Karstetter, Allan B. "Toward a Theory of Rhetorical Irony." *Communication Monographs* 31 (1964):162–78.

Kaufer, David S. "Irony and Rhetorical Strategy." *Philosophy and Rhetoric* 10 (1977):90–110.

———. "Point of View in Rhetorical Situations: Classical and Romantic Contrasts and Contemporary Implications." *Quarterly Journal of Speech* 65 (1979):171–86.

Kent, Thomas L. "The Classification of Genres." *Genre* 16 (1983):1–20.

King, Robert L. "Transforming Scandal into Tragedy: A Rhetoric of Political Apology." *Quarterly Journal of Speech* 71 (1985):289–301.

Kinneavy, James L. *A Theory of Discourse: The Aims of Discourse*. Englewood Cliffs, N.J.: Prentice-Hall, 1971.

Kruse, Noreen. "The Scope of Apologetic Discourse: Establishing Generic Parameters." *Southern Speech Communication Journal* 46 (1981):278–91.

Lakoff, George, and Mark Johnson. *Metaphors We Live By*. Chicago: University of Chicago Press, 1980.

Larson, Richard. "Lloyd Bitzer's 'Rhetorical Situation' and the Classification of Discourse: Problems and Implications." *Philosophy and Rhetoric* 3 (1970):165–68.

McKeon, Zahava Karl. *Novels and Arguments: Inventing Rhetorical Criticism*. Chicago: University of Chicago Press, 1982.

Miller, Arthur B. "Rhetorical Exigence." *Philosophy and Rhetoric* 5 (1972):111–18.

Miller, Carolyn R. "Genre as Social Action." *Quarterly Journal of Speech* 70 (1984):151–67.

Milner, Earl. "On the Genesis and Development of Literary Systems." *Critical Inquiry* 5 (1978): Part I, pp. 339–53; Part II, pp. 553–68.

Mohrmann, G. P., and Michael Leff. "Lincoln at Cooper Union: A Rationale for Neo-Classical Criticism." *Quarterly Journal of Speech* 60 (1974):459–67.

Murphy, Richard. "The Speech as Literary Genre." *Quarterly Journal of Speech* 45 (1958): 117–27.

Newcomb, Horce M. "On the Dialogic Aspects of Mass Communication." *Critical Studies in Mass Communication* 1 (1984):34–50.

Osborn, Michael M. "The Evolution of the Theory of Metaphor in Rhetoric." *Western Journal of Speech Communication* 31 (1967):121–31.

Osborn, Michael M., and Douglas Ehninger. "The Metaphor in Public Address." *Communication Monographs* 29 (1962):223–34.

Patton, John H. "Causation and Creativity in Rhetorical Situations: Distinctions and Implications." *Quarterly Journal of Speech* 65 (1979):36–55.

————. "Generic Criticism: Typology at an Inflated Price." *Rhetoric Society Quarterly* 10 (1980):128–34.

Perelman, Ch., and L. Olbrechts-Tyteca. *The New Rhetoric: A Treatise on Argumentation.* John Wilkinson and Purcell Weaver, trans. Notre Dame, Ind.: University of Notre Dame Press, 1969.

Pocock, J. G. A. "Verbalizing a Political Act: Toward a Politics of Speech." *Political Theory* 1 (1973):27–45.

Reichert, John F. " 'Organizing Principles' and Genre Theory." *Genre* 1 (1968):1–11.

Richter, David H. "Pandora's Box Revisited: A Review Article." *Critical Inquiry* 1 (1974):453–78.

Rosenfield, Lawrence W. "The Anatomy of Critical Discourse." *Communication Monographs* 35 (1968):50–69.

Sanders, Robert E., and Donald P. Cushman. "Rules, Constraints, and Strategies in Human Communication." In *Handbook of Rhetorical and Communication Theory*, Carroll C. Arnold and John Waite Bowers, eds. Boston: Allyn & Bacon, 1984; pp. 230–69.

Scott, Robert L. "Intentionality in the Rhetorical Process." In *Rhetoric in Transition: Studies in the Nature and Uses of Rhetoric*, Eugene E. White, ed. University Park: Pennsylvania State University Press, 1980; pp. 39–60.

Shimanoff, Susan B. *Communication Rules.* Beverly Hills, Calif.: Sage Publications, 1980.

Simons, Herbert W. " 'Genre-alizing' about Rhetoric: A Scientific Approach." In *Form and Genre: Shaping Rhetorical Action*, Karlyn Kohrs Campbell and Kathleen Hall Jamieson, eds. Falls Church, Va.: Speech Communication Association, 1978; pp. 33–50.

Smith, Craig R. "A Reinterpretation of Aristotle's Notion of Form." *Western Journal of Speech Communication* 43 (1979):14–25.

Stewart, Charles J. "A Functional Approach to the Rhetoric of Social Movements." *Central States Speech Journal* 31 (1980):298–305.

Strelka, Joseph, ed. *Theories of Literary Genre.* University Park: Pennsylvania State University Press, 1978.

Suleiman, Susan Robin. *Authoritarian Fictions: The Ideological Novel as a Literary Genre.* New York: Columbia University Press, 1983.

Swanson, David L. "The Requirements of Critical Justifications." *Communication Monographs* 44 (1977):306–20.

Todorov, Tzvetan. *The Fantastic: A Structural Approach to a Literary Genre.* Ithaca, N.Y.: Cornell University Press, 1975.

————. "The Origins of Genres." Richard W. Berrong, trans. *New Literary History* 8 (1976):159–70.

Vatz, Richard E. "The Myth of the Rhetorical Situation." *Philosophy and Rhetoric* 6 (1973):154–61.

Vivas, Eliseo. "Literary Classes: Some Problems." *Genre* 1 (1968):97–105.

Wasby, Stephen. "Rhetoricians and Political Scientists: Some Lines of Converging Interest." *Southern Speech Communication Journal* 36 (1971):231–42.

Weaver, Richard. *The Ethics of Rhetoric.* South Bend, Ind.: Gateway Editions, 1953.

Wellek, Rene, and Austin Warren. *Theory of Literature.* New York: Harcourt, Brace, 1942.

Wilkerson, K. E. "On Evaluating Theories of Rhetoric." *Philosophy and Rhetoric* 3 (Spring 1970):82–95.

Zarefsky, David. "A Skeptical View of Movement Studies." *Central States Speech Journal* 31 (1980):245–54.

FORM AND GENRE STUDIES

Aly, Bower. "The Gallows Speech: A Lost Genre." *Southern Speech Communication Journal* 34 (1969):204–13.

Anderson, Ray. "The Rhetoric of the *Report from Iron Mountain.*" *Communication Monographs* 37 (1970):219–31.

Andrews, James R. "They Chose the Sword: Appeals to War in Nineteenth-Century American Public Address." *Communication Quarterly* 17, no. 3 (1969):3–8.

Bailey, F. G. *The Tactical Uses of Passion: An Essay on Power, Reason, and Reality.* Ithaca, N.Y.: Cornell University Press, 1983.

Baird, John E. "The Rhetoric of Youth in Controversy against the Religious Establishment." *Western Journal of Speech Communication* 34 (1970):53–61.

Banninga, Jerald. "Sherman Adams' Resignation Address." *Central States Speech Journal* 11 (1960):191–93.

Bantz, Charles R. "Public Arguing in the Regulation of Health and Safety." *Western Journal of Speech Communication* 45 (1981):71–87.

Barefield, Paul A. "Republican Keynoters." *Communication Monographs* 37 (1970):232–39.

Barton, Stephen Nye, and John B. O'Leary. "The Rhetoric of Rural Physician Procurement Campaigns: An Application of Tavistock." *Quarterly Journal of Speech* 60 (1974):144–54.

Baskerville, Barnet. "The Illusion of Proof." *Western Journal of Speech Communication* 25 (1961): 236–42.

Bass, Jeff D. "The Rhetoric in Opposition to Controversial Wars: Rhetorical Timing as a Generic Consideration." *Western Journal of Speech Communication* 43 (1979):180–91.

———. "The Romance as Rhetorical Dissociation: The Purification of Imperialism in *King Solomon's Mines.*" *Quarterly Journal of Speech* 67 (1981):259–69.

Bennett, W. Lance. "Assessing Presidential Character: Degradation Rituals in Presidential Campaigns." *Quarterly Journal of Speech* 67 (1981):312–21.

361

———. "Myth, Ritual, and Political Control." *Journal of Communication* 30, no. 4 (1980):166–77.

———. "The Paradox of Public Discourse: A Framework for the Analysis Political Accounts." *Journal of Politics* 42 (1980):792–817.

———. "The Ritualistic and Pragmatic Bases of Political Campaign Discourse." *Quarterly Journal of Speech* 63 (1977):219–38.

Bercovitch, Sacvan. *The American Jeremiad.* Madison: University of Wisconsin Press, 1978.

Black, Edwin. "Electing Time." *Quarterly Journal of Speech* 54 (1973):125–29.

———. "The Second Persona." *Quarterly Journal of Speech* 56 (1970):109–19.

———. "The Sentimental Style as Escapism, or the Devil with Dan'l Webster." In *Form and Genre: Shaping Rhetorical Action*, Karlyn Kohrs Campbell and Kathleen Hall Jamieson, eds. Falls Church, Va.: Speech Communication Association, 1978; pp. 75–86.

Boase, Paul. *The Rhetoric of Christian Socialism.* New York: Random House, 1969.

Boase, Paul H., ed. *The Rhetoric of Protest and Reform, 1878–1898.* Athens: Ohio University Press, 1980.

Bormann, Ernest G. "A Fantasy Theme Analysis of the Television Coverage of the Hostage Release and the Reagan Inaugural." *Quarterly Journal of Speech* 68 (1982):133–45.

———, ed. *Forerunners of Black Power.* Englewood Cliffs, N.J.: Prentice-Hall, 1971.

Bosmajian, Haig, and Hamida Bosmajian. *The Rhetoric of the Civil Rights Movement.* New York: Random House, 1969.

Bostrom, Robert N. "Convention Nominating Speeches: A Product of Many Influences." *Central States Speech Journal* 11 (1960):194–97.

———. " 'I Give You a Man'—Kennedy's Speech for Adlai Stevenson." *Communication Monographs* 35 (1968):129–36.

Bowers, John Waite, and Donovan J. Ochs. *The Rhetoric of Agitation and Control.* Reading Mass.: Addison-Wesley, 1971.

Braden, Waldo W., ed. *Oratory in the New South.* Baton Rouge: Louisiana State University Press, 1979.

———. *Oratory in the Old South, 1828–1860.* Baton Rouge: Louisiana State University Press, 1970.

———. "The Rhetoric of a Closed Society." *Southern Speech Communication Journal* 45 (1980):333–51.

———. "The Rhetoric of Exploitation: Southern Demagogues in Action." In *The Oral Tradition in the South*, Waldo W. Braden, ed. Baton Rouge: Louisiana State University Press, 1983; pp. 83–106.

Bradley, Bert E. "Jefferson and Reagan: The Rhetoric of Two Inaugurals." *Southern Speech Communication Journal* 48 (1983):119–36.

———. "A Response to 'Two Inaugurals': A Second Look.' " *Southern Speech Communication Journal* 48 (1983):386–90.

Breen, Myles, and Farrel Corcoran. "Myth in the Television Discourse." *Communication Monographs* 49 (1982):127–36.

Brockriede, Wayne, and Robert L. Scott. *Moments in the Rhetoric of the Cold War*. New York: Random House, 1970.

Brooks, Robert D. "Black Power: The Dimensions of a Slogan." *Western Journal of Speech Communication* 34 (1970):108–14.

Brummett, Barry. "Burke's Representative Anecdote as a Method in Media Criticism." *Critical Studies in Mass Communication* 1 (1984):161–76.

———. "Gary Gilmore, Power, and the Rhetoric of Symbolic Forms." *Western Journal of Speech Communication* 43 (1979):3–13.

———. "Gastronomic Reference, Synecdoche, and Political Images." *Quarterly Journal of Speech* 67 (1981):138–45.

———. "Premillennial Apocalyptic as a Rhetorical Genre." *Central States Speech Journal* 35 (1984):84–93.

———. "Symbolic Form, Burkean Scapegoating, and Rhetorical Exigency in Alioto's Response to the 'Zebra' Murders." *Western Journal of Speech Communication* 44 (1980):64–73.

Bryson, Lyman. "The Rhetoric of Conciliation." *Quarterly Journal of Speech*, 39 (1953):437–443.

Burgchardt, Carl R. "Two Faces of American Communism: Pamphlet Rhetoric of the Third Period and the Popular Front." *Quarterly Journal of Speech* 66 (1980):375–91.

Burgess, Parke G. "Crisis Rhetoric: Coercion vs. Force." *Quarterly Journal of Speech* 59 (1973):61–73.

———. "The Rhetoric of Black Power: A Moral Demand." *Quarterly Journal of Speech* 54 (1968):122–33.

———. "The Rhetoric of Moral Conflict: Two Critical Dimensions." *Quarterly Journal of Speech* 56 (1970):120–30.

Burke, William L. "Notes on a Rhetoric of Lamentation." *Central States Speech Journal* 29 (1979):109–21.

Butler, Sherry Devereaux. "The Apologia, 1971 Genre." *Southern Speech Communication Journal* 26 (1972):281–89.

Campbell, Karlyn Kohrs. "Feminity and Feminism: To Be or Not To Be a Woman." *Communication Quarterly* 31 (1983):101–8.

———. "The Rhetoric of Radical Black Nationalism: A Case Study in Self-Conscious Criticism." *Central States Speech Journal* 22 (1971):151–60.

———. "The Rhetoric of Women's Liberation: An Oxymoron." *Quarterly Journal of Speech* 59 (1973):74–86.

Carlson, A. Cheree. "John Quincy Adams' 'Amistad Address': Eloquence in a Generic Hybrid." *Western Journal of Speech Communication* 49 (1985):14–26.

Carlton, Charles. "The Rhetoric of Death: Scaffold Confessions in Early Modern England." *Southern Speech Communication Journal* 49 (1983):66–79.

Carpenter, Ronald H. "The Historical Jeremiad as Rhetorical Genre." In *Form*

363

and Genre: Shaping Rhetorical Action, Karlyn Kohrs Campbell and Kathleen Hall Jamieson, eds. Falls Church, Va.: Speech Communication Association, 1978; pp. 103–17.

Carpenter, Ronald H., and Robert V. Seltzer. "Situational Style and the Rotunda Eulogies." *Central States Speech Journal* 22 (1971):11–15.

Carson, Herbert L. "War Requested: Wilson and Roosevelt." *Central States Speech Journal* 10 (1958):28–32.

Carter, Burhham, Jr. "President Carter's Inaugural Address." *College Composition and Communication* 14 (1963):36–40.

Ceaser, James W., Glen E. Thurow, Jeffrey Tulis, and Joseph M. Bessette. "The Rise of the Rhetorical Presidency." *Presidential Studies Quarterly* 11 (1981):576–82.

Cheney, George. "The Rhetoric of Identification and the Study of Organizational Communication." *Quarterly Journal of Speech* 69 (1983):143–58.

Chesebro, James W. "Cultures in Conflict—A Generic and Axiological View." *Communication Quarterly* 21, no. 2 (1973):11–20.

———. "Rhetorical Strategies of the Radical Revolutionary." *Communication Quarterly* 20, no. 1 (1972):37–48.

———, ed. *Gayspeak: Gay Male and Lesbian Communication.* New York: Pilgrim Press, 1981.

Chesebro, James W., and Caroline D. Hamsher. "The Concession Speech: The MacArthur–Agnew Analog." *Speaker and Gavel* 11 (1974):39–51.

Chester, Edward W. "A New Look at Presidential Inaugural Addresses." *Presidential Studies Quarterly* 10 (1980):571–87.

———. "Shadow or Substance? Critiquing Reagan's Inaugural Address." *Presidential Studies Quarterly* 11 (1981):158–71.

Clark, Thomas D. "An Analysis of Recurrent Features of Contemporary American Radical, Liberal, and Conservative Political Discourse." *Southern Speech Communication Journal* 44 (1979):399–422.

———. "An Exploration of Generic Aspects of Contemporary Campaign Orations." *Central States Speech Journal* 30 (1979):122–33.

Collins, Catherine Ann. "Kissinger's Press Conferences, 1972–1974: An Exploration of Form and Role Relationship in News Management." *Central States Speech Journal* 28 (1977):185–93.

Conrad, Charles. "The Rhetoric of the Moral Majority: An Analysis of Romantic Form. *Quarterly Journal of Speech* 69 (1983):159–70.

———. "The Transformation of the 'Old Feminist' Movement." *Quarterly Journal of Speech* 67 (1981):284–97.

Cook, Terrence E. "Political Justifications: The Use of Standards in Political Appeals." *Journal of Politics* 42 (1980):511–37.

Corcoran, Farrel. "The Bear in the Back Yard: Myth, Ideology, and Victimage Ritual in Soviet Funerals." *Communication Monographs* 50 (1983):305–20.

Cox, J. Robert. "The Rhetoric of Child Labor Reform: An Efficacy-Utility Analysis." *Quarterly Journal of Speech* 60 (1974):359–70.

Crable, Richard E., and Steven L. Vibbert. "Argumentative Stance and Political Faith Healing: 'The Dream Will Come True.' " *Quarterly Journal of Speech* 69 (1983):290–301.

Cusella, Louis P. "Biography as Rhetorical Artifact: The Affirmation of Fiorello H. LaGuardia." *Quarterly Journal of Speech* 69 (1983):302–16.

Denton, Robert E., Jr. "The Rhetorical Functions of Slogans: Classifications Characteristics." *Communication Quarterly* 28, no. 2 (1980):10–26.

Diamond, Edwin, and Stephen Bates. *The Spot: The Rise of Political Advertising on Television.* Cambridge, Mass.: The M.I.T. Press, 1984.

Downey, Sharon D., and Richard A. Kallan. "Semi-Aesthetic Detachment: The Fusing of Fictional and External Worlds in the Situational Literature of Leon Uris." *Communication Monographs* 49 (1982):192–204.

Duffy, Bernard K. "The Anti-Humanist Rhetoric of the New Religious Right." *Southern Speech Communication Journal* 49 (1984):339–60.

Duncan, Roger Dean. "Rhetoric of the Kidvid Movement: Ideology, Strategies and Tactics." *Central States Speech Journal* 27 (1976):129–35.

Ehninger, Douglas. "Toward a Taxonomy of Prescriptive Discourse." In *Rhetoric in Transition: Studies in the Nature and Uses of Rhetoric*, Eugene E. White, ed. University Park: Pennsylvania State University Press, 1980; pp. 89–100.

Erlich, Howard S. " '. . . And by Opposing, End them.' The Genre of Moral Justification for Legal Transgression." *Communication Quarterly* 23, no. 1 (1975):13–16.

———. "Populist Rhetoric Reassessed: A Paradox." *Quarterly Journal of Speech* 63 (1977):140–51.

Farrell, Thomas B. "Political Conventions as Legitimation Ritual." *Communication Monographs* 45 (1978):293–305.

Farrell, Thomas B., and G. Thomas Goodnight. "Accidental Rhetoric: The Root Metaphors of Three Mile Island." *Communication Monographs* 48 (1981):271–300.

Finkelstein, Leo, Jr. "The Calendrical Rite of the Ascension to Power." *Western Journal of Speech Communication* 45 (1981):51–59.

Fisher, Randall M. "A Rhetoric of Over-Reaction." *Central States Speech Journal* 17 (1966):251–56.

Fisher, Walter R. "Reaffirmation and Subversion of the American Dream." *Quarterly Journal of Speech* 59 (1973):160–67.

———. "Romantic Democracy, Ronald Reagan, and Presidential Heroes." *Western Journal of Speech Communication* 46 (1982):299–310.

Foss, Sonja K. "Abandonment of Genus: The Evolution of Political Rhetoric." *Central States Speech Journal* 33 (1982):367–78.

Frank, David A. " 'Shalom Achshav'—Rituals of the Israeli Peace Movement." *Communication Monographs* 48 (1981):165–82.

Germino, Dante. *Inaugural Addresses of American Presidents: The Public Philosophy of Rhetoric.* Lanham, Md.: University Press of America, 1984.

Gillespie, Patti P. "Feminist Theatre: A Rhetorical Phenomenon." *Quarterly Journal of Speech* 64 (1978):284–94.

Goedkoop, Richard J. "Taking the Sword from the Temple: Walter Flowers and the Rhetoric of Form." *The Pennsylvania Speech Communication Annual* 38 (1982):25–31.

Gold, Ellen Reid. "Political Apologia: The Ritual of Self-Defense." *Communication Monographs* 45 (1978):306–16.

Golden, James L., and Richard D. Rieke. *The Rhetoric of Black Americans.* Columbus, Ohio: Charles E. Merrill, 1971.

Goodin, George. *The Poetics of Protest: Literary Form and Political Implication in the Victim-of-Society Novel.* Carbondale, Ill.: Southern Illinois University Press, 1985.

Goodman, Richard J., and William I. Gorden. "The Rhetoric of Desecration." *Quarterly Journal of Speech* 57 (1971):23–31.

Goodnight, G. Thomas, and John Poulakos. "Conspiracy Rhetoric: From Pragmatism to Fantasy in Public Discourse." *Western Journal of Speech Communication* 45 (1981):299–316.

Goodwin, Paul D., and Joseph W. Wenzel. "Proverbs and Practical Reasoning: A Study in Socio-Logic." *Quarterly Journal of Speech* 65 (1979):289–302.

Graves, Michael P. "Functions of Key Metaphors in Early Quaker Sermons, 1671–1700." *Quarterly Journal of Speech* 69 (1983):364–78.

Gregg, Richard B. "The Rhetoric of Political Broadcasting." *Central States Speech Journal* 28 (1977):221–37.

Gregg, Richard B., A. Jackson McCormack, and Douglas J. Pedersen. "The Rhetoric of Black Power: A Street-Level Interpretation." *Quarterly Journal of Speech* 55 (1969):151–60.

Gribbin, William. "The Juggernaut Metaphor in American Rhetoric." *Quarterly Journal of Speech* 59 (1973):297–303.

Griffin, Leland M. "The Rhetoric of Historical Movements." *Quarterly Journal of Speech* 37 (1952):184–88.

———. "The Rhetorical Structure of the Antimansonic Movement." *The Rhetorical Idiom*, Donald Bryant, ed. Ithaca, N.Y.: Cornell University Press, 1958; pp. 145–49.

———. "The Rhetorical Structure of the 'New Left' Movement: Part I." *Quarterly Journal of Speech* 50 (1964):113–35.

Gronbeck, Bruce E. "Celluloid Rhetoric: On Genres of Documentary." In *Form and Genre: Shaping Rhetorical Action*, Karlyn Kohrs Campbell and Kathleen Hall Jamieson, eds. Falls Church, Va.: Speech Communication Association, 1978, pp. 139–161.

———. "The Functions of Presidential Campaigning." *Communication Monographs* 45 (1978):268–80.

———. "The Rhetoric of Political Corruption: Sociolinguistic, Dialectical, and Ceremonial Processes." *Quarterly Journal of Speech* 64 (1978):155–72.

———. "The Rhetoric of Social-Institutional Change: Black Action at Michi-

366

gan." In *Explorations in Rhetorical Criticism*, G. P. Mohrmann, Charles J. Stewart, and Donovan J. Ochs, eds. University Park: Pennsylvania State University Press, 1973; pp. 96–123.

Gunderson, Robert G. "The Oxymoron Strain in American Rhetoric." *Central States Speech Journal* 28 (1977):92–95.

Hahn, Dan F. "Ask Not What a Youngster Can Do for You: Kennedy's Inaugural Address." *Presidential Studies Quarterly* 12 (1982):610–14.

———. "Nixon's Second (Hortatory) Inaugural." *Speaker and Gavel* 10 (1973):111–13.

Hahn, Dan F., and Anne Morlando. "A Burkean Analysis of Lincoln's Second Inaugural Address." *Presidential Studies Quarterly* 9 (1979):376–79.

Hahn, Dan F., and Ruth M. Gonchar. "Political Myth: The Image and the Issue." *Communication Quarterly* 20, no. 3 (1972):57–65.

Halloran, Michael. "Doing Public Business in Public." In *Form and Genre: Shaping Rhetorical Action*, Karlyn Kohrs Campbell and Kathleen Hall Jamieson, eds. Falls Church, Va.: Speech Communication Association, 1978; pp. 118–38.

Hancock, Brenda. "Affirmation by Negation in the Women's Liberation Movement." *Quarterly Journal of Speech* 58 (1972):264–71.

Hankins, Sarah Russell. "Archetypal Alloy: Reagan's Rhetorical Image." *Central States Speech Journal* 34 (1983):33–43.

Harris, Barbara Ann. "The Inaugural of Richard Milhous Nixon: A Reply to Robert L. Scott." *Western Journal of Speech Communication* 34 (1970):231–34.

Hart, Roderick P. *The Political Pulpit*. West Lafayette, Ind.: Purdue University Press, 1977.

———. "The Rhetoric of the True Believer." *Communication Monographs* 38 (1971):249–61.

Hattenhauer, Darryl. "The Rhetoric of Architecture: A Semiotic Approach." *Communication Quarterly* 32 (1984):71–77.

Hayes, Joseph J. "Gayspeak." *Quarterly Journal of Speech* 62 (1976):256–66.

Heald, John C. "Apocalyptic Rhetoric: Agents of Anti-Christ from the French to the British." *Communication Quarterly* 23, no. 2 (1975):33–37.

Heath, Robert L. "Dialectical Confrontation: A Strategy of Black Radicalism." *Central States Speech Journal* 24 (1973):168–77.

Heisey, D. Ray. "The Rhetoric of the Arab-Israeli Conflict." *Quarterly Journal of Speech* 56 (1970):12–21.

Hikins, James W. "The Rhetoric of 'Unconditional Surrender' and the Decision to Drop the Atomic Bomb." *Quarterly Journal of Speech* 69 (1983):379–400.

Hill, Forbes I. "Conventional Wisdom—Traditional Form: The President's Message of November 3, 1969." *Quarterly Journal of Speech* 58 (1972):373–86.

Hillbruner, Anthony. "Archetype and Signature: Nixon and the 1973 Inaugural." *Central States Speech Journal* 25 (1974):169–81.

367

Hoban, James L., Jr. "Rhetorical Rituals of Rebirth." *Quarterly Journal of Speech* 66 (1980):275–88.

Hofstadter, Richard. *The Paranoid Style in American Politics and Other Essays.* New York: Alfred A. Knopf, 1966.

Hope, Diana Schaich. "Redefinition of Self: A Comparison of the Rhetoric of the Women's Liberation and Black Liberation Movements." *Communication Quarterly* 23, no. 1 (1975):17–25.

Hopper, Robert, and Robert A. Bell. "Broadening the Deception Concept." *Quarterly Journal of Speech* 67 (1984):287–302.

Ilkka, Richard J. "Rhetorical Dramatization in the Development of American Communism." *Quarterly Journal of Speech* 63 (1977):413–27.

Ivie, Robert L. "Images of Savagery in American Justifications for War." *Communication Monographs* 47 (1980):277–94.

———. "The Metaphor of Force in Prowar Discourse: The Case of 1812." *Quarterly Journal of Speech* 68 (1982):240–53.

———. "Presidential Motives for War." *Quarterly Journal of Speech* 40 (1974):337–45.

———. "Progressive Form and Mexican Culpability in Polk's Justification for War." *Central States Speech Journal* 30 (1979):311–20.

Jablonski, Carol J. "Promoting Radical Change in the Roman Catholic Church: Rhetorical Requirements, Problems and Strategies of the American Bishops." *Central States Speech Journal* 31 (1980):282–89.

———. "Richard Nixon's Irish Wake: A Case Study in Generic Transference." *Central States Speech Journal* 30 (1979):164–73.

Jabusch, David M. "The Rhetoric of Civil Rights." *Western Journal of Speech Communication* 30 (1966):176–84.

Jackson, Harrell, B. L. Ware, and Wil A. Linkugel. "Failure of Apology in American Politics: Nixon on Watergate." *Communication Quarterly* 42 (1975):245–61.

Jackson, James H. "Clarence Darrow's 'Plea in Defense of Himself.' " *Western Speech* 20 (1956):185–95.

Jamieson, Kathleen Hall. "The Metaphoric Cluster in the Rhetoric of Pope Paul VI and Edmund G. Brown, Jr." *Quarterly Journal of Speech* 66 (1980):51–72.

Jensen, J. Vernon. "British Voices on the Eve of the American Revolution: Trapped by the Family Metaphor." *Quarterly Journal of Speech* 63 (1977):43–50.

Jensen, Richard. "Armies, Admen, and Crusaders: Types of Presidential Election Campaigns." *The History Teacher* 2 (1969):33–50.

Karsten, Peter. *Patriot-Heroes in England and America: Political Symbolism and Changing Value over Three Centuries.* Madison: University of Wisconsin Press, 1978.

Katula, Richard A. "The Apology of Richard M. Nixon." *Communication Quarterly* 23, no. 4 (1975):1–5.

368

Kerr, Harry P. "The Election Sermon: Primer for Revolutionaries." *Communication Monographs* 29 (1962):13–22.

———. "Politics and Religion in Colonial Fast and Thanksgiving Sermons, 1763–1783." *Quarterly Journal of Speech* 46 (1960):372–82.

King, Andrew A. "Power: The Rhetoric of Mobilization." *Central States Speech Journal* 29 (1978):147–54.

———. "The Rhetoric of Power Maintenance: Elites at the Precipice." *Quarterly Journal of Speech* 62 (1976):127–34.

King, Andrew A., and Floyd Douglas Anderson. "Nixon, Agnew, and the 'Silent Majority': A Case Study in the Rhetoric of Polarization." *Western Journal of Speech Communication* 35 (1971):243–55.

Kirkwood, William G. "Storytelling and Self-Confrontation: Parables as Communication Strategies." *Quarterly Journal of Speech* 69 (1983):58–74.

Knapp, Mark L., Roderick P. Hart, Gustav W. Friedrich, and Gary M. Shulman. "The Rhetoric of Goodbye: Verbal and Non-verbal Correlates of Human Leave-Taking." *Communication Monographs* 40 (1973):182–98.

Kruse, Noreen W. "The Apologia in Team Sport." *Quarterly Journal of Speech* 67 (1981):270–83.

———. "Motivational Factors in Non-Denial Apologia." *Central States Speech Journal* 28 (1977):13–23.

Lake, Randall A. "Enacting Red Power: The Consummatory Function in Native American Protest Rhetoric." *Quarterly Journal of Speech* 69 (1983):127–42.

Lang, Gladys Engel, and Kurt Lang. "Order and Disorder in Anti-Abortion Rhetoric." *Quarterly Journal of Speech* 70 (1984):425–43.

———. *Politics and Television Re-Viewed.* Beverly Hills, Calif.: Sage Publications, 1984.

Larson, Barbara A. "The Election Eve Address of Edmund Muskie: A Case Study of the Televised Public Address." *Central States Speech Journal* 33 (1972):78–85.

Larson, Charles U. "The Trust Establishing Function of the Rhetoric of Black Power." *Central States Speech Journal* 21 (1970):52–56.

Larson, Frederick. "Patriotism in Carmine: 162 years of July 4th Oratory." *Quarterly Journal of Speech* 26 (1940):12–25.

Lasky, Melvin J. *Utopia and Revolution: On the Origins of a Metaphor, or Some Illustrations of the Problem of Political Temperament and Intellectual Climate and How Ideas, Ideals, and Ideologies Have Been Historically Related.* Chicago: University of Chicago Press, 1976.

Leathers, Dale G. "Fundamentalism of the Radical Right." *Southern Speech Communication Journal* 33 (1968):245–58.

Leff, Michael C., and Gerald P. Mohrmann. "Lincoln at Cooper Union: A Rhetorical Analysis of the Text." *Quarterly Journal of Speech* 60 (1974):346–58.

Ling, David A. "A Pentadic Analysis of Senator Edward Kennedy's Address 'To the People of Massachusetts,' July 25, 1969." *Central States Speech Journal* 21 (1970):81–86.

Linkugel, Wil A., and Nancy Razak. "Sam Houston's Speech of Self-Defense in the House of Representatives." *Southern Speech Journal* 34 (1969):263–75.

Lomas, Charles W. *The Agitator in American Society.* Englewood Cliffs, N.J.: Prentice-Hall, 1968.

Lucas, Stephen E. *Portents of Rebellion: Rhetoric and Revolution in Philadelphia, 1765–1776.* Philadelphia: Temple University Press, 1976.

Martin, Howard H. "The Fourth of July Oration." *Quarterly Journal of Speech* 44 (1958):393–401.

———. "A Generic Exploration: Staged Withdrawal, the Rhetoric of Resignation." *Central States Speech Journal* 27 (1976):247–57.

———. "The Rhetoric of Academic Protest. *Central States Speech Journal* 17 (1966):244–50.

McBath, James H., and Walter R. Fisher. "Persuasion in Presidential Campaign Communication." *Quarterly Journal of Speech* 55 (1969):17–25.

McDiarmind, J. "Presidential Inaugural Addresses—A Study of Verbal Symbols." *Public Opinion Quarterly* 1 (1937):79–82.

McEdwards, Mary G. "Agitative Rhetoric: Its Nature and Effect." *Western Journal of Speech Communication* 32 (1968):36–43.

McGee, Michael Calvin. "The 'Ideograph': A Link between Rhetoric and Ideology." *Quarterly Journal of Speech* 66 (1980):1–16.

McGuire, Michael. "Mythic Rhetoric in *Mein Kampf*: A Structuralist Critique." *Quarterly Journal of Speech* 63 (1977):1–13.

McGuckin, Henry. "A Value Analysis of Richard Nixon's 1952 Campaign-Fund Speech." *Southern Speech Communication Journal* 53 (1968):259–69.

Meadow, Robert G. "The Political Dimensions of Nonproduct Advertising." *Journal of Communication* 31, no. 3 (1981):69–82.

Measell, James. "A Comparative Study of Prime Minister William Pitt and President Abraham Lincoln on Suspension of Habeas Corpus." In *Form and Genre: Shaping Rhetorical Action*, Karlyn Kohrs Campbell and Kathleen Hall Jamieson, eds. Falls Church, Va.: Speech Communication Association, 1978; pp. 87–102.

Medhurst, Martin J. "American Cosmology and the Rhetoric of Inaugural Prayer." *Central States Speech Journal* 28 (1977):272–82.

———. "The First Amendment vs. Human Rights: A Case Study in Community Sentiment and Argument from Definition." *Western Journal of Speech Communication* 46 (1982):1–19.

Medhurst, Martin J., and Michael A. Desousa. "Political Cartoons as Rhetorical Form: A Taxonomy of Graphic Discourse." *Communication Monographs* 48 (1981):197–236.

Miles, Edwin A. "The Keynote Speech at National Nominating Conventions." *Quarterly Journal of Speech* 46 (1960):26–31.

370

Minnick, Wayne C. "The New England Execution Sermon, 1639–1800." *Communication Monographs* 35 (1968):77–89.

Mixon, Harold D. "Boston's Artillery Election Sermons and the American Revolution." *Communication Monographs* 34 (1967):43–50.

Mohrmann, G. P., and F. Eugene Scott. "Popular Music and World War II: The Rhetoric of Continuation." *Quarterly Journal of Speech* 62 (1976):145–56.

Morello, John T. "The Public Apology of a Private Matter: Representative Wayne Hays' Address to Congress." *Speaker and Gavel* 16 (1979):19–26.

Mumly, Dennis K., and Carole Spitzack. "Ideology and Television News: A Metaphoric Analysis of Political Stories." *Central States Speech Journal* 34 (1983):162–71.

Nichols, Marie Hochmuth. "Lincoln's First Inaugural Address." In *Antislavery and Disunion, 1858–1861: Studies in the Rhetoric of Compromise and Conflict*, J. Jeffery Auer, ed. New York: Harper & Row, 1963; pp. 392–414.

Nickel, W. Sandra. "The Rhetoric of Union: A Stylized Utterance." *Central States Speech Journal* 24 (1973):137–42.

Novak, Michael. *Choosing Our King: Powerful Symbols in Presidential Politics.* New York: Macmillan, 1974.

Ohmann, Richard. "Politics and Genre in Non-Fiction Prose." *New Literary History* 11 (1980):237–44.

Orr, C. Jack. "Reporters Confront the President: Sustaining a Counterpoised Situation." *Quarterly Journal of Speech* 66 (1980):17–30.

Osborn, Michael. "Archetypal Metaphor in Rhetoric: The Light-Dark Family." *Quarterly Journal of Speech* 53 (1967):115–26.

———. "The Evolution of the Archetypal Sea in Rhetoric and Poetic." *Quarterly Journal of Speech* 63 (1977):347–63.

Phifer, Gregg. "Two Inaugurals: A Second Look." *Southern Speech Communication Journal* 48 (1983):378–85.

Philipsen, Gerry. "Speaking 'Like a Man' in Teamsterville: Culture Patterns of Role Enactment in an Urban Neighborhood." *Quarterly Journal of Speech* 61 (1975):13–22.

Quimby, Rollin W. "Agnew's Plea Bargain: Between Rhetorics of Consensus and Confrontation." *Central States Speech Journal* 28 (1977):163–72.

———. "Recurrent Themes and Purposes in the Sermons of the Union Army Chaplains." *Communication Monographs* 31 (1964):425–36.

Railsback, Celeste Condit. "The Contemporary American Abortion Controversy: Stages in the Argument." *Quarterly Journal of Speech* 70 (1984):410–24.

Rasmussen, Karen. "An Interaction Analysis of Justificatory Rhetoric." *Western Speech* 37 (1973):111–17.

Raum, Richard D., and James S. Measell. "Wallace and His Ways: A Study of Rhetorical Genre of Polarization." *Central States Speech Journal* 25 (1974):28–35.

Reid, Ronald F. "Apocalypticism and Typology: Rhetorical Dimensions of a Symbolic Reality." *Quarterly Journal of Speech* 69 (1983):229–48.

———. "New England Rhetoric and the French War, 1754–1760." *Communication Monographs* 43 (1976):259–86.

Richter, David H. *Fable's End: Completeness and Closure in Rhetorical Fiction.* Chicago: University of Chicago Press, 1974.

Ritter, Kurt W. "American Political Rhetoric and the Jeremiad Tradition: Presidential Nomination Acceptance Addresses, 1960–1976." *Central States Speech Journal* 31 (1980):153–70.

———. "Ronald Reagan and 'The Speech': The Rhetoric of Public Relations Politics." *Western Journal of Speech Communication* 32 (1968):50–58.

Ritter, Kurt W., and James R. Andrews. *The American Ideology: Reflections of the Revolution in American Rhetoric.* Falls Church, Va.: Speech Communication Association, 1978.

Rogers, Richard S. "The Rhetoric of Militant Deism." *Quarterly Journal of Speech* 54 (1968):247–51.

Rogus, Raymond S. "Generic Tendencies in Majority and Non-Majority Supreme Court Opinions: The Case of Justice Black." *Communication Quarterly* 30 (1982):232–36.

Rosenfield, Lawrence W. "A Case Study in Speech Criticism: The Nixon-Truman Analog." *Communication Monographs* 35 (1968):435–50.

———. "George Wallace Plays Rosemary's Baby." *Quarterly Journal of Speech* 55 (1969):36–44.

Rude, Leslie G. "The Rhetoric of Farmer Labor Agitators." *Central States Speech Journal* 20 (1969):280–85.

Rushing, Janice Hocker. "The Rhetoric of the American Western Myth." *Communication Monographs* 50 (1983):14–32.

Ryan, Halford Ross. "Kategoria and Apologia: On Their Rhetorical Criticism as a Speech Set. *Quarterly Journal of Speech* 68 (1982):254–61.

———. "Roosevelt's First Inaugural: A Study of Technique." *Quarterly Journal of Speech* 65 (1979):137–49.

Schwichtenberg, Cathy. "*Dynasty*: The Dialectic of Feminine Power." *Central States Speech Journal* 34 (1983):151–61.

Scott, Marvin B., and Stanford M. Lyman. "Accounts." *American Sociological Review* 33 (1968):46–62.

Scott, Robert L. "The Conservative Voice in Radical Rhetoric: A Common Response to Division." *Communication Monographs* 40 (1973):123–35.

———. "Rhetoric That Postures: An Intrinsic Reading of Richard M. Nixon's Inaugural Address." *Western Journal of Speech Communication* 34, (1970):46–52.

Scott, Robert L., and Donald K. Smith. "The Rhetoric of Confrontation." *Quarterly Journal of Speech* 55 (1969):1–8.

Scott, Robert L., and Wayne Brockriede, eds. *The Rhetoric of Black Power.* New York: Harper & Row, 1969.

Simons, Herbert W. "Confrontation as a Pattern of Persuasion in University Settings." *Central States Speech Journal* 20 (1969):163–69.

Smiley, Sam. *The Drama of Attack: Didactic Plays of the American Depression.* Columbia: University of Missouri Press, 1972.

Smith, Arthur L. *Rhetoric of Black Revolution.* Boston: Allyn & Bacon, 1969.

Smith, Charles D. "Lord North's Posture of Defense." *Quarterly Journal of Speech* 45 (1959):29–38.

Smith, Craig Allen. "The Hofstadter Hypothesis Revisited: The Nature of Evidence in Politically 'Paranoid' Discourse." *Southern Speech Communication Journal* 42 (1977):274–89.

Smith, Craig R. "The Republican Keynote Address of 1968: Adaptive Rhetoric for the Multiple Audience." *Western Journal of Speech Communication* 39 (1975):32–39.

———. "Television News as Rhetoric." *Western Journal of Speech Communication* 41 (1977):147–59.

Smith, Ralph R., and Russell R. Windes. "The Rhetoric of Mobilization: Implications for the Study of Movements." *Southern Speech Communication Journal* 42 (1976):1–19.

Solomon, Martha. "The 'Positive Woman's' Journey: A Mythic Analysis of the Rhetoric of STOP ERA." *Quarterly Journal of Speech* 65 (1979):262–74.

———. "Redemptive Rhetoric: The Continuity Motif in the Rhetoric of Right to Life." *Central States Speech Journal* 31 (1980):52–62.

———. "The Rhetoric of STOP ERA: Fatalistic Reaffirmation. *Southern Speech Communication Journal* 44 (1978):42–59.

———. "Stopping ERA: A Pyrrhic Victory." *Communication Quarterly* 31, no. 2 (1983):109–17.

Spencer, Martin I. "Politics and Rhetorics." *Social Research* 37 (1970):597–623.

Stelzner, Hermann G. "Analysis by Metaphor." *Quarterly Journal of Speech* 51 (1965):52–61.

———. "Ford's War on Inflation: A Metaphor That Did Not Cross." *Communication Monographs* 44 (1977):284–97.

———. "The Quest Story and Nixon's November 3, 1969 Address." *Quarterly Journal of Speech* 57 (1971):163–72.

Stuart, Charlotte L. "The Constitution as 'Summational Anecdote.' " *Central States Speech Journal* 25 (1974):111–18.

Sudol, Ronald A. "The Rhetoric of Strategic Retreat: Carter and the Panama Canal Debates." *Quarterly Journal of Speech* 65 (1979):379–91.

Thompson, Wayne N. "Barbara Jordan's Keynote Address: Fulfilling Dual and Conflicting Purposes." *Central States Speech Journal* 30 (1979):272–77.

Trent, Judith S. "Presidential Surfacing: The Ritualistic and Crucial First Act." *Communication Monographs* 45 (1978):281–92.

Trent, Judith S., and Robert V. Friedenberg. "Recurring Forms of Political Campaign Communication." In *Political Campaign Communication,* Judith

373

S. Trent and Robert Friedenberg, eds. New York: Praeger, 1983; pp. 197–231.

Valley, David B. "Significant Characteristics of Democratic Presidential Nomination Speeches." *Central States Speech Journal* 25 (1974):56–62.

Van Graber, Marilyn. "Functional Criticism: A Rhetoric of Black Power." In *Explorations in Rhetorical Criticism*, G. P. Mohrmann, Charles J. Stewart, and Donovan J. Ochs, eds. University Park: Pennsylvania State University Press, 1973; pp. 207–22.

Vartabedian, Robert A. "From Checkers to Watergate: Richard Nixon and the Art of Contemporary Apologia." *Speaker and Gavel* 22 (1985):52–61.

Wander, Philip. "The Rhetoric of American Foreign Policy." *Quarterly Journal of Speech* 70 (1984):339–61.

Ware, B. L., and Wil A. Linkugel. "The Rhetorical *Persona*: Marcus Garvey as Black Moses." *Communication Monographs* 49 (1982):50–62.

———. "They Spoke in Defense of Themselves: On Generic Criticism of Apologia." *Quarterly Journal of Speech* 59 (1973):273–83.

Warnick, Barbara. "Conservative Resistance Revisited—A Reply to Medhurst." *Western Journal of Speech Communication* 46 (1982):373–78.

———. "The Rhetoric of Conservative Resistance." *Southern Speech Communication Journal* 42 (1977):256–73.

Weaver, Ruth Ann. "Acknowledgment of Victory and Defeat: The Reciprocal Ritual." *Central States Speech Journal* 33 (1982):480–89.

Weiler, Michael. "The Rhetoric of Neo-Liberalism." *Quarterly Journal of Speech* 70 (1984):362–78.

Wiethoff, William E. "*Topoi* of Religious Controversy in the American Catholic Debate over Vernacular Reform." *Western Journal of Speech Communication* 45 (1981):172–81.

Wilson, Gerald L. "A Strategy of Explanation: Richard M. Nixon's August 8, 1974, Resignation Address." *Communication Quarterly* 24 (1976):14–20.

Wilson, John F. *Public Religion in American Culture*. Philadelphia: Temple University Press, 1979.

Windt, Theodore Otto, Jr. "The Diatribe: Last Resort for Protest." *Quarterly Journal of Speech* 58 (1972):1–14.

———. "The Presidency and Speeches on International Crisis: Repeating the Rhetorical Past." *Speaker and Gavel* 2 (1973):6–14.

Wolfarth, Donald L. "John F. Kennedy in the Tradition of Inaugural Speeches." *Quarterly Journal of Speech* 47 (1961):124–32.

Woodward, Gary C. "Reagan as Roosevelt: The Elasticity of Pseudo-Populist Appeals." *Central States Speech Journal* 34 (1983):44–58.

Wooten, Cecil W. "The Ambassador's Speech: A Particularly Hellenistic Genre of Oratory." *Quarterly Journal of Speech* 59 (1973):209–12.

Zarefsky, David. "President Johnson's War on Poverty: The Rhetoric of Three 'Establishment' Movements." *Communication Monographs* 44 (1977): 352–73.

374

Zvesper, John. "The Problem of Liberal Rhetoric." *Review of Politics* 44 (1982):546–58.
Zyskind, Harold. "A Rhetorical Analysis of the Gettysburg Address." *Journal of General Education* 4 (1950):202–12.

INTRODUCTIONS TO MORE SPECIALIZED LITERATURE IN POLITICAL RHETORIC

GOVERNMENT PROPAGANDA

Altheide, David L., and John M. Johnson. *Bureaucratic Propaganda.* Boston: Allyn & Bacon, 1980.

PLANNED SOCIAL AND POLITICAL CHANGE

Zaltman, Gerald, and Robert Duncan. *Strategies for Planned Change.* New York: John Wiley, 1976.

POLITICAL ADVERTISING

Jamieson, Kathleen Hall. *Packaging the Presidency: A History of Presidential Campaign Advertising.* New York: Oxford University Press, 1984.
Kaid, Lynda Lee. "Political Advertising." In *Handbook of Political Communication,* Dan D. Nimmo and Keith R. Sanders, eds. Beverly Hills, Calif.: Sage Publications, 1981; pp. 249–72.

POLITICAL AND SOCIAL MOVEMENTS

Simons, Herbert W.; Elizabeth W. Mechling; and Howard N. Schreier. "The Functions of Human Communication in Mobilizing for Action from the Bottom Up: The Rhetoric of Social Movements." In *Handbook of Rhetorical and Communication Theory,* Carroll C. Arnold and John Waite Bowers, eds. Boston: Allyn & Bacon, 1984; pp. 792–867.
Stewart, Charles; Craig Smith; and Robert E. Denton. *Persuasion and Social Movements.* Prospects Heights, Ill.: Waveland Press, 1984.

POLITICAL DEBATES

Kraus, Sidney, and Dennis K. Davis. "Political Debates." In *Handbook of Political Communication,* Dan D. Nimmo and Keith R. Sanders, eds. Beverly Hills, Calif.: Sage Publications, 1981; pp. 273–96.
Martel, Myles. *Political Campaign Debates.* New York: Longman, 1983.

POLITICAL LANGUAGE, POLITICAL SYMBOLS

Edelman, Murray. *Political Language: Words That Succeed and Policies That Fail.* New York: Academic Press, 1977.
———. *Politics as Symbolic Action: Mass Arousal and Quiescence.* Chicago: Markham, 1971.
Elder, Charles D., and Roger W. Cobb. *The Political Uses of Symbols.* New York: Longman, 1983.
Graber, Doris A. "Political Languages." In *Handbook of Political Communication.* Dan D. Nimmo and Keith R. Sanders, eds. Beverly Hills, Calif.: Sage Publications, 1981; pp. 195–224.
Mueller, Claus. *The Politics of Communication: A Study in the Political Sociology of Language, Socialization, and Legitimation.* New York: Oxford University Press, 1974.
Nimmo, Dan, and James E. Combs. *Subliminal Politics: Myths and Mythmakers in America.* Englewood Cliffs, N.J.: Prentice-Hall, 1980.
Rothman, Rozann. "Political Symbolism." In *Handbook of Political Behavior.* 5 vols. Vol. 2, Samuel L. Long, ed. New York: Plenum Press, 1981; pp. 285–340.
Shapiro, Michael J., ed. *Language and Politics.* New York: New York University Press, 1984.

POLITICAL THEORY AS POLITICAL DISCOURSE

Nelson, John S. "Political Theory as Political Rhetoric." In *What Should Political Theory Be Now?* John S. Nelson, ed. Albany: State University of New York Press, 1983; pp. 169–240.

POLITICS AND NEWSMAKING

Altheide, David L. *Creating Reality: How TV News Distorts Events.* Beverly Hills, Calif.: Sage Publications, 1977.
Bennett, W. Lance. *News, the Politics of Illusion.* New York: Longman, 1983.
Tuchman, Gaye. *Making News: A Study in the Construction of Reality.* New York: Free Press, 1978.

POLITICS AND THE POPULAR ARTS

Medhurst, Martin J., and Thomas W. Benson, eds. *Rhetorical Dimensions in Media: A Critical Casebook.* Dubuque, Iowa: Kendall/Hunt, 1984.

PRESIDENTIAL NEWS MANAGEMENT

French, Blaire Atherton. *The Presidential Press Conference: Its History and Role in the American Political System.* Washington, D.C.: University Press of America, 1982.
Grossman, Michael Baruch, and Martha Joynt Kuman. *Portraying the President:*

The White House and the News Media. Baltimore, Md.: Johns Hopkins University Press, 1981.
Spear, Joseph C. *Presidents and the Press: The Nixon Legacy*. Cambridge, Mass.: M.I.T. Press, 1984.

RHETORIC OF POLITICAL CAMPAIGNS

Arterton, F. Christopher. *Media Politics: The News Strategies of Presidential Campaigns*. Lexington, Mass.: Lexington Books, 1984.
Davis, James W. *Presidential Primaries: Road to the White House*. Westport, Conn.: Greenwood Press, 1980.
Kessel, John. *Presidential Campaign Politics*. Homewood, Ill.: Dorsey, 1980.
Mauser, Gary A. *Political Marketing: An Approach to Campaign Strategy*. New York: Praeger, 1983.
Sabato, Larry. *The Rise of Political Consultants: New Ways of Winning Elections*. New York: Basic Books, 1981.
Trent, Judith S., and Robert V. Friedenberg. *Political Campaign Communication: Principles and Practices*. New York: Praeger, 1983.
Vermeer, Jan Pons. *"For Immediate Release": Candidate Press Releases in American Political Campaigns*. Westport, Conn.: Greenwood Press, 1982.

RHETORIC OF THE PRESIDENCY

Neustadt, Richard E. *Presidential Power: The Politics of Leadership*. New York: John Wiley, 1960.
Seymour-Ure, Colin. *The American President: Power and Communication*. London: Macmillan, 1982.
Windt, Theodore, and Beth Ingold, eds. *Essays in Presidential Rhetoric*. Dubuque, Iowa: Kendall/Hunt, 1983.

TELEVISION COVERAGE OF POLITICAL CAMPAIGNS

Barber, James David, ed. *Race for the Presidency: The Media and the Nominating Process*. Englewood Cliffs, N.J.: Prentice-Hall, 1978.
Joslyn, Richard. *Mass Media and Elections*. Reading, Mass.: Addison-Wesley, 1984.
Saldich, Anne Rawley. *Electronic Democracy: Television's Impact on the American Political Process*. New York: Praeger, 1978.

377